BETWEEN CHRIST AND CAESAR

CLASSIC AND CONTEMPORARY TEXTS ON CHURCH AND STATE

by

CHARLES VILLA-VICENCIO

DAVID PHILIP
CAPE TOWN

WILLIAM B. EERDMANS PUBLISHING COMPANY
GRAND RAPIDS, MICHIGAN

Printed in the United States of America

First published 1986 by Wm. B. Eerdmans Publishing Co.,
255 Jefferson Ave. SE, Grand Rapids, Mich. 49503

Published 1986 in South Africa by
David Philip, Publisher (Pty) Ltd., 217 Werdmuller Centre,
Claremont 7700, South Africa.

David Philip ISBN 0-86486-070-6

Library of Congress Cataloging-in-Publication Data

Between Christ and Caesar.

Includes bibliographies.
1. Church and state—History. I. Villa-Vicencio,
Charles.
BV631.S24 1986 261.7'09 86-16514

ISBN 0-8028-0240-0

For Eileen, Heidi,
and Tanya

The publishers gratefully acknowledge the organizations cited below for permission to reprint the following excerpts:

Thomas Aquinas, *On Kingship*: Reprinted from Thomas Aquinas, *On Kingship, to the King of Cyprus*, trans. Gerald B. Phelan, rev. I. Th. Eschmann, OP, by permission of the publishers. ©1949, 1982, by Pontifical Institute of Medieval Studies, Toronto.

The Augsburg Confession and Martin Luther, "Secular Authority": Reprinted by permission of Fortress Press.

The Schleitheim Confession: Reprinted by permission of Basil Blackwell, Oxford, and John Knox Press.

Other Anabaptist writings: The quotations on pp. 74–76 are reprinted by permission from *Anabaptism in Outline*, ed. Walter Klaassen, copyright 1981 by Herald Press, Scottdale, Pa. 15683.

Dietrich Bonhoeffer, *No Rusty Swords:* Reprinted by permission of Christian Verlag, Munich.

Dietrich Bonhoeffer, *Ethics:* Reprinted with permission of Macmillan Publishing Company and SCM Press Ltd., from *Ethics* by Dietrich Bonhoeffer. Copyright 1955 by SCM Press Ltd.

The Medellin Conference: Reprinted by permission of Consejo Episcopal Latinamericano, Bogota.

Two excerpts from the report of the Kampala Assembly of the AACC: Reprinted by permission of Lutterworth Press, Cambridge, England.

WCC Commission reports on pp. 185 and 191: Reprinted by permission of the World Council of Churches, Geneva.

CONTENTS

FOREWORD

This is a superb book—at once timely and in time! Its theme is the relation between church and state both as doctrine and in practice. Its purpose is "to identify the moment of prophetic resistance to the state, which is theologically related to the affirmation of government as a God-given institution for the common good of society."

Charles Villa-Vicencio explores the book's theme in historical perspective, with special reference to the fact that "the Christian doctrine of church and state is today being assessed and rewritten in virtually every situation of conflict around the world." And the book's purpose is most explicitly identified in the final document, the 1985 Kairos Document, in which a group of theologians publicly recognizes the moment of truth in South African society, the moment when justice and power have been so deeply separated by the governing authorities as to put the body politic in danger of self-destruction. The Kairos theologians offer a sharp critique of both "state theology" and "church theology," recognizing instead the need for a "prophetic theology" as the authentic mind and voice of the church in calling itself and the state to account and in taking responsibility for bringing justice and power together for the freedom, peace, and human good of all.

Nowhere is this situation of conflict more intense and urgent than in South Africa. There the churches have been increasingly drawn into the struggle with a government committed to the disenfranchisement and oppression of the black majority of its citizens in the name of the separatist politics of apartheid—and often also in the name of a biblical and Christian theological insistence upon obedience to the constituted authorities, divinely appointed to uphold law and order as the primary responsibility of government and as the necessary precondition of justice, freedom, and peace in human society. The timeliness of this conflict is its inclusiveness and inescapability. No member of South African society can avoid being involved either in its resolution or in its destructive persistence. Since the shock-waves of the conflict have already carried beyond its epicenters in Pretoria, Cape Town, and Johannesburg, no member of the human community anywhere in the world can avoid responsibility for its promise or its fate.

The timeliness of this book is evident from its emergence from the very eye of the storm, as an intentional response from within the Christian community to the crisis confronting and confounding church and state in South Africa and ineluctably in the world community. A postgraduate seminar in the Department of Religious Studies of the University of Cape Town, directed by Professor Villa-Vicencio during the second semester of 1984, was the occasion for the book's origin. Naturally, such an academic forum would take a historical perspective and would examine the pertinent textual sources to document that perspective. But Professor Villa-Vicencio's pages make it plain that he and his students were embarked upon no conventional investigation of a problem and of the ways in which the thought and actions of any given past can illuminate and guide a random present. On the contrary, they were acutely aware that "the engagement of church and state is no longer simply in the pages of theological statements. It is in the streets of every city, township, and rural district. It is within the churches, and it is the substance of political interrogations inside of prisons throughout South Africa." The concrete context of the present has prompted the probing of the past in a unique reciprocity between past and present that underlines the vital meaning and importance of tradition. Whether the search for knowledge, understanding, and guidance proceeds from the present to the past or from the past to the present, the bond between thought and action is forged by an unalloyed respect and responsibility for past and present alike. By this bond, faith and action, truth and life, commitment and involvement are effectively joined and lifted beyond ideology and utopia. They are set free from the self-justifying self-righteousness of possibilities that have played themselves out. They become instead the bearers of the future by making room in the present for "what is low and despised in the world, even things that are not, to bring to nothing things that are" (1 Corinthians 1:28).

Not all timely books, however, arrive in time. Some—substantive and timely as they are—arrive too late. The critical issues addressed in these books have already found second-best resolutions or have been significantly overtaken by events. Others—perceptive, profound, and wise as they may be—are too early. Cassandra or Elijah-like, they are not the voice for the ears and consciences to which they are addressed. But Professor Villa-Vicencio's acute discernment and competent probing of "the meaning of this time" (Luke 12:56) has made available *in time* a guidebook and a sourcebook of such telling, reliable, and succinctly formulated insight, analysis, challenge, and documentation as to make it an indispensable manual for "the gathering storm," signalled on the horizon of the present by the future coming our way. As, in retrospect, the 1934 Barmen Declaration appears to have been too barely *in* time to be *on* time, *Between Christ and Caesar* is so much on target for these times as to be available in time indeed, as a providentially provided first draft of a manifesto of deliverance, dedication, and direction from and for the Christian community, to and for the political community, for the sake of the human community on behalf of which church and state bear joint responsibility. The cry of suffering which has prompted this book has been transfigured as a call to renewal and responsibility of church and state, in themselves and in their dealings one with another throughout the whole inhabited earth.

The call is a magnificent expression of the ecumenical reality of the church amid the present dividedness and disorder of the church and of the world. In a time of social and cultural fragmentation, quantification, relativization, and bureaucratization of private and public values and life, a primer is at hand for the discovery of a prospect and path toward the rebirth of a commonwealth of human faith and hope, meaning and learning, life and action. In a time when tradition is in disarray and disregard (not least in theological faculties) and a cacophany of ideological pragmatisms distorts seeing and deafens hearing, a document is available for taking up again the conversation of present with past and past with present in a responsible move toward Martin Marty's "usable future." Those who govern and those who are governed, believers and unbelievers, learned and unlearned, the renowned and the unknown, the seekers and the cynics are invited through these pages to become involved again—or for the first time in their lives—in what it takes to be and to stay human in the world, by beginning at a critical and unavoidable beginning.

Whether and in how far books significantly alter the course of human events is admittedly moot. Be that as it may, Professor Villa-Vicencio's book deserves a major commitment of serious study, reflection, and conversation within the community of faith and action. Should church congregations and governing bodies take it up for regular and repeated reading; should theological faculties give it frequent place among their curricular offerings at foundational and graduate levels; should the reading and searching of this book ever and again become the companions of the reading and searching of the Scriptures; then at church conferences, study centers, and in the ongoing nurture of baptized belivers, it is more than a little likely that the church will find itself overtaken by a pentecostal visitation for the renewal of its own faith and practice, of the society for which the church shares responsibility with the state, and thus also of the state itself. The sign of such a visitation will be the gift to the church of the wisdom and the power "to identify the moment of prophetic resistance to the state" and the way of obedient and saving faith.

This is indeed a superb book—at once timely and in time! I have been much instructed by it and am thankful for its availability and for the privilege of commending for it the widest attention and use.

PAUL LEHMANN

PREFACE

The Christian doctrine of church and state is today being assessed and rewritten in virtually every situation of conflict around the world. South Africa is one of those situations. A remarkable aspect of this debate, even in its more "radical" forms, is its continuity with the history of the doctrine of church-state relations as it emerged in the classical and contemporary periods of church history.

The purpose of this book is to introduce in a concise way the history of church-state relations from the time of the early church to the present. More specifically, it is to identify the moment of prophetic resistance to the state, which is theologically related to the affirmation of government as a God-given institution for the common good of society. This prophetic tradition is an enduring dimension of the life of the church, in spite of the complex and at times compromising relationship between church and state which has manifested itself throughout history.

To introduce this extensive debate between the covers of a single volume is an audacious exercise. There is, however, some virtue to be found in gaining an overall perspective of the history of this doctrine, as a basis for further study, within which the necessary nuances which belong to each historical period can be assessed.

In order to provide a historical frame of reference against which to consider the prevailing debate, I have chosen two major periods from the history of the church: the classical period, extending from the patristic era to the Puritan reformation; and the contemporary period, extending from the Confessing church during the time of the Third Reich to contemporary thought in Roman Catholicism, Eastern Orthodoxy, and liberation and black theologies. A third section deals specifically with the church in South Africa, as a contextual study in church-state relations.

In each chapter, I attempt to introduce the church-state debate within the context of a specific period in the history of the church. The debate is grounded in one or more primary texts from the period, which are included in each chapter. In many cases I have abridged the texts in the interests of space, but have attempted in each case to do justice to the total text, excluding only those sections of the longer texts that do not deal directly with church-state relations. The actual words of the cited text have been strictly adhered to, and none of the texts appears in a summarized form.

The idea for a book of this nature originated among students in my post-graduate seminar on "Church and State in Historical Perspective," which I taught during the second semester of 1984 in the Department of Religious Studies at the University of Cape Town. It is therefore right that I acknowledge the stimulation which I received from the students who participated in that seminar. I am especially grateful to Alan Brews, Stephen de Gruchy, and Robin Petersen, who have assisted me in the selection process of the texts included in this volume, culled from a much larger selection of documents which formed part of the required reading for the seminar. A further incentive to produce this volume came from my involvement early last year in a theological working group assigned the task of producing a document in support of the South African Council of Churches' call to prayer for the end to unjust rule. This document (included in this volume) cites as its "rationale" the larger context of the history of the doctrine of church-state relations. Collecting these references in a single volume seemed a needed and useful service.

It is almost a cliche to say that "things are moving fast" in South Africa, and the debate over church-state relations is included among those fast-moving "things." This means that a book of this nature can never contain the latest document in the debate, although I have tried to be as current as possible. The Kairos document, for example, was published after this manuscript was submitted to the publishers, but we have been able to include it nevertheless. Since then the debate has taken on other contours which simply cannot be included. What is perhaps most significant is that the engagement of church and state is no longer simply in the pages of theological statements. It is in the streets of every city, township, and rural district. It is within the churches, and it is the substance of political interrogations inside of prisons throughout South Africa. Christians are engaged in the struggle against the present regime motivated by their faith in Jesus Christ.

In assembling a book on the doctrine of church and state while working within the South African context, one inevitably thinks of those in this country who have lived lives that exemplify the finest moments of the church. The names of these, both of former generations and the present age, both black and white, Afrikaans and English, often rejected by the state and at times by the church, are too many to mention. Many of them, either through the written word, communal tradition, or personal association, have had a formative influence on my perception of the doctrine of church and state. Each incarnates a different emphasis of the prophetic witness of the church in our time. I acknowledge the sustaining influence of their lives in all that follows, and find myself particularly indebted to Beyers Naudé and Allan Boesak. Each took a personal interest in the selection process of the documents which are contained between these covers.

A wide-ranging study of this kind necessitates consultation with people beyond one's own area of academic specialization. My colleagues in the Department of Religious Studies have been helpful in this respect. David Chidester, John de

Gruchy, Bill Domeris, Gabriel Setiloane, and Chuck Wanamaker were of particular assistance. I am also indebted to Father Chrisostomos Frank for the dialogue which resulted in the essay on the Eastern Orthodox church, and to Fathers Samangaliso Mkhatshwa and Albert Nolan for their comments regarding the chapters on Roman Catholic and liberation theology. I am equally grateful to James Cone who, during a visit to Cape Town in July 1985, read the chapter on black theology. Professor Andrew Ross of Edinburgh University was also of assistance in editing the modernization of the texts from the pen of John Knox, a task performed by Jean and Alex Scholes. I appreciate their assistance. I also acknowledge, with much gratitude, the assistance of Arlene Stephenson, who proofread this manuscript.

I am particularly indebted to Ed Hueneman, an American soul mate, who contributed in a variety of ways to the publication of this book and to my understanding of the doctrine of church and state. He introduced me to the Eastern Orthodox tradition during a visit to Beirut in 1980 and provided helpful comments on the chapter on the Eastern Orthodox church. He also introduced me to Paul Lehmann. These theological events sharpened my political understanding of the relationship between Christ and Caesar, and resulted in the affirmation of a theological imperative that demands a political option transcending both tyranny and anarchy. In celebrating this imperative Professor Lehmann's writings have for many years inspired, disturbed, and shaped my theological pilgrimage. He has graciously written the foreword to this volume. I am deeply honored by such generosity. It is customary to say, and this I happily do, that none of the people whose assistance I acknowledge can be held accountable for any of the inadequacies in this study.

My investigation of the history of the doctrine of church and state is part of a larger research project in relation to a senior research grant received from the Human Sciences' Research Council. I gladly acknowledge this assistance. William B. Eerdmans responded positively to the idea of this publication, and I wish to express my thanks to him. David Philip, in turn, immediately agreed to being responsible for the South African edition, and I am equally grateful to him.

Whenever there is a publisher's deadline to be met one's family bears the brunt. My wife Eileen has assisted with much of the editorial work, and our daughters Heidi and Tanya have managed to remember that "dad is working in the study." I am grateful to them and dedicate this book to them.

Cape Town, January 1986 CHARLES VILLA-VICENCIO

INTRODUCTION

CHURCH AND STATE IN HISTORICAL PERSPECTIVE

Many have argued that religion is by nature a legitimation of ruling-class ideology. Others have promoted it as a spiritual resource for revolutionary change. An objective analysis of the history of religion in the West seems to suggest that it can be both. It is a multifaceted, many-leveled, complex, and ambiguous reality. Gregory Baum suggests, for example, that it is possible to read the Bible as a textbook on the pathology of religion—giving rise to hypocrisy, idolatry, group-egotism, and collective blindness. On the other hand it can also be read as a textbook on the therapeutic nature of religion—overcoming the maladies of society by being a source of social and political renewal.[1]

The Christian church has played an ambiguous political role throughout its history. At times it has blessed and legitimated the state. This has, at least since the Constantinian settlement, been the dominant position of the church. This it has done either by direct support or by default, through affirming a "future happiness" divorced from the existing order. At other times the church, although more often minority groups within the church, has rejected the status quo by affirming the rule of God, which has often meant a renunciation of the existing social order. To take this argument one step further, on occasions, and more often than not, the same church has played two different social functions in society, depending on the cultural and ideological milieu which has impinged on that particular church at a given time.

The role of the white Nederduitse Gereformeerde Kerk (NGK) in South African politics illustrates this phenomenon in a pertinent manner. Today it is the church of the political establishment. It provides theological legitimation for apartheid, while its leaders repeatedly attack the World Council of Churches (WCC), the South African Council of Churches (SACC), black theology, and liberation theology for allegedly using religion for political ends. There was a time, however, when the NGK was firmly committed to the cause of poor and oppressed Afrikaner workers. This much is clear from the submission to the Volkskongres in 1947 by the Reverend C. D. Brink:

> The aim of the church is to bring about social justice. Justice must be done to the poor and the oppressed, and if the present system does not serve this purpose, the public conscience must be roused to demand another. If the church does not exert itself for justice in society, and together with the help she can offer also be prepared to serve as champion for the cause of the poor, others will do it. The poor have their right today: I do not ask for your charity, but I ask to be given an opportunity to live a life of human dignity.[2]

When the church of the oppressed becomes the church of the oppressor, the danger is that its theology will be remolded accordingly. The NGK is not the only church in history to have undergone this transition. The challenge to continue to speak prophetically after the fortunes of history have changed faces all churches which are committed to the liberation of an oppressed people.

Forming an integral part of the socio-economic structures of their respective societies, institutional churches become trapped in those structures, reflecting the ruling class ideas of their time. There is certainly little evidence, since the Edict of Milan in 313, of the churches ever having been able to do otherwise. In spite of this sociological propensity toward the status quo there has also been a contradictory theological identity which has not been consonant with this tradition. It is *this* tradition, recognized by the church in the most diverse circumstances, which speaks in what follows. It is a tradition which disturbs the most complacent social manifestations of the church and which keeps alive the possibility of churches being activated, under certain circumstances, to support the process of radical social change in a given situation. This tradition constitutes the social conscience not only of the state, but primarily of the church itself.

The pathological influence of religion in the political sphere and the idealistic fallacy that the gospel contains a political ideology or program tailor-made to solve the social and economic problems of the day have caused many to argue in favor of strictly secular politics, contending that religion must be kept out of politics. Recognizing the dangers inherent in confusing religion and politics, Míguez Bonino warns against the temptation to allow Christianity to become politicized by political groupings either to the left or the right. At the same time, he maintains that the church must not withdraw from the political challenges facing it. "We urgently need a Christian ethics of politics," he argues, "precisely in order that we may avoid a wrong politicization of Christianity."[3]

BETWEEN ORDER AND FREEDOM

When the church has promoted the ideology of the ruling class or legitimated a particular revolutionary cause, it has found itself in ideological captivity. The central Christian theological tradition has, however, at its best managed to avoid both these extremes. It has recognized and affirmed the need for good social order while allowing for the possibility of rejecting and removing from office those rulers who do not rule in accordance with the divine demand for justice and peace. Given the magnitude of socio-political and economic forces in society, the church has in the course of its history often tilted in favor of the existing system, while at other times segments within the church, influenced by the forces of change, have been on the side of revolutionary change. At times, as is presently the case in the church in South Africa, the church has been divided against itself. Those whose interests are served by the present regime favor a church of the status quo, while those who suffer under the prevailing political system affirm that part of the Christian tradition which rejects the existing order.

The biblical tradition

Biblical teaching on church-state relations is a study in its own right. We can not deal with it here in any detail. The history of the doctrine of church and state from biblical times to the present does, however, make it clear that each succeeding generation of Christians has, in its own way, sought to do justice to the biblical tradition.

Even the briefest consideration of the debate over biblical teaching on church-state relations indicates that the ideological dualism already referred to is an inherent part of the Judeo-Christian tradition. Walter Brueggemann's detailed analysis of the history of Israel identifies "two trajectories" in Old Testament literature, the "Mosaic liberation" trajectory and the "royal consolidation" trajectory. The latter constitutes for him the "paganization of Israel," within which "the social innovation of Moses and its theological novelty of a God aligned with the marginal ones" was abandoned for a static religion which legitimated the monarchy.[4] While arguing that these two trajectories are often exclusive of each other, he also discerns an ongoing confrontation between prophets and kings during other periods of the history of Israel. This ensures a continuation, in the Judeo-Christian tradition, of both the Mosaic affirmation of freedom—even at the cost of political stability—and the Davidic-Solomonic commitment to order and continuity.

The New Testament reveals a similar double emphasis on both stability and renewal. C. E. B. Cranfield's useful essay, "The Christian's Political Responsibility According to the New Testament," draws these two emphases together in what he argues is the "sobriety and realism" of New Testament political teaching. The sinfulness of human nature, he argues, leads biblical writers to the realization of the limits to what can be achieved in the sphere of politics. This means that limited goals ought not to be despised or rejected under the spotlight of what God's kingdom will ultimately be like. At the same time, the Christian's political responsibility ought to be a manifestation of "confidence and hope," grounded in the sure faith that Christ is the Lord over all authorities.[5] For Cranfield this means that it is necessary for the Christian not only to submit to the government of the day, but "in certain circumstances and within certain limits to join in military action at the command of the government." On the other hand, in certain extreme circumstances, it may be necessary "to engage in armed rebellion in order to overthrow a government that is intolerably unjust and to replace it." Cranfield's argument is that while there is no unambiguous New Testament teaching that prescribes the Christian response in either of these circumstances, "the Christian would be failing to take his government absolutely seriously—and so failing to render it the subjection which the New Testament enjoins—if, in the last resort, he were not ready even to use force against it, should it ever degenerate into mere tyranny."[6]

The tradition of the church

This dual attitude to government has remained the theological basis of church-state relations throughout the history of the church. Ernst Troeltsch identified these two emphases in religion in distinguishing between "compromising" and "uncompromising" religion. This gave rise to his classical distinction between "church" and "sect." The former, he argued, motivated by a desire for acceptance by and the control of great masses of people, found it difficult to avoid a compromise with the state, the prevailing social order, and the dominant economic ideology of the time. He defined the sect, on the other hand, as affirming the Sermon on the Mount as its ideal, laying stress on the simple but radical opposition of the kingdom of God to all secular interests and institutions.[7] Troeltsch's strict distinction between "church" and "sect" is of questionable use today, for there are some churches which resist the state and the dominant ideology of the time, while many sects defend that ideology. Troeltsch's analysis does, however, give expression to two traditions within Christian history, often separated from one another, but—at least within the doctrinal writing mainstream tradition of the church, if not always in practice—held in a creative tension.

While it is not possible to generalize about two thousand years of history or to ignore the fundamental cultural and contextual differences which have led to the emergence of various models of church-state relations, some salient common emphases have appeared and endured throughout this period. A careful study of this history reveals vastly different doctrinal emphases that have characterized different ecclesiastical groupings, but it also reveals a common tradition. This tradition, contained in part in the texts included in this book, is regarded by the church as "orthodoxy," despite differences of interpretation within the parameters of this consensus. Heresy is a deviation from these parameters. J. W. C. Wand held that the early church fathers used three criteria in determining whether or not a particular belief was heretical. A heresy was, first, something regarded to be novel. This is not to suggest that the Christian faith is static and cannot be addressed to new issues. On the contrary, this is the continuing task of theology. This application must, however, not be at variance with or alien to the tradition of the church. The second mark of heresy was partiality, the affirmation of a part of the Christian tradition to the exclusion of other equally important aspects of the tradition. Third, according to Wand, the church fathers believed that heresy included "an element of stubbornness and disobedience."[8]

The implication of biblical teaching on church-state relations, as articulated by Brueggemann and Cranfield, is that both social stability grounded in the common good of society and the continuing renewal of society in the light of God's impending kingdom constitute the basis of a viable political community. Wand's definition of heresy, in turn, suggests that the partial, one-sided, or incomplete affirmation of these two emphases, when held with stubborn resolve, constitute a disruptive or heretical understanding of church-state relations. That is, either to emphasize social stability at the cost of renewal in the light of God's impending kingdom or to insist on the indiscriminate dismissal of the existing social order in affirmation of God's eschatological kingdom is to form a novel and alien doctrine of church-state relations. The former constitutes the legitimation of the existing order, while the latter amounts to the legitimation of revolution. Such predisposed ideological positions constitute a serious deviation from the tradition of the church.

A HISTORICAL SUMMARY

The church has throughout its history struggled in a variety of ways, while subjected to changing socio-political and economic forces, to respond positively to this dual emphasis in which God is seen as both the giver of good, just, and orderly rule and the God of liberation from unjust and tyrannical rule. These two emphases, in fact, constitute one synthesized theological principle, namely, that God is a God of justice—which means that he is the liberator from all structures, whether of the "old" or the "new" regime, which oppress people.

The limits of political structures and the sinfulness of human nature seem to indicate that there are limits to what can be achieved in the sphere of politics. Yet there is an eschatological hope of the coming kingdom, impinging in both judgment and renewal on all political systems, which constitutes a dominant theme both within the Scriptures and throughout the tradition of the church. It functions as a social lure, drawing society forward to that day when "the wolf shall dwell with the lamb, and the leopard shall lie down with the kid" (Isa. 11:6); when "nation shall not lift up sword against nation, neither shall they learn war any more" (Isa. 2:4); when Christ shall deliver "the kingdom to God the Father after destroying every rule and every authority and power" (1 Cor. 15:24); when there shall be "a new heaven and a new earth" (Rev. 21:1). The symbol of the impending kingdom of God, understood in this way, has provided a revolutionary dimension which has destabilized and even overthrown governments, but also renewed societies that have been able to respond more positively to the vision of what ought to be—and by God's grace can be—instituted on earth as it is in heaven. This kind of anticipation of the kingdom of God is in direct continuity with the prayer that Christians pray daily: "thy kingdom come, thy will be done on earth as it is in heaven." As politics is said to be the art of the possible, so this kind of prayer anticipates what may not be possible today, but may be possible tomorrow. Without this vision society stands always in danger of becoming moribund in its preoccupation with preserving its own structures.

The moment of crisis in church-state relations has repeatedly dawned for the church through the ages when there has been a direct confrontation between the church's restrained and yet expectant aspirations for society and the naked and at times tyrannical power of the state. In this situation the inevitable question has emerged: are capitulation, compromise, or martyrdom the only alternatives available to the church? The different doctrines of church and state that have emerged throughout history are attempts by the church to take its responsibility to the state with the utmost seriousness. This responsibility concerns primarily the obligation to ensure that the state provides just and orderly government for the benefit of all its citizens. At the same time, it is the obligation of the church to concern itself with the eventuality which arises when the state resolutely refuses to heed the call of its people for justice and uses its power to impose tyranny rather than good order.

The texts included in this book show different cultural and ideological tendencies. Yet each of them, some more or less, manifests a theological commitment to just government for the benefit of all people in response to the demands of God's impending kingdom. Each text, in turn, addresses the possibility of a church confronted with a civil authority that is either incapable of instituting orderly government or willfully responsible for unjust and tyrannical rule. Differently stated, each text is by implication a response to the biblical injunction which demands that Christians obey God rather than human authority, should that authority command what is contrary to the declared will of God (Acts 5:29).

What follows is a brief synopsis of the common tradition on church-state relations, which is provided in more detail in the introductions and texts that follow. At times the dialectic in this tradition between stability and renewal is less clear than at other times. On occasions one part of this dialectic is obscured by an overemphasis on the other. Despite these deviations, the essential emphases of the common Christian tradition on church-state relations can be defined as follows:

1. Theology has, generally speaking, throughout history affirmed a political option beyond both tyranny and anarchy.

The political order has been seen by the dominant tradition of the church as more than a holding position to ward off chaos. This order has in fact tended to be taken more seriously by the church than by secular government. It has been looked to, at least since the time of Constantine, as instituted by God in order to fulfil his purpose in society, recognizing that should the civil authorities fail to do good and govern justly they are in constant danger of being removed from office. In the early church, influenced by the expectation of the imminent *eschaton;* amidst Luther's fear of political disintegration and chaos; and in some contemporary affirmations of the existing order, a similar theological affirmation has emerged. This is the recognition that the surest deterrent against revolutionary chaos is the affirmation of human rights and social justice. In some situations and in some theologies this concern has taken on a definite prophetic dimension in which the cause of those who are oppressed is specifically affirmed as being the particular or preferential concern of God. In other places this concern is more implicit. But what can be said without qualification is that the entire Christian tradition requires that government be just and merciful.

This theological rejection of political repression has not, however, led to an affirmation of revolution as the negation of repression at the cost of chaos. The rejection of tyranny must not be a means to precipitate anarchy, but rather as a way to create good order, justice, and peace. This has given rise to repeated warnings by some theologians, throughout the history of the church, against the possibility of political chaos which may result from repudiating the existing order, however unjust. Others, subjected to different historical demands, have given more attention to the injustices and chaos perpetuated by the existing order and argued that whatever the nature of the problems that might follow, they cannot be used as an excuse to allow the present tyranny to continue.

Rejecting both tyranny and anarchy, the church has nevertheless throughout its history—although with some notable exceptions—maintained a stubborn and restless hope for something more than what any existing socio-political order has been able to provide. Again, this hope has been experienced with differing degrees of intensity. Karl Barth gives more emphasis to this restless hope than many others. He speaks of the "great positive possibility" of the gospel, which promises the dawning of the kingdom of God on earth, and constitutes a restless subversion that disturbs the political complacency of every regime:

> We call "love" the "great positive possibility," precisely because in the act of love the revolutionary meaning of all ethos is exposed, because love actually has to do with the negation and breaking down of that which exists. It is love that ultimately declares the reactionary man to be wrong, in spite of the wrong that the revolutionary does. For insofar as we love one another, we *cannot* wish to maintain the status quo. Instead, we do in love the new thing that casts down what has become old. Thus what we are talking about is a breach in the wall of incomprehensible inaction, which is the still more incomprehensible action of love.[9]

Lehmann's superb discussion on this passage from Barth relates this subversion to both the existing authority and the revolution, showing the need to transcend both tyranny and revolution. Reaching beyond mere compromise between tyranny and anarchy, there is a theological option which points to what is qualitatively different. This becomes a theological incentive to continuing political renewal. It is what Lehmann affirms as a "permanent revolution," more radical in political extent and more penetrating in personal identity than what the most zealous revolutionary can offer. Says Lehmann, the need is "the freedom to be and to stay human in the world." "Obedience to God and the practice of love for the neighbor are the twin safeguards against the fury by which the revolution in the exercise of power begins to devour itself."[10]

2. The church is not exempt from the difficult exercise of making political choices. As difficult as it may have found such choices, its noblest tradition is one of undaunted decision making. The age of the martyrs in the early church provides evidence of this, while each succeeding generation has looked to this tradition as an option to be emulated in the face of state tyranny. St. Thomas Aquinas spoke of martyrdom as an appropriate response to tyrannical rule in some circumstances, Bonhoeffer committed himself to the cause of the despised of his land knowing that this might well end in martyrdom for him, and contemporary martyrs can be found in many oppressive situations around the world.

The church also has a less decisive side. Without the urgency which compels the oppressed church to decide, the church of the establishment is often trapped in a paralysis of uncertainty and indecision when it ponders the inevitable question whether a particular decision will produce the desired end. Risk and uncertainty are, however, an inevitable part of political and theological decision making. "Not to act and not to take a stand," argued Bonhoeffer, "simply for fear of making a mistake, when others have to make infinitely more difficult decisions every day, seems to me to be almost a contradiction of love."[11]

3. The obligation to make political choices is an inherent part of the theological necessity for the church to be obedient to God. The ethical implications of radical monotheism which forced the early church to reject emperor veneration became the cornerstone of church-state relations. When obedience to civil authority means disobedience to God, the Christian is obliged to disobey civil authority. The church has affirmed this guiding principle throughout its history, even in its most politically conservative phases.

The texts in this volume identify different options which theologians have proposed as possible ways of dealing with a situation which emerges when there is a clash between civil and divine obedience. Some have pointed to martyrdom; some to organized political confrontation; some have suggested that God would raise up avengers to punish the unjust rulers; some have suggested it is the church's obligation to turn to God in prayer for deliverance; some have argued that an unjust ruler may be God's way of punishing a people; and others have even argued that it is the Christian's obligation to engage in armed rebellion. Whatever the different strategies advocated to remove unjust rulers—and such differences are important—a broadly based historical consensus exists that the church is to concern itself with political structures and that in certain circumstances it is obliged, in obedience to God, to resist and oppose the existing order.

4. More often than not the conflict within the church concerning the state is related to the question whether the particular point of confrontation has been reached. To state this more bluntly: most theologians agree that it is the church's obligation to oppose a tyrant, but it is more difficult to reach a common mind within the church, as to whether a particular government is tyrannical. Those who suffer the direct consequences of a particular government's oppressive policies see the situation differently than those who do not suffer as a result of the repressive measures of the tyrant.

The post-Vatican II Roman Catholic church, in continuity with the special concern shown in the Bible for the poor, widows, orphans, and those marginalized by society, has given a decisive lead to the entire church by maintaining a "preferential option for the poor." "The poor are not morally or spiritually superior to others, but they see reality from a different angle or location—and therefore differently."[12] It is this "underside" of reality which the church can only ignore at the cost of neglecting its prophetic tradition which has its roots in the ministry of Jesus. While this particular prophetic emphasis of the church has been accentuated in recent times, it too is a perspective which the church has never totally negated, even in its most conforming moments. The poor have always been of concern in the mission of the church. What is new in post-Vatican II, and especially in liberation theology, is not merely stressing the need to alleviate the suffering of the poor by acts of charity, but affirming the need for the poor to free themselves from the structures of poverty, even at the cost of the well-being of the rich. This too has been a concern which has endured in the church's history, though it has never been a dominant one. The ascetic tradition, monasticism, the church of the radical Reformation, the witness of Barth and Bonhoeffer during the time of the Third Reich, and more recently the witness of parts of the church in the Third World have all, in different ways, sought to keep alive this preference for the poor and oppressed.

5. Running through all the numerous accounts of God's revelation in the Old and New Testaments is the sense that God's majesty is inextricably bound to social justice and holiness. "Here," suggests Gregory Baum, "the sacred becomes the bearer of a judgment on human life and society, and of a promise for the righting of present ills. Religion has to do with human transformation. The early church believed that God's ultimate self-revelation took place not in a startling theophany, but in a human being, the man Jesus Christ."[13] Elsewhere he observes, "in the major trends of biblical religion divine transcendence is inextricably linked with holiness and justice. God's majesty makes men tremble not only because God wholly transcends human proportions, but because God judges the sinful world, and God's holiness is attractive not only because it offers consolation but because it promises to turn right-side up a world that has been placed upside down by sin."[14] The ever recurring need of the church is to discover what it means to confess the transcendent God of the Bible within the political structures of a particular place. It has something to do with the affirmation of this world as the place within which to live free and stay human in submission to God, made known in Jesus Christ.

6. There is no common mind in the theological tradition of the church concerning the means at the church's disposal to oppose unjust rulers. Closely related to this debate is the question of violence—both in the defense of the state and revolutionary violence. This problem needs to be treated in a book of its own, and it is not under consideration here.

There are different attitudes to violence in the Christian tradition. After the Edict of Milan the pacifism of the early church gave way to a willingness to fight for the Christian Empire. The promotion of violence by the church through the period of the Crusades remains perhaps the most hideous scar in the history of Christianity. The doctrine of just war was an attempt on the part of some to limit war, but there remains a narrow line between "just," "justified," and "holy" war. It is against this background that the challenge of pacifism and nonviolent resistance remains a challenge that the world cannot afford to ignore. Some cannot affirm pacifism *in principle,* not wanting to rule out the possibility of resorting to arms in certain extreme circumstances while honoring nonviolence as normative practice for a Christian. Others have thoughtlessly supported state and institutional violence while expecting those who suffer most as a result of such action to be pacifists—or merely passive. If the church recognizes any form of violence as anything but a desperate last resort when all else has been tried, what Barth called a *Grenzfall* situation, the spiral of violence can only escalate until all that is worth living for no longer exists. Simple sanity suggests that there may come a moment when an oppressed or violated people can do no other than take up arms to defend themselves against the aggressor. Honest reflection, in turn, tells us that few Christians have with planned consistency explored the options of direct nonviolent action as an alternative. This debate has not been explored with any measure of sustained vigor in the mainline churches through the course of their history, and certainly not with the kind of urgency that is demanded by the many violent situations in the world today.

THE CHURCH IN SOUTH AFRICA

It has often been said that South Africa is a high-profile microcosm of the problems of the world. Certainly the relationship of the church to the state in South Africa is an overt example of less obvious strains between church and state in other parts of the world. This level of explicitness can be attributed to a variety of factors: the intensity with which the apartheid policy of this country has been theologically promoted, the continuing effects of neo-Calvinist Afrikaner nationalism, religio-cultural resistance to the impact of secularism, the abiding success of missionary activity, and the intensity of African religiosity.

The relevance of the South African debate also applies at another level. The church in South Africa is as heterogeneous as elsewhere. This has given rise to a variety of different church-state models, providing a concrete case study of the interrelationship between different, and at times conflicting, doctrines of church and state. In spite of this, in each instance when the church has engaged the state it has theologically affirmed the need to confront and, in some situations, disobey the state in order that it might obey divine rather than human authority. This is documented in Part Three on the church in South Africa. These churches have divided against one another, and not infrequently within their own ranks, primarily because of different assessments of the prevailing political situation. This has, in turn, been strongly influenced by the social location of a particular church at a particular time in history.

A further dimension to the church-state debate in South Africa which makes it relevant to broader ecumenical debate is the *traditional* nature of this debate. The documents included in Part Three show that the church-state debate in South Africa has, for historical reasons, been dominated by traditional Protestant theology, while the Roman Catholic church has sustained the commitment to resist apartheid at every opportunity. The "Call to Prayer for the End to Unjust Rule" provides a summary statement of this tradition which calls Christians to resist unjust rulers. This "traditional" approach to theology in South Africa refutes the judgment of the South African government and those churches supporting the present regime there which attribute the conflict between church and state to the "alien" influences of modern politicized forms of theology.[15] In more recent times the influence of black and liberation theologies in South Africa has become more dominant, a trend which is in line with theological developments in other parts of the world. The debate in South Africa has, however, retained a traditional Reformed, and in some cases orthodox Catholic, dimension which is different from most black and some liberation theologies elsewhere in the world.

The debate on church-state relations has, however, taken a significant shift—although theologically it is primarily a shift in emphasis—with the publication of the Kairos document. Like the "Call to Prayer for the End to Unjust Rule," it calls the church to be quite explicitly against the present regime in South Africa. The Kairos document is overtly in continuity with trends discerned in liberation theologies written elsewhere in the world. It constitutes a specific call for theology to emerge from theory to praxis and to initiate action against the oppressive structures of apartheid, both racial and economic. Yet in so doing it is also in continuity with trends already discerned in other recent statements on church-state relations in South Africa. Its major significance is the base from which it emerged. While signed by many academic theologians, clerics, and theologically trained laypersons who are not in the frontline of oppression in South Africa, it primarily constitutes the communal thinking of "community-based" theologians, the majority of whom are black. Herein is its potential power. It is not theology imposed from *above* by church leaders or one or two academic theologians. It constitutes a serious attempt from *below*, by people engaged in the struggle to discover what it means to be a Christian amidst the oppression, primarily in the black townships of South Africa. The significance of this kind of theology has not yet been fully realized, although it constitutes a new point of departure in church-state relations in this country.

The documents on the church in South Africa are an attempt to provide a contextual focus for the historical debate which constitutes the larger part of this book. Bishop Desmond Tutu once argued that it is much easier to be a Christian in South Africa than elsewhere in the world, because the issues are so much clearer here. The church is on trial in places like South Africa, and if it fails to be the church in this kind of situation, it has perhaps forfeited the right to exist in less explicitly oppressive situations. Its task here is no different from what it has been throughout history. It is to be the church in obedience to Jesus Christ, and by so being it will enable the state to be the state. "This," according to the SACC response to the Eloff Commission of Inquiry into its activities, "is the most loyal service which the church can render to the state, to a particular government and to itself—it is to protect the government from itself and from unreasonable demands by its people."[16] It should strive to ensure that civil authority fulfils its office as instituted by God, that is to rule with justice, goodness, and love (Rom. 13). In awareness of this responsibility to the state and in the interest of the common good, Christians have prayed that they may be governed in a quiet and Godlike way. More recently in South Africa, they have prayed that God will remove from office those who persist in defying his laws. It is also this responsibility which has motivated the debate on the nature of tyranny in the Christian tradition within the Kairos document.

NOTES

1. Gregory Baum, *Religion and Alienation: A Theological Reading of Sociology* (New York: Paulist, 1975), pp. 62–84.
2. In *Kerk en Stad* (Cape Town: NG Kerk Boekhandel, 1947). Quoted by Desmond Tutu in his submission to the Eloff Commission of Inquiry into the SACC; see *The Divine Intention* (Braamfontein: An SACC Publication, 1982).

3. José Míguez Bonino, *Toward a Christian Political Ethics* (Philadelphia: Fortress, 1983), p. 17.
4. Walter Brueggemann, "Trajectories in Old Testament Literature and the Sociology of Ancient Israel," in *The Bible and Liberation: Political and Social Hermeneutics* (Maryknoll, N.Y.: Orbis, 1983), p. 313.
5. C. E. B. Cranfield, *The Service of God* (London: Epworth Press, 1965), pp. 62, 65.
6. Ibid., p. 62.
7. Ernst Troeltsch, *The Social Teaching of the Christian Churches*, vol. 1 (New York: Macmillan, 1956), pp. 328–43.
8. J. W. C. Wand, *The Four Great Heresies* (London: SCM, 1955), pp. 377f. For an application of this definition of heresy to apartheid and the white NGK, see John W. de Gruchy, "Towards a Confessing Church: The Implications of Heresy," in John W. de Gruchy and Charles Villa-Vicencio, eds., *Apartheid is a Heresy* (Grand Rapids: Eerdmans, 1983), pp. 83–86.
9. The translation of this quotation from Barth's *Römerbrief* is by Paul Lehmann in *The Transfiguration of Politics* (New York: Harper & Row, 1975), p. 44. See also Karl Barth, *The Epistle to the Romans* (London: Oxford University Press, 1960).
10. Lehmann, pp. 41–48.
11. Dietrich Bonhoeffer, *Gesammelte Schriften*, VI (Munich: Christian Kaiser Verlag, 1974), p. 350.
12. Míguez Bonino, p. 43.
13. Gregory Baum, "The Sociology of Roman Catholic Theology," in D. Martin, J. O. Mills, and U. S. F. Pickering, eds., *Sociology and Theology: Alliance and Conflict* (Brighton: The Harvester Press, 1980), p. 135.
14. Gregory Baum, "Peter Berger's Unfinished Symphony," in Gregory Baum, ed., *Sociology and Human Destiny* (New York: Seabury, 1980), p. 119.
15. See Charles Villa-Vicencio, "Theology in the Service of the State: The Steyn and Eloff Commissions," in Charles Villa-Vicencio and John W. de Gruchy, eds., *Resistance and Hope: South African Essays in Honour of Beyers Naudé* (Grand Rapids: Eerdmans, 1985), pp. 112–25.
16. See "Response to the Evaluation of the Activities of the SACC Division of Justice and Reconciliation in the Memorandum of the South African Police," submitted to the Eloff Commission by the director of the SACC Division of Justice and Reconciliation, Dr. Wolfram Kistner.

PART ONE

THE CLASSICAL PERIOD

CHAPTER 1

THE EARLY CHURCH

The earliest encounter between the Christian church and the Roman state is, with good reason, commonly known as the age of martyrs. Certainly the apostle Paul could appeal to his Roman citizenship as a basis for demanding legal justice (Acts 16:38), but ultimately he was imprisoned for his faith (2 Cor. 11:23; Phil. 1:16–17), and according to tradition both he and Peter were martyred by the state. Spiritual perfection as the goal of the Christian faith was seen to be attainable through faithful and obedient living and death, and this soon manifested itself in a cult of Christian martyrdom (Rev. 2:13f.; 17:6f.). The martyr's death came to be regarded as a second baptism through which one could become a true disciple and a perfect imitator of Christ.[1]

POLYCARP

The significance of the martyr's death for the life of the early church is seen nowhere more clearly than in *The Epistle Concerning the Martyrdom of Polycarp*, a text commonly regarded as the earliest of all the *martyria*, although some regard it as having been interpolated at several points and date it later than the middle of the second century to which it is commonly ascribed.[2] It tells of the persecution and death of Polycarp. Although it describes the bones of the saint as "more precious than the most exquisite jewels, and more purified than gold" (the burial places of such bones were among the most important centers of worship for early Christians), it affirms, "the martyrs . . . we love," but "the Son of God we worship." In affirming the example of those who witnessed unto death, radical monotheism—in the sense of being obedient to God alone whatever the consequences—became the cornerstone of church-state relations in the early church. It also saved the normative witness of the early church from aberrant and deviant forms of relic and saint worship such as emerged in later years.

Central to Christian martyrdom was a distinction between spiritual and political realms, a distinction perpetuated in church-state relations in medieval and Reformation times and one which continues to have decisive and at times contradictory implications for church-state relations today. In the early church this distinction was interpreted to mean that spiritual authority impinged on the political realm in both judgment and renewal. For early Christians this was a distinction grounded in a theological suspicion of, if not hostility to, the state—whether Jewish or Roman—shown by the followers of Jesus who claimed that his kingdom was not of this world (John 18:36). It never occurred to them that Caesar could become a Christian. They anticipated a permanent minority status and interpreted their trials and persecution as signs of the imminent return of Christ (1 Pet. 4:7–14). In this milieu they saw their task to be uncompromised obedience to God alone in anticipation of the *eschaton* as they prayed "*Marana-tha*," "Our Lord come" (1 Cor. 16:22).

This theology of political noninvolvement, however, did not imply indifference to society. Civil authority was seen to be given by God for the sake of orderly and just government. Such authority was regarded as deserving the respect and honor of Christians, and obedience to such authority was seen to be in accordance with the will of God (Rom. 13:1–7; 1 Pet. 2:13–15). It was this reality that would become the basis of the traditional prayer within Christianity that people may be quietly and justly governed. The New Testament community was equally clear that when legitimate, God-given authority was transgressed and Christians were confronted with a choice between obedience to civil authority and the commandments of God, it was "for us to obey God rather than man" (Acts 5:29). It was the possibility of this situation that caused the church to recognize that civil authority can be a source of blasphemy against God (Rev. 13).

The actual conflict between the early church and the state was occasioned by the introduction of a qualification to the tried and tested Roman policy of religious toleration. Emperor veneration was first introduced, although never seriously enforced, by Caesar Augustus (27 B.C.E.–14 C.E.). Such veneration was required even though people were, as a rule, free to practice the many other religions in the Empire. The debate surrounding this practice is a long one, but the conventional explanation is the need to provide a religio-cultural sense of cohesion in a sprawling and diverse Empire. Not many emperors imposed veneration of themselves and, as a rule, it was only at death that emperors were seen to be enrolled on an ever-increasing list of gods. Caligula (Gaius) (37–41), who required that his image be installed in the temple in Jerusalem, was apparently the first emperor to impose worship of himself with any amount of zeal, and his assassination was probably not unrelated to his self-perception and demand for religious veneration. In time other emperors, Nero (54–68) and Domitian (81–96) among them, also demanded divine recognition during their lifetimes. Perhaps it is no coincidence that these two, like Caligula, were eventually assassinated.

Certainly Nero and Domitian were hostile toward Christianity. They regarded the church as a source of superstition, which was a capital offense, and viewed with deep mistrust its secret and closed meetings. No doubt they were influenced by rumors that Christians were indulging in immoral practices, atheism, adultery and incest. For them this all added up to the danger of social instability and political intrigue.[3] Much has also been made by some scholars of the fact that the Jews, also monotheists who refused emperor worship, were exempt from the kind of persecution which the Christians faced. The explanation which they offer is that while the Jews exercised political and economic influence in the Empire, the Christians were, generally speaking, from the poorer classes and without influence.[4] In more recent times this thesis concerning the deprived social status of Christians has, however, also come to be challenged.[5]

The conflict between church and state in the Roman Empire came out of different concepts of what constituted good citizenship.[6] The Christian apologists never tired of stressing the good and virtuous nature of Christian citizenship. In obeying God and expecting the just and consistent execution of ethically defensible laws, they believed they were rendering the most loyal submission that any government could expect of its citizens. The Roman state in turn understood citizenship to entail unquestioning obedience to its laws. This included the right to demand veneration of the emperor as a public act of allegiance to the state. The total rejection of this and the obligation to render uncompromising obedience to God alone were regarded by Christians as the essence of true faith. To refuse to sacrifice was to confess Christ; to give way and comply was to deny him. The church rejected any possibility for compromise, and the ensuing confrontation was inevitable. There is, in fact, evidence that some early Christians were, by today's standards, quite unreasonable in refusing to conform to the demands of civil law. "It was little wonder," concludes Cadoux, "that even reasonable and humane magistrates were struck with the obstinacy of the Christians."[7]

TERTULLIAN

It was this conflict which gave rise to a succession of Christian apologists, among whom Tertullian (150–220) was certainly one of the most skilled and articulate. He is generally regarded as surpassed only by Augustine as an exponent of Latin Christianity. His *Apology*, extracts from which are included here, is a masterpiece of apologetics, legal argument, and Christian theology. Addressing Roman sensibilities, he appealed to their own sense of morality: "Your gods have more reason to complain of you than Christians." He considered the relationship between law and justice, arguing that if law was not based on justice it was tyranny, and affirmed a strong notion of conscientious commitment to what is good, even if it meant disobeying a law: "If I have found what your law prohibits to be good . . . has it not lost its power to debar me from it?" Furthermore, it is not only to be justly administered, it must be seen to be just by those affected by it: ". . . it is not enough that a law is just, nor that a judge should be convinced of its justice; those from whom obedience is expected should have that conviction too." At the same time the familiar distinction between the divine and human spheres of early patristic thought is affirmed: "As the divine and human are ever opposed to each other, when we are condemned by you, we are acquitted by the Highest." Ultimately it was this kind of radical obedience to God alone which formed the basis of Tertullian's response to the state, generating as it did both uncompromising resistance and a measure of indifference to the complexities of civil rule. While there is some evidence of Christians being in the service of the state, the norm was nonparticipation, which led to the charge of political irresponsibility frequently levelled against them. Such indifference could, however, be interpreted as part of their resistance to a particular form of civic rule, because when the political structures were changed under Constantine, Christians apparently flocked to participate in the civil service and the army and to accept political office.

Given his framework of reference and expectations, Tertullian was not primarily interested in political renewal at all. What he wanted was merely a government that would leave the church to affirm its obedience to God. It was this *theological* commitment that resulted in the political confrontation that existed between the church and the Roman state. The highest loyalty and honor which Tertullian believed he could bring to the state was to convince it that its authority was under that of God. In this context prayer for the state to find its rightful place in relation to God was the essence of the early church's loyalty to, and paradoxically its resistance against, the state.

EUSEBIUS OF CAESAREA

The sharp distinction between the pre- and post-Constantinian church is shown in clear outline by comparing Tertullian's *Apology* with Eusebius's (260–337) panegyric written to celebrate the thirtieth anniversary of Constantine's reign on July 25, 335.

One can almost excuse Eusebius's uncritical adulation. The unthinkable had happened. Having suffered under Diocletian's persecution, he saw the publication of the Edict of Milan in 312 allowing the church freedom of worship and ordering the return of confiscated properties as an acknowledgement of divine authority. Constantine had become the supreme ruler in the West, having seen, according to a tradition preserved by Eusebius, the sign of the cross in the sky with the words *In hoc signo vinces*, "in this sign you will conquer," the day before the decisive battle. Within a little more than a decade he was the sole ruler of the Empire—largely as a result of a series of bloody and treacherous deeds—and he made Christianity the official religion of the Empire. Imperial power was suddenly seen to be on God's side, whereas before it was seen to be demonic—and therefore to be despised and rejected by Christians. The fundamental shift in the church's perception of the state concerned its attitude to political power. Alistair Kee observes: "Constantine achieved by kindness what his predecessors had not been able to achieve by force. Without a threat or a blow, and all unsuspecting, the Christians were led into captivity and their religion transformed into a new imperial cult."[8] With this a new consciousness was assumed by Christians.

Monotheism, in whatever form it was appropriated by Constantine, stripped the emperor of his divinity. Certainly Eusebius recognized that the emperor was not divine, but neither was he regarded as a mere mortal. He came to regard the emperor as the favored one whom God "receives," "a transcript of divine sovereignty," "an imitation of God himself," a representative of the divine Logos who "reigns from ages which had no beginning." He was a "friend" of God, and "an interpreter of the Word of God," one who frames "his earthly government according to the pattern of that divine original, feeling strength in its conformity to the Monarchy of God." A decisively new phase of church-state relations had been reached. The political implications of the early church's radical monotheism were thrust aside. The monarchy had been sacralized, and it would take the church centuries to unravel this kind of legitimation, which elevated civil authority to a status not hitherto known within Christianity. "The cosmic theology, which regarded Jesus as the incarnation of the Cosmic Logos, could be used to integrate the political realm with the cosmic realm, regarding Constantine as representing the providential rule in the political cosmos that Christ represents in the natural and metaphysical cosmos."[9] Henceforth the concept of political rule would enjoy a theological legitimation against which opponents of a particular civil authority could only prevail in the most extenuating circumstances. From this basis the Judeo-Christian tradition would be reinterpreted by Christian orthodoxy with only minor deviations until well into the present century. Hornus concedes that while Constantine was in an immediate and material sense "an outstanding benefactor of the church," he was also "the initiator of the oppressive Caesaro-papism for which the church was often to suffer during the ensuing centuries."[10] To be more accurate, it was rather the church's theological legitimation of Constantine which sealed its political captivity.

Eusebius, as Norman Baynes shows, used and adapted the Hellenistic model of *mimesis*, whereby the king came to be regarded as an imitation of the king in heaven, to legitimate the rule of Constantine.[11] Alistair Kee, in turn, asks with Feuerbach whether the reverse is not true, namely, that God in heaven is recreated in the image of the earthly king.[12] Certainly the history of theologized political legitimation provides sufficient evidence to substantiate the claim that once the ideological foundation had been laid, the way is open to such exploitation. It is this close relationship between church and state that has ultimately caused many of the great schisms of the church. This kind of theological justification of a particular political ideology has been used and abused in different situations through the ages to give divine sanction to a host of different political dictatorships and oligarchies that could scarcely be measured against the scriptural norms of justice, righteousness, and peace and not be found wanting.

The texts that follow—extracts from the *Martyrdom of Polycarp*, Tertullian's *Apology*, and the oration of Eusebius *In Praise of Constantine* — are intended to enable the reader to see the fundamental transition which took place in the church's view of the state in the patristic period, a shift that was to set the course for centuries to come.

NOTES

1. Tertullian, *On Baptism*, in Alexander Roberts and James Donaldson, eds., *The Ante-Nicene Fathers* (Grand Rapids: Eerdmans, n.d.), 3:677; Ignatius of Antioch, Epistle to the Romans, ibid., 1:75–76.

2. "Introductory Note," Epistle Concerning the Martyrdom of Polycarp, ibid., 1:37.
3. See Harry R. Boer, *A Short History of the Early Church* (Grand Rapids: Eerdmans, 1979), pp. 45–48; and C. J. Cadoux, *The Early Church and the World* (Edinburgh: T. & T. Clark, 1925), pp. 97–115.
4. A. Deissmann, *Light from the Ancient Near East* (London: Hodder and Stoughton, 1927), p. 144.
5. See R. H. Smith, "Were the Early Christians Middle Class? A Sociological Analysis of the New Testament," in N. K. Gottwald, ed., *The Bible and Liberation* (Maryknoll, N.Y.: Orbis, 1985), pp. 441–57, and Gerd Theissen, *The Social Setting of Pauline Christianity* (Philadelphia: Fortress, 1982), pp. 69–120.
6. See Cadoux, p. 251.
7. Ibid., p. 253.
8. Alistair Kee, *Constantine Versus Christ* (London: SCM, 1982), p. 154.
9. Rosemary Radford Ruether, "Augustine and Christian Political Theology," *Interpretation*, 29 (1975), 256.
10. Jean-Michel Hornus, *It Is Not Lawful For Me To Fight* (Scottdale, Pa.: Herald Press, 1980), p. 212.
11. Norman H. Baynes, *Byzantine Studies and Other Essays* (London: Athlone Press, 1955), pp. 168–72.
12. Kee, p. 132.

SELECT BIBLIOGRAPHY

Baynes, Norman H. *Byzantine Studies and Other Essays.* London: Athlone Press, 1955.

Boer, H. R. *A Short History of the Early Church.* Grand Rapids: Eerdmans, 1979.

Daniélou, J., and H. Marrou, eds. *The First Six Hundred Years,* Vol. 1 of *The Christian Centuries,* ed. L. J. Rogier, R. Aubert, and M. D. Knowles. New York: McGraw-Hill, 1964.

Hornus, J.-M. *It Is Not Lawful For Me To Fight.* Scottdale, Pa.: Herald Press, 1980.

Kee, A. *Constantine Versus Christ.* London: S.C.M., 1982.

Pelikan, J. *The Christian Tradition,* vol. 1: *The Emergence of the Catholic Tradition.* Chicago: University of Chicago Press, 1971.

Walker, W. *A History of the Christian Church.* Edinburgh: T. & T. Clark, 1976.

Willis, J. R. *A History of Christian Thought from Apostolic Times to St. Augustine.* Hicksville, N.Y.: Exposition Press, 1976.

CONCERNING THE MARTYRDOM OF THE HOLY POLYCARP

THE ENCYCLICAL EPISTLE OF THE CHURCH AT SMYRNA

THE CONFESSION OF POLYCARP

Chap. IX And when he came near, the proconsul asked him whether he was Polycarp. On his confessing that he was, [the proconsul] sought to persuade him to deny [Christ], saying, "Have respect to thy old age," and other similar things, according to their custom, [such as], "Swear by the fortune of Caesar; repent, and say, Away with the Atheists." But Polycarp, gazing with a stern countenance on all the multitude of the wicked heathen then in the stadium, and waving his hand towards them, while with groans he looked up to heaven, said, "Away with the Atheists." Then, the proconsul urging him, and saying, "Swear, and I will set thee at liberty, reproach Christ;" Polycarp declared, "Eighty and six years have I served Him, and He never did me any injury: how then can I blaspheme my King and my Saviour?"

Chap. X And when the proconsul yet again pressed him, and said, "Swear by the fortune of Caesar," he answered, "Since thou art vainly urgent that, as thou sayest, I should swear by the fortune of Caesar, and pretendest not to know who and what I am, hear me declare with boldness, I am a Christian.

Chap. XIV They did not nail him, but simply bound him. And he, placing his hands behind him, and being bound like a distinguished ram [taken] out of a great flock for sacrifice, and prepared to be an acceptable burnt-offering unto God, looked up to heaven, and said, "O Lord God Almighty, the Father of thy beloved and blessed Son Jesus Christ, by whom we have received the knowledge of Thee, the God of angels and powers, and of every creature, and of the whole race of the righteous who live before thee, I give Thee thanks that Thou hast counted me worthy of this day and this hour, that I should have a part in the number of Thy martyrs, in the cup of thy Christ, to the resurrection of eternal life, both of soul and body, through the incorruption [imparted] by the Holy Ghost.

THE DEATH OF POLYCARP

Chap. XV When he had pronounced this *amen*, and so finished his prayer, those who were appointed for the purpose kindled the fire. And as the flame blazed forth in great fury, we, to whom it was given to witness it, beheld a great miracle, and have been preserved that we might report to others what then took place. For the fire, shaping itself into the form of an arch, like the sail of a ship

---

[Source: Alexander Roberts and James Donaldson, eds., *The Ante-Nicene Fathers*, vol. 1: *The Apostolic Fathers with Justin Martyr and Irenaeus* (Grand Rapids: Eerdmans, n.d.).]

when filled with the wind, encompassed as by a circle the body of the martyr. And he appeared within not like flesh which is burnt, but as bread that is baked, or as gold and silver glowing in a furnace. Moreover, we perceived such a sweet odour [coming from the pile], as if frankincense or some such precious spices had been smoking there.

Chap. XVI At length, when those wicked men perceived that his body could not be consumed by the fire, they commanded an executioner to go near and pierce him through with a dagger.

THE SON OF GOD WE ADORE, THE MARTYRS WE LOVE

Chap. XVII But when the adversary of the race of the righteous, the envious, malicious, and wicked one, perceived the impressive nature of his martyrdom, and [considered] the blameless life he had led from the beginning, and how he was now crowned with the wreath of immortality, having beyond dispute received his reward, he did his utmost that not the least memorial of him should be taken away by us, although many desired to do this, and to become possessors of his holy flesh. For this end he suggested it to Nicetes, the father of Herod and brother of Alce, to go and entreat the governor not to give up his body to be buried, "lest," said he, "forsaking Him that was crucified, they begin to worship this one." This he said at the suggestion and urgent persuasion of the Jews, who also watched us, as we sought to take him out of the fire, being ignorant of this, that it is neither possible for us ever to forsake Christ, who suffered for the salvation of such as shall be saved throughout the whole world (the blameless one for sinners), nor to worship any other. For Him indeed, as being the Son of God, we adore; but the martyrs, as disciples and followers of the Lord, we worthily love on account of their extraordinary affection towards their own King and Master, of whom may we also be made companions and fellow-disciples!

THE BONES OF POLYCARP MORE PURIFIED THAN GOLD

Chap. XVIII The centurion then, seeing the strife excited by the Jews, placed the body in the midst of the fire, and consumed it. Accordingly, we afterwards took up his bones, as being more precious than the most exquisite jewels, and more purified than gold, and deposited them in a fitting place, whither, being gathered together, as opportunity is allowed us, with joy and rejoicing, the Lord shall grant us to celebrate the anniversary of his martyrdom, both in memory of those who have already finished their course, and for the exercising and preparation of those yet to walk in their steps.

Chap. XIX This, then, is the account of the blessed Polycarp, who, being the twelfth that was martyred in Smyrna (reckoning those also of Philadelphia), yet occupies a place of his own in the memory of all men, insomuch that he is everywhere spoken of by the heathen themselves. He was not merely an illustrious teacher, but also a pre-eminent martyr, whose martyrdom all desire to imitate, as having been altogether consistent with the Gospel of Christ.

TERTULLIAN

APOLOGY

JUSTICE + THE LAW

Chap. IV We shall reply to the accusation of all the various crimes we are said to be guilty of in secret, such as we find them committing in the light of day, and as being guilty of which we are held to be wicked, senseless, worthy of punishment, deserving of ridicule. But since, when our truth meets you successfully at all points, the authority of the laws as a last resort is set up against it, so that it is either said that their determinations are absolutely conclusive, or the necessity of obedience is, however unwillingly, preferred to the truth, I shall first, in this matter of the laws, grapple with you as with their chosen protectors. Now first, when you sternly lay it down in your sentences, "It is not lawful for you to exist," and with unhesitating rigour you enjoin this to be carried out, you exhibit the violence and unjust domination of mere tyranny, if you deny the thing to be lawful, simply on the ground that you wish it to be unlawful, not because it ought to be. But if you would have it unlawful because it *ought* not to be lawful, without doubt that should have no permission of law which does harm; and on this ground, in fact, it is already determined that whatever is beneficial is legitimate. Well, if I have found what your law prohibits to be good, as one who has arrived at such a previous opinion, has it not lost its power to debar me from it, though that very thing, if it were evil, it would justly forbid to me? If your law has gone wrong, it is of human origin, I think; it has not fallen from heaven. Is it wonderful that man should err in making a law, or come to his senses in rejecting it? . . .

How many laws lie hidden out of sight which still require to be reformed! For it is neither the number of their years nor the dignity of their maker that commends them, but simply that they are just; and therefore, when their injustice is recognized, they are deservedly condemned, even though they condemn. . . .

It is not enough that a law is just, nor that the judge should be convinced of its justice; those from whom obedience is expected should have that conviction too. Nay, a law lies under strong suspicions which does not care to have itself tried and approved: it is a positively wicked law, if, unproved, it tyrannizes over men.

REFUSAL TO WORSHIP THE GODS: GOD ALONE DISPENSES KINGDOMS

Chap. X "You do not worship the gods," you say; "and you do not offer sacrifices for the emperors." Well, we do not offer sacrifice for others, for the same reason that we do not for ourselves,—namely, that your gods are not at all the objects of our worship. So we are accused of sacrilege and treason. This is the chief

---

[Source: Alexander Roberts and James Donaldson, eds., *The Ante-Nicene Fathers*, vol. 3: *Latin Christianity: Its Founder, Tertullian* (Grand Rapids: Eerdmans, n.d.).]

ground of charge against us—nay, it is the sum-total of our offending; and it is worthy then of being inquired into, if neither prejudice nor injustice be the judge, the one of which has no idea of discovering the truth, and the other simply and at once rejects it. We do not worship your gods, because we know that there are no such beings.

Chap. XVII The object of our worship is the One God, He who by His commanding word, His arranging wisdom, His mighty power, brought forth from nothing this entire mass of our world, with all its array of elements, bodies, spirits, for the glory of His majesty; whence also the Greeks have bestowed on it the name of Κόσμος. The eye cannot see Him, though He is (spiritually) visible. He is incomprehensible, though in grace He is manifested. He is beyond our utmost thought, though our human faculties conceive of Him. He is therefore equally real and great. But that which, in the ordinary sense, can be seen and handled and conceived, is inferior to the eyes by which it is taken in, and the hands by which it is tainted, and the faculties by which it is discovered; but that which is infinite is known only to itself. This it is which gives some notion of God, while yet beyond all our conceptions—our very incapacity of fully grasping Him affords us the idea of what He really is. He is presented to our minds in His transcendent greatness, as at once known and unknown. And this is the crowning guilt of men, that they will not recognize One, of whom they cannot possibly be ignorant. Would you have the proof from the works of His hands, so numerous and so great, which both contain you and sustain you, which minister at once to your enjoyment, and strike you with awe; or would you rather have it from the testimony of the soul itself? Though under the oppressive bondage of the body, though led astray by depraving customs, though enervated by lusts and passions, though in slavery to false gods; yet, whenever the soul comes to itself, as out of a surfeit, or a sleep, or a sickness, and attains something of its natural soundness, it speaks of God; using no other words, because this is the peculiar name of the true God. "God is great and good"—"Which may God give," are the words on every lip. It bears witness, too, that God is judge, exclaiming, "God sees," and, "I commend myself to God," and, "God will repay me." O noble testimony of the soul by nature Christian! Then, too, in using such words as these, it looks not to the Capitol, but to the heavens. It knows that there is the throne of the living God, as from Him and from thence itself came down.

Chap. XXVI Examine then, and see if *He* be not the dispenser of kingdoms, who is Lord at once of the world which is ruled, and of man himself who rules; if He have not ordained the changes of dynasties, with their appointed seasons, who was before all time, and made the world a body of times; if the rise and the fall of states are not the work of Him, under whose sovereignty the human race once existed without states at all.

THE WORSHIP OF GOD ALONE ENSURES THE PROTECTION OF THE STATE

Chap. XXX For we offer prayer for the safety of our princes to the eternal, the true, the living God, whose favour, beyond all others, they must themselves desire. They know from whom they have obtained their power; they know, as they are men, from whom they have received life itself; they are convinced that He is God alone, on whose power alone they are entirely dependent, to whom they are second, after whom they occupy the highest places, before and above all the gods. Why not, since they are above all living men, and the living, as living, are superior to the dead? They reflect upon the extent of their power, and so they come to understand the highest; they acknowledge that they have all their might from Him against whom their might is nought. Let the emperor make war on heaven; let him lead heaven captive in his triumph; let him put guards on heaven; let him impose taxes on heaven! He cannot. Just because he is less than heaven, he is great. . . .

Without ceasing, for all our emperors we offer prayer. We pray for life prolonged; for security to the empire; for protection to the imperial house; for brave armies, a faithful senate, a virtuous people, the world at rest, whatever, as man or Caesar, an emperor would wish. These things I cannot ask from any but the God from whom I know I shall obtain them, both because He alone bestows them and because I have claims upon Him for their gift, as being a servant of His. . . .

With our hands thus stretched out and up to God, rend us with your iron claws, hang us up on crosses, wrap us in flames, take our heads from us with the sword, let loose the wild beasts on us,—the very attitude of a Christian praying is one of preparation for all punishment. Let this, good rulers, be your work: wring from us the soul, beseeching God on the emperor's behalf. Upon the truth of God, and devotion to His name, put the brand of crime.

Chap. XXXIII But why dwell longer on the reverence and sacred respect of Christians to the emperor, whom we cannot but look up to as called by our Lord to his office? So that on valid grounds I might say Caesar is more ours than yours, for our God has appointed him. Therefore, as having this propriety in him, I do more than you for his welfare, not merely because I ask it of Him who can give it, or because I ask it as one who deserves to get it, but also because, in keeping the majesty of Caesar within due limits, and putting it under the Most High, and making it less than divine, I commend him the more to the favour of Deity, to whom I make him alone inferior. But I place him in subjection to one I regard as more glorious than himself. Never will I call the emperor God, and that either because it is not in me to be guilty of falsehood; or that I dare not turn him into ridicule; or that not even himself will desire to have that high name applied to him. If he is but a man, it is his interest as man to give God His higher place. Let him think it enough to bear the name of emperor. That, too, is a great name of God's giving. To call him God, is to rob him of his title. If he is not a man, emperor he cannot be.

Chap. XXXIV Give all reverence to God, if you wish Him to be propitious to the emperor. Give up all worship of, and belief in, any other being as divine. Cease also to give the sacred name to him who has need of God himself. If such adulation is not ashamed of its lie, in addressing a man as divine, let it have some dread at least of the evil omen which it bears. It is the invocation of a curse, to give Caesar the name of god before his apotheosis.

THE CHRISTIAN BENEFIT TO SOCIETY

Chap. XXXVII If we are enjoined, then, to love our enemies, as I have remarked above, whom have we to hate? If injured, we are forbidden to retaliate, lest we become as bad ourselves: who can suffer injury at our hands? In regard to this, recall your own experiences. How often you inflict gross cruelties on Christians, partly because it is your own inclination, and partly in obedience to the laws! How often, too, the hostile mob, paying no regard to you, takes the law into its own hand, and assails us with stones and flames! . . .

Yet, banded together as we are, ever so ready to sacrifice our lives, what single case of revenge for injury are you able to point to, though, if it were held right among us to repay evil by evil, a single night with a torch or two could achieve an ample vengeance?

Chap. XXXVIII We have no pressing inducement to take part in your public meetings; nor is there aught more entirely foreign to us than affairs of state. We acknowledge one all-embracing commonwealth—the world. We renounce all your spectacles, as strongly as we renounce the matters originating them, which we know were conceived of superstition, when we give up the very things which are the basis of their representations. Among us nothing is ever said, or seen, or heard, which has anything in common with the madness of the circus, the immodesty of the theatre, the atrocities of the arena, the useless exercises of the wrestling-ground. Why do you take offence at us because we differ from you in regard to your pleasures? If we will not partake of your enjoyments, the loss is ours, if there be loss in the case, not yours. We reject what pleases you. You, on the other hand, have no taste for what is our delight.

Chap. XXXIX I shall at once go on, then, to exhibit the peculiarities of the Christian society, that, as I have refuted the evil charged against it, I may point out its positive good. We are a body knit together as such by a common religious profession, by unity of discipline, and by the bond of a common hope. We meet together as an assembly and congregation, that, offering up prayer to God as with united force, we may wrestle with Him in our supplications. This violence God delights in. We pray, too, for the emperors, for their ministers and for all in authority, for the welfare of the world, for the prevalence of peace, for the delay of the final consummation. We assemble to read our sacred writings, if any peculiarity of the times makes either forewarning or reminiscence needful. . . .

Though we have our treasure-chest, it is not made up of purchase-money, as of a religion that has its price. On the monthly day, if he likes, each puts in a small donation. . . .

These gifts are, as it were, piety's deposit fund. For they are not taken thence and spent on feasts, and drinking-bouts, and eating-houses, but to support and bury poor people, to supply the wants of boys and girls destitute of means and parents, and of old persons confined now to the house; such, too, as have suffered shipwreck; and if there happen to be any in the mines, or banished to the islands, or shut up in the prisons, for nothing but their fidelity to the cause of God's Church, they become the nurslings of their confession. But it is mainly the deeds of a love so noble that lead many to put a brand upon us. . . .

We are in our congregations just what we are when separated from each other; we are as a community what we are as individuals; we injure nobody, we trouble nobody. When the upright, when the virtuous meet together, when the pious, when the pure assemble in congregation, you ought not to call that a faction, but a *curia*—[i.e., the court of God.]

Chap. XLIV Yes, and no one considers what the loss is to the common weal,—a loss as great as it is real, no one estimates the injury entailed upon the state, when, men of virtue as we are, we are put to death in such numbers; when so many of the truly good suffer the last penalty. And here we call your own acts to witness, you who are daily presiding at the trials of prisoners, and passing sentence upon crimes. Well, in your long lists of those accused of many and various atrocities, has any assassin, any cutpurse, any man guilty of sacrilege, or seduction, or stealing bathers' clothes, his name entered as being a Christian too? Or when Christians are brought before you on the mere ground of their name, is there ever found among them an ill-doer of the sort? It is always with your folk the prison is steaming, the mines are sighing, the wild beasts are fed: it is from you the exhibitors of gladiatorial shows always get their herds of criminals to feed up for the occasion. You find no Christian there, except simply as being such; or if one is there as something else, a Christian he is no longer.

Chap. XLIX But in a thing of the kind, if this be so indeed, we should be adjudged to ridicule, not to swords, and flames, and crosses, and wild beasts, in which iniquitous cruelty not only the blinded populace exults and insults over us, but in which some of you too glory, not scrupling to gain the popular favour by your injustice.

PUNISHMENT IS SELF-DEFEATING: THE BLOOD OF MARTYRS IS THE SEED OF THE CHURCH

Chap. L But go zealously on, good presidents, you will stand higher with the people if you sacrifice the Christians at their wish, kill us, torture us, condemn us, grind us to dust; your injustice is the proof that we are innocent. Therefore God suffers that we thus suffer; for but very lately, in condemning a Christian woman to the *leno* rather than to the *leo*, you made confession that a taint on our purity is considered among us something more terrible than any punishment and any death. Nor does your cruelty, however exquisite, avail you; it is rather a temptation to us. The oftener we are mown down by you, the more in number we grow; *the blood of Christians is seed.*

EUSEBIUS

THE ORATION IN PRAISE OF THE EMPEROR CONSTANTINE PRONOUNCED ON THE THIRTIETH ANNIVERSARY OF HIS REIGN

THE EMPEROR AS THE PRE-EMINENT SERVANT OF GOD

Chap. II This only begotten Word of God reigns, from ages which had no beginning, to infinite and endless ages, the partner of his Father's kingdom. And [our emperor] ever beloved by him, who derives the source of imperial authority from above, and is strong in the power of his sacred title, has controlled the empire of the world for a long period of years. Again, that Preserver of the universe orders these heavens and earth, and the celestial kingdom, consistently with his Father's will. Even so our emperor whom he loves, by bringing those whom he rules on earth to the only begotten Word and Saviour renders them fit subjects of his kingdom. And as he who is the common Saviour of mankind, by his invisible and Divine power as the good shepherd, drives far away from his flock, like savage beasts, those apostate spirits which once flew through the airy tracts above this earth, and fastened on the souls of men; so this his friend, graced by his heavenly favor with victory over all his foes, subdues and chastens the open adversaries of the truth in accordance with the usages of war. He who is the pre-existent Word, the Preserver of all things, imparts to his disciples the seeds of true wisdom and salvation, and at once enlightens and gives them understanding in the knowledge of his Father's kingdom. Our emperor, his friend, acting as interpreter to the Word of God, aims at recalling the whole human race to the knowledge of God; proclaiming clearly in the ears of all, and declaring with powerful voice the laws of truth and godliness to all who dwell on the earth. Once more, the universal Saviour opens the heavenly gates of his Father's kingdom to those whose course is thitherward from this world. Our emperor, emulous of his Divine example, having purged his earthly dominion from every stain of impious error, invites each holy and pious worshiper within his imperial mansions, earnestly desiring to save with all its crew that mighty vessel of which he is the appointed pilot. And he alone of all who have wielded the imperial power of Rome, being honored by the Supreme Sovereign with a reign of three decennial periods, now celebrates this festival, not, as his ancestors might have done, in honor of infernal demons, or the apparitions of seducing spirits, or of the fraud and deceitful arts of impious men; but as an act of thanksgiving to him by whom he has thus been honored, and in acknowledgment of the blessings he has received at his hands.

[Source: Philip Schaff and Henry Wace, eds., *Nicene and Post-Nicene Fathers*, 2nd ser., vol. 1: *Eusebius* (Grand Rapids: Eerdmans, n.d.).]

Chap. III He it is who appoints him this present festival, in that he has made him victorious over every enemy that disturbed his peace: he it is who displays him as an example of true godliness to the human race. And thus our emperor, like the radiant sun, illuminates the most distant subjects of his empire through the presence of the Caesars, as with the far piercing rays of his own brightness . . . invested as he is with a semblance of heavenly sovereignty, he directs his gaze above, and frames his earthly government according to the pattern of that Divine original, feeling strength in its conformity to the monarchy of God. And this conformity is granted by the universal Sovereign to man alone of the creatures of this earth: for he only is the author of sovereign power, who decrees that all should be subject to the rule of one. And surely monarchy far transcends every other constitution and form of government: for that democratic equality of power, which is its opposite, may rather be described as anarchy and disorder.

Chap. V And in this hope [of the kingdom of heaven] our divinely-favored emperor partakes even in this present life, gifted as he is by God with native virtues, and having received into his soul the out-flowings of his favor. His reason he derives from the great Source of all reason: he is wise, and good, and just, as having fellowship with perfect Wisdom, Goodness, and Righteousness: virtuous, as following the pattern of perfect virtue: valiant, as partaking of heavenly strength. And truly may he deserve the imperial title, who has formed his soul to royal virtues, according to the standard of that celestial kingdom.

GOD CHOSE CONSTANTINE TO OPPOSE THE FORCES OF EVIL

Chap. VII For whereas we are composed of two distinct natures, I mean of body and spirit, of which the one is visible to all, the other invisible, against both these natures two kinds of barbarous and savage enemies, the one invisibly, the other openly, are constantly arrayed. The one oppose our bodies with bodily force: the other with incorporeal assaults besiege the naked soul itself. Again, the visible barbarians, like the wild nomad tribes, no better than savage beasts, assail the nations of civilized men, ravage their country, and enslave their cities, rushing on those who inhabit them like ruthless wolves of the desert, and destroying all who fall under their power. But those unseen foes, more cruel far than barbarians, I mean the soul-destroying demons whose course is through the regions of the air, had succeeded, through the snares of vile polytheism, in enslaving the entire human race, insomuch that they no longer recognized the true God, but wandered in the mazes of atheistic error. . . .

The ruling powers of those times [were] enslaved by the force of error, to appease their gods with the blood of their own countrymen and kindred; to whet their swords against those who stood forward to defend the truth; to maintain a ruthless war and raise unholy hands, not against foreign or barbarian foes, but against men bound to them by the ties of family and affection, against brethren, and kinsmen, and dearest friends, who had resolved, in the practice of virtue and true piety, to honor and worship God.

Chap. IX These adversaries of the Lord of all, confident in the aid of a multitude of gods, advanced to the attack with a powerful array of military force, preceded by certain images of the dead, and lifeless statues, as their defense. On the other side our emperor, secure in the armor of godliness, opposed to the numbers of the enemy the salutary and life-giving Sign, as at the same time a terror to the foe, and a protection against every harm; and returned victorious at once over the enemy and the demons whom they served. And then, with thanksgiving and praise, the tokens of a grateful spirit, to the Author of his victory, he proclaimed this triumphant Sign, by monuments as well as words, to all mankind, erecting it as a mighty trophy against every enemy in the midst of the imperial city, and expressly enjoining on all to acknowledge this imperishable symbol of salvation as the safe-guard of the power of Rome and of the empire of the world. . . .

Accordingly these signal proofs of our emperor's magnificence forthwith appeared in the provinces and cities of the empire, and soon shone conspicuously in every country; convincing memorials of the rebuke and overthrow of those impious tyrants who but a little while before had madly dared to fight against God.

CONSTANTINE ACKNOWLEDGES CHRIST AS LORD

Chap. XVII And now the time is come for us to consider the works of our Saviour in our own age, and to contemplate the living operations of the living God. For how shall we describe these mighty works save as living proofs of the power of a living agent, who truly enjoys the life of God? . . .

Who else has power to make war after death, to triumph over every enemy, to subjugate each barbarous and civilized nation and city, and to subdue his adversaries with an invisible and secret hand? Lastly, and chief of all, what slanderous lip shall dare to question that universal peace to which we have already referred, established by his power throughout the world? . . .

But why should we still vainly aim at detailing those Divine proofs of our Saviour's power which no language can worthily express; which need indeed no words of ours, but themselves appeal in loudest tones to those whose mental ears are open to the truth? Surely it is a strange, a wondrous fact, unparalleled in the annals of human life; that the blessings we have described should be accorded to our mortal race, and that he who is in truth the only, the eternal Son of God, should thus be visible on earth.

Chap. XVIII These words of ours, however, [gracious] Sovereign, may well appear superfluous in your ears, convinced as you are, by frequent and personal experience, of our Saviour's Deity; yourself also, in actions still more than words, a herald of the truth to all mankind. Yourself, it may be, will vouchsafe at a time of leisure to relate to us the abundant manifestations which your Saviour has accorded you of his presence, and the oft-repeated visions of himself which have attended you in the hours of sleep. I speak not of those secret suggestions which to us are unrevealed; but of those principles which he has instilled into your own mind, and which are fraught with general interest and benefit to the human race. You will yourself relate in worthy terms the visible protection which your Divine shield and guardian has extended in the hour of battle; the ruin of your open and secret foes; and his ready aid in time of peril. To him you will ascribe relief in the midst of perplexity; defence in solitude; expedients in extremity; foreknowledge of events yet future; your forethought for the general weal; your power to investigate uncertain questions; your conduct of most important enterprises; your administration of civil affairs; your military arrangements, and correction of abuses in all departments; your ordinances respecting public right; and, lastly, your legislation for the common benefit of all.

CHAPTER 2

THE MEDIEVAL CHURCH

Many dates have been suggested as the exact beginning of the Middle Ages—and none of them would include the late fourth and early fifth centuries of the African monk and bishop of Hippo, St. Augustine (354–430). Augustinian theology was, however, used by medieval theologians as a basis for interpreting life as two clearly distinguishable and yet related temporal and spiritual spheres of existence. It represents a change in the development of church-state relations clearly distinguishable from both the pre- and post-Constantinian church.

It may, of course, well be argued that the antecedent of medieval church-state relations was rather to be found with Augustine's mentor, St. Ambrose (339–387). Ambrose probably did more than any other person to "correct" the overt Constantinian domination of the church. In so doing he laid the foundation for medieval papal hegemony which would, in turn, need to be repudiated in the Catholic and Protestant Reformations of the sixteenth century. His greatest moment of triumph came when Theodosius suppressed a seditious movement in Thessalonica with brutal violence. Ambrose refused him the sacrament of holy communion until he openly repented. "The emperor," he insisted, "was within the church and not over it." Augustine would not show the same political assertiveness as Ambrose, but inherent in his theology was a dynamic that would shape church-state relations for centuries to come. St. Thomas Aquinas would, in turn, systematize, develop, and build on Augustine's thought in a way that would dominate the High Middle Ages.

ST. AUGUSTINE OF HIPPO

To look to Augustine for a "universal history" applicable to all ages is to overlook the stark demands of the particular occasion which gave rise to *The City of God*. Rome had been sacked by Alaric the Goth in 410, and refugees began to stream into North Africa, nostalgically lamenting the betrayal of traditional Roman values and religious ideals in favor of Constantine's Christian faith. In this milieu, Augustine set himself the task of explaining the fall of Rome. The city of Rome had symbolized the security of a whole civilized way of life which had clearly provided the identity for his own cultural and social existence, as it did for most educated citizens of the Empire. "If Rome can perish," wrote St. Jerome, "what can be safe?"[1] Such was the nature of this event that it was experienced as a cataclysmic "day of the Lord" by the Catholic church throughout the Empire.

Augustine was enough of a Roman to argue that the Empire rose by real merit and for providential purposes. At the same time he was concerned to challenge the view of those who suggested that life attains its ultimate purpose in the glorious achievements of human civilizations. He regarded the sacrifices and self-denial of the ancient Romans as an inspiration to Christians, although he insisted that they did this for an earthly crown and "have received their reward." Turning to the fate of the refugees, he advised Christians that no amount of loss of property, suffering, deprivation, or even death should be regarded as an ultimate loss. Their fortune and hope was in things eternal. This immediate contextual sense of pastoral urgency should not be overlooked in any assessment of Augustine's response to the momentous collapse of the Empire.

A second factor to be born in mind in reading Augustine's *City of God* is the Constantinian synthesis of church and state that characterized the ethos of the Catholic church and that to a large extent contributed to the Donatist schism. A variety of factors accounted for groups such as the Donatists that existed on the fringe of the Empire: they had been conquered by the forces of the Roman Empire and were simply not able to submit to assimilation into the dominant Catholic church, fused as it was to the very Empire that had conquered them. The persecution which followed persuaded them that they were the true heirs of the church of the martyrs, keeping alive the apocalyptic hope of God's imminent intervention to end the age of moral compromise and social apostasy. Donatism was a schism that reached back to the persecution of Diocletian in 303–305. Caecilian, the bishop of Carthage, was said to have been ordained by a *traditor*, one who had under persecution surrendered the Scriptures to state prosecutors. This precipitated the election of an alternative bishop—Donatus—by the Numidian Christians. Augustine, as bishop of the North African see of Hippo, felt compelled to confront these dissident apocalyptic forces, dominant as they were in the African church. Eventually when his acts of coercion met with resistance from the Donatists—which threatened to develop into what has been referred to as "a peasants' revolt in embryo"[2]—imperial authority intervened, and many of the resisting Donatists were executed. In addition to all the other divisiveness involved in schism, Augustine had accepted the cultural and political ethos of the Empire as the identity of the Catholic church, rejecting the marginalized church of the Donatists as contrary to the needs of the Empire, and therefore heretical.[3] Rosemary Ruether's critique is a telling one: "When faced with the test of a non-Roman identity, Augustine, as much as Eusebius, proved that his catholicity was a closed universe, bounded by the Greco-Roman oecumene."[4]

The City of God was written toward the end of Augustine's life, after the fall of Rome, and he was clearly less infatuated with the possibilities of the Roman Empire than he had been earlier. He moved away from the Eusebian tendencies that appear to have been latently present in his thought in his first dealings with the Donatists, shortly after he returned to Africa.[5] In *The City of God*, in fact, he drew on the ideas of the Donatists in viewing the kingdoms of this world—and therefore the Empire—as the kingdom of Satan, with which he contrasted the kingdom of God. In so doing, he turns his readers' attention from the glory of the Roman past to "the most glorious City of God" of the future, which is always "enduring its existence on earth, always sighing for heaven."[6] At the same time he seems to recall the dualism of the Manichaean system which he affirmed in his youth. He writes of a division within history between light and darkness, but now it is internalized as he distinguishes between two human wills which constitute, for him, the essence of the human predicament. He sees mankind as occupying a battleground between two loyalties, heavenly and earthly, the self-denying love of God and the God-denying love of self. Edward Hardy is correct: Augustine is "describing a human conflict rather than propounding a political programme."[7] The political implications of Augustinian anthropology cannot, however, be avoided. To turn away from the grandiose claims of the state in affirmation of a heavenly city and its demands provides a potential deabsolutizing attitude that contradicts all chauvinistic forms of nationalism. It also forms the basis of a politically significant eschatological critique of the state.

Latent within this theology is a doctrine of church and state as cogent as any, and when Augustine addresses himself to the implications of this doctrine its significance is indisputable: it is the obligation of the Christian to bring the earthly city into as much conformity to the heavenly city as is possible. An Empire that is without justice is little more than a band of robbers. Peace is more than the absence of hostilities; it is the ordered harmony of its citizens. A legitimate *res publica* is for Augustine "an assemblage of reasonable beings bound together by a common agreement as to the objects of their love."[8] Central to this exposition is, however, also ambiguity. The two cities commingle in history, and "earthly peace" is necessarily temporal and imperfect, one which must be tolerated and used until such time as "this mortal life shall give place to one that is eternal." Christians are required to sojourn in history and make the most of "the peace of Babylon" while the final separation between the two cities takes place eschatologically.[9] It is this resignation to the inevitability of evil, with history having no more than temporal meaning in God's total scheme of things, that causes Rosemary Ruether to argue that "Augustine, in his struggle to retain truths, but to reject the errors of both the apocalyptic dualism of Donatism and the sacramental fusion of empire and the kingdom of Eusebius, discovers for the first time in theological history a principle of secularity in a way which recognizes the political order as fully legitimate in its own terms."[10]

To this an important qualification must, however, be added. Augustine had normative or orthodox government in mind, which for him meant government acting in obedience to God. In effect, Augustine exempted the state from the radical demands of the gospel, and the historical expectation of the kingdom was removed from the political realm, which was abandoned to those whose task it was to hold together the tentative peace of what Augustine calls "Babylon." For Augustine, the Christian sojourns in history, but this is not the Christian's "true home." The kingdom of God is not expected to begin in history, and thus history loses the kind of theological pertinency that is found in the Judeo-Christian hope for messianic redemption within history itself. The heavenly city is hidden within history, always commingled with the earthly city, causing it to be renewed and transformed, but there is for Augustine no decisive turning point *in* history to be equated with the millennial reign.

Augustine's primary concern with the heavenly city, which is essentially beyond history, causes Edward Hardy to suggest that "Augustine would have done more justice to his own thought if he had formally described the state, like our earthly life generally, as a battleground of good and evil."[11] Instead of this, while allowing for its function in history to be influenced by the heavenly city, Augustine ultimately abandoned the state to the earthly city's "love of self" and "contempt of God." In a similar vein, Peter Brown argues that "the 'true church' of Augustine is not only the 'body of Christ,' the 'heavenly Jerusalem,' it is also deeply tinged with the metaphysical ideas of Plotinus."[12] The "concrete church" on earth can be no more than an imperfect shadow of the spiritual church which is the true church. For all the realism of Augustinian thought, it allows neither civil society nor the concrete manifestation of church to be taken with the kind of seriousness that is required to resolve the most stubborn problems of history. In this way Augustine plays down the political significance of the eschatological critique of the gospel. If politics is the art of the possible in this earthly city with all its restraints of self-affirming love and pride, the function of theology is surely to witness to the antagonism between the earthly city and the demands of the heavenly city. Simply because there can never be, in terms of Augustinian presuppositions, a final synthesis between Christian hope and political reality, the role of the church in relation to the state must be one of renewing critique rather than conforming submission. It is this interpretation of history, implicit but undeveloped in the thought of Augustine, which is given theological emphasis in the later affirmations of the principles of his thought, both in Reformation and contemporary forms of Augustinian thought.[13]

ST. THOMAS AQUINAS

It is often said that St. Thomas Aquinas had no theology of history or political philosophy. Certainly he kept aloof from the strife of the turbulent age in which he lived. He wrote very little on politics and virtually nothing on the social events of his day. Probably only the first section and a small part of the second section of the book entitled *De Regimine Principum (On Princely Government*, or *On Kingship)* can be attributed to him. His commentaries on Aristotle's *Ethics* and *Politics* suggest that his views differed only slightly from those of Aristotle himself, and the other relevant material is scattered throughout his more systematic writings. Valuable collections of these writings are to be found in D. Bigongiari's *The Political Ideas of St. Thomas Aquinas* and in A. P. D'Entreves's *Aquinas: Selected Political Writings*. This having been said, Thomas's somewhat limited and often less than explicit theological thought on political theory has made a formative contribution to Christian thinking on church-state relations.

Thomas lived in an age of transition and crisis. There was an intellectual awakening in Europe. Aristotelian texts had been rediscovered and translated into Latin, and an otherworldly interpretation of Augustinian theology which had provided the theological identity of the church for so long was being reworked in relation to Aristotelian empiricism. This was never, however, a form of empirical preoccupation with particulars. It was rather—certainly in the case of Thomas—a form of deductive concern in which the major task was to discern and analyze the principles behind the empirical concerns of the day with a view to clarifying the implications of such principles for ethical behavior.[14]

For Thomas the implications of people living together in community, which is the basis of politics, is grounded in nature or reality itself. As such it is accessible to reason, and while marred by sin, it is not totally destroyed. Nor is it negated by God's grace. It is rather perfected. On this basis the pursuit of truth—whether pursued by Aristotle or Augustine—is the common end of all humanity. Yet the obligation and necessity to establish a viable and just practice of coexistence is, for Thomas, not the ultimate end of humanity. It is this that exercises such an important function in his political thought and that constitutes a point of deviation from Aristotle. For him, the *perfecta beatitudo,* fully attainable only in the future life, is one of contemplation.[15] It is a unity with, and a peace which is found in, God alone.

In this context *natural law* is not only central to Thomas's understanding of the state, but it is also the object of the quest for all truth. It declares the nature of God's rational order of the universe.[16] To know it is to gain insight into God's intended purpose for his world, and to act in accordance with it is the source of communal order and human happiness on earth. With this Thomas provided the church with an understanding of state that was first anticipated by Augustine. He legitimated it as part of God's natural order of things, yet never as an end in itself. Ultimately there is, for him, always a higher end which is the faithful contemplation of God.

To affirm a natural explanation of the state is, in turn, to ground the idea of the state in the nature of humanity. For Thomas, the human being is "a political animal because he is a social animal."[17] As such he or she is subject to a *triplex ordo*: divine law, reason, and political authority.[18] Yet since humans were placed in authority over the animals of the field but not over fellow human beings, the degradation of any section of the population or of one individual by another is seen to be contrary to nature. "Since every person is a part of a political community he cannot be good unless he be adjusted to the common good."[19] At the same time submission to political authorities is regarded as being in accordance with nature, for, Thomas argues, "there is an order also found among men themselves. Indeed, those who excel in understanding naturally gain control."[20] For Thomas, such control should, however, never result in the loss of personal identity. There is something within the individual that the state can never satisfy. This is a person's highest end which is realized in God alone. "All that a man is, and all that he can do, and all that he has is within God's order."[21] It is this emphasis which denies any absolute authority to the state.

Thomas's political theory is ultimately an affirmation of medieval theocracy, although certainly not in its abused form. His is the medieval form of government at its model best, in which civil authority is part of a hierarchical society that defines its place under God. The closest thing to a systematic treatment of this relationship within the context of the problem of state and church is found in the fourteenth chapter of the treatise *On Kingship*, which is included in this selection of texts. Here Thomas insists that the highest form of government to which Christians are called to be obedient is "such government [which] belongs only to that King who is both man, and also God: that is to Jesus Christ, our Lord, Who, making men to be sons of God has led them to the glory of heaven."

Thomas's inevitable mirroring of his own context is seen in his preference for being governed by "one man" rather than by "many," as chapter two of the following text illustrates. He clearly recognizes the limits of such government and discusses these at some length in various places in his writing. Dino Bigongiari's analysis of the different forms of government contemplated by Thomas provides a useful discussion of this problem. The solution for Thomas, he writes, was found in "a form of government in which the king's power would be limited and the people's desire satisfied. That form of government is called the 'mixed regime.' "[22] This government involves the participation of the people, through their representatives, in the government, akin to the seventy-two elders chosen by the people to advise Moses, so that there was an element of aristocracy. But it was a democratical government in so far as the rulers were chosen by the people."[23]

Thomas also faces the inevitable question: What actions are open to those ruled by a tyrant who is motivated by self-interest and who persistently refuses to obey the higher authority of God? Because Thomas is convinced that orderly rule and social stability are an integral part of nature itself, his bias in responding to this question is on the side of preserving the existing order rather than with individual *political* rights.[24] For Thomas, as indicated in the citation from the *Summa Theologica* given below, it is not sedition to disturb a tyrannical government. But his inherent caution in such matters is evident in his warning that such activity be only permitted provided "the disturbance be [not] so excessive that the people suffer more from it than the tyrannical regime." It may well be, he argues in chapter six of his treatise *On Kingship* also reproduced below, that a bad king has been placed in authority by God for a particular purpose, because God sometimes permits tyrants to rule in order to punish his subjects for their sinful conduct. He also suggests that if the particular form of tyranny is not too bad, subjects should accept it, because given his presuppositions about the nature of order, this is preferable to chaos. At the same time he recognizes that this may well result in martyrdom as it did in the early church. Thomas seems to suggest that martyrdom should be considered an option by those who are subjected to such rule. He rejects the possibility of private individuals intervening to take the life of a tyrant, allowing three means for removing the tyrant from office. If elected by the people, it is their right to correct him or, if necessary, remove him from office. If a tyrant exercises power in response to the leadership of another, it is the responsibility of that person to remove the tyrant from office. Third, if all human procedures of remediation fail, Thomas's advice is that we turn to God in prayer. In this situation it may please God to convert the tyrant to his ways, or he may judge it necessary that the people suffer under unjust rule, or he may remove the ruler from power. What Thomas does not do is suggest by what method God would dispense of a ruler.

Thomas's understanding of social order as a reflection of the natural order of things can not be separated from his own place in and experience of medieval society of which he was a part. The fear of chaos, as reflected in the years following the fall of Rome commonly referred to as the Dark Ages, seemed to leave an indelible mark on the medieval worldview. The question needs to be asked to what extent, as Alistair Kee asked in relation to Eusebius, Thomas's understanding of the natural order was a reflection of his own values and those of the ruling group in medieval Europe. The consequence of this is that, for Thomas, order is more important than justice. What he fails to do is face the inevitable question concerning the obligation of Christians who are confronted with a state that is not the reflection of order but is the source of the very chaos which he so decidedly fears. This is a situation which Thomas recognizes as a possibility—where the tyrannical ruler is the source of sedition, as he suggests in the *Summa Theologica* text quoted below. Like Augustine, Thomas reserves the advent of God's kingdom for beyond history, and in so doing, in spite of his theological rejection of tyranny, he provides theological legitimation for a form of statecraft which is less than what is anticipated in the prophetic teachings of the Judeo-Christian tradition. In so doing he also ultimately fails to develop the political significance of humanity's end in God, impinging in judgment and renewal on the affairs of state, with the kind of persistence that a viable political theology seems to demand.

An area of thought that is central to medieval theology but which we do not consider here is the doctrine of just war. Suffice it to say that the attention given to this doctrine by Augustine and subsequently accepted by Thomas constitutes a theological initiative to *limit* war and to endeavor to further the ends of justice,[25] even though the church was simultaneously promoting a theology of holy war. Recently, some theologians have proposed a doctrine of just revolution based on the principles of just war theory as expressed in the thought of Augustine and Thomas. This discussion is beyond the limits of our study, although it signals one instance of the latent political and indeed the revolutionary potential of the theology of two theologians, bound to their own context, who continue to hold significance for the contemporary debate on church-state relations in its most radical sense.

NOTES

1. Peter Brown, *Augustine of Hippo* (Berkeley: University of California Press, 1969), p. 289.
2. Ibid., p. 241.
3. W. H. C. Frend, *The Donatist Church: A Movement of Protest in North Africa* (Oxford: Clarendon Press, 1952), pp. 131–38.
4. Rosemary Radford Ruether, "Augustine and Christian Political Theology," *Interpretation*, 29 (1975), 258.

5. R. A. Markus, *Saeculum: History and Society in the Theology of St. Augustine* (Cambridge: Cambridge University Press, 1970), pp. 28–44.
6. See discussion in Brown, pp. 314–15.
7. Edward R. Hardy, "The City of God," in Roy W. Battenhouse, ed., *A Companion to the Study of St. Augustine* (Grand Rapids: Baker, 1979), p. 257.
8. St. Augustine, *City of God*, XIX, 24; see also 21.
9. See discussion in T. J. Bigham and A. T. Mollegen, "The Christian Ethic," in Battenhouse, pp. 388–95.
10. Ruether, p. 261. See also Markus, pp. 172f.
11. Hardy, p. 279.
12. Brown, p. 222.
13. For a contemporary form of Augustinian thought of this kind see, *inter alia*, J. Ellul, *The Meaning of the City* (Grand Rapids: Eerdmans, 1970); *The Politics of God and the Politics of Man* (Grand Rapids: Eerdmans, 1972); *The False Presence of the Kingdom* (New York: Seabury, 1970).
14. D. Knowles, *The Evolution of Medieval Thought* (London: Longman, 1962), pp. 185–92. Also A. P. D'Entreves, ed., *Aquinas: Selected Political Writings* (Oxford: Blackwell, 1970), p. viii.
15. St. Thomas Aquinas, *Summa Theologica* (London: Blackfriars, 1964), la/2ae. 111, 5; 66, 3; 2a/2ae. 179, 1 and 2; 2a/2ae. 47, 2.
16. Ibid., 2a/lae. 90–96.
17. D'Entreves, p. xv. Also Dino Bigongiari, ed., *The Political Ideas of St. Thomas Aquinas* (New York: Hafner, 1969), pp. vii–xi.
18. *Summa Theologica*, la/2ae. 72, 4.
19. Ibid., la/2ae. 92, 1.
20. St. Thomas Aquinas, *Summa Contra Gentiles* (South Bend, Ind.: University of Notre Dame Press, 1975), 111, 81.
21. *Summa Theologica*, la/2ae. 21, 4.
22. Bigongiari, p. xxx.
23. *Summa Theologica*, la/2ae. 105, 1.
24. Bigongiari, pp. xxxi–xxxiii.
25. See T. A. Shannon, ed., *War or Peace?* (Maryknoll, N.Y.: Orbis, 1980), especially pp. 17–18. See also pp. 3–71.

SELECT BIBLIOGRAPHY

Battenhouse, R. W., ed. *A Companion to the Study of St. Augustine.* Grand Rapids: Baker, 1979.

Brown, P., *Augustine of Hippo.* Berkeley: University of California Press, 1969.

Bigongiari, D., ed. *The Political Ideas of St. Thomas Aquinas.* New York: Hafner, 1969.

Deane, H. A., *The Political and Social Ideas of St. Augustine.* New York: Columbia University Press, 1963.

D'Entreves, A. P., ed. *Aquinas: Selected Political Writings.* Oxford: Blackwell, 1970.

Hill, B. D., ed. *Church and State in the Middle Ages.* New York: John Wiley, 1970.

Marshall, R. T., *Studies in the Political and the Social-Religious Terminology of the* De Civitate Dei. Washington, D.C.: Catholic University Press, 1952.

Maritain, J., *Man and the State.* Chicago: University of Chicago Press, 1951.

ST. AUGUSTINE

THE CITY OF GOD

KINGDOMS WITHOUT JUSTICE ARE BUT GREAT ROBBERIES

III, 3 Wherefore if the true God is worshipped, and if He is served with genuine rites and true virtue, it is advantageous that good men should long reign both far and wide. Nor is this advantageous so much to themselves, as to those over whom they reign. For, so far as concerns themselves, their piety and probity, which are great gifts of God, suffice to give them true felicity, enabling them to live well the life that now is, and afterwards to receive that which is eternal. In this world, therefore, the dominion of good men is profitable, not so much for themselves as for human affairs. But the dominion of bad men is hurtful chiefly to themselves who rule, for they destroy their own souls by greater license in wickedness; while those who are put under them in service are not hurt except by their own iniquity. For to the just all the evils imposed on them by unjust rulers are not the punishment of crime, but the test of virtue. Therefore the good man, although he is a slave, is free; but the bad man, even if he reigns, is a slave, and that not of one man, but, what is far more grievous, of as many masters as he has vices; of which vices when the divine Scripture treats, it says, "For of whom any man is overcome, to the same he is also the bond-slave."

III, 4 Justice being taken away, then, what are kingdoms but great robberies? For what are robberies themselves, but little kingdoms? . . .

THE ORIGIN OF THE CITY OF GOD AND THE CITY OF MAN

XI, 9 I have undertaken to treat of the origin of the holy city, and first of the holy angels, who constitute a large part of this city, and indeed the more blessed part, since they have never been expatriated.

XI, 11 Those spirits whom we call angels were never at any time or in any way darkness, but, as soon as they were made, were made light; yet they were not so created in order that they might exist and live in any way whatever, but were enlightened that they might live wisely and blessedly. Some of them, having turned away from this light, have not won this wise and blessed life, which is certainly eternal and accompanied with the sure confidence of its eternity; but they have still the life of reason, though darkened with folly, and this they cannot lose even if they would.

XI, 33 That certain angels sinned, and were thrust down to the lowest parts of this world, where they are, as it were, incarcerated till their final damnation in the day of judgment, the Apostle Peter very plainly declares. . . .

[Source: Augustine, *The City of God*, in Philip Schaff, ed., *Nicene and Post-Nicene Fathers*, 1st ser., vol. 2 (Grand Rapids: Eerdmans, n.d.).]

The one the minister of God's goodness to the utmost of their good pleasure, the other held in by God's power from doing the harm it would; the former laughing at the latter when it does good unwillingly by its persecutions, the latter envying the former when it gathers in its pilgrims. These two angelic communities, then, dissimilar and contrary to one another, the one both by nature good and by will upright, the other also good by nature but by will depraved.

XI, 34 Since, then, we have now said what seemed needful regarding these two diverse and contrary communities of angels, in which the origin of the two human communities (of which we intend to speak anon) is also found, let us at once bring this book also to a conclusion.

THE NATURE OF THE TWO CITIES

XIV, 1 We have already stated in the preceding books that God, desiring not only that the human race might be able by their similarity of nature to associate with one another, but also that they might be bound together in harmony and peace by the ties of relationship, was pleased to derive all men from one individual, and created man with such a nature that the members of the race should not have died, had not the two first . . . merited this by their disobedience; for by them so great a sin was committed, that by it the human nature was altered for the worse, and was transmitted also to their posterity, liable to sin and subject to death. And the kingdom of death so reigned over men, that the deserved penalty of sin would have hurled all headlong even into the second death, of which there is no end, had not the undeserved grace of God saved some therefrom. And thus it has come to pass, that though there are very many and great nations all over the earth, whose rites and customs, speech, arms, and dress, are distinguished by marked differences, yet there are no more than two kinds of human society, which we may justly call two cities, according to the language of our Scriptures. The one consists of those who wish to live after the flesh, the other of those who wish to live after the spirit; and when they severally achieve what they wish, they live in peace, each after their kind.

THE LOVE OF SELF AND THE LOVE OF GOD

XIV, 13 Humility is specially recommended to the city of God as it sojourns in this world, and is specially exhibited in the city of God, and in the person of Christ its King; while the contrary vice of pride, according to the testimony of the sacred writings, specially rules his adversary the devil. And certainly this is the great difference which distinguishes the two cities of which we speak, the one being the society of the godly men, the other of the ungodly, each associated with the angels that adhere to their party, and the one guided and fashioned by love of self, the other by love of God.

XIV, 28 Accordingly, two cities have been formed by two loves: the earthly by the love of self, even to the contempt of God; the heavenly by the love of God, even to the contempt of self. The former, in a word, glories in itself, the latter in the Lord. For the one seeks glory from men; but the greatest glory of the other is God, the witness of conscience. The one lifts up its head in its own glory; the other says to its God, "Thou art my glory, and the lifter up of mine head." In the one, the princes and the nations it subdues are ruled by the love of ruling; in the other, the princes and the subjects serve one another in love, the latter obeying, while the former take thought for all. The one delights in its own strength, represented in the persons of its rulers; the other says to its God, "I will love Thee, O Lord, my strength." And therefore the wise men of the one city, living according to man, have sought for profit to their own bodies or souls, or both, and those who have known God "glorified Him not as God, neither were thankful, but became vain in their imaginations, and their foolish heart was darkened; professing themselves to be wise,"—that is, glorying in their own wisdom, and being possessed by pride,—"they became fools, and changed the glory of the incorruptible God into an image made like to corruptible man, and to birds, and four-footed beasts, and creeping things." For they were either leaders or followers of the people in adoring images, "and worshipped and served the creature more than the Creator, who is blessed for ever." But in the other city there is no human wisdom, but only godliness, which offers due worship to the true God, and looks for its reward in the society of the saints, of holy angels as well as holy men, "that God may be all in all."

THE CITY OF GOD—A SHIP IN STORMY WATERS

XV, 26 God commanded Noah, a just man, and, as the truthful Scripture says—a man perfect in his generation—to make an ark, in which he might be rescued from the destruction of the flood, along with his family, *i.e.*, his wife, sons, and daughters-in-law, and along with the animals who, in obedience to God's command, came to him into the ark: this is certainly a figure of the city of God sojourning in this world; that is to say, of the church, which is rescued by the wood on which hung the Mediator of God and men, the man Christ Jesus.

PEACE IN THIS WORLD AND IN THE ONE TO COME

XIX, 11 And thus we may say of peace, as we have said of eternal life, that it is the end of our good; and the rather because the Psalmist says of the city of God, the subject of this laborious work, "Praise the Lord, O Jerusalem; praise thy God, O Zion: for He hath strengthened the bars of thy gates; He hath blessed thy children within thee; who hath made thy borders peace." For when the bars of her gates shall be strengthened, none shall go in or come out from her; consequently we ought to understand the peace of her borders as that final peace we are wishing to declare. For even the mystical name of the city itself, that is, *Jerusalem*, means, as I have already said, "Vision of Peace." But as the word peace is employed in connection with things in this world in which certainly life eternal has no place, we have preferred to call the end or supreme good of this city life eternal rather than peace.

XIX, 12 Pride in its perversity apes God. It abhors equality with other men under Him; but, instead of His rule, it seeks to impose a rule of its own upon its equals. It abhors, that is to say, the just peace of God, and loves its own unjust peace; but it cannot help loving peace of one kind or other. For there is no vice so clean contrary to nature that it obliterates even the faintest traces of nature.

He, then, who prefers what is right to what is wrong, and what is well-ordered to what is perverted, sees that the peace of unjust men is not worthy to be called peace in comparison with the peace of the just. And yet even what is perverted must of necessity be in harmony with, and in dependence on, and in some part of the order of things, for otherwise it would have no existence at all.

XIX, 13 Peace between man and man is well-ordered concord. Domestic peace is the well-ordered concord between those of the family who rule and those who obey. Civil peace is a similar concord among the citizens. The peace of the celestial city is the perfectly ordered and harmonious enjoyment of God, and of one another in God. The peace of all things is the tranquillity of order. Order is the distribution which allots things equal and unequal, each to its own place.

THE HEAVENLY CITY IS A STRANGER IN THE EARTHLY CITY AND MAY BE COMPELLED TO DISSENT

XIX, 17 The earthly city, which does not live by faith, seeks an earthly peace, and the end it proposes, in the well-ordered concord of civic obedience and rule, is the combination of men's wills to attain the things which are helpful to this life. The heavenly city, or rather the part of it which sojourns on earth and lives by faith, makes use of this peace only because it must, until this mortal condition which necessitates it shall pass away. Consequently, so long as it lives like a captive and a stranger in the earthly city, though it has already received the promise of redemption, and the gift of the Spirit as the earnest of it, it makes no scruple to obey the laws of the earthly city, whereby the things necessary for the maintenance of this mortal life are administered; and thus, as this life is common to both cities, so there is a harmony between them in regard to what belongs to it. But, as the earthly city has had some philosophers whose doctrine is condemned by the divine teaching, and who, being deceived either by their own conjectures or by demons, supposed that many gods must be invited to take an interest in human affairs . . . and as the celestial city, on the other hand, knew that one God only was to be worshipped, and that to Him alone was due that service which the Greeks call **λατρεία**, and which can be given only to a god, it has come to pass that the two cities could not have common laws of religion, and that the heavenly city has been compelled in this matter to dissent, and to become obnoxious to those who think differently, and to stand the brunt of their anger and hatred and persecutions, except in so far as the minds of their enemies have been alarmed by the multitude of the Christians and quelled by the manifest protection of God accorded to them. This heavenly city, then, while it sojourns on earth, calls citizens out of all nations, and gathers together a society of pilgrims of all languages, not scrupling about diversities in the manners, laws, and institutions whereby earthly peace is secured and maintained, but recognizing that, however various these are, they all tend to one and the same end of earthly peace. It therefore is so far from rescinding and abolishing these diversities, that it even preserves and adopts them, so long only as no hindrance to the worship of the one supreme and true God is thus introduced. Even the heavenly city, therefore, while in its state of pilgrimage, avails itself of the peace of earth, and, so far as it can without injuring faith and godliness, desires and maintains a common agreement among men regarding the acquisition of the necessaries of life, and makes this earthly peace bear upon the peace of heaven; for this alone can be truly called and esteemed the peace of the reasonable creatures, consisting as it does in the perfectly ordered and harmonious enjoyment of God and of one another in God. When we shall have reached that peace, this mortal life shall give place to one that is eternal, and our body shall be no more this animal body which by its corruption weighs down the soul, but a spiritual body feeling no want, and in all its members subjected to the will. In its pilgrim state the heavenly city possesses this peace by faith; and by this faith it lives righteously when it refers to the attainment of that peace every good action towards God and man; for the life of the city is a social life.

THOMAS AQUINAS

1. ON KINGSHIP

ON FORMS OF GOVERNMENT

I, 8 If, then, it is natural for man to live in the society of many, it is necessary that there exist among men some means by which the group may be governed. For where there are many men together and each one is looking after his own interest, the multitude would be broken up and scattered unless there were also an agency to take care of what appertains to the common weal. . . .

Consequently, there must exist something which impels toward the common good of the many, over and above that which impels toward the particular good of each individual. . . .

Therefore in every multitude there must be some governing power.

I, 10 Now it happens in certain things which are ordained toward an end that one may proceed in a right way and also in a wrong way. So, too, in the government of a multitude there is a distinction between right and wrong. A thing is rightly directed when it is led toward a befitting end, wrongly when it is led toward an unbefitting end. Now the end which befits a multitude of free men is different from that which befits a multitude of slaves, for the free man is one who exists for his own sake, while the slave, as such, exists for the sake of another. If, therefore, a multitude of free men is ordered by the ruler toward the common good of the multitude, that rulership will be right and just, as is suitable to free men. If, on the other hand, a rulership aims, not at the common good of the multitude, but at the private good of the ruler, it will be an unjust and perverted rulership.

I, 11 If an unjust government is carried on by one man alone, who seeks his own benefit from his rule and not the good of the multitude subject to him, such a ruler is called a "tyrant"—a word derived from "strength"—because he oppresses by might instead of ruling by justice. Thus among the ancients all powerful men were called tyrants. If an unjust government is carried on, not by one but by several, and if they be few, it is called an "oligarchy," that is, the rule of a few. This occurs when a few, who differ from the tyrant only by the fact that they are more than one, oppress the people by means of their wealth. If, finally, the bad government is carried on by the multitude, it is called a "democracy," i.e., control by the populace, which comes about when the plebeian people by force of numbers oppress the rich. In this way the whole people will be as one tyrant.

I, 12 In like manner we must divide just governments. If the government is administered by many, it is given the name common to all forms of government,

---

[Source: Dino Bigongiari, ed., *The Political Ideas of St. Thomas Aquinas* (New York: Hafner, 1969).]

viz., "polity," as for instance when a group of warriors exercise dominion over a city or province. If it is administered by a few men of virtue, this kind of government is called an "aristocracy," i.e., noble governance, or governance by noble men, who for this reason are called the "Optimates." And if a just government is in the hands of one man alone, he is properly called a "king." Wherefore the Lord says by the mouth of Ezechiel: "My servant, David, shall be king over them and all of them shall have one shepherd."

ON TYRANTS

VI, 41 Therefore, since the rule of one man, which is the best, is to be preferred, and since it may happen that it be changed into a tyranny, which is the worst (all this is clear from what has been said), a scheme should be carefully worked out which would prevent the multitude ruled by a king from falling into the hands of a tyrant.

VI, 42 First, it is necessary that the man who is raised up to be king by those whom it concerns should be of such condition that it is improbable that he should become a tyrant. . . .

Then, once the king is established, the government of the kingdom must be so arranged that opportunity to tyrannize is removed. At the same time his power should be so tempered that he cannot easily fall into tyranny.

VI, 43 Finally, provision must be made for facing the situation should the king stray into tyranny.

VI, 44 Indeed, if there be not an excess of tyranny it is more expedient to tolerate the milder tyranny for a while than, by acting against the tyrant, to become involved in many perils more grievous than the tyranny itself. For it may happen that those who act against the tyrant are unable to prevail and the tyrant then will rage the more. But should one be able to prevail against the tyrant, from this fact itself very grave dissensions among the people frequently ensue: the multitude may be broken up into factions either during their revolt against the tyrant or in process of the organization of the government, after the tyrant has been overthrown. Moreover, it sometimes happens that while the multitude is driving out the tyrant by the help of some man, the latter, having received the power, thereupon seizes the tyranny. Then, fearing to suffer from another what he did to his predecessor, he oppresses his subjects with an even more grievous slavery.

VI, 45 If the excess of tyranny is unbearable, some have been of the opinion that it would be an act of virtue for strong men to slay the tyrant and to expose themselves to the danger of death in order to set the multitude free.

VI, 46 But this opinion is not in accord with apostolic teaching. For Peter admonishes us to be reverently subject to our masters, not only to the good and gentle but also the forward: "For if one who suffers unjustly bear his trouble for conscience' sale, this is grace."

VI, 47 Should private persons attempt on their own private presumption to kill the rulers, even though tyrants, this would be dangerous for the multitude as well as for their rulers.

VI, 48 Furthermore, it seems that to proceed against the cruelty of tyrants is an action to be undertaken, not through the private presumption of a few, but rather by public authority.

VI, 49 If to provide itself with a king belongs to the right of a given multitude, it is not unjust that the king be deposed or have his power restricted by that same multitude if, becoming a tyrant, he abuses the royal power. It must not be thought that such a multitude is acting unfaithfully in deposing the tyrant, even though it had previously subjected itself to him in perpetuity, because he himself has deserved that the covenant with his subjects should not be kept, since, in ruling the multitude, he did not act faithfully as the office of a king demands.

VI, 50 If, on the other hand, it pertains to the right of a higher authority to provide a king for a certain multitude, a remedy against the wickedness of a tyrant is to be looked for from him.

VI, 51 Should no human aid whatsoever against a tyrant be forthcoming, recourse must be had to God, the King of all, Who is a helper in due time in tribulation. For it lies in his power to turn the cruel heart of the tyrant to mildness.

VI, 52 But to deserve to secure this benefit from God, the people must desist from sin, for it is by divine permission that wicked men receive power to rule as a punishment for sin.

X, 76 It is to be added further, however, that the very temporal advantages for which tyrants abandon justice work to the greater profit of kings when they observe justice.

X, 77 First of all, among all worldly things there is nothing which seems worthy to be preferred to friendship. Friendship unites good men and preserves and promotes virtue. Friendship is needed by all men in whatsoever occupations they engage. In prosperity it does not thrust itself unwanted upon us, nor does it desert us in adversity. It is what brings with it the greatest delight, to such an extent that all that pleases is changed to weariness when friends are absent, and all difficult things are made easy and as nothing by love. There is no tyrant so cruel that friendship does not bring him pleasure.

X, 78 Yet, although tyrants desire this very benefit of friendship, they cannot obtain it, for when they seek their own good instead of the common good there is little or no communion between them and their subjects. . . .

Good kings, on the contrary, are loved by many when they show that they love their subjects and are studiously intent on the common welfare, and when their subjects can see that they derive many benefits from this zealous care.

X, 79 The consequence of this love is that the government of good kings is stable, because their subjects do not refuse to expose themselves to any danger whatsoever on behalf of such kings.

X, 80 The government of tyrants, on the other hand, cannot last long because it is hateful to the multitude, and what is against the wishes of the multitude cannot be long preserved. For a man can hardly pass through this present life without suffering some adversities, and in the time of his adversity occasion cannot be lacking to rise against the tyrant; and when there is an opportunity there will not be lacking at least one of the multitude to use it. Then the people will fervently favor the insurgent, and what is attempted with the sympathy of the multitude will not easily fail of its effects. It can thus scarcely come to pass that the government of a tyrant will endure for a long time.

X, 81 This is very clear, too, if we consider the means by which a tyrannical government is upheld. It is not upheld by love, since there is little or no bond of friendship between the subject multitude and the tyrant, as is evident from what we have said. On the other hand, tyrants cannot rely on the loyalty of their subjects, for such a degree of virtue is not found among the generality of men that they should be restrained by the virtue of fidelity from throwing off the yoke of unmerited servitude, if they are able to do so. Nor would it perhaps be a violation of fidelity at all, according to the opinion of many, to frustrate the wickedness of tyrants by any means whatsoever. It remains, then, that the government of a tyrant is maintained by fear alone, and consequently they strive with all their might to be feared by their subjects. Fear, however, is a weak support. Those who are kept down by fear will rise against their rulers if the opportunity ever occurs when they can hope to do it with impunity, and they will rebel against their rulers all the more furiously the more they have been kept in subjection against their will by fear alone.

HUMANITY'S FINAL END

III, 105 But there is a further destiny for man after this mortal life; that final blessedness and enjoyment of God which he awaits after death. . . .

III, 106 Our conclusion must be the same, whether we consider the destiny of one person or of a whole community. Consequently, if the end of man were to be found in any perfection existing in man himself, the final object of government in a community would lie in the acquisition of such perfection and in its preservation once acquired. So that if such an end, whether of an individual or of a community, were life and bodily health, doctors would govern. If, on the other hand, it were abundance of riches, the government of the community could safely be left in the hands of the economist. If it were knowledge of truth, the king, whose task it is to guide the community, would have the duties of a professor. But the object for which a community is gathered together is to live a virtuous life. For men consort together that they may thus attain a fullness of life which would not be possible to each living singly: and the full life is one which is lived according to virtue. Thus the object of human society is a virtuous life. . . .

III, 107 Now the man who lives virtuously is destined to a higher end, which consists, as we have already said, in the enjoyment of God: and the final object of human association can be no different from that of the individual man. Thus the final aim of social life will be, not merely to live in virtue, but rather through virtuous life to attain to the enjoyment of God. If, indeed, it were possible to attain this object by natural human virtue, it would, in consequence, be the duty of kings to guide men to this end. We believe, however, that it is the supreme power in temporal affairs which is the business of a king. Now government is of a higher order according to the importance of the ends it serves. For it is always the one who has the final ordering of affairs who directs those who carry out what pertains to the attainment of the final aim: just as the sailor who must navigate the ship advises the shipwright as to the type of ship which will suit his purpose; and the citizen who is to bear arms tells the smith what weapons to forge. But the enjoyment of God is an aim which cannot be attained by human virtue alone, but only through divine grace, as the Apostle tells us (*Romans*, VI, 23): 'The grace of God is eternal life.' Only a divine rule, then, and not human government, can lead us to this end. Such government belongs only to that King who is both man, and also God: that is to Jesus Christ, our Lord, Who, making men to be Sons of God, has led them to the glory of heaven.

This, then, is the government entrusted to Him: a dominion which shall never pass away, and in virtue of which He is called in the Holy Scriptures, not only a priest but a king; as *Jeremias* says (XXIII, 5): 'A king shall reign and shall be wise.' It is from Him that the royal priesthood derives; and, what is more, all the Faithful of Christ, being members of Him, become thus, priests and kings. The ministry of this kingdom is entrusted not to the rulers of this earth but to priests, so that temporal affairs may remain distinct from those spiritual: and, in particular, it is delegated to the High Priest, the successor of Peter and Vicar of Christ, the Roman Pontiff; to whom all kings in Christendom should be subject, as to the Lord Jesus Christ Himself.

2. SUMMA THEOLOGICA

THE RIGHT TO RESIST TYRANNY

2a2ae.42,2 A tyrannical government is unjust because it is not directed to the common good, but to the private good of the ruler, as Aristotle says. Consequently, disturbing such a government has not the nature of sedition, unless perhaps the disturbance be so excessive that the people suffer more from it than from the tyrannical regime. Indeed it is the tyrant rather that is more guilty of sedition, since he fosters discord and dissension among his subjects in order to lord over them more securely. For this is tyranny, to govern for the ruler's personal advantage to the people's harm.

[Source: Thomas Aquinas, *Summa Theologica*, trans. J.P. Reid (London: Eyre & Spottiswoode; New York: McGraw-Hill, 1972).]

THE LIMITS TO OBEDIENCE

2a2ae.104,5 There are two ways it can happen that a subordinate is not bound to obey a superior in everything. The first is because of the precept of a higher superior; a gloss on *Romans*, *He that resisteth the power, resisteth the ordinance of God;* comments, *Should a commissioner issue an order, are you to comply if it be contrary to the bidding of a proconsul? Again, if the proconsul command one thing and the emperor another, would you hesitate to disregard the first and observe the other? Therefore if the emperor order one thing and God another, it is God who is to be obeyed.*

The second way is for a command to be given in a matter where no subjection to the superior exists. Seneca's remark is to the point, *He is mistaken who supposes that slavery takes in the whole person. It touches not the better part; the body may be subject and consigned to an owner, but thoughts are free.* The force of this is that we are not bound to obey man but God alone in matters which concern the inner life of the will.

Those matters in which one man is bound to obey another are outward actions involving the body. Even so, he is not bound to obey humans but God alone in regard to what belongs to the very nature of physical life, since in these matters all men are equal: for example in what concerns taking food and begetting children. This is why there is no obligation either of slaves towards their master or of children towards their parents to obey with regard to contracting marriage, vowing virginity, or the like. In what relates to the control of human conduct and affairs, a subject is bound to obey his superiors within the limits of the authority in question—a soldier, his commander in military matters; a slave, his master in carrying out the labours of his service; a child, its parents in what concerns upbringing, running the household, etc.

2a2ae.104,6 Further, we have no obligation to obey thieves accosting us, and Augustine has it that *where justice is wanting, what is the regime but a band of brigands?* Since, then, the regime of secular rulers is often marked by injustice, or else they have unjustly usurped power, it seems that Christians should not obey them.

On the other hand there are these texts, *Admonish them to be subject to princes and powers; Be ye subject to every human creature for God's sake, whether it be to kings as excelling or to governors as sent by him.*

Reply: Following *Romans*, *The justice of God by faith of Jesus Christ,* faith in Christ is the source and support of all righteousness. For this reason the order of justice is not abolished but strengthened through the faith of Christ. Now the order of justice calls for inferiors to be subject to their superiors; otherwise it would be impossible to maintain stability in human affairs. Thus, their faith in Christ does not exempt the faithful from the duty to obey civil authority. . . .

The obligation to obey civil authority is measured by what the order of justice requires. For this reason when any regime holds its power not by right but by usurpation, or commands what is wrong, subjects have no duty to obey, except for such extraneous reasons as avoidance of scandal or risk.

CHAPTER 3

THE CHURCH OF THE REFORMATION

The Reformation, like any other historical period, produced a variety of different models of church and state. Dominant were those of Martin Luther (1483–1546) and John Calvin (1509–1564) who both inherited many of the medieval presuppositions on church-state relations to which reference has already been made.

In addition, they professed other common emphases of faith: *sola Scriptura*, justification by faith, predestination, and the priesthood of all believers. Both affirmed a covenantal relationship between God and his people, although this played a more formative role in Calvin's theology than in Luther's understanding of church-state relations. Similarly, both maintained a doctrine of two kingdoms, although differently interpreted, and both stressed the importance of the law and the gospel, although they had a significantly different understanding of the function of the law in the life of the Christian. These factors, together with the different historical contexts within which their respective emphases emerged, ultimately resulted in two related but different understandings of church-state relations.

There continues to be debate on the extent to which the Augsburg Confession of 1530 can legitimately be regarded as representative of Luther's own theology and whether it was seriously affirmed by Calvin.[1] It does, however, exemplify certain key categories in church-state relations as they emerged in the magisterial Reformation. Articles 16 and 28 of the confession (extracted here) illustrate the different emphases of Luther and Calvin regarding these categories.

MARTIN LUTHER

The often maligned "two kingdoms" doctrine was confessed as part of the Protestant faith in the Augsburg Confession. This doctrine distinguished the spiritual and the political spheres of existence in much the same way that Augustine did. Yet, article 16 also recognized that the political realm was part of the divine order, and as such it was to be engaged in by Christians. Those who conscientiously renounced this realm, such as the Anabaptists, were condemned. They failed, according to article 16, to understand that the gospel simply did not address our relationship to such external things as political action. It was rather concerned with the "righteousness of the heart." Here is the essence of the evangelical doctrine of salvation which teaches that salvation cannot be earned by good works—nor by refraining from any particular activity. Salvation is a free gift of God. This, rightly understood, frees the individual to participate in society in a selfless and uninhibited manner. At the same time it excludes any form of ethical quietism because, to quote Luther, a Christian is one who "lives in Christ through faith and his neighbor through love."[2] The intention of article 16 is clear. It is to appraise the state positively, and to see it as a realm within which the Christian is to love the neighbor and to exercise the works of his or her calling.

Article 16 also stressed the need for Christians to be subject to civil authority and to obey its commands and laws, provided such obedience did not involve sin. This point is made clear in Luther's treatise on *Secular Authority: To What Extent It Should Be Obeyed*, part of which is included in this selection of texts. His words were decisive; there was "a limit to temporal authority, for if we have to do everything that temporal authority wanted there would have been no point to say, 'We must obey God rather than men.' " Luther was as determined in stating that short of a law which compels one to sin, the Christian was obliged to submit to the government of the day. The separation of the two realms was equally clear in article 28, which censured bishops for their engagement in political affairs. Their authority was "to preach the Gospel and administer the sacraments," while "temporal authority is concerned with matters altogether different from the Gospel."

Luther's teaching on church-state relations was obviously more extensive than what can be summarized in the two articles of the Augsburg Confession, written as it was by Melanchthon, although apparently in consultation with Luther. Different situations demanded different responses from the pen of Luther, and it would be quite wrong to select writings from any one of these situations and to regard it as representative of all that Luther said on the topic. A convenient collection of Luther's most significant political writings is found in J. M. Porter's *Luther: His Political Writings*, which includes *Secular Authority*, written in 1523. As one of Luther's less polemical documents on church-state relations, it provided an over-all theory of this doctrine. But while considering this text, we should also be aware of Luther's more polemical and less tenable writings concerning the Peasants' Revolt of 1525. Few today would care to defend Luther's views on that conflict.

Whatever one's assessment of Luther's political thought, it is important to recall that while he was never uncritical of the German princes—and at times he was severe in his criticism of their rule—he was essentially supportive of them. This needs to be contextually understood. Like his medieval predecessors, Luther regarded history as, at best, a place of tentative peace to be endured while awaiting the age to come. Like them also, he was predisposed toward a sense of natural order in society under a legitimate ruler, and he lived throughout his life in fear of political chaos and disintegration. For him, there was a natural hierarchy of order in society, and the German princes were the legitimate rulers best equipped "to patch and darn as best we can while we live, punish the abuses and lay bandages and poultices over the sores," within a temporal realm which Luther believed "God does not think as much of . . . as he does of his spiritual realm."[3] This observation needs to be qualified by certain fragmentary indications in Luther's writings which seem to glimpse the possibility of more positive and optimistic functions of government.[4] These were, however, not fully developed nor were they positively promoted. In later generations, they were in fact lost from sight under the influence of nineteenth-century German nationalism, to the point of completely denying the church a prophetic role in the political realm. In order to do Luther's two kingdoms justice one needs to reach beyond the literature of his nineteenth-century descendants as well as those in the Third Reich period to the teaching of Luther himself.[5]

It must also be remembered that Luther's views of church-state relations took form under the benign and conscientious reigns of Frederick the Wise, whose judicious refusal to become involved in a religious dispute was what ensured the survival of Luther's Reformation in its early days, Frederick's brother John who succeeded him, and his son, the young John Frederick who looked to Luther as a mentor. Luther involved himself in politics and urged his followers to do likewise, but it never occurred to him to engage in the overthrow of the existing rulers. He did not shrink from warning the princes that their subjects would not endure their abuses much longer, nor would they be tolerated by God. But when the peasants rose in revolt he advised the princes to kill them. Such is the complexity of Luther's church-state doctrine. What is clear is that Luther's analysis of the milieu of his times was obviously influenced by his social place within it.

It was, however, also his understanding of the threefold use of the law that influenced his theological perception of the state. Contrary to the more rigid approach of Calvin, the *political* function of the law was for Luther one of reason, negotiation, and even compromise. The *teaching* or guiding function of the law was, in turn, not applicable to the Christian at all, although, as *Secular Authority* makes clear, this was not to be used as an excuse for political laxity. Luther's point was, however, that the *convicting* use of the law, which was God's Word of both grace and judgment, redeemed the Christian and implanted God's law within his or her desire. In a word, the rigid demands of prescriptive law were simply not part of Luther's doctrine, making for a more relaxed—and potentially ambivalent—attitude to morality than comes with Calvin's covenantal theology.

The important question is whether Luther's understanding of church-state relations was largely timebound, or whether it was even fundamentally wrong? For him the secular forces of chaos needed to be subjected to Christian hierarchical control. Today it is realized that this hierarchy is often itself the source of chaos. The governed, in turn, no longer see themselves merely as subjects but as citizens whose political responsibility goes well beyond submission to, and prayer for, those who rule over them. Given this shift in the history of politics, it could be argued that Luther's doctrine needs merely to be adjusted to meet this new situation, extending the concept of "political office" to include people from outside the existing order, with every citizen having the right to oppose civil authority as part of his or her political responsibility.[6] It could similarly be argued that given today's understanding of the parameters of Christian responsibility, Luther's clear teaching that a prince should be disobeyed if he advocates what is sinful or wrong takes on a pertinent dimension of political resistance that was not as obvious in his day. The burning question that remains unanswered is whether Luther's ethic can be updated to deal with the complexities of those situations where people do *not* enjoy citizenship rights, as is clearly the case for the majority of people in South Africa. Or to recast the question in relation to Luther's own situation, what were the options open to the peasants whose rebellion caused Luther to call them "prophets of murder" and "mad dogs" and to suggest that those who died in defeating them could not die a more blessed death?[7]

Virtually every dictatorship in the world affirms its own version of the two kingdoms doctrine to reject church "interference" in the affairs of the state. The doctrine has also been interpreted as a basis for limiting the power of the state and to legitimate the church's resistance to dictatorships. This contradictory use of Luther's two kingdoms doctrine must, at least partially, be attributed to the lack of uniformity in Luther's own writing on the doctrine.[8] Luther, in fact, often used the doctrine of the two kingdoms to different and contradictory ends. For Luther, like Augustine before him, the fall of humanity raised the world in rebellion against God, but the world continued to be God's world. The kingdom of Christ was thus both *against* the world, and *for* the world. At times Luther placed his emphasis on the former and at times on the latter. At times the *regnum Dei* (kingdom of God) was seen in opposition to the *regnum mundi* (kingdom of this world) understood as the *regnum diaboli* (kingdom of the devil). But at other times the *regnum mundi* was understood as the *regnum terrena* (God's kingdom on earth). In the former case the argument is that the church ought to address itself only to spiritual matters, leaving the state to deal with the harsh and diabolic problems of this world. In the latter case, the church can well claim, as it often has done, that it too has a responsibility for this world, simply because it is God's world. In this situation, the church is obliged to take politics, economics, and social affairs seriously.

A balanced understanding of Luther's two kingdoms doctrine suggests that the "spiritual kingdom" (which is the concern of the church) and the "temporal kingdom" (which is the concern of the civil authorities) are both manifestations of the "kingdom of Christ" over against the "kingdom of the devil." Luther's point, however, was that the temporal and the spiritual realms were to be responded to in different ways. Moltmann clarifies this point:

> Luther's two kingdoms doctrine is in truth a critical-polemical separation between God and Caesar. It permits neither a Caesaro-papalism nor a clerical theocracy. It intended to teach that the world and politics may not be deified, nor may they be religiously administered. One should give to Caesar what belongs to Caesar—no more and no less—and give to God that which is God's. One should turn the self-deified world into the world, and let God be God. One should deal rationally with the world, with the law, and with force. The world is not and it never will become the kingdom of God; rather it is a good earthly order against evil chaos. One should

deal spiritually—which means with faith—with God and his gospel. The gospel does not create a new world but saves people through faith.[9]

JOHN CALVIN

Calvin's response to Luther's scheme of things was less accommodating and emphasized the direct lordship of Christ over every area of life. As already noted, he too took his stand on a two kingdoms doctrine, with each realm having its "different kings and different laws."[10] What made his doctrine of church-state relations different from Luther's was what he said in addition to Luther, in exhibiting what Paul Lehmann calls a "livelier sense" of the possibilities of government.[11] This much is seen in the texts excerpted below.

Certainly Calvin had a stronger prescriptive sense of God's law for Christians and non-Christians alike. The task of civil authority was, for him, not merely to "patch and darn." Such "powers are from God, not as pestilence, and famine, and wars and other visitations of sin are said to be from him, but because he has appointed them for the legitimate and just government of the world."[12] What is important for our purposes is Calvin's anticipation of something new in political rule: the Little Council in the city of Geneva met regularly for the purpose of mutual criticism of the rulers and the ruled. Calvin thus put into practise a system of rule of "aristocracy bordering on popular government."[13] "The magistracy under the pressure of the people," suggests Lehmann, was Calvin's "functional instrument for obeying God rather than men in human affairs."[14] Like Luther, he stressed the need for obedience to rulers, "whatever they may be like," while warning that God would raise up "avengers among his servants, and arm them with his command to punish the wicked government and deliver his people." This vengeance, though, belongs to the Lord: "Let us not think it is entrusted to us, to whom no command has been given except to obey and to suffer." This is part of the undeveloped political theology of Calvin—God will use people with both good and bad motives to remove unjust rulers, but not those who are his followers. The magistrates, as the leaders of the people, were given a grave responsibility with regard to wicked leaders. It was their duty to resist such rulers, although in extreme situations—less cautiously than Luther—Calvin advised ordinary Christians that if rulers commanded anything that contradicted the purposes of God, "let it go unesteemed."

John T. McNeill in his excellent essay on "John Calvin and Civil Government" amplifies this emphasis in relation to Calvin's other writings. Commenting on Calvin's *Instruction and Confession of Faith,* written in 1537, he writes as follows:

> . . . obedience even to tyrannical rulers is expressly enjoined "until we be freed from their yoke." Here, however, stress is also laid on the solemn obligation of rulers. They must do nothing unworthy of their office as ministers and lieutenants of God, and they must maintain religion in its purity and by good laws guide the life of their subjects and secure their welfare. Obedience to superiors is very explicitly restricted by the prior obligation of obedience to God. . . . For Calvin, firm gov-

> ernment is a matter of prime importance. It is an agency of God's sovereign purpose and it is indispensable for man's peaceable existence. For ruler and ruled "the public good" . . . is placed within religious obligation, and obedience to rulers is emphatically limited by primary obedience to God.[15]

Calvin's emphasis on and application of his doctrine of church and state, like Luther's, must also be understood contextually. Geneva was an independent and self-contained city, which had actually voted for reform prior to Calvin's arrival. One thousand clergy and church workers had been expelled from Geneva to be replaced by a group of nineteen clergy of whom Calvin was one. They were not permitted to hold political office or own property, and soon all except Calvin were dismissed. Within eighteen months of his arrival, he too was dismissed. Given this background, we can understand why, even after he was invited to return to Geneva to begin his major program of reform which would continue to his death in 1664, he simply never enjoyed the complete confidence of the rulers, nor did he fully trust them. It was ultimately Calvin's sense of covenant, of being the people of God with the responsibility to be obedient to God in every area of existence, nurtured in an era of persecution in a city with a broad-based program of reform, that gave his theology a dynamic which Luther, operating essentially with the same principles of reform, was not able to realize.

The point is a rather simple one. Context does influence one's way of doing theology. Fundamentally there is significant agreement in many of the formulations on the encounter between church and state in the writings of Luther and Calvin. But Luther was writing from the perspective of the rulers of a German elite, while Calvin wrote from the perspective of a city of refugees.

Luther understood the reality of political power which was developing in Europe at the time. Politics was becoming an entity separate from religion. This was a process already identified in the writing of Augustine and further developed in the thought of Thomas, in which civil authority began to attain an identity and legitimacy of its own, apart from the church. This authority was, for Luther, God's indirect way of ruling his creation. Later generations of Lutherans transformed this emphasis into a static doctrine of separate orders of creation: institutions of government, schools, the home, and so on. Although these orders were to be used by Christians and non-Christians alike with a view to establishing the best form of government and societal order in response to the complex problems of the day, they often tended to become restrictive institutions, remote from the direct influence of the church. For all the appeal of this approach to church-state relations, which must have provided a welcome relief from the theocratic teaching of the medieval world, it relaxed the demands of the gospel on the state. In a world which Luther saw to be necessarily less than perfect, one to be tolerated and endured, it opened the way to later abuses and excesses by civil rulers, who would regard the church's influence as restricted to a separate, spiritual sphere.

Calvin, in turn, understood the political responsibility of the church in relation to the state to be more explicit and direct. If, for Luther, politics were the *affairs of people*, for Calvin, politics were the *affairs of God*, and, as such, it was the obligation of the church to discern and ensure the enactment of God's laws in society.

The danger of Lutheran politics is the separation of the two realms, thrusting religion into an other-worldly form of piety and politics into unbridled nationalism. The danger of Calvinism is the assimilation of religion and politics into an uncompromising theocracy. It has often been argued that the teachings of Luther and Calvin themselves provide the necessary safeguards against these dangers, to which subsequent generations have not given sufficient attention. The pertinent question is to what extent the reformers themselves were latently responsible for the deviant ways of their followers. A further question concerns the extent to which different historical situations demand different religious models. Certainly history suggests that Calvinism has appealed to oppressed people around the world as a source of their political liberation. It has also, in a different guise, provided the legitimation of many an oppressive regime. Lutheran theology has, in turn, often earned the wrath of the oppressed and the praise of more stabilized societies.

NOTES

1. B. A. Gerrish, *The Old Protestantism and the New: Essays on the Reformed Heritage* (Edinburgh: T. and T. Clark, 1982), pp. 248–54. For an English translation of the Augsburg Confession see T. G. Tappert, ed., *The Book of Concord* (Philadelphia: Fortress, 1959). See also my article, "Augsburg, Barmen and Ottawa: The Protestant Quest for a Political Theology," *Journal of Theology for Southern Africa*, 47 (June 1984), 47–58; reprinted in *International Review of Missions*, 73 (1984).
2. Martin Luther, "The Freedom of a Christian," *Works of Martin Luther (LW)* (Philadelphia: Muhlenberg Press, 1959), vol. 31, p. 341.
3. Martin Luther, "Interpretation of Psalm 101," quoted in H. G. Haile, *Luther: An Experiment in Biography* (Princeton, N.J.: Princeton University Press, 1980), p. 101.
4. See among others "Treatise on Good Works," *LW*, vol. 44, p. 95; "To the Christian Nobility," *LW*, vol. 44, pp. 212–15; "To the Nobles of Germany," *LW*, vol. 45, pp. 355–78.
5. Ulrich Duchrow, *Zwei Reiche und Regimente* (Gütersloh: Gütersloher Verlagshaus Gerd Mohn, 1977) and *Christenheit und Weltverantwortung* (Stuttgart: Ernst Klett Verlag, 1970), has been decisive in distinguishing between Luther's political theology and nineteenth-century two kingdom theology.
6. Gerrish, p. 260.
7. Martin Luther, "Against the Robbing and Murdering Hordes of Peasants," *LW*, vol. 46, pp. 49–55.
8. Jürgen Moltmann, *On Human Dignity: Political Theology and Ethics* (London: SCM, 1984), p. 63.
9. Ibid., pp. 70–71.
10. John Calvin, *Institutes of the Christian Religion (CI)*, trans. Henry Beveridge (Grand Rapids: Eerdmans, n.d.), III, xix, 15.
11. Paul Lehmann, *The Transfiguration of Politics* (New York: Harper & Row, 1975), p. 40.
12. John Calvin, *Commentaries on the Epistle of Paul the Apostle to the Romans*, trans. John Owen (Grand Rapids: Eerdmans, 1948), p. 479.
13. *CI*, IV, xx, 8.
14. Lehmann, p. 41.

15. John T. McNeill, "John Calvin on Civil Government," in G. L. Hunt, ed., *Calvinism and the Political Order* (Philadelphia: Westminister, 1965), pp. 31–32. See also P. T. Fuhrmann, *Calvin: Instruction in Faith* (Philadelphia: Westminster, 1947), pp. 76f.

SELECT BIBLIOGRAPHY

Bornkamm, H. *Luther's Doctrine of the Two Kingdoms*. Philadelphia: Fortress, 1966.

Calvin, J. *On God and Political Duty*, ed. by J. T. McNeill. Indianapolis: Bobbs-Merrill, 1956.

Graham, W. F. *The Constructive Revolution: John Calvin and His Socio-Economic Instinct*. Richmond, Va.: John Knox Press, 1971.

Gerrish, B. A. *The Old Protestantism and the New: Essays in the Reformed Heritage*. Edinburgh: T. and T. Clark, 1982.

Hertz, K. *Two Kingdoms and One World*. Minneapolis: Augsburg, 1976.

Hunt, G. L., ed. *Calvinism and the Political Order*. Philadelphia: Westminster, 1965.

Kirchner, H. *Luther and the Peasants' War*. Philadelphia: Fortress, 1972.

Kuyper, A. *Lectures on Calvinism*. Grand Rapids: Eerdmans, 1970.

Lehmann, P. *The Transfiguration of Politics*. New York: Harper & Row, 1975.

Moltmann, J. *On Human Dignity: Political Theology and Ethics*. London: SCM, 1984, especially section 2.

Porter, J. M., ed. *Luther: Selected Political Writings*. Philadelphia: Fortress, 1974.

THE AUGSBURG CONFESSION, 1530

ARTICLE 16: CIVIL GOVERNMENT

It is taught among us that all government in the world and all established rule and laws were instituted and ordained by God for the sake of good order, and that Christians may without sin occupy civil offices or serve as princes and judges, render decisions and pass sentence according to imperial and other existing laws, punish evildoers with the sword, engage in just wars, serve as soldiers, buy and sell, take required oaths, possess property, be married, etc. . . .

Condemned here are the Anabaptists who teach that none of the things indicated above is Christian.

Also condemned are those who teach that Christian perfection requires the forsaking of house and home, wife and child, and the renunciation of such activities as are mentioned above. Actually, true perfection consists alone of proper fear of God and real faith in God, for the Gospel does not teach an outward and temporal but an inward and eternal mode of existence and righteousness of the heart. The Gospel does not overthrow civil authority, the state, and marriage but requires that all these be kept as true orders of God and that everyone, each according to his own calling, manifest Christian love and genuine good works in his station of life. Accordingly Christians are obliged to be subject to civil authority and obey its commands and laws in all that can be done without sin. But when commands of the civil authority cannot be obeyed without sin, we must obey God rather than men (Acts 5:29).

ARTICLE 28: THE POWER OF BISHOPS

This power of keys or of bishops is used and exercised only by teaching and preaching the Word of God and by administering the sacraments (to many persons or to individuals, depending on one's calling). In this way are imparted not bodily but eternal things and gifts, namely, eternal righteousness, the Holy Spirit, and eternal life. These gifts cannot be obtained except through the office of preaching and of administering the holy sacraments, for St. Paul says, "The gospel is the power of God for salvation to everyone who has faith." Inasmuch as the power of the church or of bishops bestows eternal gifts and is used and exercised only through the office of preaching, it does not interfere at all with government or temporal authority. Temporal authority is concerned with matters altogether different from the Gospel. Temporal power does not protect the soul, but with the sword and physical penalties it protects body and goods from the power of others.

Therefore, the two authorities, the spiritual and the temporal, are not to be mingled or confused, for the spiritual power has its commission to preach the

---

[Source: T. G. Tappert, ed., *The Book of Concord* (Philadelphia: Fortress, 1959).]

Gospel and administer the sacraments. Hence it should not invade the function of the other, should not set up and depose kings, should not annul temporal laws or undermine obedience to government, should not make or prescribe to the temporal power laws concerning worldly matters. Christ himself said, "My kingship is not of this world," and again, "Who made me a judge or divider over you?" Paul also wrote in Phil. 3:20, "Our commonwealth is in heaven," and in II Cor. 10:4, 5, "The weapons of our warfare are not worldly but have divine power to destroy strongholds and every proud obstacle to the knowledge of God."

Thus our teachers distinguish the two authorities and the functions of the two powers, directing that both be held in honor as the highest gifts of God on earth.

In cases where bishops possess temporal authority and the sword, they possess it not as bishops by divine right, but by human, imperial right, bestowed by Roman emperors and kings for the temporal administration of their lands. Such authority has nothing at all to do with the office of the Gospel.

According to divine right, therefore, it is the office of the bishop to preach the Gospel, forgive sins, judge doctrine and condemn doctrine that is contrary to the Gospel, and exclude from the Christian community the ungodly whose wicked conduct is manifest. All this is to be done not by human power but by God's Word alone. On this account parish ministers and churches are bound to be obedient to the bishops according to the saying of Christ in Luke 10:16, "He who hears you hears me." On the other hand, if they teach, introduce, or institute anything contrary to the Gospel, we have God's command not to be obedient in such cases, for Christ says in Matt. 7:15, "Beware of false prophets." St. Paul also writes in Gal. 1:8, "Even if we, or an angel from heaven, should preach to you a gospel contrary to that which we preached to you, let him be accursed," and in II Cor. 13:8, "We cannot do anything against the truth, but only for the truth." Again Paul refers to "the authority which the Lord has given me for building up and not for tearing down." Canon law requires the same in Part II, Question 7, in the chapters "Sacerdotes" and "Oves."

St. Augustine also writes in his reply to the letters of Petilian that one should not obey even regularly elected bishops if they err or if they teach or command something contrary to the divine Holy Scriptures.

Whatever other power and jurisdiction bishops may have in various matters (for example, in matrimonial cases and in tithes), they have these by virtue of human right. However, when bishops are negligent in the performance of such duties, the princes are obliged, whether they like to or not, to administer justice to their subjects for the sake of peace and to prevent discord and great disorder in their lands.

MARTIN LUTHER

SECULAR AUTHORITY: TO WHAT EXTENT IT SHOULD BE OBEYED

Some time ago I addressed a little book to the German nobility, setting forth their Christian office and functions. How far they acted on my suggestions is only too evident. Hence, I must change my tactics and write them, this time, what they should omit and not do. I fear this new effort will have as little effect on them as the other, and that they will continue to be princes and never become Christians. For God the Almighty has made our rulers mad; they actually think they can do—and order their subjects to do—whatever they please. And the subjects make the mistake of believing that they, in turn, are bound to obey their rulers in everything. It has gone so far that the rulers have begun ordering the people to get rid of certain books, and to believe and conform to what the rulers prescribe. They are thereby presumptuously setting themselves in God's place, lording it over men's consciences and faith, and schooling the Holy Spirit according to their own crackbrained ideas. Nevertheless, they let it be known that they are not to be contradicted, and are to be called gracious lords all the same.

THE TWO KINGDOMS

We must divide the children of Adam and all mankind into two classes, the first belonging to the kingdom of God, the second to the kingdom of the world. Those who belong to the kingdom of God are all the true believers who are in Christ and under Christ, for Christ is King and Lord in the kingdom of God, as Psalm 2 [:6] and all of Scripture says. For this reason he came into the world, that he might begin God's kingdom and establish it in the world. Therefore, he says before Pilate, "My kingdom is not of the world, but every one who is of the truth hears my voice" [John 18:36–37]. . . .

Now observe, these people need no temporal law or sword. If all the world were composed of real Christians, that is, true believers, there would be no need for or benefits from prince, king, lord, sword, or law. They would serve no purpose, since Christians have in their heart the Holy Spirit, who both teaches and makes them to do injustice to no one, to love everyone, and to suffer injustice and even death willingly and cheerfully at the hands of anyone. Where there is nothing but the unadulterated doing of right and bearing of wrong, there is no need for any suit, litigation, court, judge, penalty, law, or sword. . . .

All who are not Christians belong to the kingdom of the world and are under the law. There are few true believers, and still fewer who live a Christian life, who do not resist evil and indeed themselves do no evil. For this reason God

---

[Source: Martin Luther, *Works*, vol. 45 (Philadelphia: Muhlenberg Press, 1959).]

has provided for them a different government beyond the Christian estate and kingdom of God. He has subjected them to the sword so that, even though they would like to, they are unable to practice their wickedness, and if they do practice it they cannot do so without fear or with success and impunity. In the same way a savage wild beast is bound with chains and ropes so that it cannot bite and tear as it would normally do, even though it would like to; whereas a tame and gentle animal needs no restraint, but is harmless despite the lack of chains and ropes. . . .

For this reason God has ordained two governments: the spiritual, by which the Holy Spirit produces Christians and righteous people under Christ; and the temporal, which restrains the un-Christian and wicked so that—no thanks to them—they are obliged to keep still and to maintain an outward peace. Thus does St. Paul interpret the temporal sword in Romans 13 [:3], when he says it is not a terror to good conduct but to bad. And Peter says it is for the punishment of the wicked [I Pet. 2:14].

If anyone attempted to rule the world by the gospel and to abolish all temporal law and sword on the plea that all are baptized and Christian, and that, according to the gospel, there shall be among them no law or sword—or need for either—pray tell me, friend, what would he be doing? He would be loosing the ropes and chains of the savage wild beasts and letting them bite and mangle everyone, meanwhile insisting that they were harmless, tame, and gentle creatures; but I would have the proof in my wounds. Just so would the wicked under the name of Christian abuse evangelical freedom, carry on their rascality, and insist that they were Christians subject neither to law nor sword, as some are already raving and ranting.

To such a one we must say: Certainly it is true that Christians, so far as they themselves are concerned, are subject neither to law nor sword, and have need of neither. But take heed and first fill the world with real Christians before you attempt to rule it in a Christian and evangelical manner. This you will never accomplish; for the world and the masses are and always will be un-Christian, even if they are all baptized and Christian in name. Christians are few and far between (as the saying is). Therefore, it is out of the question that there should be a common Christian government over the whole world, or indeed over a single country or any considerable body of people, for the wicked always outnumber the good. . . .

For this reason one must carefully distinguish between these two governments. Both must be permitted to remain; the one to produce righteousness, the other to bring about external peace and prevent evil deeds. Neither one is sufficient in the world without the other. No one can become righteous in the sight of God by means of the temporal government, without Christ's spiritual government. Christ's government does not extend over all men; rather, Christians are always a minority in the midst of non-Christians. Now where temporal government or law alone prevails, there sheer hypocrisy is inevitable, even though the commandments be God's very own. For without the Holy Spirit in the heart no one becomes truly righteous, no matter how fine the work he does. On the other hand, where the spiritual government alone prevails over land and people, there wickedness is given free rein and the door is open for all manner of rascality, for the world as a whole cannot receive or comprehend it.

THE LIMITS OF TEMPORAL AUTHORITY

We come now to the main part of this treatise. Having learned that there must be temporal authority on earth, and how it is to be exercised in a Christian and salutary manner, we must now learn how far its arm extends and how widely its hand stretches, lest it extend too far and encroach upon God's kingdom and government. It is essential for us to know this, for where it is given too wide a scope, intolerable and terrible injury follows; on the other hand, injury is also inevitable where it is restricted too narrowly. In the former case, the temporal authority punishes too much; in the latter case, it punishes too little. To err in this direction, however, and punish too little is more tolerable, for it is always better to let a scoundrel live than to put a godly man to death. The world has plenty of scoundrels anyway and must continue to have them, but godly men are scarce.

It is to be noted first that the two classes of Adam's children—the one in God's kingdom under Christ and the other in the kingdom of the world under the governing authority, as was said above—have two kinds of law. For every kingdom must have its own laws and statutes; without law no kingdom or government can survive, as everyday experience amply shows. The temporal government has laws which extend no further than to life and property and external affairs on earth, for God cannot and will not permit anyone but himself to rule over the soul. Therefore, where the temporal authority presumes to prescribe laws for the soul, it encroaches upon God's government and only misleads souls and destroys them. We want to make this so clear that everyone will grasp it, and that our fine gentlemen, the princes and bishops, will see what fools they are when they seek to coerce the people with their laws and commandments into believing this or that. . . .

No one shall or can command the soul unless he is able to show it the way to heaven; but this no man can do, only God alone. Therefore, in matters which concern the salvation of souls nothing but God's word shall be taught and accepted. . . .

How he believes or disbelieves is a matter for the conscience of each individual, and since this takes nothing away from the temporal authority the latter should be content to attend to its own affairs and let men believe this or that as they are able and willing, and constrain no one by force. For faith is a free act, to which no one can be forced. . . .

But, you say: Paul said in Romans 13 [:1] that every soul [*seele*] should be subject to the governing authority; and Peter says that we should be subject to every human ordinance (I Pet. 2:13]. Answer: Now you are on the right track, for these passages are in my favor. St. Paul is speaking of the governing authority. Now you have just heard that no one but God can have authority over souls. Hence, St. Paul cannot possibly be speaking of any obedience except where there can be corresponding authority. From this it follows that he is not speaking of faith, to the effect that temporal authority should have the right to command faith. He is speaking rather of external things, that they should be ordered and governed on earth. . . .

This is also what St. Peter means by the phrase, "Human ordinance" [I Pet. 2:13]. A human ordinance cannot possibly extend its authority into heaven and over souls; it is limited to the earth, to external dealings men have with one another, where they can see, know, judge, evaluate, punish, and acquit.

Christ himself made this distinction, and summed it all up very nicely when he said in Matthew 22 [:21], "Render to Caesar the things that are Caesar's and to God the things that are God's." Now, if the imperial power extended into God's kingdom and authority, and were not something separate, Christ would not have made this distinction. . . .

That is, over what is on earth and belongs to the temporal, earthly kingdom, man has authority from God; but whatever belongs to heaven and to the eternal kingdom is exclusively under the Lord of heaven. . . .

This is the meaning as St. Peter says in Acts 4 [5:29], "We obey God rather than men." Thereby, he clearly sets a limit to the temporal authority, for if we had to do everything that the temporal authority wanted there would have been no point in saying, "We must obey God rather than men."

WHEN CIVIL AUTHORITY CAN BE DISOBEYED

If your prince or temporal ruler commands you to side with the pope, to believe thus and so, or to get rid of certain books, you should say, "It is not fitting that Lucifer should sit at the side of God. Gracious sir, I owe you obedience in body and property; command me within the limits of your authority on earth, and I will obey. But if you command me to believe or to get rid of certain books, I will not obey; for then you are a tyrant and overreach yourself, commanding where you have neither the right nor the authority," etc. Should he seize your property on account of this and punish such disobedience, then blessed are you; thank God that you are worthy to suffer for the sake of the divine word. Let him rage, fool that he is; he will meet his judge. For I tell you, if you fail to withstand him, if you give in to him and let him take away your faith and your books, you have truly denied God.

Let me illustrate. In Meissen, Bavaria, the Mark, and other places, the tyrants have issued an order that all copies of the New Testament are everywhere to be turned in to the officials. This should be the response of their subjects: They should not turn in a single page, not even a letter, on pain of losing their salvation. Whoever does so is delivering Christ up into the hands of Herod, for these tyrants act as murderers of Christ just like Herod. If their homes are ordered searched and books or property taken by force, they should suffer it to be done. Outrage is not to be resisted but endured; yet we should not sanction it, or lift a little finger to conform, or obey. For such tyrants are acting as worldly princes are supposed to act, and worldly princes they surely are. But the world is God's enemy; hence, they too have to do what is antagonistic to God and agreeable to the world, that they may not be bereft of honor, but remain worldly princes. Do not wonder, therefore, that they rage and mock at the gospel; they have to live up to their name and title.

You must know that since the beginning of the world a wise prince is a mighty rare bird, and an upright prince even rarer. They are generally the biggest fools or the worst scoundrels on earth; therefore, one must constantly expect the worst from them and look for little good, especially in divine matters which concern the salvation of souls. . . .

For there are very few princes who are not regarded as fools or scoundrels; that is because they show themselves to be so. The common man is learning to think, and the scourge of princes (that which God calls *contemptum*) is gathering force among the mob and with the common man. I fear there will be no way to avert it, unless the princes conduct themselves in a princely manner and begin again to rule decently and reasonably. Men will not, men cannot, men refuse to endure your tyranny and wantonness much longer. Dear princes and lords, be wise and guide yourselves accordingly. God will no longer tolerate it. The world is no longer what it once was, when you hunted and drove the people like game. Abandon therefore your wicked use of force, give thought to dealing justly, and let God's word have its way, as it will anyway and must and shall; you cannot prevent it.

THE RESPONSIBILITIES OF A CHRISTIAN PRINCE

Now that we know the limits of temporal authority, it is time to inquire also how a prince should use it. We do this for the sake of those very few who would also like very much to be Christian princes and lords, and who desire to enter into the life in heaven. . . .

He who would be a Christian prince must certainly lay aside any intent to exercise lordship or to proceed with force. For cursed and condemned is every sort of life lived and sought for the benefit and good of self; cursed are all works not done in love. . . .

A prince must have the law as firmly in hand as the sword, and determine in his own mind when and where the law is to be applied strictly or with moderation, so that law may prevail at all times and in all cases, and reason may be the highest law and the master of all administration of law. . . .

He must take care to deal justly with evildoers. Here he must be very wise and prudent, so he can inflict punishment without injury to others. . . .

Let this be his rule: Where wrong cannot be punished without greater wrong, there let him waive his rights, however just they may be. He should not have regard to his own injury, but to the wrong others must suffer in consequence of the penalty he imposes.

CONSCIENTIOUS OBJECTION

Here you will ask: "Is a prince then not to go to war, and are his subjects not to follow him into battle?" Answer: This is a far-reaching question, but let me answer it very briefly. To act here as a Christian, I say, a prince should not go to war against his overlord. . . .

If, however, the antagonist is your equal, your inferior, or of a foreign government, you should first offer him justice and peace, as Moses taught the children of Israel. If he refuses, then—mindful of what is best for you—defend yourself against force by force. . . .

In this matter subjects are in duty bound to follow, and to devote their life and property, for in such a case one must risk his goods and himself for the sake of others. . . .

What if a prince is in the wrong? Are his people bound to follow him then too? Answer: No, for it is no one's duty to do wrong; we must obey God (who desires the right) rather than men [Acts 5:29]. . . .

JOHN CALVIN

INSTITUTES OF THE CHRISTIAN RELIGION

CIVIL GOVERNMENT

IV,xx,1 Having shown above that there is a twofold government in man, and having fully considered the one which, placed in the soul or inward man, relates to eternal life, we are here called to say something of the other, which pertains only to civil institutions and the external regulation of manners.

IV,xx,2 But as we lately taught that [civil] government is distinct from the spiritual and internal kingdom of Christ, so we ought to know that they are not adverse to each other. The former, in some measure, begins the heavenly kingdom in us, even now upon earth, and in this mortal and evanescent life commences immortal and incorruptible blessedness, while to the latter it is assigned, so long as we live among men, to foster and maintain the external worship of God, to defend sound doctrine and the condition of the Church, to adapt our conduct to human society, to form our manners to civil justice, to conciliate us to each other, to cherish common peace and tranquility. All these I confess to be superfluous, if the kingdom of God, as it now exists within us, extinguishes the present life. But if it is the will of God that while we aspire to true piety we are pilgrims upon the earth, and if such pilgrimage stands in need of such aids, those who take them away from man rob him of his humanity.

THE RESPONSIBILITY OF THOSE IN CIVIL GOVERNMENT: TO RULE WITH JUSTICE

IV,xx,4 With regard to the function of magistrates, the Lord has not only declared that he approves and is pleased with it, but, moreover, has strongly recommended it to us by the very honourable titles which he has conferred upon it. To mention a few. When those who bear the office of magistrate are called gods, let no one suppose that there is little weight in that appellation. It is thereby intimated that they have a commission from God, that they are invested with divine authority, and, in fact, represent the person of God, as whose substitutes they in a manner act. . . . Their functions were expressly approved by the Lord. Wherefore no man can doubt that civil authority is, in the sight of God, not only sacred and lawful, but the most sacred, and by far the most honourable, of all stations in mortal life.

IV,xx,6 This consideration ought to be constantly present to the minds of magistrates, since it is fitted to furnish a strong stimulus to the discharge of duty, and

---

[Source: John Calvin, *Institutes of the Christian Religion*, trans. Henry Beveridge (Grand Rapids: Eerdmans, n.d.).]

also afford singular consolation, smoothing the difficulties of their office, which are certainly numerous and weighty. What zeal for integrity, prudence, meekness, continence, and innocence, ought to sway those who know that they have been appointed ministers of the divine justice! How will they dare to admit iniquity to their tribunal, when they are told that it is the throne of the living God? How will they venture to pronounce an unjust sentence with that mouth which they understand to be an ordained organ of divine truth? With what conscience will they subscribe impious decrees with that hand which they know has been appointed to write the acts of God? In a word, if they remember that they are the vicegerents of God, it behoves them to watch with all care, diligence, and industry, that they may in themselves exhibit a kind of image of the Divine Providence, guardianship, goodness, benevolence, and justice.

ON TYPES OF GOVERNMENT

IV,xx,8 And certainly it were a very idle occupation for private men to discuss what would be the best form of polity in the place where they live, seeing these deliberations cannot have any influence in determining any public matter. Then the thing itself could not be defined absolutely without rashness, since the nature of the discussion depends on circumstances. And if you compare the different states with each other, without regard to circumstances, it is not easy to determine which of these has the advantage in point of utility, so equal are the terms on which they meet. Monarchy is prone to tyranny. In an aristocracy, again, the tendency is not less to the faction of a few, while in popular ascendancy there is the strongest tendency to sedition. When these three forms of government, of which philosophers treat, are considered in themselves, I, for my part, am far from denying that the form which greatly surpasses the others is aristocracy, either pure or modified by popular government, not indeed in itself, but because it very rarely happens that kings so rule themselves as never to dissent from what is just and right, or are possessed of so much acuteness and prudence as always to see correctly. Owing, therefore, to the vices or defects of men, it is safer and more tolerable when several bear rule, that they may thus mutually assist, instruct, and admonish each other, and should any one be disposed to go too far, the others are censors and masters to curb his excess. This has already been proved by experience, and confirmed also by the authority of the Lord himself, when he established an aristocracy bordering on popular government among the Israelites, keeping them under that as the best form, until he exhibited an image of the Messiah in David. And as I willingly admit that there is no kind of government happier than where liberty is framed with becoming moderation, and duly constituted so as to be durable, so I deem those very happy who are permitted to enjoy that form, and I admit that they do nothing at variance with their duty when they strenuously and constantly labour to preserve and maintain it. Nay, even magistrates ought to do their utmost to prevent the liberty, of which they have been appointed guardians, from being impaired, far less violated. If in this they are sluggish or little careful, they are perfidious traitors to their office and their country.

THE CITIZEN'S DUTY TO THE CIVIL GOVERNMENT: HONOR AND SUBJECTION

IV,xx,22 The first duty of subjects towards their rulers, is to entertain the most honourable views of their office, recognising it as a delegated jurisdiction from God, and on that account receiving and reverencing them as the ministers and ambassadors of God.

IV,xx,23 From this, a second consequence is, that we must with ready minds prove our obedience to them, whether in complying with edicts, or in paying tribute, or in undertaking public offices and burdens, which relate to the common defence, or in executing any other orders. "Let every soul," says Paul, "be subject unto the higher powers." . . . Let no man here deceive himself, since we cannot resist the magistrate without resisting God.

IV,xx,24 But as we have hitherto described the magistrate who truly is what he is called—viz. the father of his country, and (as the Poet speaks) the pastor of the people, the guardian of peace, the president of justice, the vindicator of innocence, he is justly to be deemed a madman who disapproves of such authority. And since in almost all ages we see that some princes, careless about all their duties on which they ought to have been intent, live, without solicitude, in luxurious sloth; others, bent on their own interest, venally prostitute all rights, privileges, judgments, and enactments; others pillage poor people of their money, and afterwards squander it in insane largesses; others act as mere robbers, pillaging houses, violating matrons, and slaying the innocent; many cannot be persuaded to recognise such persons for princes, whose command, as far as lawful they are bound to obey. For while in this unworthy conduct, and among atrocities so alien, not only from the duty of the magistrate, but also of the man, they behold no appearance of the image of God, which ought to be conspicuous in the magistrate, while they see not a vestige of that minister of God, who was appointed to be a praise to the good and a terror to the bad, they cannot recognise the ruler whose dignity and authority Scripture recommends to us. And, undoubtedly, the natural feeling of the human mind has always been not less to assail tyrants with hatred and execration, than to look up to just kings with love and veneration.

IV,xx,25 But if we have respect to the word of God, it will lead us farther, and make us subject not only to the authority of those princes who honestly and faithfully perform their duty toward us, but all princes, by whatever means they have so become, although there is nothing they less perform than the duty of princes. For though the Lord declares that a ruler to maintain our safety is the highest gift of his beneficence, and prescribes to rulers themselves their proper sphere, he at the same time declares, that of whatever description they may be, they derive their power from none but him. Those, indeed, who rule for the public good, are true examples and specimens of his beneficence, while those who domineer unjustly and tyrannically are raised up by him to punish the people for their iniquity. Still all alike possess that sacred majesty with which he has invested lawful power.

IV,xx,27 If we constantly keep before our eyes and minds the fact, that even the most iniquitous kings are appointed by the same decree which establishes all regal authority, we will never entertain the seditious thought, that a king is to be treated according to his deserts, and that we are not bound to act the part of good subjects to him who does not in his turn act the part of a king to us.

GOD CRUSHES UNJUST KINGS: LET PRINCES HEAR AND BE AFRAID

IV,xx,29 And let us reflect that it belongs not to us to cure these evils, that all that remains for us is to implore the help of the Lord, in whose hands are the hearts of kings, and inclinations of kingdoms. . . . Before his face shall fall and be crushed all kings and judges of the earth, who have not kissed his anointed, who have enacted unjust laws to oppress the poor in judgment, and do violence to the cause of the humble, to make widows a prey, and plunder the fatherless.

IV,xx,30 Herein is the goodness, power, and providence of God wondrously displayed. At one time he raises up manifest avengers from among his own servants, and gives them his command to punish accursed tyranny, and deliver his people from calamity when they are unjustly oppressed; at another time he employs, for this purpose, the fury of men who have other thoughts and other aims.

IV,xx,31 But whatever may be thought of the acts of the men themselves, the Lord by their means equally executed his own work, when he broke the bloody sceptres of insolent kings, and overthrew their intolerable dominations. Let princes hear and be afraid; but let us at the same time guard most carefully against spurning or violating the venerable and majestic authority of rulers, an authority which God has sanctioned by the surest edicts, although those invested with it should be most unworthy of it, and, as far as in them lies, pollute it by their iniquity. Although the Lord takes vengeance on unbridled domination, let us not therefore suppose that that vengeance is committed to us, to whom no command has been given but to obey and suffer.

THE RIGHT TO CIVIL DISOBEDIENCE

IV,xx,32 But in that obedience which we hold to be due to the commands of rulers, we must always make the exception, nay, must be particularly careful that it is not incompatible with obedience to Him to whose will the wishes of all kings should be subject, to whose decrees their commands must yield, to whose majesty their sceptres must bow. And, indeed, how preposterous were it, in pleasing men, to incur the offence of Him for whose sake you obey men! The Lord, therefore, is King of kings. When he opens his sacred mouth, he alone is to be heard, instead of all and above all. We are subject to the men who rule over us, but subject only in the Lord. If they command anything against Him let us not pay the least regard to it, nor be moved by all the dignity which they possess as magistrates—a dignity to which no injury is done when it is subordinated to the special and truly supreme power of God. On this ground Daniel denies that he had sinned in any respect against the king when he refused to obey his impious decree (Dan. vi. 22), because the king had exceeded his limits, and not only been injurious to men, but, by raising his horn against God, had virtually abrogated his own power. On the other hand, the Israelites are condemned for having too readily obeyed the impious edict of the king. For, when Jeroboam made the golden calf, they forsook the temple of God, and, in submissiveness to him, revolted to new superstitions (1 Kings xii. 28). With the same facility posterity had bowed before the decrees of their kings. For this they are severely upbraided by the Prophet (Hosea v. 11). So far is the praise of modesty from being due to that pretence by which flattering courtiers cloak themselves, and deceive the simple, when they deny the lawfulness of declining anything imposed by their kings, as if the Lord had resigned his own rights to mortals by appointing them to rule over their fellows, or as if earthly power were diminished when it is subjected to its author, before whom even the principalities of heaven tremble as suppliants. I know the imminent peril to which subjects expose themselves by this firmness, kings being most indignant when they are contemned. As Solomon says, "The wrath of a king is as messengers of death" (Prov. xvi. 14). But since Peter, one of heaven's heralds, has published the edict, "We ought to obey God rather then men" (Acts v. 29), let us console ourselves with the thought, that we are rendering the obedience which the Lord requires, when we endure anything rather than turn aside from piety. And that our courage may not fail, Paul stimulates us by the additional consideration (1 Cor. vii. 23), that we were redeemed by Christ at the great price which our redemption cost him, in order that we might not yield a slavish obedience to the depraved wishes of men, far less do homage to their impiety.

CHAPTER 4

THE CHURCH OF RADICAL PROTESTANTISM

"Radical Protestantism" is used here as a collective term referring to both the sixteenth-century radical Reformation in Europe, and the Puritan reformations in both England and Scotland which emerged during the second half of the same century.

Attention is given first to Anabaptism within the larger movement of the European radical Reformation, as representative of that form of Protestantism which radically defined the Christian faith as being in contradiction to the demands of the state. Second, attention is given to a form of Protestantism which radically affirmed participation in the affairs of state as definitive of Christian living, namely English Puritanism, influenced essentially by Calvinism and to a lesser extent by some forms of Anabaptism. Third, consideration is given to Scottish Presbyterianism, specifically the writings of John Knox, dominated as they were by radical Calvinism and zealous Scottish nationalism.

ANABAPTISM

The radical Reformation was a structured manifestation of sixteenth-century religious renewal, quite distinct from the magisterial Reformation of Luther, Calvin, Zwingli, and others. Indeed, those denominations which today stand in continuity with this tradition—the Mennonites, certain of the Brethren, the Amish, some Unitarians who developed their own distinctive character, and less directly the Baptists—each in their own way, to a greater or lesser extent, continue to affirm this identity as a basis for church-state relations. In this continuity they are unlike other Protestant groups for whom extraneous social, cultural, and doctrinal factors have often influenced and even dominated their contemporary positions with regard to matters of church and state.

The sixteenth-century radical Reformation is usually understood in relation to three groups: the Anabaptists, the Spiritualists, and the Evangelical Rationalists.[1] Collectively they are often referred to as the "left wing of the Reformation."

There were many differences among these groups, but the reality which bound them together was their common rejection of any alliance between church and state, grounded in a distinctive doctrine of the church. What ultimately distinguished the different groups was their respective emphases on related but different understandings of authority. The Anabaptists organized themselves in strict adherence to the teachings of the New Testament; the Spiritualists in submission, often quietistically and individualistically, to the guidance of the Holy Spirit; and the Evangelical Rationalists in response to a form of natural piety related to intuitive and speculative reason as a form of authority alongside the Scriptures.

Each group had its subgroups and its deviant followers. There were, to mention the better known names, the Zwickau prophets and other "revolutionaries" who have caught the imagination of historians. The magisterial reformers seemed to use the names of Thomas Müntzer, Carlstadt, and others to caricature indiscriminately the entire left wing of the Reformation, so often loosely and collectively referred to as Anabaptists. In order to gain an accurate understanding of the radical Reformation it is necessary to reach beyond the polemical writings of both the magisterial reformers and many contemporary historians to the writings of those who have represented the center of this movement since the sixteenth century. Pertinent to this scholarship is the rejection of the thesis which links Anabaptism with the fanaticism of Thomas Müntzer and the Zwickau prophets, locating the origin of Anabaptism instead in the Zwinglian Reformation, more specifically in the *pacifist* manifestation of this tradition.[2]

The call of Anabaptism was to affirm unambiguously the church of the apostolic age through the affirmation of Scripture alone. Yoder's observation in this regard is important for our purposes: "This did not mean (at least not necessarily) a slavishly legalistic use of Scripture; it meant only that no *other* norm be set up beside the Bible."[3] In so doing, Anabaptism gave a quite distinctive expression to the doctrine of the two cities or kingdoms that Christianity had wrestled with ever since the time of Augustine. Where mainstream Christianity (both Roman Catholic and Protestant) has given expression to various forms of integration between the two, Anabaptism, like the early church, saw the heavenly kingdom to be diametrically opposed to the earthly kingdom, believed to be dominated by the rule of Satan. Unlike the early church, sixteenth-century Anabaptists regarded the true church as a concrete expression of "the present kingdom of Christ which is being established in the midst of and alongside of the kingdom of this world; not . . . deferred to some millennial future."[4] In a word, the Anabaptist vision is a boldly historical one, giving rise to the theological concept of an alternative community.[5]

It is this commitment which constitutes the essence of the Anabaptist understanding of the church. It flows from the importance attached to believer's baptism as a sign of entry into the church and the concept of discipleship in obedience to the teaching of Christ, especially the Sermon on the Mount, as the praxis of the church. It is more than an invisible church, unrealizable in history, that is affirmed. It is the anticipation of the coming kingdom of God and is concretely to be seen in contradiction to the existing political order. As such, it can never be "simply an administrative subdivision of a monolithic society, charged with giving that society moral sanction and psychological stability, nor an invisible mystic communion of true believers, but a new kind of disciplined fellowship, taking shape within history by the gathering of confessing believers."[6] The radical Reformation broke with the Catholic-Protestant *corpus Christianum* enshrined in the formula "*cuius regio eius religio*" which gave every political authority the right to determine what religion was to be practiced in that territory. In its place the radical Reformation affirmed the *corpus Christi* of true believers.

From this flowed a doctrine of church and state in reaction to the residual forms of Constantinianism found in the dominant forms of church-state relations in the sixteenth century. Robert Kreider summarizes this Anabaptist position in a helpful manner, providing a clear basis for distinguishing it from the magisterial Protestant position.[7] The Christian, it is argued, is a citizen of the kingdom of Christ, which is sharply separated from the kingdoms of this world. Such citizenship demands radical obedience to God alone and willingly accepts the persecution of this world. This distinction was also interpreted by most, but not all, Anabaptists to mean that Christians should not occupy the office of magistrate. For most such an appointment was regarded as a violation of the precepts of Scripture, while some others allowed for the possibility of a Christian magistrate, but concluded that the strict contradiction between the spirit of Christ and the spirit of the world would not allow a Christian to survive as a magistrate.[8] Essentially, however, the question never seriously arose whether a sixteenth-century Anabaptist could be a magistrate—it was as impossible an option to contemplate as it would have been for a Christian in the pre-Constantinian church. Sixteenth-century Anabaptism advocated disestablishment and rejected those clergy who participated in government as "hirelings of the rulers." "The true church," to quote Kreider, "should be a gathered, exclusive, heroic, disciplined church of believers completely severed from all control by the state." It further meant that they would refuse to take the oath of loyalty to a civic or national authority, while rejecting all means of violence to either maintain or overthrow the state.

In more recent times some deviations from this position of strict noninvolvement have occurred. Certainly the writings of John Howard Yoder, which constitute to those who stand in mainstream Protestant and Roman Catholic circles perhaps the most articulate and appealing form of contemporary Anabaptist and Mennonite thought, have given rise to different interpretations of the extent to which a Christian may selectively and conscientiously participate in government. For him this is, however, "more an occasion to speak to the authorities than an opportunity to be an agent of the government,"[9] and thus the norm remains the same. Such participation would be motivated not by a concern for power, but rather to serve the common good and to exercise a prophetic role. The extent to which it may be possible for an Anabaptist Christian to hold civil office must therefore be necessarily limited by what Kreider has referred to as "disestablishment" ethics. The following texts by Hubmaier, Denck, Marpeck, and Menno Simons illustrate the intensity of this debate even within the earliest times of this movement.

The Schleitheim Confession of 1527, included in this anthology, is the authoritative statement of the Anabaptist movement. It gives expression to the discipline of Anabaptism and forms the basis for what can be regarded as an Anabaptist doctrine of church-state relations.[10] It is not written primarily against the magisterial Reformation, and certainly not against the civil authorities, but against "certain false brethren among us . . . in the way they intend to practice and observe the freedom of the Spirit and of Christ." Briefly stated, it is written against the antinomian and the revolutionary excesses which appeared on the fringes of the movement. It provides clear evidence of a break with the magisterial—in this case the Zwinglian—view, that the saints or elect of God are known only to God. The true church was seen to be a visible manifestation of the people of God, and the ban was used as an important disciplinary measure affecting all those baptized into the membership of the church. It is also clear, in the sixth article, that a position was adopted against those who supported the idea of a Christian magistracy. Similarly, any support for the idea of future struggle at the end of the age when the saints of God would rule this world is rejected. Christians are to resist temporal power as Christ resisted it. "Since Christ is as it is written of Him, His members must also be the same."

The appeal of the *corpus Christi* emphasis of Anabaptism is a powerful and an enduring one which has reasserted itself in a variety of forms in recent times. A pertinent question, from the perspective of the mainline Protestant and Catholic churches, is whether the Anabaptist model of church-state relations provides the kind of political base and participation that is required for removing the stubborn socio-economic and political obstacles to just government. Theologically stated, it could be asked whether this model takes the doctrine of creation as seriously as it should: The tantalizing counterquestion is whether the mainline churches have avoided the compromise of residual Constantinianism in their engagement with the always more powerful structures of political and economic power.

ENGLISH PURITANISM

Puritanism had a variety of different manifestations, represented in persons as widely divergent as the scholarly Thomas Cartwright, the recalcitrant Robert Browne, the poet John Milton, the industrious Ben Jonson, and the militant Oliver Cromwell, the Lord Protector of the Commonwealth. The spiritual father of the Puritans was essentially John Calvin, whose religious fervor was transmitted to England either by Continental exiles or by English refugees returning during the rule of Elizabeth I. On the other hand, some Puritans, and notably those who became known as Congregationalists, had come under the influence of Anabaptist groups and held firmly to the idea of a "gathered church," with a strict separation of church and state.

With the death of Catholic Queen Mary, "bloody Mary" as she was known to the Protestants, and the accession of Elizabeth I to the throne, the nonconforming Protestants, long banished from the establishment, many into exile, took heart at the thought of having a Protestant on the throne. Elizabeth's Protestantism, however, was much like that conceived by her father, Henry VIII—a modified Catholicism with herself as the head of the church. Her Acts of Supremacy and Uniformity satisfied neither the Catholics nor the Puritans. To the former she was a heretic, to the latter a papist, and neither had any intention of remaining silent.

Puritan protest against her religious policy manifested itself in three major groups: those within the established church; the separatists, who would become known as Independents or Congregationalists and Baptists; Presbyterians; and, as the protest grew, a variety of smaller more radical groups such as the Levellers, the Diggers, the Ranters, the Quakers, and other subgroups. The more impatient *separatist* groups were ready to pay the price of schism for immediate reform, while the *conforming* group, which remained within the established church, instigated for the reform of the church through Parliament.

The Congregationalists focused on the local congregation as the community of Christ. In the words of an early leader Robert Browne (1550–1633), "The Church planted or gathered is a company or number of Christians or believers, which, by a willing covenant made with their God, are under the government of God and Christ, and keep his laws in one holy communion: because Christ hath redeemed them unto holiness and happiness for ever, from which they were fallen by the sin of Adam."[11] Robert Harrison, a close associate of Browne, regarded correct church polity as fundamental to Christian discipleship and argued that the structure of the church as determined by English law was in contradiction to the apostolic pattern of the church found in the New Testament. At the same time he insisted that it was incompatible with the New Testament to allow the civil authorities to determine the character of the church at all—this was a matter to be handled by the church of Christ itself.[12] For these fundamental reasons the separatists felt compelled to withdraw from the established church. Preachers and church leaders who made the excuse that they were bound by the law of the state and could not act in obedience to the demands of the New Testament were condemned in the strongest language by both Browne and Harrison. As is clear in the text that follows, Browne regarded such preachers as neglecting their spiritual heritage and as enemies of Christ's kingdom. The sense of divine calling in Puritan thought is a powerful category.

Browne was adamant that separation from the established church did not imply disloyalty to either the queen or the civil authorities. For preachers and teachers to neglect their God-given calling to reform and order the life of the church in accordance with the New Testament, leaving this task to the unwilling magistrates, was regarded as sacrilege. Browne makes it clear in the text that it is the task of Christians to obey God and to accept whatever consequences might follow. The Anabaptist strain among these separatists was unmistakable. P. T. Forsyth is correct that Congregationalist separatism "was Calvinism flushed and fertilised by Anabaptism on English ground. It drew from Calvinism its positive and theological Gospel of the Word, from Anabaptism its personal and subjective religion of the spirit."[13]

Ultimately this blend of Calvinist and Anabaptist thought would give the Congregationalists a theology and an ecclesiology which would set them apart from other separatists, including the Presbyterians, who were more conformist. The Congregationalist strain involved a covenantal relationship with God and discipline to deal with those who deviate from the required obedience in both doctrine and morals. The integration of the established church and civil authority in England at the time was such that this was to have far-reaching political implications. For the separatists, the theological issues were straightforward. The civil authority hindered their faithful worship of God, and therefore this authority needed ultimately to be opposed. Civil authorities, in turn, regarded these demands to be part of a broader popular demand for political and civil rights, while the established church bishops perceived their own authority to be under question. Separatist leaders were driven into exile and thrown into prison, but resolutely sought to obey God alone and to do his will in both church and society. Browne was imprisoned a total of thirty-two times, ultimately breaking under interrogation and torture. Forced to recant, he was despised by his followers and opponents alike.

The English Presbyterians—not to be confused with Scottish Presbyterianism, although John Knox worked among Presbyterians on both sides of the border—were opposed by both the Church of England and the Congregationalists. What distinguished them from the Church of England was, among other things, their insistence that the Bible knew nothing of bishops but only a church governed by elders or presbyters, elected not by bishops but by the congregations. Having a less radical doctrine of the church than the Congregationalists, they were content with a national church rather than a community of believers called by God into a separate existence. Browne was little impressed, arguing that should Episcopacy be replaced by Presbyterianism, "then instead of one pope we should have a thousand, and of some lord Bishops in name a thousand, lordly tyrants indeed which now do disdain the names."[14] Presbyterianism was not predisposed to the idea of a "gathered church," as the Congregationalists were. Directly influenced by Calvin's Geneva and John Knox in the north, their hope was for a national Presbyterian church in England.

The essential divergence between the Puritans, whether conforming or nonconforming, and the established Church of England came from their different conceptions of the authority of the Scriptures within the tradition of the church. For the established church the Bible, tempered by reason, was regarded as authoritative in matters of doctrine and personal conduct. For the Puritans, reason was distorted by original sin, and the Bible contained the infallible divine pattern for church government, worship, discipline, public morals, and belief. From this the program of Puritan reform followed, extending from liturgical reform and the abolition of vestments to social reform and the recruitment of every Christian to be a saint. The Puritan movement was an ecclesiastical and political revolution of the saints. There could be no compromise, because it was God's revolution. To quote Robert Browne, it was "a reformation without tarrying for any." Puritanism of whatever stripe—for ultimately there was little doctrinal conflict between the different groups—had its origin in an intensity of religion which scorned nominal church membership and held firmly to the teaching of Scripture alone, expressed in the priesthood of all believers. What distinguished it from other religious groups with similar views, and ultimately from Anabaptism, was the Calvinist sense of compulsion which flowed from these convictions, as a basis for reforming not only the Christian community but the entire political order. This, suggests Horton Davies, was to become "the seedplot of democratic government."[15]

The religio-political history of English Puritanism cannot be considered in any detail here. Paul Sangster's *A History of the Free Churches* provides a most readable account of these events.[16] The separatists were imprisoned in the Tower, often awaiting death, as they wrote pamphlets defending separatism and the urgency of reform in church and society. The Presbyterians were gaining ground in Parliament, and a Puritan ideology of frugal living, hard work, and political participation was being felt throughout England. By the time of Elizabeth's death the Puritans were a powerful minority in both the political and ecclesiastical realms. They were divided among themselves, but Elizabeth saw fit to write to her successor, James I, saying: "Let me warn you that there has risen, both in your realm and mine, a sect of perilous consequence, such as would have no kings but a presbytery, and take our place while they enjoy our privilege." As the Puritans had their early hopes shattered when Elizabeth came to the throne, so they were disappointed by James. He resisted all their petitions, and, to quote Sangster, "the greatest contribution that King James made to religion was in America." His laws compelled some of his most creative and dynamic subjects to seek religious toleration and liberty in the "new world," taking with them not only ideals concerning the separation of church and state but also the sense of divine vocation that would influence the growing sense of independence in the colonies and indeed the American form of civil religion for centuries to come.

When Charles I came to the throne, he overruled parliament and appointed William Laud as Archbishop of Canterbury. Laud ruthlessly sought to impose religious uniformity on the dissenting groups. Popular unrest grew, the king was forced to recall Parliament, and the people demanded the total abolition of the present form of government. In 1642 Parliament presented the king with the "Grand Remonstration," a statement of grievances and suggested solutions. Civil war was imminent. Oliver Cromwell raised an army "who upon a matter of conscience engaged in this quarrel," arguing that "he that prays best fights best." Charles was beheaded. Sangster's summation seems to do justice to the sequence of events: "The army had become a church militant in the most literal sense. Every kind of Christian was in it, united for one purpose, God's purpose in freeing England from the tyranny of that 'man of blood,' Charles Stuart." Cromwell's religious settlement was a compromise that failed to satisfy the extremists. He was the defender of no particular faith, but the protector of all. Leaving aside his personal preference for Independency, his solution for England was that the Episcopalians, the Presbyterians, and the Independents learn to coexist. But toleration was not popular with Cromwell's supporters, and eventually the rule of the Stuarts would be restored with the return of Charles II from exile.

The Puritan revolution must be understood in relation to the crucial years of conflict between 1530, when Henry VIII began his assault on papal control in England, and 1660, when the Protectorate ended and Charles II was welcomed back from exile as the rightful successor to the throne. For Walzer it was an ideology of transition.[17] Radical Protestantism provided the theological and ideological motivation for Britain's middle class struggle against the establishment of church and state epitomized in James I's famous dictum, "No Bishop, No King."

A. G. Dickens's observation is important for an accurate understanding of the Puritan revolution: "Even while Puritanism seemed to be creating division, in another and deeper sense it was uniting the kingdom."[18] To pose the question whether Puritanism was essentially a religious or a political movement is to introduce a debate on the social identity of religious ideas which takes us well beyond the confines of this essay. Suffice it to say that it was a movement motivated and sustained by a religious ideology which extended deep into the political arena—in fact into Parliament—and which contributed to extensive constitutional reforms.

Such resolute unity seldom endures when the common enemy is removed from the scene. England was no exception. The Commonwealth lasted for a little more than a decade. During this time Congregationalists turned away from participation in the Commonwealth, which was supported largely by the Presbyterians and Erastian Anglicans. Motivated by a strain of Anabaptism, clinging to a strong sense of the gathered community of Christ, and desiring the kind of freedom that an alliance of religious and secular forces could not give, this step was perhaps inevitable. The irony of history is such that their quest for greater liberty indirectly contributed to Cromwell accepting the office of Lord Protector to enforce law and order, which ultimately contradicted their greatest theological aspirations.[19] As sincere Independents, fired by a determination—in obedience to God—to be separate and different from the best society could offer, they would again find their true identity in opposition to the newly emerged political and religious establishment, in much the same way as they had opposed the earlier order. As time passed the Congregationalists, the Presbyterians, and the Baptists were again united in their common sufferings as a result of the penalties due to all nonconformists. Their struggle for civil liberties continued well into the nineteenth century, when the Corporation Act of 1661 and the Test Act of 1673—which effectively excluded all nonconformists from holding civil, ecclesiastical, or military posts—were finally repealed.

Upon the return of the Stuarts in the person of Charles II, the Act of Uniformity was passed. The Church of England was as dominant as before. There was toleration of those who now became known as the "Nonconformers" or "Dissenters"—at the cost of second-class religious citizenship and periodic forms of persecution. Another chapter in the history of the "separatist" or Free churches had started. Growth, stagnation, and revival would all make their mark on both the established church and among those who chose to dissent. But what needs to be reiterated is that the story of Puritanism is a story of radical obedience to God with profound political consequences that have manifested themselves in a variety of forms in different countries around the world. Reference has already been made to America in this regard, and similar trends would emerge in South Africa, which will be discussed later. And the most explicit, and from a certain perspective "successful," integration of politics and religion in the sixteenth century occurred in Scotland.

SCOTTISH PRESBYTERIANISM

John Knox (1514–1572) succeeded as perhaps no one else did to relate religious fervor and political nationalism. He mobilized his followers, reformed his church, and ultimately removed Mary, Queen of Scots, from the throne. Presbyterianism in Scotland no less than in England—and indeed Knox himself—opposed the Elizabethan settlement and in this sense was part of the Puritan movement.

Knox was living in exile in France, for his earlier involvement in the Protestant-based rebellion in his homeland, when he was invited to England to serve as a royal chaplain to the young Edward VI. Like so many other Puritans he had earlier fled from Mary's rule to join other Protestant refugees in Geneva. There he seized upon an aspect of Calvinism, already encountered in the theology of Browne, hitherto not fully developed in relation to politics—that of "office" and "calling." Knox believed that individual inadequacy and corruption were overcome by the discipline of duty and divinely ordained status. "God's ministers," Knox wrote, "as they be the sons of men, of nature are they liars, unstable and vain; but His eternal Word which he putteth in their mouths and whereof they are made ambassadors is of . . . truth, stability and assurance."[20] This same distinction between the person of those whom God calls and the work which he accomplishes through them is seen in the following letters written by Knox to both the leaders and the common people of Scotland. It is this fundamental sense of divine calling to reform the nation that characterized all that Knox would be engaged in. Yet for him, this calling extended beyond himself and the leaders of church and state to the common people—to all believers. This too is clear in Knox's letter to the "Commonality of Scotland."

In the meantime relations between England and Scotland continued to deteriorate, while Mary of Guise, acting as regent for her young daughter Mary, Queen of Scots, not only looked to France for protection but also favored the Catholic faith. After returning briefly to Scotland Knox wrote his famous *First Blast of the Trumpet Against the Monstrous Regiment of Women* aimed at Mary, although it earned the wrath of Elizabeth as well. It was at more or less the same time that he wrote the treatises which are excerpted in this collection. At the instigation of the Scottish nobles and people he returned to Scotland in 1559. Protestantism and nationalism were bound together, and Knox was seen as the leader of this movement. Eventually England sent troops to counter the French presence in Scotland, but within a little more than a year Scottish independence was reasserted, and a Calvinist confession of faith, written largely by Knox, was adopted as the creed of the realm. The relevant section on obedience to those whom God has placed in authority "so long as they do not exceed the bounds of their office" is appended below. Within months of this triumph, the young Mary, who had married Francis II of France, was widowed and returned to Scotland. Knox denounced her masses and court life, was locked in controversy with her, and ultimately demanded her execution. After her abdication he preached at the coronation of her son, James VI of Scotland, who also became James I of England.

The overt revolutionary emphasis of Knox's brand of religion is not the epitome of all brands of radical Calvinism or the broader model of Puritanism.

It does, however, provide a typological example of the political prowess of a particular manifestation of the Protestant faith, shared in less explicit ways by the broad base of Puritanism. Knox had moved to a position beyond Calvin, who located the right to rebellion in duly constituted officials or magistrates. In Knox's view this duty was laid on all believers. All were called to be saints, Christ died for all, and no one had the right to surrender to another the primary responsibility to redress the faults and crimes of rulers. Indeed, to be silent in the face of tyranny implied, for him, complicity in the tyranny.[21]

The stark options facing radical Protestants continue to be those of disestablishment and aggressive participation in the affairs of state. Both have their consequences. If the former can be criticized for failing to provide a programmatic strategy for political transformation, the latter stands constantly in danger of confusing nationalistic zeal and theological truth.[22]

NOTES

1. See the introductory essay in *Spiritual and Anabaptist Writers*, ed. G. H. Williams and Angel M. Mergal (Philadelphia: Westminster, 1957). Also G. H. Williams, *The Radical Reformation* (Philadelphia: Westminster, 1975), pp. xxiii–xxxi.
2. Williams and Mergal, pp. 27–28.
3. John Howard Yoder, "The Prophetic Dissent of the Anabaptists," in *The Recovery of the Anabaptist Vision*, ed. G. H. Hershberger (Scottdale, Pa.: Herald Press, 1962), p. 93.
4. R. Friedmann, "The Doctrine of Two Worlds," in Hershberger.
5. See Franklin H. Littell, *The Anabaptist Vision of the Church* (Boston: Starr King Press, 1958).
6. Yoder, in Hershberger, p. 93.
7. Robert Kreider, "The Anabaptist Understanding of the State," in Hershberger.
8. Walter Klaassen, ed., *Anabaptism in Outline: Selected Primary Sources* (Kitchener, Ont.: Herald Press, 1981), p. 245.
9. John Howard Yoder, *Christian Witness to the State* (Newton, Kans.: Faith and Life Press, 1964), p. 28. See also *The Politics of Jesus* (Grand Rapids: Eerdmans, 1972), pp. 193f.; and "The Christian Case for Democracy," *Journal of Religious Ethics*, 5 (1977).
10. Williams, pp. 181–85.
11. Paul Sangster, *A History of the Free Churches* (London: Heinemann, 1983), p. 46.
12. Robert Harrison, *A Treatise of the Church and the Kingdom of Christ*, in *The Writings of Robert Harrison and Robert Browne*, ed. A. Peel and L. H. Carlson; vol. 2 of *Elizabethan Nonconformist Texts* (London: Allen and Unwin, 1953), pp. 47–48.
13. P. T. Forsyth, *Faith, Freedom and the Future* (New York: Hodder & Stoughton, n.d.; rpt. Independent Press, 1955), p. 50.
14. Sangster, p. 31.
15. Horton Davies, *The English Free Churches* (London: Oxford University Press, 1963), p. 33.
16. The history that follows is dependent on Sangster; A. G. Dickens, *The English Reformation* (London: Batsford, 1964); and G. F. Nuttall, *Visible Saints: The Congregational Way, 1640–1660* (Oxford: Blackwell, 1957).
17. Michael Walzer, *The Revolution of the Saints: A Study in the Origins of Radical Politics* (New York: Atheneum, 1976), p. 312.

18. Dickens, p. 319.
19. Davies, p. 63.
20. See G. Donaldson, *The Scottish Reformation* (Cambridge: Cambridge University Press, 1960); John Knox, *The History of the Reformation of Religion*, ed. C. J. Guthrie (Edinburgh: Banner of Truth Trust, 1982); Lord Eustace Percy, *John Knox* (London: Hodder and Stoughton, n.d.).
21. Walzer, p. 98. See also E. Muir, *Portrait of a Calvinist* (London: SCM, 1939), which provides an important study on the tension between "man" and "instrument" in the Calvinist tradition.
22. J. G. Davies, *Christians, Politics and Violent Revolution* (Maryknoll, N.Y.: Orbis, 1976), pp. 54–65.

SELECT BIBLIOGRAPHY

Davies, H. *The English Free Churches*. London: Oxford University Press, 1963.

Davies, J. G. *Christians, Politics and Violent Revolution*. Maryknoll, N.Y.: Orbis, 1976.

Dickens, A. G. *The English Reformation*. London: Batsford, 1964.

Donaldson, G. *The Scottish Reformation*. Cambridge: Cambridge University Press, 1960.

Durnbaugh, D. F. *The Believers' Church: The History and Character of the Radical Reformation*. London: Macmillan, 1968.

Hershberger, G. F., ed. *The Recovery of the Anabaptist Vision*. Scottdale, Pa.: Herald Press, 1962.

Knox, J. *The History of the Reformation of Religion*, ed. C. J. Guthrie. Edinburgh: Banner of Truth Trust, 1982.

Klaassen, W., ed., *Anabaptism in Outline: Selected Primary Sources*. Kitchener, Ont.: Herald Press, 1981.

Littell, F. H. *The Anabaptist Vision of the Church*. Boston: Starr King Press, 1958.

Nuttall, G. F. *Visible Saints: The Congregational Way, 1640–1660*. Oxford: Blackwell, 1957.

Percy, Lord E. *John Knox*. London: Hodder and Stoughton, n.d.

Sangster, P. *A History of the Free Churches*. London: Heinemann, 1983.

Walzer, M. *The Revolution of the Saints*. New York: Atheneum, 1976.

Williams, G. H. *The Radical Reformation*. Philadelphia: Westminster, 1975.

Williams, G. H., and Angel M. Mergal, eds. *Spiritual and Anabaptist Writings*. Philadelphia: Westminster, 1959.

Yoder, J. H. *The Christian Witness to the State*. Newton, Kans.: Faith and Life Press, 1964.

———. *The Politics of Jesus*. Grand Rapids: Eerdmans, 1972.

THE SCHLEITHEIM CONFESSION, 1527

Dear brethren and sisters, we who have been assembled in the Lord at Schleitheim on the Border, make known in points and articles to all who love God that as concerns us we are of one mind to abide in the Lord as God's obedient children, [His] sons and daughters, we who have been and shall be separated from the world in everything, [and] completely at peace. To God alone be praise and glory without the contradiction of any brethren. In this we have perceived the oneness of the Spirit of our Father and of our common Christ with us. For the Lord is the Lord of peace and not of quarreling, as Paul points out. That you may understand in what articles this has been formulated you should observe and note [the following].

A very great offense has been introduced by certain false brethren among us, so that some have turned aside from the faith, in the way they intend to practice and observe the freedom of the Spirit and of Christ. But such have missed the truth and to their condemnation are given over to the lasciviousness and self-indulgence of the flesh. They think faith and love may do and permit everything, and nothing will harm them nor condemn them, since they are believers.

Observe, you who are God's members in Christ Jesus, that faith in the heavenly Father through Jesus Christ does not take such form. It does not produce and result in such things as these false brethren and sisters do and teach. Guard yourselves and be warned of such people, for they do not serve our Father, but their father, the devil.

But you are not that way. For they that are Christ's have crucified the flesh with its passions and lusts. You understand me well and [know] the brethren whom we mean. Separate yourselves from them for they are perverted. Petition the Lord that they may have the knowledge which leads to repentance, and [pray] for us that we may have constancy to persevere in the way which we have espoused, for the honor of God and of Christ, His Son, Amen.

The articles which we discussed and on which we were of one mind are these: 1. Baptism; 2. The Ban [Excommunication]; 3. Breaking of Bread; 4. Separation from the Abomination; 5. Pastors in the Church; 6. The Sword; and 7. The Oath.

ON SEPARATION FROM THE WORLD

We are agreed [as follows] on separation: A separation shall be made from the evil and from the wickedness which the devil planted in the world; in this manner, simply that we shall not have fellowship with them [the wicked] and not run with them in the multitude of their abominations. This is the way it is: Since all who do not walk in the obedience of faith, and have not united themselves with God

---

[Source: *Creeds of the Churches*, ed. J. H. Leith (Oxford: Blackwell, 1973).]

so that they wish to do His will, are a great abomination before God, it is not possible for anything to grow or issue from them except abominable things. For truly all creatures are in but two classes, good and bad, believing and unbelieving, darkness and light, the world and those who [have come] out of the world, God's temple and idols, Christ and Belial; and none can have part with the other.

To us then the command of the Lord is clear when He calls upon us to be separate from the evil and thus He will be our God and we shall be His sons and daughters.

He further admonishes us to withdraw from Babylon and the earthly Egypt that we may not be partakers of the pain and suffering which the Lord will bring upon them.

From this we should learn that everything which is not united with our God and Christ cannot be other than an abomination which we should shun and flee from. By this is meant all popish and antipopish works and church services, meetings and church attendance, drinking houses, civic affairs, the commitments [made in] unbelief and other things of that kind, which are highly regarded by the world and yet are carried on in flat contradiction to the command of God, in accordance with all the unrighteousness which is in the world. From all these things we shall be separated and have no part with them for they are nothing but an abomination, and they are the cause of our being hated before our Christ Jesus, Who has set us free from the slavery of the flesh and fitted us for the service of God through the Spirit Whom He has given us.

Therefore there will also unquestionably fall from us the unchristian, devilish weapons of force—such as sword, armor and the like, and all their use [either] for friends or against one's enemies—by virtue of the word of Christ, Resist not [him that is] evil.

THE USE OF THE SWORD

We are agreed as follows concerning the sword: The sword is ordained of God outside the perfection of Christ. It punishes and puts to death the wicked, and guards and protects the good. In the Law the sword was ordained for the punishment of the wicked and for their death, and the same [sword] is [now] ordained to be used by the worldly magistrates.

In the perfection of Christ, however, only the ban is used for a warning and for the excommunication of the one who has sinned, without putting the flesh to death—simply the warning and the command to sin no more.

Now it will be asked by many who do not recognize [this as] the will of Christ for us, whether a Christian may or should employ the sword against the wicked for the defence and protection of the good, or for the sake of love.

Our reply is unanimously as follows: Christ teaches and commands us to learn of Him, for He is meek and lowly in heart and so shall we find rest to our souls. Also Christ says to the heathenish woman who was taken in adultery, not that one should stone her according to the law of His Father (and yet He says, As the Father has commanded me, thus I do), but in mercy and forgiveness and warning, to sin no more. Such [an attitude] we also ought to take completely according to the rule of the ban.

Secondly, it will be asked concerning the sword, whether a Christian shall pass sentence in worldly disputes and strife such as unbelievers have with one another. This is our united answer. Christ did not wish to decide or pass judgment between brother and brother in the case of the inheritance, but refused to do so. Therefore we should do likewise.

Thirdly, it will be asked concerning the sword, Shall one be a magistrate if one should be chosen as such? The answer is as follows: They wished to make Christ king, but He fled and did not view it as the arrangement of His Father. Thus shall we do as He did, and follow Him, and so shall we not walk in darkness. For He Himself says, He who wishes to come after me, let him deny himself and take up his cross and follow me. Also, He Himself forbids [employment of] the force of the sword saying, The worldly princes lord it over them, etc., but not so shall it be with you. Further, Paul says, Whom God did foreknow He also did predestinate to be conformed to the image of His Son, etc. Also Peter says, Christ has suffered (not ruled) and left us an example, that ye should follow His steps.

Finally it will be observed that it is not appropriate for a Christian to serve as a magistrate because of these points: The government magistracy is according to the flesh, but the Christians' is according to the Spirit; their houses and dwelling remain in this world, but the Christians' are in heaven; their citizenship is in this world, but the Christians' citizenship is in heaven; the weapons of their conflict and war are carnal and against the flesh only, but the Christians' weapons are spiritual, against the fortification of the devil. The worldlings are armed with steel and iron, but the Christians are armed with the armor of God, with truth, righteousness, peace, faith, salvation and the Word of God. In brief, as is the mind of Christ toward us, so shall the mind of the members of the body of Christ be through Him in all things, that there may be no schism in the body through which it would be destroyed. For every kingdom divided against itself will be destroyed. Now since Christ is as it is written of Him, His members must also be the same, that His body may remain complete and united to its own advancement and upbuilding.

OTHER ANABAPTIST WRITINGS ON CHURCH AND STATE

BALTHASAR HUBMAIER, "CONCERNING THE SWORD," 1527

Even a blind man can see that a Christian may with a good conscience be a judge and a council member to judge and decide in temporal matters. Even though the contentious and the litigious sin, yet would they sin far more if they were to bring their matters before unbelieving judges. Now if a Christian may and ought to be a judge in his pronouncements in the power of the divine Word, so he may also be a protector with the hand of justice and a punisher of the unrighteous. For of what good were law, court, and judge if one were not obliged to execute and carry out the penalty on the wicked? What good is a shoe if one dare not wear it? Observe, dear brothers, that councils, courts and laws are not unjust. The judge too may and ought to be a Christian even though the contentious parties sin and are not prepared to be wronged. Thus also a Christian may—according to the order of God—bear the sword in God's stead against the evildoer and punish him. For it has been so ordered by God because of wickedness for the protection of the pious (Rom. 13).

HANS DENCK, "CONCERNING TRUE LOVE," 1527

It is not that power in itself is wrong seen from the perspective of the evil world, for [the government] serves God in his wrath, but rather that love teaches her children a better way, namely to serve the graciousness of God. For it is the nature of love not to will or desire the hurt of anyone, but as much as is possible to serve for the betterment of everyone. A housefather should treat his wife and child, menservants and maids as he would that God should treat him. That is not incompatible with love. And insofar as it were possible for a government to act in this way it could well be Christian in its office. Since however the world will not tolerate it, a friend of God should not be in the government but out of it, that is if he desires to keep Christ as a Lord and master. Whoever loves the Lord loves him regardless of his station. But he should not forget what characterizes a true lover [of God], namely that for the Lord's sake he renounce all power and to be subject to no one but the Lord.

PILGRAM MARPECK, "CONFESSION," 1532

I admit worldly, carnal, and earthly rulers as servants of God in earthly matters, but not in the kingdom of Christ. According to the words of Paul, to them

---

[Source: *Anabaptism in Outline: Selected Primary Sources*, ed. Walter Klaassen (Kitchener, Ont.: Herald Press, 1981).]

rightfully belongs all carnal honour, fear, obedience, tax, toll, and tribute. However, when such persons who hold authority become Christians (which I heartily wish and pray for) they may not use the aforementioned carnal force, sovereignty or ruling in the kingdom of Christ. It cannot be upheld by any Scripture. To allow the external authority to rule in the kingdom of Christ brings blasphemy of the Holy Spirit, who alone is Lord and Ruler without any human assistance. And if false teachers desire to lead astray, the true sheep do not listen to the voice of strangers; they are soon known by them. Where the governmental authority is used, as it was in the Old Testament, to root out the false prophets, Christ's Word and Spirit are weakened, and are turned into a servile spirit designed to uphold insufficient and weak laws. For the Word of God is the sharp, two-edged sword, separating and chastising false and true, good and evil.

MENNO SIMONS, "FOUNDATION," 1539

Therefore, dear sirs, take heed; this is the task to which you are called: namely, to chastise and punish, in the true fear of God with fairness and Christian discretion, manifest criminals, such as thieves, murderers, Sodomites, adulterers, seducers, sorcerers, the violent, highwaymen, robbers, etc. Your task is to do justice between a man and his neighbor, to deliver the oppressed out of the hand of the oppressor; also to restrain by reasonable means, that is, without tyranny and bloodshed, manifest deceivers who so miserably lead poor helpless souls by hundreds of thousands into destruction. Whether the deceivers are priests, monks, preachers, baptized or unbaptized, it is your task to restrain them so that they may no longer detract from the power of the almighty majesty of God, our only and eternal Saviour, Christ Jesus, the Holy Ghost, and the Word of grace; nor introduce such ridiculous abuses and idolatry under the semblance of truth as has been done until now. In this way, in all love, without force, violence, and blood, you may enlarge, help, and protect the kingdom of God with gracious consent and permission, with wise counsel and a pious, unblamable life. . . .

O highly renowned, noble lords, believe Christ's Word, fear God's wrath, love righteousness, do justice to widows and orphans, judge rightly between a man and his neighbor, fear no man's highness, despise no man's littleness, hate all avarice, punish with reason, allow the Word of God to be taught freely, hinder no one from walking in the truth, bow to the scepter of him who called you to this high service. Then shall your throne stand firm forever. . . .

Sirs, dear sirs, humble yourselves. Righteous is he who will hear your case, and mighty is he who will sentence. His name is the Ruler of rulers; He is the Almighty, the holy and terrible, the highly adorable and wonderworking God who has created heaven and earth, and grips in the hands of his strength all majesty, power, and dominion. Him learn to know; him learn to fear. Rouse yourselves; the time is not far off when you will hear. Give an account of your stewardship; for thou mayest no longer be steward. Lk. 16:2. . . .

O kings and rulers of the land, where indeed is your faith and love with their pious nature? Where is the fear of your God, your burning lamp, your humble heart dead unto sin? Where is your blameless, godly life which is of

God? Is it not Simon-pure world and carnality which you seek and protect? We find in your houses and courts nothing but sparkling pomp and showy dress, boldness and presumptuousness of heart, insatiable avarice, hatred and envy, backbiting, betraying, harloting, seduction, gambling, gaming, carousing, dancing, swearing, stabbing, and violence. This is your chivalrous custom and courtly conduct all the days of your lives. You never once reflect through what misery, tribulation, humility, love, and righteousness the Lord of lords and King of kings walked his way before you, what he taught the children of men, and what pattern or example he left them. The pitiful moaning and misery of the wretched men does not reach your ears. The sweat of the poor we find in your house, and the innocent blood on your hands. Their gifts and presents are received to pervert judgment and you take counsel against the Lord and his anointed. The prophets of Jezebel and the priests of Baal, men who talk to your taste and fawn all over you, these are in big demand and swarm all over you. These are in big demand with you, men who sit on easy cushions and have a fine time.

ROBERT BROWNE

A TREATISE OF REFORMATION WITHOUT TARRYING FOR ANY

It is often asked why we are reviled and persecuted, and leave our country. Our enemies say: ". . . They are evilly disposed to their queen and country, and they forsake and condemn the Church of God. They are condemned by all, and discredit and bring into contempt the [authentic] preachers of the Gospel." In reply to them, we say that they, and not we, bring trouble to Israel and evil to the prince. They forsake and condemn the Church, not we. Our faithfulness to queen and country, and our attitude to the civil authorities, is as follows. . . .

We affirm and have often taught that neither the Pope nor any other minor "Pope" has any authority over either her or the Church of God, and that the Pope is the Antichrist, who does not have any jurisdiction over the queen or over the Church. . . . In civil jurisdiction, the queen is second in power only to God, within her dominion. She has authority over all. She may execute all who deserve it, in terms of the law of the Church or of the State. None may resist her, or her officials, when they enforce the law; not by force, nor by slander. . . .

We hold accursed those teachers and preachers who refuse to carry out their duties until compelled by the civil authorities. . . . Can the Lord's spiritual rule not be carried out apart from the civil authorities? These preachers and teachers have broken away from the spiritual power of the Church, and now they want the civil rulers to exercise the discipline which they have shunned. They wish the rulers to be greater than God but worse than animals. They hold that the pastor should be subject to the civil administration, and that Church government should cease if the civil authorities refuse to exercise ecclesiastical power.

Unless the magistrates are content with their own ruin under the wrath of God, they should subject themselves to the rule of Christ. They must be under pastoral care, and must obey the sceptre of Christ if they are Christians. But how should the pastor, who has oversight of the magistrate, if he is a member of his flock, exercise this oversight when the magistrate can unjustly and wrongfully discharge him. . . .

On the one hand, the preachers exalt the throne of the magistrates, and in so doing they restrict the Kingdom of Christ. . . . Most of them refuse to confront the magistrates but choose rather to flatter them, so that they may, in turn, be honoured by the magistrates. Yet, on the other hand, turning away from their own responsibility, they say that it is the fault of the magistrates that reform does not take place. So they in fact speak against them, laying all the burden on them, but the pastors themselves do not move a single finger to promote reform. In

---

[Source: *The Writings of Robert Harrison and Robert Browne*, ed. A. Peel and L. H. Carlson; vol. 2 of *Elizabethan Nonconformist Texts* (London: Allen and Unwin, 1953). Spelling and punctuation have been modernized by the editor.]

some cases they are quite outspoken against the magistrates, making them their enemies, saying that the magistrates do not exercise adequate control over the Church. Yet in expecting them to exercise this control, they make enemies also of the Lord's Kingdom and righteousness. . . .

If the magistrates are enemies of the Lord's Kingdom, why should it be assumed that they are better able to reform the Church? The preachers have surrendered their spiritual power to the magistrates and to the ecclesiastical courts, and cannot therefore call themselves the Church of God, or its legitimate ministers. Christ is at the right hand of God in heaven, where he rules the angels and powers. How then can his Kingdom await the pleasure of the civil rulers, unless they think the rulers are better able to uphold the Kingdom of Christ than Christ himself?

Christ said: My Kingdom is not of this world. Yet bishops and civil rulers are placed on his spiritual throne, to make it of this world, and to place these men rulers over Christ. . . . The civil rulers are indeed first in the state, but they have no ecclesiastical authority, and are ordinary Christians, if Christians at all. . . . Woe unto you, you priests and doctors, hypocrites, you are a snare to the people, and complete their iniquity, while you pretend that it is the magistrates who have [spiritual] authority. Will any man give up his calling or limit the execution thereof? When the magistrates forbid them, will they cease their teaching or guiding of their households, and fail to execute their duties? Should the labourers in God's spiritual order surrender and cease to function? It is God's order and not theirs. The Church is his and not theirs. We have authority from God, we need not fear the opposition of kings and nations, and need not abandon our calling on their account. How long will the priests take this inheritance from its rightful owner [the Church] and give it to the servant [the civil authorities]? The spiritual power of Christ and of his Church, and the keys of binding and loosing, they have taken from Christ and given it to the magistrate. The magistrates have the civil sword, and out of fear that they will strike them with it, the priests give them the ecclesiastical sword as well. "If only we were prophets and apostles," they say, "then we would preach even if the magistrates forbade us, but we are only pastors and preachers and therefore fear the threats of the magistrates and keep silent." These preachers need to explain in what way the magistrates have less power over the apostles than they have over other pastors. Were the apostles more exempted from being obedient to the magistrates than other pastors? The Scriptures say, "Let *every* soul be subject to the higher powers." Therefore as they could not displace nor discharge apostles from their office and calling, so they cannot displace lawful pastors and preachers. [The question facing every preacher is] whether it be right in the sight of God to obey men rather than God. . . . God has distributed to every man certain gifts and called everyone to a special vocation. If the magistrate orders a soldier to become a minister, or a preacher to resign or change his job, they are not to obey him . . . but if the ruler calls one to a higher position, for which he is competent, he should obey, for it is God's call. In all things, we must first establish what is the Lord's will and command, and only then the will of man. Paul tells us we are bought with a price, and we are not therefore the servants of the unlawful commands of men.

If a civil ruler, or another, wants to take our liberty from us, we must not yield . . . as this liberty is the free use of our gifts, in accordance with our understanding of the Word of God, and to his glory. . . . The calling [to preach] is not given by the civil authority, but by God, and is ratified by the Church. Therefore, as the ruler did not issue the calling, so he cannot rescind it. . . . In doing so, he would not be a Christian, but an apostate. How can office in the Church depend on one who is not of the Church? . . . The welfare of the Church is a higher concern than that of whole kingdoms and countries. . . . Too many priests fear the civil rulers, flatter them and curry their favour, . . . but the Lord's faithful servants . . . are commanded to arise and speak to them all that the Lord commands.

Do you not know, you wicked preachers, that those who are called and have sufficient authority [from God] are not to seek further authority [from the civil powers]? Does not every legitimate pastor or preacher have all the authority he needs? . . . Be ashamed, foolish shepherds, that you need to be forced by the ruler, one of your sheep, before you do your duty. . . . The Lord's Kingdom is not built by force . . . as are the kingdoms of this world.

Now let the wise understand these things, and the Lord be merciful, and deliver us from these unreasonable and evil men. For there is no end to the pride and cruelty of those who assume the rulers' seat, and oppress the people with a continual plague, and deal violently with those who do not obey them. But the Lord shall bring them down to the dust and to the pit, as abominable carcasses. . . . Those who presume the throne of Christ Jesus, and usurp authority in his Church, while being opposed to this kingdom and his rule, . . . accuse us of denying the authority of the civil rulers, because we do not exalt them, or the rulers, above Christ Jesus and his glorious Kingdom. . . . If any man, ruler or not, persecutes Christ's witnesses, the fire of their message will devour them.

The Church has more authority in Church government than the civil rulers. . . . Though the rulers have civil authority over all, they are nevertheless subject to the censure of the Church if they are Christians, and when they have sinned, they are to humble themselves in repentance, publicly and sincerely. . . . All powers shall serve and obey Christ, and that nation which refuses to serve his Church will perish.

Spiritual power and ecclesiastical reform must proceed without reference to the civil authorities. In civic matters, the rulers must intervene to set matters right, and none may usurp their power. We know that when the rulers have been most antagonistic to the Church, it has flourished most. . . . Let us leave to the rulers their rightful powers, to govern the state with justice. But let the Church rule in spiritual matters, and not in a worldly manner.

They pollute my name, says the Lord. Yet they ask, "How have we polluted your name?" In that you allow wickedness among you, says the Lord, and say that it is tolerable and cannot be remedied. . . . By toleration, they make unlawful things lawful, and justify all sin. . . . Go away, you tolerant preachers, you have no place among the righteous, or in the body of the Church.

THE SCOTS CONFESSION, 1560

THE WORKS WHICH ARE COUNTED GOOD BEFORE GOD

We confess and acknowledge that God has given to man his holy law, in which not only all such works as displease and offend his godly majesty are forbidden, but also those which please him and which he has promised to reward are commanded. These works are of two kinds. The one is done to the honor of God, the other is to the profit of our neighbor, and both have the revealed will of God as their assurance. To have one God, to worship and honor him, to call upon him in all our troubles, to reverence his holy Name, to hear his Word and to believe it, and to share in his holy sacraments, belong to the first kind. To honor father, mother, princes, rulers, and superior powers; to love them, to support them, to obey their orders if they are not contrary to the commands of God, to save the lives of the innocent, to repress tyranny, to defend the oppressed, to keep our bodies clean and holy, to live in soberness and temperance, to deal justly with all men in word and deed, and, finally, to repress any desire to harm our neighbor, are the good works of the second kind, and these are most pleasing and acceptable to God as he has commanded them himself. Acts to the contrary are sins, which always displease him and provoke him to anger, such as, not to call upon him alone when we have need, not to hear his Word with reverence, but to condemn and despise it, to have or worship idols, to maintain and defend idolatry, lightly to esteem the reverend name of God, to profane, abuse, or condemn the sacraments of Christ Jesus, to disobey or resist any whom God has placed in authority, so long as they do not exceed the bounds of their office, to murder, or to consent thereto, to bear hatred, or let innocent blood be shed if we can prevent it. In conclusion, we confess and affirm that the breach of any other commandment of the first or second kind is sin, by which God's anger and displeasure are kindled against the proud, unthankful world. So that we affirm good works to be those alone which are done in faith and at the command of God who, in his law, has set for the things that please him. We affirm that evil works are not only those expressly done against God's command, but also, in religious matters and the worship of God, those things which have no other warrant than the invention and opinion of man. From the beginning God has rejected such, as we learn from the words of the prophet Isaiah and of our master, Christ Jesus, "In vain do they worship Me, teaching the doctrines and commandments of men."

[Source: *The Proposed Book of Confession* (Presbyterian Church in the United States, 1976).]

JOHN KNOX

1. A LETTER TO THE PROFESSORS, THE LORDS, AND OTHERS PROFESSING THE TRUTH IN SCOTLAND

God's favour and fatherly care are given to all his children in things pertaining to life everlasting, while everyone receives such grace as is necessary for the completion and confirmation of the good work which God has initiated. Yet, in distributing temporal blessings, God takes special care of those whom he has appointed to be rulers, comforters and maintainers of others.

Above all else it is diligently to be observed, that before all such special graces given to rulers, we must be able to discern the fear of God implanted in their hearts. The fear of the Lord is the beginning and continuance of wisdom, such wisdom which is worthy of the name of wisdom, a special gift of God given to those through whom he resolves to accomplish such work which is to his glory. This does not, however, mean that it is only those who are shown particular privileges or revelations of secret things that have fear in their hearts. The fear of God resides also in the hearts of all those inspired by God, and who with reverence receive the counsel and admonitions given by God's messengers who are determined to obey his holy will, even though at times their message seems to surpass human power and understanding.

The ways of God cannot be fully understood by the imagination of man, yet this must be emphasized: wheresoever the true fear of God is planted in the heart, there shall be added wisdom and other graces, necessary and profitable not only to the receiver but also to others. But where this road of virtue and wisdom, grounded in the true fear of God is absent from the heart, there can be no obedience which is acceptable to God, neither can there be enduring love for his messengers. Where this fear is absent there can be no wisdom to search and seek for things that are profitable, nor can there be grace to follow in the ways of God, in spite of the striking manner of this revelation. The wholesome counsel and admonition of God is given for the removal of iniquity, the reformation of temporal privileges, and conservation of realms and commonwealths. Princes and rulers of these institutions have, however, not understood this counsel and admonition, treating God's messengers disdainfully and with contempt.

In order that society may be governed with Godly purpose, God appoints and sends to battle his best and most approved soldiers. He ensures that they trust not in themselves or in the arm of any man. They are rather raised up in the boldness of his strength, and by the promise of his mercy, and in this manner does he salve their troubled conscience. In this dejection, humiliation, and denial

---

[Source: *The Works of John Knox*, ed. David Laing (Edinburgh: James Thin, 1846– 1864). The text has been modified to conform to modern usage.]

of themselves, he works in both their conscience and lack of confidence in worldly power. He humbles the conscience of all people opening the eyes of their minds that they may know of the miseries of their own nature, and the just condemnation which their sins deserve. As individuals contemplate this reality, God brings them to the portals of hell, to an unfeigned hatred of themselves and of sin. This is the initial step toward the true fear of God, but in this estate he does not leave them. He rather manifests to them his undeserved love and favour in Christ Jesus, his only son; he relieves their conscience and raises them up so that in all these assaults they may trust in his free mercy.

The simple estate of Gideon, and the contemptuous youth and infancy of David, are not concealed by the Holy Ghost. These are, in fact, used to instruct us that in appointing his messengers, God does not concern himself with these things which the world considers so important. In so doing God counteracts the arrogance and pride of all flesh to ensure that no man may glory in those works which God accomplishes through someone he has chosen from the dunghill (as David suggests), in order to place him with the princes of his people, while having no merit of his own, or reason to trust in his own ancestors.

But now, not wanting to trouble you further at this time, I will only advise you of such rumours as are spoken in some places. There are some in the realm who are rising in contradiction and rebellion against [civil] authority. My conscience does not allow me to withhold my counsel from you in this regard. My judgment and commandment, which I offer you in God's fear, and by the assurance of his truth, is that none of you that seek to promote the glory of Christ may disobey or displease the established authority in things lawful. Yet, neither should you assist or promote those causes which further your own particular end or those of some worldly cause which should trouble the realm. But in the bowels of Christ Jesus I exhort you, with all simplicity and lawful obedience, to join with boldness in God, and with open confession of your faith, to seek the co-operation of the authorities, that by these means (if this be possible) the cause in which you labour may be promoted, or at least not acted against. If after having made your humble request to the authorities, and your goals still cannot be attained, then, with open and solemn protestation of such obedience which must be given to the authorities in all things not plainly repugnant to God, you lawfully may attempt the extreme. This is to provide, whether the authorities will consent or not, that the Christian gospel may be truly preached, and his holy sacraments rightly ministered to you, and to your brethren, the subjects of the realm. And further, you may lawfully, and are bound to, defend your brethren from persecution and tyranny, even if it be against all the power the princes and rulers can muster, provided, as I have said, that you do not withhold lawful obedience.

Nor should you assist or promote those that seek authority and the preeminence of worldly glory for their own ends, with a view to the suppression and destruction of others. I refer to him* who in the beginning of his authority and

*This reference is to James, Duke of Châtelherault, Governor of Scotland. In his *History of the Reformation in Scotland*, Knox describes him as one who, when first elected governor, favored Protestant doctrine and social reform, but who was later influenced in the opposite direction.

government began to profess Christ's truth, but then suddenly became a cruel persecutor of Christ's members, a manifest and open oppressor of all true subjects, and a supporter of all mischievous men. In so doing he, his faction and assistants, including his nearest kinsmen and chiefs, continue in horrible vice to this day. They maliciously rule according to their own power, which God in his just judgment shall shortly suppress. For not only the blood of those constant martyrs of Christ Jesus, Mr. George Wischert, simple Adam Wallace, and others who suffer for Christ's cause, but also the blood of those who, for alleged civil crimes, has most unjustly been shed, shall cry in the ears of the Lord of hosts till a just and open vengeance is poured forth on all those who contributed to this process, but chiefly on him who was in authority at the time, unless sincere and speedy repentance prevent God's judgment. I shall be judged sharp, but be admonished to flee all association with that generation. I speak and write in the name of him before whose eyes the blood of his saints is so precious, that no worldly power which delights in the shedding of blood has ever been able to endure against it. Therefore, until such time as you see some signs of repentance in them, I say yet again, avoid close familiarity with them.

That I now persuade you to show lawful obedience to authority, is not in contradiction to what I wrote to you on an earlier occasion. There is a great difference between lawful obedience, and a fearful flattering of princes.

2. A LETTER TO THE COMMONALITY OF SCOTLAND

God has ordained that in the order and administration of civil policy, there should be distinctions and differences between kings and subjects, between rulers and common people. But with regard to the hope of life to come, he has made all equal. For as in Christ Jesus, the Jew has no greater prerogative than the Gentile, or man than woman, or learned than unlearned, or master than servant, because all are one in him, so is there only one way and means to partake of his benefits and spiritual graces, which is a lively faith manifesting itself in charity. This applies in no lesser sense to you. Beloved brethren, ensure that your faith and religion is grounded and established on the true and trusted Word of God, rather than on princes or rulers.

In order to ensure us of his promise that he is with us, Christ has established signs of his presence among us, which is his spiritual tabernacle, namely the true

---

[Source: *The Works of John Knox*, ed. David Laing (Edinburgh, 1846–1864). Modernized by the editor.]

preaching of his Word, and the right administration of his sacraments. We are all bound to the maintenance thereof, the subject no less than the prince, and the poor no less than the rich. As the price given for man's redemption is one, so God requires of all who benefit from this redemption a similar duty, which is a plain confession that it is by Christ Jesus alone that we have received all that was lost in Adam. Of the prince, God requires that he deny himself and that he follow Christ Jesus, and of the subject he requires the same. Of kings and judges it is required that they kiss the Son, that is, give honour, subjection, and obedience to him, and from such reverence the subject is not exempted. This means that there is an equality between kings and subjects, and between the most rich and noble on the one hand, and the poorest and lowest of people on the other. This equality means that everyone is obliged to believe in the heart, and confess with the mouth, that the Lord Jesus is the only Saviour of the world.

The poorest and the most simple person on earth, who in the face of cruel persecution, firmly believes in Christ, and boldly confesses him before his wicked generation, is no less acceptable before God, nor is he judged in God's sight to have done any less in promoting the cause of Christ than the king, who, by sword and power, which he received from God, has rooted out idolatry and in so doing advanced Christ's glory. But to return to our purpose. It is no less required of the subject than it is of the prince and king to believe in Christ, and to profess his true religion. It shall therefore not excuse you, in the sight of God, to allege that you are not chief rulers, and that the care and reformation of religion are therefore not your responsibility.

You ought to prefer the glory of God, the promoting of the gospel of Christ, and the salvation of your souls, to anything else on earth. Although you are merely subjects, you may lawfully require of your superiors, be it of your king, lords, rulers, or any other person in authority, that they provide true preachers, expelling those who, under the pretense of being pastors, devour and destroy the flock instead of nourishing them in the manner which Christ Jesus has commanded. If in this regard your superiors be negligent, or maintain tyrants in their tyranny, you may justly provide true teachers for yourselves, be it in your cities, towns, or villages. You may maintain and defend them against all who persecute them, with a view to defrauding you of the necessary food for your souls, which is the gospel of Christ that is truly preached.

If (may God forbid), the love of friends, the fear of princes, and the wisdom of the world draws you away from God and from his Son, Christ Jesus, you shall drink the cup of his vengeance. This applies to all who disregard or despise the loving call of your heavenly Father. It will not excuse you, dear brethren, in the sight of God, neither will it benefit you in the day of his visitation, to say, we were but simple subjects, we could not redress the faults and crimes of our rulers, bishops, and clergy. It will profit you nothing to say we desired reformation and called for it but the bishops were brothers of the lords, their sons were abbots, and the friends of great men had the possession of the church compelling us to be obedient to all they demanded. These vain excuses will not profit you in the sight of God, who requires no less of subjects than he does of rulers. Both are to refrain from evil and do good. Both are to abstain from idolatry, superstition, blasphemy, murder, and other such horrible crimes which his law forbids, even though they are openly committed and maliciously defended in this miserable realm. And if you think that you are innocent, because you are not the chief perpetrators of such iniquity, you are utterly deceived. God does not only punish the chief offenders, he also damns those who together with them consent to iniquity, that is those who, knowing that impiety is committed, do not protest against it. To speak more plainly: as your princes and rulers are guilty together with your bishops for their idolatry, and of all the innocent blood that is shed in testimony to Christ's truth, because they maintain them in their tyranny, you too (that is, as many of you as do not plainly confess to the contrary) are also both criminal and guilty, with your princes and rulers, of the same crimes, because you assist and maintain your princes in their blind rage, offering no protest against their tyranny.

The iniquity of your bishops is clearly manifest, their filthy lives contaminate the air, and the innocent blood which they shed cries for vengeance in the ears of our God. The idolatry and abomination which they continue openly to commit without punishment corrupts and defiles the entire land. Yet none among you has earnestly demanded any redress for these enormities. Will God, with regard to this matter, judge you as innocent? Be not deceived, dear brethren. God has in the past punished not only proud tyrants, filthy persons, and cruel murderers. He has also punished those together with them who have been responsible for the yoke of iniquity, whether by flattering their offences, obeying their unjust commandments, or overlooking their manifest iniquity. God has, in the past, punished all such offenders, together with the chief offenders. Be assured, brethren, that as God is immutable of nature, so will he not pardon in you what he has so severely punished in others. And now there is even less reason why he should pardon you, because he has warned you of the dangers to come, and offered you his mercy, before pouring forth his wrath and displeasure on the disobedient.

PART TWO

THE CONTEMPORARY PERIOD

CHAPTER 5

THE CHURCH AND THE THIRD REICH

The story of the church during the time of the Third Reich is told in many places and need not be repeated in full here.[1] It is enough to consider the theological commitment of two people whose names have become synonymous with the Confessing church at the time and whose doctrine of church-state relations is in every respect an affirmation of the Barmen Declaration. A new translation of this declaration, which provided the doctrinal center for the Confessing church in Germany, is reprinted below.

KARL BARTH

It is often argued that the signing of a manifesto by ninety-three German intellectuals, including most of Barth's former theological teachers, in support of the war policy of Kaiser Wilhelm II on August 1, 1914, the first day of World War I, caused Barth's disenchantment with liberal theology. His disenchantment might better be understood as the culmination of a series of events which resulted in his double disillusionment with both the socialist praxis of the time and liberal theology. Both signified for him humanity's trust in its own resources; when linked as this was to the self-aggrandizement of *Kulturprotestantismus*, such hubris could lead only to disaster.

With this the stage was set for Barth's lifelong quest for a theology which affirmed an "infinite qualitative distinction" between God and humanity and between time and eternity. Barth's theology addressed the political realm with a sustained and relentless commitment without ever allowing a particular political program to be theologically absolutized. Barth reaffirmed radical encounter between theology and politics many years later when he observed, "No sentence is more dangerous or revolutionary than that God is One and there is no other like him. . . . It was on the truth of the sentence that God is One that the 'Third Reich' of Adolf Hitler made shipwreck."[2]

Barth had a passion to love God and to fear God above all else, giving an unqualified precedence to the sovereign Word of God which never tired of saying "no" to all human effort. Perhaps it was only what has been called Barth's one-sided emphasis on the separation of the divine from the human that was able to save German Protestantism from total capitulation to German nationalism. It was also this that moved Paul Tillich to warn that "an instrument that is a mighty weapon in warfare may be an inconvenient tool for use in the building trade."[3] Yet for Barth there was also God's "yes" to the human race in Christ. He gives powerful expression to this in the text cited below from "The Christian Community and the Civil Community." Because Christ is the Lord of all creation, his kingdom is an ideal for both church and state. On this view, the state is more than merely a force against evil, as the Lutheran tradition so strongly emphasized. It is a vehicle for good. Barth sees the kingdom of God as an analogy and parable, not only for the church but also for the state. In a similar manner, in his *Epistle to the Romans*, the affirmation of the "great positive possibility" which demanded at once both Herculean human commitment and complete self-surrender to Christ in an all-embracing love, located the *otherness* of God in the midst of the human or civil community.[4] It was this that gave to Barth a lifelong commitment to God's revolution within the civil community. In so doing he showed a firm commitment to a form of democratic socialism as "the best present—and hence provisional—political parable of the Kingdom of God,"[5] while always adopting a critical attitude to this movement which he located under the judgment and renewing power of God's impending kingdom. These political and social ideals, grounded as they were in his theology, placed him firmly "against the lofty and on behalf of the lowly; against those who already enjoy right and privilege and on behalf of those who are denied it and deprived of it."[6] It is this that inspired Barth to declare himself against the reactionary, "despite the wrongness of the revolutionary."[7]

In order to understand the church and state doctrine of Barth as it emerged in relation to the Third Reich, three essays written by Barth between 1935 and 1946 constitute a formative entity: "Gospel and Law," "Church and State," originally published as *Rechtfertigung und Recht* ("Justification and Justice"), and "The Christian Community and the Civil Community."[8]

In the first essay Barth reversed the relationship between law and gospel, marking a significant development beyond the Reformation debate on this matter, and more particularly beyond the Lutheran emphasis on the German institutional church. Affirming an uncompromising Christocentric approach to theology, Barth insisted that "we must first of all know the gospel in order to know about the law, and not vice versa." In fact "the law is nothing else but the form of the gospel, whose content is grace," both of which are proclaimed and manifest in the person of Jesus Christ. What this meant for church-state relations was that there could be no separation between heavenly and earthly kingdoms. The gospel was directly related to that sphere of existence commonly regarded as being under the law. Orthodoxy and ortho-belief were inherently related to ortho-praxis, and ethics became for Barth the predicate of Christology.

It was this emphasis which accounted for Barth's rigid rejection of natural theology, which gave culture, human achievement, and nationalism such prominence in the synthesis of ideology and theology in the German-Christian movement of the Third Reich. There could, for Barth, never be an identification of law and gospel, or political ideology and gospel. The former was always under the dominance of the latter. Yet he allowed for an analogous or parabolic relationship between heaven and earth; the fullness of God's glory could be anticipated on earth. It is this "positive possibility," present in Barth's thought as early as the writing of his commentary on *The Epistle to the Romans*, which rejects the sacralization of human effort, declaring that "there is no human action which is not in itself fashioned according to the form of this world; and yet there are actions which seem almost to bear in themselves the mark of the divine protest against the great error."[9]

Barth further developed this inherent link between gospel and law in his essay entitled "Church and State," in which he demonstrated the inherent relationship between justification and justice. In this essay, the state, as one of the angelic powers mentioned in the New Testament, was understood to be under the constant threat of demonization, the "temptation of making itself an absolute." When the state takes on theonomous pretensions, it does so not only through its presumption of autonomy but also through its renunciation of its true dignity and authority given and affirmed in submission to God. Thus the greatest service which the church could render the state was to ensure that it never perverted its authority. To quote Barth: "Jesus would, in actual fact, have been an enemy of the state if He had *not* dared to call King Herod a 'fox' (Luke 13:32). If the State has perverted its God-given authority, it cannot be honoured better than by this criticism which is due it in all circumstances." God's radical "no" to human effort is therefore ultimately the basis of his "yes" to cultural and political achievement: "Reconciliation in Christ is the restoration of the lost promise. It renews the status of the creation with its great 'Yes' to man, with its reasonableness of reason. It gives man again insight into the meaning of his activity."[10] Politics and culture were not undervalued in Barth's theological critique; rather, they became the basis of political and cultural liberation in relation to God's ultimate *telos*.

In the third essay, "Christian Community and the Civil Community," Barth emphasized the unity between state and church while stressing the need to recognize that they are two different communities. His major concern with regard to church-state relations in this essay, as elsewhere, was that "the church must remain the church." Using the image of two concentric circles to represent the relationship between the two communities—with the church as the inner circle—his concern was that the church proclaim the lordship of Christ as a basis for both a hope for and a critique of the civil community. Barth neither divinized politics nor politicized theology. For him politics and theology were rather held in constant tension. Nor was there a simple relationship between theological ideals and political reality. The church was to hold before the state an analogy or ideal of what could and ought to be. "By concentrating on the proclamation of Christ as Lord, the Christian community keeps political processes in operation and open to the Kingdom of God. . . . It brings politics humanly into suspension of permanent improvability and historical imperfectibility."[11] To quote from the excerpt printed below: "It is reliance on a spiritual norm that makes the Christian community free to support the cause of the civil community honestly and calmly." Having allegiance to Christ alone, the church is freed from the political intrigue which so often characterizes the function of other groups within the civil community. Yet at the same time it is obliged to take sides in the political process.

To fail to emphasize the *contextual* nature of Barth's theology is to fail to understand the pathos of it. His context demanded an uncompromising "no" to the Promethean efforts of the Third Reich which had lost its true dignity by presumptuously feigning autonomous authority. Different situations, such as those which prevail in many oppressive settings today where human dignity and effort has been destroyed by sustained forms of political oppression, may demand a different kind of theology. What Barth's theology can offer this kind of situation is a way of escaping what Míguez Bonino has warned can so easily result in "wittingly or unwittingly deifying history or humanity."[12] Barth's understanding of church-state relations is one that gives to the church enormous responsibilities with regard to the state. The "true church" has a responsibility to ensure that there is a "true state." Moltmann's telling observation is that this "true church" simply does not exist in reality and that the affirmation of the Lordship of Christ over all the earth, witnessed to in New Testament thought, is "an enthusiastic congregational piety" which tends to be forgetful of the crucified Christ. Yet Barth is aware that the church, no less than the state, fails to realize its full potential. The kingdom is no more fully realized in the church than in the state. This much is stated in the following text. His vision of the "true church" is a powerful eschatological symbol that challenges the church to be the church and the state, which is obedient to God, to be the state. It is this, argues Moltmann correctly, that makes Barth's ethic of church-state relations primarily an ethic for Christians, rather than a metaphysics of the state.[13] Barth would presumably agree!

DIETRICH BONHOEFFER

Dietrich Bonhoeffer's name is almost synonymous with the church struggle in the Third Reich. Like Barth's, his theology was boldly Christocentric. Larry Rasmussen has described his anti-Nazi conspiratorial activity as "his Christology enacted with utter seriousness."[14] On April 9, 1945, Dietrich Bonhoeffer was executed on a charge of treason for his part in the plot to assassinate Adolf Hitler. He never tried to justify his involvement in the plot theologically or morally. He had a radical sense of sin and a profound sense of social responsibility. It never occurred to him that he could claim nonresponsibility for the deeds of Hitler, or that he could avoid guilt by not sharing in the plot. Yet clearly he was a reluctant martyr, with his doctrine of church-state relations being grounded in the legacy of nineteenth-century German adaptations of Lutheranism, organic interpretations of the state, and the German quest for communal holism and an organic understanding of humanity.[15] A debate has, in fact, emerged concerning whether his martyrdom flowed from his theology at all. Alistair Kee has observed, "he acted as a responsible and brave man but his action was not the outcome of his theology which he was still in the process of evolving."[16] Yet certainly, Bonhoeffer's developed theology forged a link between theology and ethics that compels us to look back on his involvement in the plot to assassinate Hitler with a different understanding of martyrdom. In this context de Gruchy argues that "Bonhoeffer's death was that of a martyr, because he died on behalf of the weak, despised, and suffering ones, and in so doing affirmed God's love for all in Christ."[17]

Clearly Bonhoeffer's early theology of the state was a conservative one. In this regard, Ruth Zerner shows the extent of Bonhoeffer's dependency on Brunner's relatively conservative understanding of the dignified role afforded the state in the theology of the Reformers, especially that of Luther. To quote Brunner: "The state is a divine order, established as a power to exert force because of sin; the state's purpose is the creation of order and the establishment of external justice. Therefore the Christian owes obedience to the state, even the bad state and the unjust law, except in the event that the state attempts to force the Christian to disobey God."[18] In the *Cost of Discipleship*, written in the midst of the German church struggle, Bonhoeffer's own teaching on the state is equally conservative: "To renounce rebellion and revolution is the most appropriate way of expressing our conviction that the Christian hope is not set on this world, but on Christ and his kingdom." "Authority is the minister of God." "Let the slave therefore remain a slave. Let the Christian remain in subjection to the powers which exercise dominion over him."[19] And later, even when pursuing his resistance activities, he affirmed a similar position: "In the exercise of the mission of government the demand for obedience is unconditional and qualitatively total; it extends both to conscience and to bodily life." The only exception is the familiar one of the Christian tradition: "His duty of obedience is binding on him until government directly compels him to offend against the divine commandment, that is to say, until government openly denies its divine commission and thereby forfeits its claim."[20] It is this "exception," allowed for in the Christian tradition, which Zerner fails to appreciate in referring to what she calls the "dramatic break" in Bonhoeffer's later theology with certain Christian traditions.[21] It would be more accurate to recognize Bonhoeffer as affirming precisely this aspect of the tradition which had been neglected by institutional Lutheranism at the time. De Gruchy's more perceptive observation is that although Bonhoeffer would move in a more radical theological direction in later life, his involvement in the conspiracy can only be appreciated when viewed against his earlier more conservative theology of the state. "Bonhoeffer had a very high regard for the state, and he put a premium on Christian submission to the authorities. He did so [conspired against the state] because he had an even higher regard for God's authority over the state, an authority from which the state derived its right to govern. It was precisely because this was so that he could begin to conceive the possibility of Christian disobedience in obedience to God."[22] The appended extract from *Ethics* illustrates the point—government is of God and must be obeyed, but government is given for the sake of Christ. Bonhoeffer's April 1933 response to the Nazi Aryan clause, "The Church and the Jewish Question," made this same point, while proceeding to address also the inevitable question concerning the obligation of the church should the government no longer serve the cause of Christ. The church, he stressed, was the "most loyal servant" of the state and has no right "to praise or to censure the laws of the state"; neither could it "exert direct political action." His classical Lutheran theology dominated his thought as he looked rather to Christian individuals and humanitarian groups to deal with the prevailing political crisis. "Every strong state needs such associations and such individual personalities," he warns. But he went on to say that ultimately "the church has an unconditional obligation to the victims of any ordering of society, even if they do not belong to the Christian community. . . . [It] is not just to bandage the victims under the wheel, but to put a spoke in the wheel itself."

At no point did Bonhoeffer fail to take the necessity of obedience to the state with utter seriousness, but his involvement in the conspiracy provided a new impulse to interpret this obedience in the light of the cross. Hitherto he had spoken of the kingdom of God manifesting itself in the world in the "two-fold form of church and state," in accordance with Lutheran doctrine.[23] Later he would say "Christ is present to us in a double form, as church and state," giving vent to what has been discerned as a stronger Calvinist emphasis.[24] There was, suggests Rasmussen, a shift from "single-minded obedience" in the *Cost of Discipleship* to responsible freedom in *Ethics*. The reason for this is christological. Sharing our guilt in redeeming us, Christ redeems those who incur "guilt in venturing deeds of free responsibility." Yet this was always for him a *Grenzfall* situation, or "the way of exception," while he stressed the need to be "very careful not to make the extraordinary normative."[25] In so doing he gave concrete meaning and expression to the possibility of tyrannicide, alluded to but only rarely developed within the Christian tradition. For Bonhoeffer the theological responsibility is awesome: "When a man takes guilt upon himself in responsibility, and no responsible man can avoid this, he imputes this guilt to himself and on no one else, he answers for it; he accepts responsibility for it. . . . Before other men the man of free responsibility is justified by necessity; before himself he is acquitted by his conscience; but before God he hopes only for mercy."[26]

The theological affinity between Barth and Bonhoeffer concerning church-state relations is clearly substantive. Much has been made of what has been identified as the gap between the earlier and "post-dialectical," "modern" Bonhoeffer. The continuity between this more radical period and the early Bonhoeffer is, however, difficult to ignore. His 1932 address "Dein Reich Komme" provided his clearest perception of church-state relations. The church and the state were seen as separate but related. "Neither is solely for itself," he stressed. "Every attempt of the one to seize possession of the other disregards that relationship of the kingdom of God to the earth. . . . The church limits the state, just as the state limits the church."

Ultimately, his direct political action against Hitler was essentially this. It was a concrete expression of what he allowed in "The Church and the Jewish Question" to be the obligation of the church in extreme situations, namely, "direct political action" because "the existence of the state, and with it its own existence, [is] threatened."[27] This emphasis is in direct continuity with Barth's observation that "if the state has perverted its God-given authority, it cannot be honoured better than by . . . criticism." For both Barth and Bonhoeffer direct political action by the church was justified on the basis of ensuring that the state fulfilled its God-given function as state. To quote Barth: "The political analogy of this truth is that violent solutions of conflicts in the political community—from police measures to law court decisions, from the armed rising against a regime that is no longer worthy of or equal to its task (in the sense of a revolt undertaken not to undermine but to restore the lawful authority of the state) to the defensive war against an external threat to the lawful state—must be approved, supported, and if necessary even suggested by the Christian community—for how could it possibly contract out in such situations."[28] The caution and care stressed by both Barth and Bonhoeffer in affirming direct action by the church in the political realm must not be lost sight of, but neither must the possible necessity of this option be minimized, central as it is to their respective theologies.

NOTES

1. See, among others, Arthur Cochrane, *The Church's Confession Under Hitler* (Philadelphia: Westminster, 1962).
2. Karl Barth, *Church Dogmatics (CD)* (Edinburgh: T. and T. Clark, 1957), II/1, 444.
3. Quoted in J. R. Stumme, *Socialism in Ecumenical Perspective* (Missoula, Mont.: Scholars Press, 1978), p. 226, from "What is Wrong with Dialectical Theology?" *Journal of Religion*, 15 (1935), 135.
4. Karl Barth, *The Epistle to the Romans* (London: Oxford University Press, 1960), p. 492.
5. Jürgen Moltmann, *On Human Dignity: Political Theology and Ethics* (Philadelphia: Fortress, 1984), p. 91.
6. Barth, *CD*, II/1, 386.
7. Barth, *Epistle to the Romans*, p. 493.
8. These essays are collected in *Community, State and Church*, ed. Will Herberg (Magnolia, Mass.: Peter Smith, 1981).
9. Barth, *Epistle to the Romans*, p. 434.
10. See R. E. Hood, "Karl Barth's Christological Basis for the State and Political Praxis," *Scottish Journal of Theology*, 33 (1980), 228.
11. Moltmann, p. 88.
12. G. Hunsinger, "Karl Barth and Liberation Theology," *Journal of Religion*, 63 (1983), 247–63.
13. Moltmann, pp. 92–95.
14. Larry L. Rasmussen, *Dietrich Bonhoeffer: Reality and Resistance* (Nashville: Abingdon, 1972), p. 15.
15. Ruth Zerner, "Dietrich Bonhoeffer's Views on the State and History," in A. J. Klassen, ed., *A Bonhoeffer Legacy* (Grand Rapids: Eerdmans, 1981), pp. 135, 137.
16. Quoted by John W. de Gruchy, *Bonhoeffer and South Africa* (Grand Rapids: Eerdmans, 1984), p. 16.
17. Ibid., p. 17.
18. Zerner, pp. 137, 144.
19. Dietrich Bonhoeffer, *The Cost of Discipleship* (London: SCM, 1959), p. 234.
20. Dietrich Bonhoeffer, *Ethics* (New York: Macmillan, 1976), p. 342.
21. Zerner, p. 151.
22. De Gruchy, pp. 95–96.

23. Dietrich Bonhoeffer, *Gesammelte Schriften (GS)* (Munich: Christian Kaiser, 1974), III, 279.
24. Dietrich Bonhoeffer, *Christology* (London: Collins, 1966), pp. 65f. Compare with footnote 19. See also de Gruchy's discussion on "Bonhoeffer, Calvin, and the Right to Resist," pp. 98–106.
25. Rasmussen, p. 30 n. 72.
26. Bonhoeffer, *Ethics*, p. 248.
27. Dietrich Bonhoeffer, in *No Rusty Swords: Letters, Lectures and Notes, 1928–1936* (New York: Harper & Row, 1965).
28. Karl Barth, "The Christian Community and the Civil Community," in *Community, State and Church*, ed. Will Herberg (Magnolia, Mass.: Peter Smith, 1981).

SELECT BIBLIOGRAPHY

Barth, K. *Community, State, and Church*, ed. Will Herberg. Garden City, N.Y.: Anchor Books, 1960.

________. *The Church and the Political Problem of Our Day.* New York: Scribner's, 1939.

________. *Ethics.* New York: Seabury, 1981.

Cochrane, A. C. *The Church's Confession Under Hitler.* Philadelphia: Westminster, 1962.

De Gruchy, J. W. *Bonhoeffer and South Africa: Theology in Dialogue.* Grand Rapids: Eerdmans, 1984.

Hunsinger, G., ed. *Karl Barth and Radical Politics.* Philadelphia: Westminster, 1976.

Kelly, G. B. *Liberating Faith.* Minneapolis: Augsburg, 1984.

Klassen, A. J., ed. *A Bonhoeffer Legacy.* Grand Rapids: Eerdmans, 1981.

Moltmann, J. *On Human Dignity: Political Theology and Ethics.* Philadelphia: Fortress, 1984, especially section two.

Rasmussen, L. L. *Dietrich Bonhoeffer: Reality and Resistance.* Nashville: Abingdon, 1972.

THE BARMEN DECLARATION, 1934

In view of the errors of the "German Christians" and of the present Reich Church Administration, which are ravaging the Church and at the same time also shattering the unity of the German Evangelical Church, we confess the following evangelical truths:

1. "I am the Way and the Truth and the Life; no one comes to the Father except through me." (Jn. 14:6)

"Truly, truly I say to you, he who does not enter the sheepfold through the door but climbs in somewhere else, he is a thief and a robber. I am the Door; if anyone enters through me, he will be saved." (Jn. 10:1,9)

Jesus Christ, as he is attested to us in Holy Scripture, is the one Word of God which we have to hear, and which we have to trust and obey in life and in death.

We reject the false doctrine that the Church could and should recognize as a source of its proclamation, beyond and besides this one Word of God, yet other events, powers, historic figures, and truths as God's revelation.

2. "Jesus Christ has been made wisdom and righteousness and sanctification and redemption for us by God." (I Cor. 1:30)

As Jesus Christ is God's comforting pronouncement of the forgiveness of all our sins, so, and with equal seriousness, he is also God's vigorous announcement of his claim upon our whole life. Through him there comes to us joyful liberation from the godless ties of this world for free, grateful service to his creatures.

We reject the false doctrine that there could be areas of our life in which we would belong not to Jesus Christ but to other lords, areas in which we would not need justification and sanctification through him.

3. "Let us, however, speak the truth in love, and in every respect grow into him who is the head, into Christ, from whom the whole body is joined together." (Eph. 4:15-16)

The Christian Church is the community of brethren in which, in Word and sacrament, through the Holy Spirit, Jesus Christ acts in the present as Lord. With both its faith and its obedience, with both its message and its order, it has to testify in the midst of the sinful world, as the Church of pardoned sinners, that it belongs to him alone and lives and may live by his comfort and under his direction alone, in expectation of his appearing.

We reject the false doctrine that the Church could have permission to hand over the form of its message and of its order to whatever it itself might wish or to the vicissitudes of the prevailing ideological and political convictions of the day.

[Source: A new translation by Douglas S. Bax in *Journal of Theology for Southern Africa*, 47 (June 1984).]

4. "You know that the rulers of the Gentiles exercise authority over them and those in high position lord it over them. So shall it not be among you; but if anyone would have authority among you, let him be your servant." (Matt. 20:25-26)

The various offices in the Church do not provide a basis for some to exercise authority over others but for the ministry with which the whole community has been entrusted and charged to be carried out.

We reject the false doctrine that, apart from this ministry, the Church could, and could have permission to, give itself or allow itself to be given special leaders *(Führer)* vested with ruling authority.

5. "Fear God, honour the King!" (I Pet. 2:17)

Scripture tells us that by divine appointment the State, in this still unredeemed world in which also the Church is situated, has the task of maintaining justice and peace, so far as human discernment and human ability make this possible, by means of the threat and use of force. The Church acknowledges with gratitude and reverence toward God the benefit of this, his appointment. It draws attention to God's Kingdom (Reich), God's commandment and justice, and with these the responsibility of those who rule and those who are ruled. It trusts and obeys the power of the Word, by which God upholds all things.

We reject the false doctrine that beyond its special commission the State should and could become the sole and total order of human life and so fulfil the vocation of the Church as well.

We reject the false doctrine that beyond its special commission the Church should and could take on the nature, tasks and dignity which belong to the State and thus become itself an organ of the State.

6. "See, I am with you always, to the end of the age." (Matt. 28:20) "God's Word is not fettered." (II Tim. 2:9)

The Church's commission, which is the foundation of its freedom, consists in this: in Christ's stead, and so in the service of his own Word and work, to deliver to all people, through preaching and sacrament, the message of the free grace of God.

We reject the false doctrine that with human vainglory the Church could place the Word and work of the Lord in the service of self-chosen desires, purposes and plans.

The Confessional Synod of the German Evangelical Church declares that it sees in the acknowledgement of these truths and in the rejection of these errors the indispensable theological basis of the German Evangelical Church as a confederation of Confessional Churches. It calls upon all who can stand in solidarity with its Declaration to be mindful of these theological findings in all their decisions concerning Church and State. It appeals to all concerned to return to unity in faith, hope and love.

Verbum Dei manet in aeternum.

KARL BARTH

THE CHRISTIAN COMMUNITY AND THE CIVIL COMMUNITY

By the "Christian community" we mean what is usually called "the Church" and by the "civil community" what is usually called "the State."

The use of the concept of the "community" to describe both entities may serve at the very outset to underline the positive relationship and connexion between them. . . .

THE DIFFERENCE BETWEEN THE CHRISTIAN AND THE CIVIL COMMUNITY

When we compare the Christian community with the civil community the first difference that strikes us is that in the civil community Christians are no longer gathered together as such but are associated with non-Christians (or doubtful Christians). The civil community embraces everyone living within its area. Its members share no common awareness of their relationship to God, and such an awareness cannot be an element in the legal system established by the civil community. . . .

For this reason the civil community can only have external, relative, and provisional tasks and aims, and that is why it is burdened and defaced by something which the Christian community can, characteristically, do without: physical force, the "secular arm" which it can use to enforce its authority. That is why it lacks the ecumenical breadth and freedom that are so essential to Christianity. . . . And that is why the State has no safeguard or corrective against the danger of either neglecting or absolutising itself and its particular system and thus in one way or the other destroying and annulling itself. One cannot in fact compare the Church with the State without realising how much weaker, poorer, and more exposed to danger the human community is in the State than in the Church.

It would be inadvisable, however, to make too much of the comparison. According to the fifth thesis of the *Theological Declaration* of Barmen (1934), the Christian community also exists in "the still unredeemed world," and there is not a single problem harassing the State by which the Church is not also affected in some way or other. . . . The Word and Spirit of God are no more automatically available in the Church than they are in the State.

THE POSITIVE RELATIONSHIP BETWEEN THE CHRISTIAN AND THE CIVIL COMMUNITIES

More important still, however, is the positive relationship between the two communities which results from the fact that the constitutive elements of the civil community are also proper and indispensable to the Christian community. . . .

[Source: *Community, State and Church*, ed. Will Herberg (Magnolia, Mass.: Peter Smith, 1981).]

The Christian community exists at all times and places as a *politeia* with definite authorities and offices, with patterns of community life and divisions of labour. . . .

In this sense, therefore, the existence of the Christian community is political. Furthermore, the object of the promise and the hope in which the Christian community has its eternal goal consists, according to the unmistakable assertion of the New Testament, not in an eternal Church but in the *polis* built by God and coming down from heaven to earth. . . . It knows that the original and final pattern of this order is the eternal Kingdom of God and the eternal righteousness of His grace. It preaches the Kingdom of God in this external form. But it also thanks God that His Kingdom has an external, relative, and provisional embodiment "in the world that is not yet redeemed," in which it is valid and effective even when the temporal order is based on the most imperfect and clouded knowledge of Jesus Christ or on no such knowledge at all. . . . The Christian community is aware of the need for the civil community, and it alone takes the need absolutely seriously. . . . It knows that without this political order there would be no Christian order. It knows and it thanks God that—as the inner circle within the wider circle (cf. O. Cullmann, *Königsherrschaft Christi und Kirche im Neuen Testament,* 1941)—it is allowed to share the protection which the civil community affords. . . . Its existence is not separate from the Kingdom of Jesus Christ; its foundations and its influence are not autonomous. It is outside the Church but not outside the range of Christ's dominion—it is an exponent of His Kingdom.

THE CHURCH AS CHURCH

The Church must remain the Church. It must remain the inner circle of the Kingdom of Christ. . . . It proclaims the rule of Jesus Christ and the hope of the Kingdom of God. This is not the task of the civil community; it has no message to deliver; it is dependent on a message being delivered to it. It is not in a position to appeal to the authority and grace of God; it is dependent on this happening elsewhere. It does not pray; it depends on others praying for it. It is blind to the whence and whither of human existence; its task is rather to provide for the external and provisional delimitation and protection of human life; it depends on the existence of seeing eyes elsewhere. It cannot call the human *hybris* into question fundamentally, and it knows of no final defence against the chaos which threatens it from that quarter; in this respect, too, it depends on ultimate words and insights existing elsewhere. . . .

The Christian community shares in the task of the civil community precisely to the extent that it fulfils its own task. By believing in Jesus Christ and preaching Jesus Christ it believes in and preaches Him who is Lord of the world as He is Lord of the Church. The Christian community prays for the civil community. It does so all the more since the civil community as such is not in the habit of praying. But by praying for it, it also makes itself responsible for it before God, and it would not be taking this responsibility seriously if it did no more than pray, if it did not also work actively on behalf of the civil community. It also expresses its active support of the civil community by acknowledging that, as an operation of a divine ordinance, the civil power is also binding on Christians and significant and just from the Christian point of view. It expresses its active support of the civil community by "subordinating" itself, in the words of the Apostle (Romans 13:1), to the cause of the civil community under all circumstances (and therefore whatever the political form and reality it has to deal with *in concreto*). . . .

In making itself jointly responsible for the civil community, the Christian community has no exclusive theory of its own to advocate in face of the various forms and realities of political life. It is not in a position to establish one particular doctrine as *the* Christian doctrine of the just State. It is also not in a position to refer to any past realisation of the perfect State or to hold out any prospect of one in the future. There is but one Body of Christ, born of the Word of God, which is heard in faith. There is therefore no such thing as a Christian State corresponding to the Christian Church; there is no duplicate of the Church in the political sphere. . . .

By making itself jointly responsible for the civil community, the Christian community participates—on the basis of and by belief in the divine revelation—in the human search for the best form, for the most fitting system of political organisation; but it is also aware of the limits of all the political forms and systems which man can discover (even with the co-operation of the Church), and it will beware of playing off one political concept—even the "democratic" concept—as *the* Christian concept, against all others. . . . It trusts and obeys no political system or reality but the power of the Word, by which God upholds all things (Hebrews 1:3; Barmen Thesis No. 5), including all political things. . . .

The Christian community "subordinates" itself to the civil community by making its knowledge of the Lord who is Lord of all its criterion, and distinguishing between the just and the unjust State, that is, between the better and the worse political form and reality; between order and caprice; between government and tyranny; between freedom and anarchy; between community and collectivism; between personal rights and individualism; between the State as described in Romans 13 and the State as described in Revelation 13. And it will judge all matters concerned with the establishment, preservation, and enforcement of political order in accordance with these necessary distinctions and according to the merits of the particular case and situation to which they refer. . . .

The Christian decisions which have to be made in the political sphere have no idea, system, or programme to refer to but a direction and a line that must be recognised and adhered to in all circumstances. This line cannot be defined by appealing to the so-called "natural law." To base its policy on "natural law" would mean that the Christian community was adopting the ways of the civil community, which does not take its bearings from the Christian centre and is still living or again living in a state of ignorance. . . .

The tasks and problems which the Christian community is called to share, in fulfilment of its political responsibility, are "natural," secular, profane tasks and problems. But the norm by which it should be guided is anything but natural: it is the only norm which it can believe in and accept as a spiritual norm, and is derived from the clear law of its own faith, not from the obscure workings of a system outside itself: it is from knowledge of this norm that it will make its decisions in the political sphere.

It is this reliance on a spiritual norm that makes the Christian community free to support the cause of the civil community honestly and calmly. In the political sphere the Church will not be fighting for itself and its own concerns. Its own position, influence, and power in the State are not the goal which will determine the trend of its political decisions. . . . Whenever the Church has entered the political arena to fight for its claim to be given public recognition, it has always been a Church which has failed to understand the special purpose of the State, an impenitent, spiritually unfree Church. . . .

The Church cannot, however, simply take the Kingdom of God itself into the political arena. The Church reminds men of God's Kingdom. This does not mean that it expects the State gradually to become the Kingdom of God. The Kingdom of God is the Kingdom where God is without shadow, without problems and contradictions, where He is All in All: it is the rule of God in the redeemed world. In the Kingdom of God the outward is annulled by the inward, the relative by the absolute, the provisional by the final. . . .

The Kingdom of God is the world dominion of Jesus Christ in honour of the Father, revealed in the clear light of day. The State as such, the neutral, pagan, ignorant State knows nothing of the Kingdom of God. It knows at best of the various ideals based on natural law. The Christian community within the State does know about the Kingdom of God, however, and it brings it to man's attention. It reminds men of the Jesus Christ who came and is to come again. But it cannot do this by projecting, proposing, and attempting to enforce a State in the likeness of the Kingdom of God. The State is quite justified if it refuses to countenance all such Christian demands. It belongs to the very nature of the State that it is not and cannot become the Kingdom of God.

THE CONCEPT OF ANALOGY

The direction of Christian judgments, purposes, and ideals in political affairs is based on the analogical capacities and needs of political organisation. Political organisation can be neither a repetition of the Church nor an anticipation of the Kingdom of God. In relation to the Church it is an independent reality; in relation to the Kingdom of God it is (like the Church itself) a human reality bearing the stamp of this fleeting world. . . .

A simple and absolute heterogeneity between State and Church on the one hand and State and Kingdom of God on the other is therefore just as much out of the question as a simple and absolute equating. The only possibility that remains—and it suggests itself compellingly—is to regard the existence of the State as an allegory, as a correspondence and an analogue to the Kingdom of God which the Church preaches and believes in. . . . Since the State forms the outer circle, within which the Church, with the mystery of its faith and gospel, is the inner circle, since it shares a common centre with the Church, it is inevitable that, although its presuppositions and its tasks are its own and different, it is nevertheless capable of reflecting indirectly the truth and reality which constitute the Christian community. Since, however, the peculiarity and difference of its presuppositions and tasks and its existence as an outer circle must remain as they are, its justice and even its very existence as a reflected image of the Christian truth and reality cannot be given once and for all and as a matter of course but are, on the contrary, exposed to the utmost danger; it will always be questionable whether and how far it will fulfil its just purposes. To be saved from degeneration and decay it needs to be reminded of the righteousness which is a reflection of Christian truth. Again and again it needs a historical setting whose goal and content are the moulding of the State into an allegory of the Kingdom of God and the fulfilment of its righteousness. . . . It needs the wholesomely disturbing presence, the activity that revolves directly around the common centre, the participation of the Christian community in the execution of political responsibility. The Church is not the Kingdom of God, but it has knowledge of it; it hopes for it; it believes in it; it prays in the name of Jesus Christ, and it preaches His Name as the Name above all others. The Church is not neutral on this ground, and it is therefore not powerless. . . . Among the political possibilities open at any particular moment it will choose those which most suggest a correspondence to, an analogy and a reflection of, the content of its own faith and gospel. . . .

The Church is based on the knowledge of the one eternal God, who as such became man and thereby proved Himself a neighbor to man, by treating him with compassion (Luke 10:36f.). The inevitable consequence is that in the political sphere the Church will always and in all circumstances be interested primarily in human beings and not in some abstract cause or other, whether it be anonymous capital or the State as such (the functioning of its departments!) or the honour of the nation or the progress of civilisation or culture or the idea, however conceived, of the historical development of the human race.

The Church is witness of the divine justification, that is, of the act in which God in Jesus Christ established and confirmed His original claim to man and hence man's claim against sin and death. The future of which the Church waits is the definitive revelation of this divine justification. This means that the Church will always be found where the order of the State is based on a commonly acknowledged law, from submission to which no one is exempt, and which also provides equal protection for all. . . .

The Church is witness of the fact that the Son of man came to seek and to save the lost. And this implies that—casting all false impartiality aside—the Church must concentrate first on the lower and lowest levels of human society. The poor, the socially and economically weak and threatened, will always be the object of its primary and particular concern, and it will always insist on the State's special responsibility for these weaker members of society. . . .

The Church is the fellowship of those who are freely called by the Word of grace and the Spirit and love of God to be the children of God. Translated into political terms, this means that the Church affirms, as the basic right which every citizen must be guaranteed by the State, the freedom to carry out his decisions in the politically lawful sphere, according to his own insight and choice, and therefore independently, and the freedom to live in certain spheres (the family, education, art, science, religion, culture), safeguarded but not regulated by law. . . .

As the fellowship of those who live in one faith under one Lord on the basis of a Baptism in one Spirit, the Church must and will stand for the equality of the freedom and responsibility of all adult citizens, in spite of its sober insight into the variety of human needs, abilities, and tasks.

Since the Church is aware of the variety of the gifts and tasks of the one Holy Spirit in its own sphere, it will be alert and open in the political sphere to the need to separate the different functions and "powers"—the legislative, executive, and judicial—inasmuch as those who carry out any one of these functions should not carry out the others simultaneously. . . .

As disciples of Christ, the members of His Church do not rule: they serve. In the political community, therefore, the Church can only regard all ruling that is not primarily a form of service as a diseased and never as a normal condition. No State can exist without the sanction of power. But the power of the good State differs from that of the bad State as *potestas* differs from *potentia*. *Potestas* is the power that follows and serves the law; *potentia* is the power that precedes the law, that masters and bends and breaks the law—it is the naked power which is directly evil.

Since the Church is ecumenical (catholic) by virtue of its very origin, it resists all abstract local, regional, and national interests in the political sphere. . . .

The Church knows God's anger and judgment, but it also knows that His anger lasts but for a moment, whereas His mercy is for eternity. The political analogy of this truth is that violent solutions of conflicts in the political community—from police measures to law court decisions, from the armed rising against a regime that is no longer worthy of or equal to its task (in the sense of a revolt undertaken not to undermine but to restore the lawful authority of the State) to the defensive war against an external threat to the lawful State—must be approved, supported, and if necessary even suggested by the Christian community—for how could it possibly contract out in such situations? On the other hand, it can only regard violent solutions of any conflict as an *ultima ratio regis*. It will approve and support them only when they are for the moment the ultimate and only possibility available. It will always do its utmost to postpone such moments as far as possible. It can never stand for absolute peace, for peace at any price. But it must and will do all it can to see that no price is considered too high for the preservation or restoration of peace at home and abroad except the ultimate price which would mean the abolition of the lawful State and the practical denial of the divine ordinance.

The translation of the Kingdom of God into political terms demands Christian, spiritual, and prophetic knowledge on every side. The points of comparison and the decisions we have quoted are in no sense equivalent to the paragraphs of a political constitution. They are merely intended to illustrate how the Church can make decisions on a Christian basis in the political sphere. . . . The essence of Christian politics is not a system or a succession of momentary brain waves but a constant direction, a continuous line of discoveries on both sides of the boundary which separates the political from the spiritual spheres, a correlation between explication and application. . . .

A further comment on the constancy and continuity of the Christian approach in politics: it may be remarked (again, with pleasure or annoyance) that the Christian line that follows from the gospel betrays a striking tendency to the side of what is generally called the "democratic" State. . . .

In conclusion, we propose to discuss the problem of how Christian decisions in the political sphere may be put into action. In the political sphere the Christian community can draw attention to its gospel only indirectly, as reflected in its political decisions, and these decisions can be made intelligible and brought to victory not because they are based on Christian premises but only because they are politically better and more calculated to preserve and develop the common life. They can witness only to Christian truths. The claim to be witnesses to Christian truths does not necessarily make them such, however! . . .

The opportunity that it is offered to fulfil this duty is simply the one that lies nearest to hand: the preaching of the whole gospel of God's grace, which as such is the whole justification of the whole man—including political man. . . . It is a bad sign when Christians are frightened by "political" sermons—as if Christian preaching could be anything but political. . . .

Perhaps the most important contribution the Church can make is to bear in mind in the shaping of its own life that, gathered as it is directly and consciously around the common centre, it has to represent the inner within the outer circle. The real Church must be the model and prototype of the real State. The Church must set an example so that by its very existence it may be a source of renewal for the State and the power by which the State is preserved. . . .

The Church must not forget that what it is rather than what it says will be best understood, not least in the State. If the Church is a Christian community it will not need a Christian party.

DIETRICH BONHOEFFER

1. THE CHURCH AND THE JEWISH QUESTION

The fact, unique in history, that the Jew has been made subject to special laws by the state solely because of the race to which he belongs and quite apart from his religious beliefs, raises new problems for the theologian. . . . What is the church's attitude to this action by the state? And what should the church do as a result of it? . . .

Without doubt, the Church of the Reformation has no right to address the state directly in its specifically political actions. It has neither to praise nor to censure the laws of the state, but must rather affirm the state to be God's order of preservation in a godless world; it has to recognise the state's ordinances, good or bad as they appear from a humanitarian point of view, and to understand that they are based on the sustaining will of God amidst the chaotic godlessness of the world. This view of the state's action on the part of the church is far removed from any form of moralism and is distinct from humanitarianism of any shade through the radical nature of the gulf between the standpoint of the Gospel and the standpoint of the Law. The action of the state remains free from the church's intervention. There are no piqued or pedantic comments from the church here. History is made not by the church, but by the state; but of course only the church, which bears witness to the coming of God in history, knows what history, and therefore what the state, is. And precisely because of this knowledge, it alone testifies to the penetration of history by God in Christ and lets the state continue to make history. Without doubt the Jewish question is one of the historical problems which our state must deal with, and without doubt the state is justified in adopting new methods here. It remains the concern of humanitarian associations and individual Christians who feel themselves called to the task, to remind the state of the moral side of any of its measures, i.e. on occasions to accuse the state of offences against morality. Any strong state needs such associations and such individuals, and will to some extent take good care of them. It is an insight into the finer arts of statesmanship which knows how to make use of these spokesmen in their relative significance. In the same way, a church which is essentially regarded as a cultural function of the state must at times contact the state with such reminders, and must do so all the more strongly as the state takes the church to itself, i.e. ascribes to it essentially moral and pedagogic tasks.

The true church of Christ, however, which lives solely from the Gospel and realises the character of the state's actions, will never intervene in the state in such a way as to criticise its history-making actions, from the standpoint of some humanitarian ideal. It recognises the absolute necessity of the use of force in this world and also the 'moral' injustice of certain concrete acts of the state

---

[Source: Dietrich Bonhoeffer, *No Rusty Swords: Letters, Lectures and Notes, 1928–1936* (New York: Harper & Row, 1965).]

which are necessarily bound up with the use of force. The church cannot in the first place exert direct political action, for the church does not pretend to have any knowledge of the necessary course of history. Thus even today, in the Jewish question, it cannot address the state directly and demand of it some definite action of a different nature. But that does not mean that it lets political action slip by disinterestedly; it can and should, precisely because it does not moralise in individual instances, continually ask the state whether its action can be justified as legitimate action of the state, i.e. as action which leads to law and order, and not to lawlessness and disorder. It is called to put this question with great emphasis where the state appears to be threatened precisely in its nature as the state, i.e. in its function of creating law and order by means of force. It will have to put this question quite clearly today in the matter of the Jewish question. In so doing it does not encroach on the state's sphere of responsibility, but on the contrary fathers upon the state itself the whole weight of the responsibility for its own particular actions. In this way it frees the state from any charge of moralising and shows precisely thus its appointed function as the preserver of the world. As long as the state continues to create law and order by its acts, even if it be a new law and new order, the church of the Creator, the Mediator and the Redeemer cannot engage in direct political action against it. It may not of course prevent the individual Christian, who knows himself called to the task, from calling the state 'inhuman' on occasion, but *qua* church it will not only ask whether the state is bringing about law and order or not.

Now here, of course, the state sees itself to be limited in two respects. Both too much law and order and too little law and order compel the church to speak. There is too little law and order where a group of men becomes lawless, though in real life it is sometimes extraordinarily difficult to distinguish real lawlessness from a formally permitted minimum of law. Even in slavery a minimum of law and order was preserved, and yet a re-introduction of slavery would mean real lawlessness. It is at any rate worth noting that Christian churches tolerated slavery for eighteen centuries and that a new law was made only at a time when the Christian substance of the church could at least be put in question, with the help of the churches, but not essentially or even solely by them. Nevertheless, a step back in this direction would be to the church the expression of a lawless state. It therefore follows that the concept of law is subject to historical change, and this in its turn once again confirms the state in its characteristic history-making law. It is not the church, but the state, which makes and changes the law.

Too little law and order stands in contrast to too much law and order. That means that the state develops its power to such an extent that it deprives Christian preaching and Christian faith (not freedom of conscience—that would be the humanitarian illusion, which is illusory because any life in a state constrains the so-called 'free conscience') of their rights—a grotesque situation, as the state only receives its peculiar rights from this proclamation and from this faith, and enthrones itself by means of them. The church must reject this encroachment of the order of the state precisely because of its better knowledge of the state and of the limitations of its action. The state which endangers the Christian proclamation negates itself.

All this means that there are three possible ways in which the church can act towards the state: in the first place, as has been said, it can ask the state whether its actions are legitimate and in accordance with its character as state, i.e. it can throw the state back on its responsibilities. Secondly, it can aid the victims of state action. The church has an unconditional obligation to the victims of any ordering of society, even if they do not belong to the Christian community. 'Do good to all men.' In both these courses of action, the church serves the free state in its free way, and at times when laws are changed the church may in no way withdraw itself from these two tasks. The third possibility is not just to bandage the victims under the wheel, but to put a spoke in the wheel itself. Such action would be direct political action, and is only possible and desirable when the church sees the state fail in its function of creating law and order, i.e. when it sees the state unrestrainedly bring about too much or too little law and order. In both these cases it must see the existence of the state, and with it its own existence, threatened. There would be too little law if any group of subjects were deprived of their rights, too much where the state intervened in the character of the church and its proclamation, e.g. in the forced exclusion of baptised Jews from our Christian congregations or in the prohibition of our mission to the Jews. Here the Christian church would find itself *in statu confessionis* and here the state would be in the act of negating itself. A state which includes within itself a terrorised church has lost its most faithful servant. But even this third action of the church, which on occasion leads to conflict with the existing state, is only the paradoxical expression of its ultimate recognition of the state; indeed, the church itself knows itself to be called here to protect the state *qua* state from itself and to preserve it. In the Jewish problem the first two possibilities will be the compelling demands of the hour. The necessity of direct political action by the church is, on the other hand, to be decided at any time by an 'Evangelical Council' and cannot therefore ever be casuistically decided beforehand.

2. STATE AND CHURCH

THE DIVINE CHARACTER OF GOVERNMENT

The claim of government, which is based on its power and its mission, is the claim of God and is binding upon conscience. Government demands obedience 'for conscience' sake' (Rom. 13.5), which may also be interpreted as 'for the Lord's sake' (I Pet. 2.13). This obedience is combined with deference (Rom. 13.7; I Pet.

[Source: Dietrich Bonhoeffer, *Ethics* (New York: Macmillan, 1955).]

2.17). In the exercise of the mission of government the demand for obedience is unconditional and qualitatively total; it extends both to conscience and to bodily life. Belief, conscience and bodily life are subject to an obligation of obedience with respect to the divine commission of government. A doubt can arise only when the contents and the extent of the commission of government become questionable. The Christian is neither obliged nor able to examine the rightfulness of the demand of government in each particular case. His duty of obedience is binding on him until government directly compels him to offend against the divine commandment, that is to say, until government openly denies its divine commission and thereby forfeits its claim. In cases of doubt obedience is required; for the Christian does not bear the responsibility of government. But if government violates or exceeds its commission at any point, for example by making itself master over the belief of the congregation, then at this point, indeed, obedience is to be refused, for conscience' sake, for the Lord's sake. It is not, however, permissible to generalize from this offence and to conclude that this government now possesses no claim to obedience in some of its other demands, or even in all its demands. Disobedience can never be anything but a concrete decision in a single particular case. Generalizations lead to an apocalyptic diabolization of government. . . .

Government is instituted for the sake of Christ; it serves Christ, and consequently it also serves the Church. Yet the dominion of Christ over all government does not by any means imply the dominion of the Church over government. But the same Lord, whom government serves, is the Head of the congregation, the Lord of the Church. The service of government to Christ consists in the exercise of its commission to secure an outward justice by the power of the sword. This service is thus an indirect service to the congregation, which only by this is enabled to 'lead a quiet and peaceable life' (I Tim. 2.2). Through its service towards Christ, government is ultimately linked with the Church. If it fulfils its mission as it should, the congregation can live in peace, for government and congregation serve the same Master.

GOVERNMENT'S CLAIM ON THE CHURCH

The claim of government to obedience and deference extends also to the Church. With respect to the spiritual office, government can indeed only demand that this office shall not interfere in the secular office, but that it shall fulfil its own mission, which does, in fact, include the admonition to obey government. Government possesses no authority over this mission itself, as it is exercised in the pastoral office and in the office of Church management. So far as the spiritual office is an office which is exercised publicly, government has a claim to supervise it, to see that everything is done in an orderly manner, that is to say, in accordance with outward justice. It is only in this connexion that it has a claim to intervene in the question of appointments and organization within the office. The spiritual office itself is not subject to government. Yet government possesses a full claim to obedience with regard to the Christian members of the congregation. In this it does not appear as a second authority side by side with the authority of Christ, but its own authority is only a form of the authority of Christ. In his obedience to government the Christian is obedient to Christ. As a citizen the Christian does not cease to be a Christian, but he serves Christ in a different way. This in itself also provides an adequate definition of the contents of the authentic claim of government. It can never lead the Christian against Christ; on the contrary, it helps him to serve Christ in the world. The person who exercises government thus becomes for the Christian a servant of God.

THE CHURCH'S CLAIM ON GOVERNMENT

The Church has the task of summoning the whole world to submit to the dominion of Jesus Christ. She testifies before government to their common Master. She calls upon the persons who exercise government to believe in Christ for the sake of their own salvation. She knows that it is in obedience to Jesus Christ that the commission of government is properly executed. Her aim is not that government should pursue a Christian policy, enact Christian laws, etc., but that it should be true government in accordance with its own special task. Only the Church brings government to an understanding of itself. For the sake of their common Master the Church claims to be listened to by government; she claims protection for the public Christian proclamation against violence and blasphemy; she claims protection for the institution of the Church against arbitrary interference, and she claims protection for Christian life in obedience to Jesus Christ. The Church can never abandon these claims; and she must make them heard publicly so long as government itself maintains its claim to acknowledge the Church. Of course, if government opposes the Church, explicitly or in fact, there may come a time when the Church no longer wastes her words, even though she still does not give up her claim; for the Church knows that, whether government performs its mission well or badly, it must always serve only its Master, and therefore also the Church. The government which denies protection to the Church thereby places the Church all the more patently under the protection of her Master. The government which blasphemes its Master testifies thereby all the more evidently to the power of this Master who is praised and glorified in the torments and martyrdoms of the congregation.

THE POLITICAL RESPONSIBILITY OF THE CHURCH

If political responsibility is understood exclusively in the sense of governmental responsibility, then it is clearly only upon government that this responsibility devolves. But if the term is taken to refer quite generally to life in the *polis*, then there are a number of senses in which it is necessary to speak of political responsibility of the Church in answer to the claim of government upon the Church. Here again we distinguish between the responsibility of the spiritual office and the responsibility of the Christians. It is part of the Church's office of guardianship that she shall call sin by its name and that she shall warn men against sin; for 'righteousness exalteth a nation', both in time and in eternity, 'but sin is perdition for the people', both temporal and eternal perdition (Prov. 14.34). If the Church did not do this, she would be incurring part of the guilt for the blood of the wicked (Ezek. 3.17ff.). This warning against sin is delivered to the congregation openly and publicly, and whoever will not hear it passes judgement upon himself. The intention of the preacher here is not to improve the world, but to summon it to belief in Jesus Christ and to bear witness to the reconciliation which has been accomplished through Him and to His dominion. The theme of the proclamation is not the wickedness of the world but the grace of Jesus Christ. It is part of the responsibility of the spiritual office that it shall devote earnest attention to the proclamation of the reign of Christ as King, and that it shall with all due deference address government directly in order to draw its attention to shortcomings and errors which must otherwise imperil its governmental office. If the word of the Church is, on principle, not received, then the only political responsibility which remains to her is in establishing and maintaining, at least among her own members, the order of outward justice which is no longer to be found in the *polis*, for by so doing she serves government in her own way.

Is there a political responsibility on the part of individual Christians? Certainly the individual Christian cannot be made responsible for the action of government, and he must not make himself responsible for it; but because of his faith and his charity he is responsible for his own calling and for the sphere of his own personal life, however large or however small it may be. If this responsibility is fulfilled in faith, it is effectual for the whole of the *polis*. According to Holy Scripture, there is no right to revolution; but there is a responsibility of every individual for preserving the purity of his office and mission in the *polis*. In this way, in the true sense, every individual serves government with his responsibility. No one, not even government itself, can deprive him of this responsibility or forbid him to discharge it, for it is an integral part of his life in sanctification, and it arises from obedience to the Lord of both Church and government.

CHAPTER 6

THE CHURCH OF VATICAN II

When eighty-year-old Pope John XXIII convened the Twenty-First Ecumenical Council on October 11, 1962—the first in ninety-two years—a new era dawned in Roman Catholic theology. Yet as the documents of the council show, every effort was made to show continuity with earlier pronouncements by the church. Certainly *Gaudium et Spes,* or the *Pastoral Constitution on the Church in the Modern World,* the major Vatican II document on social teaching, was a synthesis of Catholic thought as it emerged in a vast corpus of papal statements on social issues from Leo XIII to Paul VI.[1] John XXIII's *Mater et Magistra* was drawn on extensively, while it in turn was understood to be in direct continuity with Leo's *Rerum Novarum.* It can therefore with some legitimacy be argued that modern Roman Catholic social teaching must be regarded, at least at the level of theory, as having its point of departure in Leo's encyclical of 1891, a document strongly influenced by the context of the time.[2] Karl Marx had established the First International approximately thirty years earlier in 1864, and the *Communist Manifesto* had been published roughly twenty years before that. The challenge of socialism and the leadership of the working class were being debated in the church, and the impact of the unification of Italy was felt throughout the Vatican. The effects of the gradual extension of suffrage beyond the traditional ruling class had resulted in a coalition of socialists and radicals in the Italian parliament, and the Italian Socialist Party was constituted in 1891.

That was the year in which *Rerum Novarum* was published. It is a complex document, critical of the structures of the new industrial Italy. Indirectly it gave support to the nobility and landowners, who, divested of their power, argued that the restoration of the *ancien regime* was the only basis for improved social conditions. On this ambivalent basis, *Rerum Novarum* was nevertheless a document in support of workers' rights, and it soon became known as "the workers' charter." It attacked socialist practice of the time, although it supported the working class. Today scholars discern an ambiguity in the document, but Leo's intention was to take a stand on the side of the exploited workers, and this seems to have been the social effect of the document. "It would be overstating the case to claim that

Rerum Novarum represents or calls for 'an option for the poor' in the sense in which that term is generally understood today; but it indicates a particular concern for the poor, and can now be seen as a major step on the road which eventually led to such an option."[3]

When John XXIII's *Mater et Magistra* was published in 1961, there had not, in fact, been a papal encyclical explicitly on social teaching since Pius XI's *Quadragesimo Anno* thirty years earlier. *Mater et Magistra* was also influenced by Italian politics. The Italian Christian Democratic Party had been struggling to reassert its earlier commitment to social justice and reform, while endeavoring to establish a working alliance with the socialists. This was a move strongly opposed by some high-ranking conservative clerics in Italy. John XXIII responded with *Mater et Magistra*, a document which marked a turning point in Catholic social thought and marked the beginning of the end of a political alliance between Roman Catholicism and socially conservative forces. Certainly the socially restrained approach of Pius XII was thrust aside, and the newly elected pope lent support to the pursuit of the welfare state and a cautious redistribution of wealth.[4] John's next encyclical, *Pacem in Terris*, dated April 11, 1963, was published during the time of Vatican II. It provided a new focus on human rights and the place of the individual in relation to the state. The section on the origin and nature of state authority is appended below, part of which reads as follows: "Governmental authority . . . is a postulate of the moral order and derives from God. Consequently, laws and decrees passed in contravention of the moral order, and hence of the divine will, can have no binding force in conscience, since 'it is right to obey God rather than man.' Indeed the passing of such laws undermines the very nature of authority and results in shameful abuse." With the publication of this encyclical letter, a new emphasis had emerged in the defense of human rights in official pronouncements of the Catholic church. John died a few months later, and the future of the council was in the hands of his successor, Paul VI, elected pope on June 21, 1963.

What Pope John XXIII had raised in general terms, the Second Vatican Council addressed more specifically in *Gaudium et Spes* (December 7, 1965). The opening message of the council had identified peace and social justice as the two major problems facing the church.[5] These are the issues addressed in *Gaudium et Spes*. The first section addresses the nature of "the Church's and man's calling" and the other "some problems of special urgency." The doctrinal foundation of the document is found in the affirmation that "the basic source of human dignity lies in man's call to communion with God." From this presupposition the council addressed the full implications of social and political living, believing that "through her individual members and her whole community, the Church believes she can contribute greatly towards making the whole family of man and its history more human." The document then proceeds to address a variety of issues: marriage and family life, human culture, life in its social, economic, and political dimensions, issues of war and the formation of a family of nations.

For our purposes it is essentially the section on the political community that is of specific interest, and this is reproduced in full in this volume. Human dignity is related to the common good: "The political community exists, consequently, for the sake of the common good, in which it finds its full justification and significance, and the source of its inherent legitimacy." This emphasis is in broad continuity with the Christian tradition as discussed in the preceding pages of this book. A refreshing emphasis in this document is the teaching that authority be concerned with more than the preservation of the existing order of things. This point is recognized at various points in the tradition of the church, but rarely developed with the kind of explicitness found in the Vatican II documents. The emphasis provides a basis for a cautious recognition of the right to resistance and revolution: "Where citizens are oppressed by a public authority overstepping its competence . . . it is legitimate for them to defend their own rights and the rights of their fellow citizens against the abuse of this authority."

Pope Paul VI's encyclical *Popularum Progressio*, dated March 26, 1967, addressed the problem of economics in a way only alluded to in the Vatican II document by confronting the problem of disparity in wealth among the nations. Relating the problem to the aftermath of colonialism and other forms of economic exploitation by the wealthy countries, Paul maintained an optimistic outlook on the problem. He appealed to wealthy countries to provide material aid, to stimulate better trading relations with the developing world, and to show universal charity. His emphasis was on development rather than radical change, while recognizing certain obstacles to development to be dominant in the world. He acknowledged the temptation facing oppressed people to resort to violence. Ultimately he rejected this option, while allowing for an exception in situations "where there is manifest, long-standing tyranny."[6]

Eighteen months after the publication of *Populorum Progressio* came the important Medellin conference in Latin America, to be considered in the next chapter. The outcome was the rejection of the developmental model of economic change, which was to have its impact on subsequent papal statements. Certainly the synod of bishops meeting in Rome in 1971 would emphasize both economic growth and political participation as necessary for human dignity to prevail, as is evident in both *Octagesimo Adveniens*, published to commemorate the eightieth anniversary of *Rerum Novarum*, and in *Justice in the World*, published later that year. Pope John Paul II's *Laborem Exercens* would eventually shift the focus of papal concern from an appeal for more understanding and charity on the part of the wealthy nations to a more thorough analysis of economics and the theological and social significance of human work. He would give "priority of labour over capitalism." Gregory Baum, commenting on these developments in Catholic thought, has suggested that while the Vatican remained critical of some aspects of Marxism, it introduced a more nuanced approach to Marxism. "It removed the taboo from socialism. It acknowledged that many Catholics had become socialists because their Christian convictions led them to this. . . . If Marxism is understood as a form of social analysis, as a sociology of oppression, then according to Paul VI, it can be useful in the struggle for justice."[7]

Pope Paul's *Evangelii Nuntiandi*, which appeared in 1974, emphasized the inherent link between evangelization and liberation. In doing so it represented a giant step forward in the theological understanding of salvation as an all-embracing reality which would constitute the essence of Medellin theology. Donal Dorr's assessment of *Evangelii Nuntiandi* is worth quoting:

> The most important thing to note here is that the word liberation is given theological respectability. But this is done in a very nuanced way that is typical of Pope Paul. The word is used in a manner that extricates it as far as possible from the very restricted meaning it had been given in recent times—for many people "liberation" had almost come to be equivalent to "revolution." The pope speaks of being liberated "from everything that oppresses people, particularly from sin and the Evil One." This clearly presses the meaning of the word far beyond political and economic liberation. Furthermore, the word liberation is used in the document in a way that does not allow it to replace the word salvation, or even to be seen as entirely equivalent to it. Instead it is given a more limited role; it becomes one of the everyday words (such as "gift" and "joy") that are used to explain the meaning of the more primordial word salvation.[8]

"Liberation" was located within a network of other theological concepts, and evangelization was understood as transcending any division between "religion and the secular" or "spiritual and temporal." Evangelization was unequivocally defined as bringing good news to every sphere of existence. Paul VI rejected violent revolution as a means to liberation, but rejoiced in the "evangelical means" that the church has at its disposal "in order to collaborate in the liberation of many." An extract from this important "apostolic exhortation" is also provided below.

Vatican II had provided an incentive for renewal in doctrine and praxis. Pope Paul VI had invited the Latin American bishops to relate this renewal to their own situations, a process already well underway by the time the pope wrote his letter.[9] The outcome of this process was the first meeting of the General Conference of the Latin American Episcopacy, held in Medellin, which is discussed in the next chapter. By the time of Paul VI's death in 1978 the second General Conference of Latin American bishops was due to be held. His successor, John Paul I's, sudden death delayed the conference further, while the new pope, John Paul II, quickly agreed that the conference be held in Puebla, Mexico. Theologically a conservative, John Paul has continued to show preference for the poor and the need for social justice. The extent of his support for the Medellin conference is also addressed in the next chapter. Suffice it to say that in spite of his many cautious statements concerning the freedom of the church in relation to all political and economic ideologies, he has consistently affirmed a preferential option for the poor. A recent document of the Congregation for the Doctrine of the Faith, approved by the pope in August 1984, has warned of the dangers of the "insufficiently critical" use of some aspects of Marxism in some liberation theologies. This same document has, however, affirmed "liberation theology" as a valid concept: ". . . it designates a theological reflection central to the biblical theme of liberation and freedom, and on the urgency of its practical realisation."[10]

The theological shift from Vatican II to Medellin was a shift from a liberal concern for the poor to a radical solidarity with the poor. The unquestioned importance of this solidarity, as a source of liberation, has been recognized by all theologians with a genuine concern for the welfare of the poor. The most dynamic liberation theologians have, at the same time, recognized the dangers of ideological captivity inherent in all political activity, while never allowing this concern to undermine their theological commitment to liberation in thought and deed. The continuing debate in the Vatican, and beyond, on liberation theology is an important part of this dialectic.

NOTES

1. A convenient collection of these documents is found in M. Welsh and Brian Davies, eds., *Proclaiming Justice and Peace* (London: Collins, 1984). See also Donal Dorr, *Option for the Poor: A Hundred Years of Vatican Social Teaching* (Maryknoll, N.Y.: Orbis, 1983).
2. Dorr, pp. 11–56.
3. Ibid., p. 15.
4. E. E. Y. Hales, *Pope John and His Revolution* (London: Eyre and Spottiswoode, 1965).
5. *Message to Humanity*, in *The Documents of Vatican II*, ed. W. M. Abbott (London: Geoffrey Chapman, 1966), pp. 5–6.
6. *Popularum Progressio*, in Walsh and Davies, p. 150.
7. Gregory Baum and D. Cameron, eds., *Ethics and Economics* (Toronto: James Lorimer, 1984), p. 24.
8. Dorr, p. 194.
9. Enrique Dussel, *A History of the Christian Church in Latin America: Colonialism to Liberation* (Grand Rapids: Eerdmans, 1981), p. 140.
10. "Instruction On Certain Aspects of the 'Theology of Liberation,' " Southern Africa Catholic Bishops' Conference series, no. 38: *Pastoral Action* (Pretoria, 1984).

SELECT BIBLIOGRAPHY

Abbott, W. M., ed. *The Documents of Vatican II*. London: Geoffrey Chapman, 1966.
Berkouwer, G. C. *The Second Vatican Council and the New Catholicism*. Grand Rapids: Eerdmans, 1965.
Charles, R. *The Social Teaching of Vatican II*. Oxford: Plater Publications, 1982.
Dorr, D. *Option for the Poor*. Maryknoll, N.Y.: Orbis, 1983.
Hales, E. E. Y. *Pope John and His Revolution*. London: Eyre and Spottiswoode, 1965.
John XXIII. *The Encyclicals and other Messages of John XXIII*. Washington, D.C.: TPS Press, 1964.
John Paul II, *John Paul II in Mexico: His Collected Speeches*. London: Collins, 1979.
O'Brien, D. J., and T. A. Shannon, eds. *Renewing the Earth: Catholic Documents on Peace, Justice and Liberation*. Garden City, N.Y.: Doubleday, 1977.
Welsh, M., and B. Davies, eds. *Proclaiming Justice and Peace*. London: Collins, 1984.

POPE JOHN XXIII

PACEM IN TERRIS, 1963

THE ORIGIN OF THE STATE'S AUTHORITY

Human society can be neither well ordered nor prosperous without the presence of those who, invested with legal authority, preserve its institutions and do all that is necessary to sponsor actively the interests of all its members. And they derive their authority from God, for, as St. Paul teaches, 'there is no power but from God.' In his commentary on this passage, St. John Chrysostom writes: 'What are you saying? Is every ruler appointed by God? No, that is not what I mean, he says, for I am not now talking about individual rulers, but about authority as such. My contention is that the existence of a ruling authority—the fact that some should command and others obey, and that all things should not come about as the result of blind chance—this is a provision of divine wisdom.' God has created men social by nature, and a society cannot 'hold together unless someone is in command to give effective direction and unity of purpose. Hence every civilized community must have a ruling authority, and this authority, no less than society itself, has its source in nature, and consequently has God for its author.'

But it must not be imagined that authority knows no bounds. Since its starting point is the permission to govern in accordance with right reason, there is no escaping the conclusion that it derives its binding force from the moral order, which in turn has God as its origin and end. Hence, to quote Pope Pius XII, 'The absolute order of living beings, and the very purpose of man—an autonomous being, the subject of duties and inviolable rights, and the origin and purpose of human society—have a direct bearing upon the State as a necessary community endowed with authority. Divest it of this authority, and it is nothing, it is lifeless . . . But right reason, and above all Christian faith, make it clear that such an order can have no other origin but in God, a personal God, our creator. Hence it is from him that state officials derive their dignity, for they share to some extent in the authority of God himself.'

Hence, a regime which governs solely or mainly by means of threats and intimidation or promises of reward, provides men with no effective incentive to work for the common good. And even if it did, it would certainly be offensive to the dignity of free and rational human beings. Authority is before all else a moral force. For this reason the appeal of rulers should be to the individual conscience, to the duty which every man has of voluntarily contributing to the common good. But since all men are equal in natural dignity, no man has the capacity to force internal compliance on another. Only God can do that, for he alone scrutinizes and judges the secret counsels of the heart.

[Source: *Proclaiming Justice and Peace*, ed. M. Welsh and Bryan Davies (London: Collins, 1984).]

Hence, representatives of the State have no power to bind men in conscience, unless their own authority is tied to God's authority, and is a participation in it.

The application of this principle likewise safeguards the dignity of citizens. Their obedience to civil authorities is never an obedience paid to them as men. It is in reality an act of homage paid to God, the provident creator of the universe, who has decreed that men's dealings with one another be regulated in accordance with that order which he himself has established. And we men do not demean ourselves in showing due reverence to God. On the contrary, we are lifted up and ennobled in spirit, for to serve God is to reign.

Governmental authority, therefore, is a postulate of the moral order and derives from God. Consequently, laws and decrees passed in contravention of the moral order, and hence of the divine will, can have no binding force in conscience, since 'it is right to obey God rather than men.' Indeed, the passing of such laws undermines the very nature of authority and results in shameful abuse. As St Thomas teaches: 'In regard to the second proposition, we maintain that human law has the *rationale* of law in so far as it is in accordance with right reason, and as such it obviously derives from eternal law. A law which is at variance with reason is to that extent unjust and has no longer the *rationale* of law. It is rather an act of violence.'

The fact that authority comes from God does not mean that men have no power to choose those who are to rule the state, or to decide upon the type of government they want, and determine the procedure and limitations of rulers in the exercise of their authority. Hence the above teaching is consonant with any genuinely democratic form of government.

THE PURPOSE OF THE STATE'S AUTHORITY

Men, both as individuals and as intermediate groups, are required to make their own specific contributions to the general welfare. The main consequence of this is that they must harmonize their own interests with the needs of others, and offer their goods and services as their rulers shall direct—assuming, of course, that justice is maintained and the authorities are acting within the limits of their competence. Those who have authority in the state must exercise that authority in a way which is not only morally irreproachable, but also best calculated to ensure or promote the state's welfare.

The attainment of the common good is the sole reason for the existence of civil authorities. In working for the common good, therefore, the authorities must obviously respect its nature, and at the same time adjust their legislation to meet the requirements of the given situation.

Among the essential elements of the common good one must certainly include the various characteristics distinctive of each individual people. But these by no means constitute the whole of it. For the common good, since it is intimately bound up with human nature, can never exist fully and completely unless the human person is taken into account at all times. Thus, attention must be paid to the basic nature of the common good and what it is that brings it about.

We must add, therefore, that it is in the nature of the common good that every single citizen has the right to share in it—although in different ways, depending on his tasks, merits and circumstances. Hence every civil authority must strive to promote the common good in the interest of all, without favouring any individual citizen or category of citizen. As Pope Leo XIII insisted: 'The civil power must not be subservient to the advantage of any one individual, or of some few persons; in as much as it was established for the common good of all.' Nevertheless, considerations of justice and equity can at times demand that those in power pay more attention to the weaker members of society, since these are at a disadvantage when it comes to defending their own rights and asserting their legitimate interests.

In this connection, we would draw the attention of our own sons to the fact that the common good is something which affects the needs of the whole man, body and soul. That, then, is the sort of good which rulers of states must take suitable measures to ensure. They must respect the hierarchy of values, and aim at achieving the spiritual as well as the material prosperity of their subjects.

These principles are clearly contained in that passage in our encyclical *Mater et Magistra* where we emphasized that the common good 'must take account of all those social conditions which favour the full development of human personality'.

Consisting, as he does, of body and immortal soul, man cannot in this mortal life satisfy his needs or attain perfect happiness. Thus, the measures that are taken to implement the common good must not jeopardize his eternal salvation; indeed, they must even help him to obtain it.

It is generally accepted today that the common good is best safeguarded when personal rights and duties are guaranteed. The chief concern of civil authorities must therefore be to ensure that these rights are recognized, respected, co-ordinated, defended and promoted, and that each individual is enabled to perform his duties more easily. For 'to safeguard the inviolable rights of the human person, and to facilitate the performance of his duties, is the principal duty of every public authority.'

Thus any government which refused to recognize human rights or acted in violation of them, would not only fail in its duty; its decrees would be wholly lacking in binding force.

THE STATE AND HUMAN RIGHTS

One of the principal duties of any government, moreover, is the suitable and adequate superintendence and co-ordination of men's respective rights in society. This must be done in such a way (1) that the exercise of their rights by certain citizens does not obstruct other citizens in the exercise of theirs; (2) that the individual, standing upon his own rights, does not impede others in the performance of their duties; (3) that the rights of all be effectively safeguarded, and completely restored if they have been violated.

In addition, heads of states must make a positive contribution to the creation of an overall climate in which the individual can both safeguard his own rights and fulfil his duties, and can do so readily. For if there is one thing we have learned in the school of experience, it is surely this: that, in the modern world especially, political, economic and cultural inequities among citizens become more and more widespread when public authorities fail to take appropriate action in these spheres. And the consequence is that human rights and duties are thus rendered totally ineffective.

The public administration must therefore give considerable care and thought to the question of social as well as economic progress, and to the development of essential services in keeping with the expansion of the productive system. Such services include road-building, transportation, communications, drinking-water, housing, medical care, ample facilities for the practice of religion and aids to recreation. The government must also see to the provision of insurance facilities, to obviate any likelihood of a citizen's being unable to maintain a decent standard of living in the event of some misfortune, or greatly increased family responsibilities. The government is also required to show no less energy and efficiency in the matter of providing opportunities for suitable employment, graded to the capacity of the workers. It must make sure that working men are paid a just and equitable wage, and are allowed a sense of responsibility in the industrial concerns for which they work. It must facilitate the formation of intermediate groups, so that the social life of the people may become more fruitful and less constrained. And finally, it must ensure that everyone has the means and opportunity of sharing as far as possible in cultural benefits.

The common welfare further demands that in their efforts to co-ordinate and protect, and their efforts to promote, the rights of citizens, the civil authorities preserve a delicate balance. An excessive concern for the rights of any particular individual or group might well result in the principal advantages of the state being in effect monopolized by these citizens. Or again, the absurd situation can arise where the civil authorities, while taking measures to protect the rights of citizens, themselves stand in the way of the full exercise of these rights. 'For this principle must always be retained: that however extensive and far-reaching the influence of the State on the economy may be, it must never be exerted to the extent of depriving the individual citizen of his freedom of action. It must rather augment his freedom, while effectively guaranteeing the protection of everyone's essential, personal rights.'

And the same principle must be adopted by civil authorities in their various efforts to facilitate the exercise of rights and performance of duties in every department of social life.

SECOND VATICAN COUNCIL

GAUDIUM ET SPES, 1965

(THE PASTORAL CONSTITUTION ON THE CHURCH IN THE MODERN WORLD)

THE LIFE OF THE POLITICAL COMMUNITY

In our day, profound changes are apparent also in the structure and institutions of peoples. These result from their cultural, economic and social evolution. Such changes have a great influence on the life of the political community, especially regarding the rights and duties of all in the exercise of civil freedom and in the attainment of the common good, and in organizing the relations of citizens among themselves and with respect to public authority.

The present keener sense of human dignity has given rise in many parts of the world to attempts to bring about a politico-juridical order which will give better protection to the rights of the person in public life. These include the right freely to meet and form associations, the right to express one's own opinion and to profess one's religion both publicly and privately. The protection of the rights of a person is indeed a necessary condition so that citizens, individually or collectively, can take an active part in the life and government of the state.

Along with cultural, economic and social development, there is a growing desire among many people to play a greater part in organizing the life of the political community. In the conscience of many there arises an increasing concern that the rights of minorities be recognized, without any neglect for their duties towards the political community. In addition, there is a steadily growing respect for men of other opinions or other religions. At the same time, there is wider co-operation to guarantee the actual exercise of personal rights to all citizens, and not only to a few privileged individuals.

However, those political systems, prevailing in some parts of the world, are to be reproved which hamper civic or religious freedom, victimize large numbers through avarice and political crimes, and divert the exercise of authority from the service of the common good to the interests of one or another faction or of the rulers themselves.

There is no better way to establish political life on a truly human basis than by fostering an inward sense of justice and kindliness, and of service to the common good, and by strengthening basic convictions as to the true nature of the political community and the purpose, right exercise, and sphere of action of public authority.

Men, families and the various groups which make up the civil community are aware that they cannot achieve a truly human life by their own unaided

---

[Source: *Proclaiming Justice and Peace*, ed. M. Welsh and Bryan Davies (London: Collins, 1984).]

efforts. They see the need for a wider community, within which each one makes his specific contribution every day towards an ever broader realization of the common good. For this purpose they set up a political community which takes various forms. The political community exists, consequently, for the sake of the common good, in which it finds its full justification and significance, and the source of its inherent legitimacy. Indeed, the common good embraces the sum of those conditions of the social life whereby men, families and associations more adequately and readily may attain their own perfection.

Yet the people who come together in the political community are many and diverse, and they have every right to prefer divergent solutions. If the political community is not to be torn apart while everyone follows his own opinion, there must be an authority to direct the energies of all citizens towards the common good, not in a mechanical or despotic fashion, but by acting above all as a moral force which appeals to each one's freedom and sense of responsibility.

It is clear, therefore, that the political community and public authority are founded on human nature and hence belong to the order designed by God, even though the choice of a political regime and the appointment of rulers are left to the free will of citizens.

It follows also that political authority, both in the community as such and in the representative bodies of the state, must always be exercised within the limits of the moral order and directed towards the common good—with a dynamic concept of that good—according to the juridical order legitimately established or which should be established. When authority is so exercised, citizens are bound in conscience to obey. Accordingly, the responsibility, dignity and importance of leaders are indeed clear.

But where citizens are oppressed by a public authority overstepping its competence, they should not protest against those things which are objectively required for the common good; but it is legitimate for them to defend their own rights and the rights of their fellow citizens against the abuse of this authority, while keeping within those limits drawn by the natural law and the Gospels.

According to the character of different peoples and their historic development, the political community can, however, adopt a variety of concrete solutions in its structures and the organization of public authority. For the benefit of the whole human family, these solutions must always contribute to the formation of a type of man who will be cultivated, peace-loving and well-disposed towards all his fellow men.

It is in full conformity with human nature that there should be juridico-political structures providing all citizens in an ever better fashion and without any discrimination with the practical possibility of freely and actively taking part in the establishment of the juridical foundations of the political community and in the direction of public affairs, in fixing the terms of reference of the various public bodies and in the election of political leaders. All citizens, therefore, should be mindful of the right and also the duty to use their free vote to further the common good. The Church praises and esteems the work of those who for the good of men devote themselves to the service of the state and take on the burdens of this office.

If the citizens' responsible co-operation is to produce the good results which may be expected in the normal course of political life, there must be a statute of positive law providing for a suitable division of the functions and bodies of authority and an efficient and independent system for the protection of rights. The rights of all persons, families and groups, and their practical application, must be recognized, respected and furthered, together with the duties binding on all citizens. Among the latter, it will be well to recall the duty of rendering the political community such material and personal services as are required by the common good. Rulers must be careful not to hamper the development of family, social or cultural groups, nor that of intermediate bodies or organizations, and not to deprive them of opportunities for legitimate and constructive activity; they should willingly seek rather to promote the orderly pursuit of such activity. Citizens, for their part, either individually or collectively, must be careful not to attribute excessive power to public authority, not to make exaggerated and untimely demands upon it in their own interests, lessening in this way the responsible role of persons, families and social groups.

The complex circumstances of our day make it necessary for public authority to intervene more often in social, economic and cultural matters in order to bring about favourable conditions which will give more effective help to citizens and groups in their free pursuit of man's total well-being. The relations, however, between socialization and the autonomy and development of the person can be understood in different ways according to various regions and the evolution of peoples. But when the exercise of rights is restricted temporarily for the common good, freedom should be restored immediately upon change of circumstances. Moreover, it is inhuman for public authority to fall back on dictatorial systems or totalitarian methods which violate the rights of the person or social groups.

Citizens must cultivate a generous and loyal spirit of patriotism, but without being narrow-minded. This means that they will always direct their attention to the good of the whole human family, united by the different ties which bind together races, people and nations.

All Christians must be aware of their own specific vocation within the political community. It is for them to give an example by their sense of responsibility and their service of the common good. In this way they are to demonstrate concretely how authority can be compatible with freedom, personal initiative with the solidarity of the whole social organism, and the advantages of unity with fruitful diversity. They must recognize the legitimacy of different opinions with regard to temporal solutions, and respect citizens, who, even as a group, defend their points of view by honest methods. Political parties, for their part, must promote those things which in their judgement are required for the common good; it is never allowable to give their interests priority over the common good.

Great care must be taken with regard to civic and political formation, which is of the utmost necessity today for the population as a whole, and especially for youth, so that all citizens can play their part in the life of the political community. Those who are suited or can become suited should prepare themselves for the difficult, but at the same time, the very noble art of politics, and should seek to practise this art without regard for their own interests or for material advantages.

With integrity and wisdom, they must take action against any form of injustice and tyranny, against arbitrary domination by an individual or a political party, and any intolerance. They should dedicate themselves to the service of all with sincerity and fairness, indeed, with the charity and fortitude demanded by political life.

It is very important, especially where a pluralistic society prevails, that there be a correct notion of the relationship between the political community and the Church, and a clear distinction between the tasks which Christians undertake, individually or as a group, on their own responsibility as citizens guided by the dictates of a Christian conscience, and the activities which, in union with their pastors, they carry out in the name of the Church.

The Church, by reason of her role and competence, is not identified in any way with the political community nor bound to any political system. She is at once a sign and a safeguard of the transcendent character of the human person.

The Church and the political community in their own fields are autonomous and independent from each other. Yet both, under different titles, are devoted to the personal and social vocation of the same men. The more that both foster healthier co-operation between themselves with due consideration for the circumstances of time and place, the more effectively will their service be exercised for the good of all. For man's horizons are not limited only to the temporal order: while living in the context of human history, he preserves intact his eternal vocation. The Church, for her part, founded on the love of the redeemer, contributes towards the reign of justice and charity within the borders of a nation and between nations. By preaching the truths of the gospel, and bringing to bear on all fields of human endeavour the light of her doctrine and of a Christian witness, she respects and fosters the political freedom and responsibility of citizens.

The apostles, their successors and those who co-operate with them, are sent to announce to mankind Christ, the saviour. Their apostolate is based on the power of God, who very often shows forth the strength of the gospel in the weakness of its witnesses. All those dedicated to the ministry of God's word must use the ways and means proper to the gospel which in a great many respects differ from the means proper to the earthly city.

There are, indeed, close links between earthly things and those elements of man's condition which transcend the world. The Church herself makes use of temporal things in so far as her own mission requires it. She, for her part, does not place her trust in the privileges offered by civil authority. She will even give up the exercise of certain rights which have been legitimately acquired, if it becomes clear that their use will cast doubt on the sincerity of her witness or that new ways of life demand new methods. It is only right, however, that at all times and in all places, the Church should have true freedom to preach the faith, to teach her social doctrine, to exercise her role freely among men, and also to pass moral judgement in those matters which concern public order when the fundamental rights of a person or the salvation of souls requires it. In this, she should make use of all the means—but only those—which accord with the gospel and which correspond to the general good with due regard to the diverse circumstances of time and place.

While faithfully adhering to the gospel and fulfilling her mission to the world, the Church, whose duty it is to foster and elevate all that is found to be true, good and beautiful in the human community, strengthens peace among men for the glory of God.

POPE PAUL VI

EVANGELII NUNTIANDI 1974

(ON EVANGELIZATION IN THE MODERN WORLD)

OBSTACLES TO DEVELOPMENT

Between evangelization and human advancement—development and liberation—there are in fact profound links. These include links of an anthropological order, because the man who is to be evangelized is not an abstract being but is subject to social and economic questions. They also include links in the theological order, since one cannot dissociate the plan of creation from the plan of redemption. The latter plan touches the very concrete situations of injustice to be combatted and of justice to be restored. They include links of the eminently evangelical order, which is that of charity: how in fact can one proclaim the new commandment without promoting in justice and in peace the true, authentic advancement of man? We ourself have taken care to point this out, by recalling that it is impossible to accept 'that in evangelization one could or should ignore the importance of the problems so much discussed today, concerning justice, liberation, development and peace in the world. This would be to forget the lesson which comes to us from the gospel concerning love of our neighbour who is suffering and in need.'

The same voices which during the synod touched on this burning theme with zeal, intelligence and courage have, to our great joy, furnished the enlightening principles for a proper understanding of the importance and profound meaning of liberation, such as it was proclaimed and achieved by Jesus of Nazareth and such as it is preached by the Church.

We must not ignore the fact that many, even generous Christians who are sensitive to the dramatic questions involved in the problem of liberation, in their wish to commit the Church to the liberation effort are frequently tempted to reduce her mission to the dimensions of a simply temporal project. They would reduce her aims to a man-centred goal; the salvation of which she is the messenger would be reduced to material well-being. Her activity, forgetful of all spiritual and religious preoccupation, would become initiatives of the political or social order. But if this were so, the Church would lose her fundamental meaning. Her message of liberation would no longer have any originality and would easily be open to monopolization and manipulation by ideological systems and political parties. She would have no more authority to proclaim freedom as in the name of God. This is why we have wished to emphasize, in the same address at the opening of the synod, 'the need to restate clearly the specifically religious finality of evangelization. This latter would lose its reason for existence if it were to

---

[Source: *Proclaiming Justice and Peace*, ed. M. Welsh and Bryan Davies (London: Collins, 1984).]

diverge from the religious axis that guides it: the kingdom of God, before anything else, in its fully theological meaning.'

With regard to the liberation which evangelization proclaims and strives to put into practice one should rather say this:

It cannot be contained in the simple and restricted dimension of economics, politics, social or cultural life; it must envisage the whole man, in all his aspects, right up to and including his openness to the absolute, even the divine absolute.

It is therefore attached to a certain concept of man, to a view of man which it can never sacrifice to the needs of any strategy, practice or short-term efficiency.

Hence, when preaching liberation and associating herself with those who are working and suffering for it, the Church is certainly not willing to restrict her mission only to the religious field and dissociate herself from man's temporal problems. Nevertheless she reaffirms the primacy of her spiritual vocation and refuses to replace the proclamation of the kingdom by the proclamation of forms of human liberation; she even states that her contribution to liberation is incomplete if she neglects to proclaim salvation in Jesus Christ.

The Church links human liberation and salvation in Jesus Christ, but she never identifies them, because she knows through revelation, historical experience and the reflection of faith that not every notion of liberation is necessarily consistent and compatible with an evangelical vision of man, of things and of events; she knows too that in order that God's kingdom should come it is not enough to establish liberation and to create well-being and development.

And what is more, the Church has the firm conviction that all temporal liberation, all political liberation—even if it endeavours to find its justification in such a page of the Old or New Testament, even if it claims for its ideological postulates and its norms of action theological data and conclusions, even if it pretends to be today's theology—carries within itself the germ of its own negation and fails to reach the ideal that it proposes for itself, whenever its profound motives are not those of justice in charity, whenever its zeal lacks a truly spiritual dimension and whenever its final goal is not salvation and happiness in God.

The Church considers it to be undoubtedly important to build up structures which are more human, more just, more respectful of the rights of the person and less oppressive and less enslaving, but she is conscious that the best structures and the most idealized systems soon become inhuman if the inhuman inclinations of the human heart are not made wholesome, if those who live in these structures or who rule them do not undergo a conversion of heart and of outlook.

The Church cannot accept violence, especially the force of arms—which is uncontrollable once it is let loose—and indiscriminate death as the path of liberation, because she knows that violence always provokes violence and irresistibly engenders new forms of oppression and enslavement which are often harder to bear than those from which they claimed to bring freedom. We said this clearly during our journey in Colombia: 'We exhort you not to place your trust in violence and revolution: that is contrary to the Christian spirit, and it can also delay instead of advancing that social uplifting to which you lawfully aspire.' 'We must say and reaffirm that violence is not in accord with the gospel, that it is not Christian; and that sudden or violent changes of structures would be deceitful, ineffective of themselves, and certainly not in conformity with the dignity of the people.'

Having said this, we rejoice that the Church is becoming ever more conscious of the proper manner and strictly evangelical means that she possesses in order to collaborate in the liberation of many. And what is she doing? She is trying more and more to encourage large numbers of Christians to devote themselves to the liberation of men. She is providing these Christian 'liberators' with the inspiration of faith, the motivation of fraternal love, a social teaching which the true Christian cannot ignore and which he must make the foundation of his wisdom and of his experience in order to translate it concretely into forms of action, participation and commitment. All this must characterize the spirit of a committed Christian, without confusion with tactical attitudes or with the service of a political system. The Church strives always to insert the Christian struggle for liberation into the universal plan of salvation which she herself proclaims.

What we have just recalled comes out more than once in the synod debates. In fact we devoted to this theme a few clarifying words in our address to the Fathers at the end of the Assembly.

It is to be hoped that all these considerations will help to remove the ambiguity which the word 'liberation' very often takes on in ideologies, political systems or groups. The liberation which evangelization proclaims and prepares is the one which Christ himself announced and gave to man by his sacrifice.

The necessity of ensuring fundamental human rights cannot be separated from this just liberation which is bound up with evangelization and which endeavours to secure structures safeguarding human freedoms. Among these fundamental human rights, religious liberty occupies a place of primary importance. We recently spoke of the relevance of this matter, emphasizing 'how many Christians still today, because they are Christians, because they are Catholics, live oppressed by systematic persecution! The drama of fidelity to Christ and of the freedom of religion continues, even if it is disguised by categorical declarations in favour of the rights of the person and of life in society!'

CHAPTER 7

THE LATIN AMERICAN CHURCH

When the Council of Trent met in 1542 no Latin American bishops were present. Although no Apostolic Brief to the effect has been found, the king of Spain informed the bishops that they were excused from attending. During the sixteenth century the Catholic church provided a definite religious facade to the process of Hispanic colonialism in Latin America and elsewhere. The Catholic church was in ideological captivity to Spain as it would find itself wedded to other political and economic ideological movements in later years. Similar forms of captivity have been recurring maladies in Protestantism, but history shows that Catholicism has also, on occasion, acquiesced to the forces of nationalism and self-interest.

A small number of Latin American prelates were allowed to attend the First Vatican Council which began in June 1868, but Latin American pastoral experience was not discussed. The identity of the Roman Catholic church was that of the Northern Hemisphere and particularly Europe. The Second Vatican Council met in October 1962 with many more Latin American delegates in attendance than had previously been the case, although they were still disproportionately outnumbered by European delegates (22.3 percent of the participating bishops were from Latin America, against 31.6 percent from Europe).[1] Nevertheless, this event marked the beginning of a shift in Roman Catholic theological perception away from an exclusively European center.

The Latin American church had been undergoing a serious process of theological, liturgical, catechetical, and parochial renewal since the turn of the century. Dussel traces this back to the First Continental Council of the Latin American Roman Catholic Church held in Rome in 1899, while pointing to the great depression of the 1930s as the turning point which forced the Latin American church to respond pastorally to the economic and political structures imposed on the region by the colonial powers. In Europe the philosophy of Jacques Maritain and others became the basis of a new focus on social and democratic action. "Christian democracy was a reaction to the rightist propensity of the Spanish Fascist government of Francisco Franco, who came to power in 1936, the year when the Christian spirits divided in a germinal way, a division that would be accentuated during the time of the Second Vatican Council."[2] At more or less the same time, ecclesiastical renewal and a sense of episcopal collegiality were emerging in Latin America. The first meeting of the General Conference of the Latin American Episcopacy (CELAM) was in 1955, and the second meeting was held in Medellin in 1968. In between these two historic conferences there were eleven regular meetings of the bishops at which expression was given to the emerging "new Christianity" of the Roman Catholic church, especially the church in Latin America.

During the course of the Second Vatican Council, CELAM held three regular meetings, and the Latin American delegates met several times in Rome. An extraordinary meeting was held at Mar del Plata within a few months of the close of the council. By this time the encyclical *Populorum Progressio* was already under discussion, although it was not promulgated until the following year. At the close of the Mar del Plata meeting the Latin American bishops, together with other Third World bishops, issued a statement entitled "Theological Reflection on Development," anticipating the Medellin Conference statement to appear two years later: "From the doctrinal point of view," they insisted, "the Church knows that the Gospel demands the first fundamental revolution which is called 'conversion,' a complete return from sin to grace, from selfishness to love, from pride to a humble willingness to serve. This conversion is not merely internal and spiritual, it affects the whole man, his physical and social as well as his spiritual and personal being." From this theological basis they systematically affirmed "independence in the face of political, social and economic systems" which they judged to be responsible for their oppression.[3]

With this statement the emphasis in Latin American theology shifted from "development" to "liberation." The theological ground had been well prepared for the 1968 Second General Conference of Latin American Bishops meeting in Medellin, with Pope Paul VI, the first pontiff ever to visit the continent, delivering the opening address. Earlier he had written to the bishops urging them to take seriously "the responsibilities of the sacred pastors in the postconciliar period." Now in his opening address he urged them to show "the clarity and the courage of the Spirit in promoting social justice and in loving and defending the poor." In so doing he specifically called for a nonviolent means of promoting the cause of the poor. He spoke to the Colombian peasants exhorting them "not to put their confidence in violence nor in revolution." In a second speech he warned that while "some conclude that the basic problem of Latin America cannot be resolved without violence . . . we must say and reaffirm that violence is neither evangelical nor Christian."[4]

The task of the Latin American bishops meeting in Medellin was largely in continuity with this quest for "another way," a nonviolent way of addressing the problems of the region. But in grappling with this issue, the Medellin conference recognized that in some situations violence may be legitimate, although it warned that this violence could lead to new injustices. Donal Dorr shows the difference in emphasis between the pope's statement and that of the Medellin documents in this way: The pope identified two elements concerning violence. "The main one is that a revolution is an unacceptable remedy for injustice because it gives rise to worse evils. The second point is the parenthesis in which the pope indicates that there might be certain rare exceptions to this general guideline. The Medellin document quotes from both parts of Pope Paul's statement—but it does so in reverse order, putting first the point that revolutionary insurrection can sometimes be legitimate, and then the point that it generally gives rise to new injustices."[5]

The Latin American church had manifested an awareness of its own "coming of age." It was ready to take the reins of its own destiny. To quote Gutiérrez:

> Vatican II speaks of the underdevelopment of peoples, of the developed countries and what they can and should do about this underdevelopment; Medellin tries to deal with the problem from the standpoint of the poor countries, characterizing them as subjected to a new kind of colonialism. Vatican II talks about a Church in the world and describes the relationship in a way which tends to neutralize the conflicts; Medellin demonstrates that the world in which the Latin American church ought to be present is in full revolution. Vatican II sketches a general outline for Church renewal; Medellin provides guidelines for a transformation of the Church in terms of its presence on a continent of misery and injustice.[6]

Acting in response to Vatican II and the papal initiative, the Latin American bishops extracted from Vatican II theology and the thought of John XXIII and Paul VI what would become the bases of Latin American liberation theology. The Medellin documents denounced oppression in terms of both "internal colonialism" and "external neocolonialism," the former referring to the exploitation of the poor by local elites and the latter to what Paul VI had referred to in *Populorum Progressio* as the "international imperialism of money." Briefly stated, the bishops recognized economic exploitation, what they called "exacerbated nationalism," and the arms race as the fundamental causes of the oppression of the poor in their respective countries. Theology, they insisted, was to be done in relation to these structures—not with a view merely to reflecting on the nature of these events, but rather with a sense of compulsion to change them.

The Medellin documents make it equally clear that the basis of the poor's liberation from this oppression is to be found in the gospel of Christ. For the bishops all social, political, and economic protest is located in Christ. This much is clear from the doctrinal affirmations in both the documents on *Justice* and on *Peace* which are excerpted below. The document on *Justice* declares: "It is the same God who, in the fullness of time, sends his Son in the flesh, so that He might come to liberate all men from the slavery to which sin has subjected them: hunger, misery, oppression and ignorance, in a word, that injustice and hatred which have their origin in human selfishness." The doctrinal reflection on *Peace* is equally clear: "Human solidarity cannot truly take effect unless it is done in Christ, who gives peace that the world cannot give. Love is the soul of justice. . . . God is the basic foundation of internal and social peace." It is declarations of faith such as these, argues Gutiérrez, which "have made priests and the religious today one of the most dynamic and restless groups in the Latin American Church."[7] Yet the Medellin documents are not without what some have regarded as compromises, ambiguities, and lacunae.[8] The doctrinal basis of the document on justice, for example, refers to both "integral human development" and "liberation." This could, however, be explained as the bishops' recognition that while development is part of the process of liberation from economic and social oppression, it must never be allowed to become a means of dependency and captivity. What is clear is that the major focus of Medellin was on *liberation*. "Medellin represented the climax of the period of preparation."[9] The shift from a theology of liberal, optimistic development had given way to a form of radical engagement in a struggle to reject the political and economic structures of oppression.

The major hermeneutical emphasis of the Medellin documents is to be found in the direct consequence of its christological affirmation. In imitation of Christ, the Christian's duty is to show *solidarity with the poor*—and it is from this perspective that the social and theological analysis of Latin American liberation theology is done. Medellin was in continuity with the preparatory work of Vatican II while it gave new content to the hermeneutical commitment to the poor. To quote the Medellin document: "We ought to sharpen the awareness of our duty of solidarity with the poor, to which charity leads us. This solidarity means that we make ours their problems and their struggles, that we know how to speak with them." The linguistic shift from the documents of Vatican II to Medellin is indicative of a shift in theology and praxis. The shift is from a concern for the poor to a preferential option in solidarity *with* the poor. It is from this perspective, recognizing the abject oppression of the poor, that the bishops warn, "we should not be surprized . . . that the 'temptation to violence' is surfacing in Latin America."

What is more significant is the introduction of the concept of "institutionalized violence" into the debate. It is this which has, in turn, become the point of departure for analyzing the options available to the oppressed, giving rise, for example, to Dom Helder Camara's notion of a spiral of violence, beginning with "institutionalized violence," leading to the "counter violence" of resistance, responded to with "repressive violence."[10] The bishops neither endorsed nor did they condemn the "counter violence" of resistance and revolution. Their concern was rather to find another solution to the problem. This they identified as "the dynamism of the awakened and organized community . . . put to the service of justice and peace." This, the bishops argued, necessitates the involvement of the church in a "conscientization" role through educational programs and the use of mass media, and the formation of "basic communities" "to encourage and favour the efforts of the people to create and develop their own grass-roots organizations for the redress and consolidation of their rights and the search for true justice." It is this notion which has acquired the title "conscienticizing evangelization" in liberation theology circles, dealing, as the document on peace states, with the pastoral "duty to educate the Christian conscience, to inspire, stimulate and help orient all of the initiatives that contribute to the formation of man."

In spite of the imperfections in the Medellin documents which have been discerned by both those affirming liberation theology and its critics, they have become a watershed in contemporary theological debate on church-state relations. The debate on liberation theology continues to rage in Latin America, more than it does in other parts of the world. Oppressive politics and dictatorial regimes have continued to dictate the quality of life in Latin America since Medellin, with a succession of military and political coups in a number of countries in the region. CELAM has continued to meet, and the Third Bishops' Conference has since met in Puebla in 1979 with Pope John Paul II present. This was a conference in which conservative bishops lined up against those defending the church's commitment to the oppressed people of the continent. Every effort was made by some bishops to destroy liberation theology. The Secretariat of the Conference of Latin American Bishops drew up a preparatory document which was rejected by those committed to liberation theology. The result was that the Puebla conference explicitly asserted its continuity with Medellin.[11] "Puebla was not nearly as original as the Second Bishops' Conference (Medellin) but it followed the same direction, which in itself is significant and to a certain degree was unexpected."[12]

Pope John Paul II has at times been quoted as also being opposed to liberation theology. In many ways he is a conservative person, with set views on sexual ethics, women's ordination, priestly celibacy, church government, and international politics and communism. He does in fact show a more cautious response to liberation theology than some would like. In many situations of conflict around the world, such caution is interpreted as ambivalence. The major theological emphasis of liberation theology, which is a preferential option for the poor, has not, however, been called into question by him. Some have criticized him for failing to show a sufficiently clear ideological alignment with the struggle of the poor. For example, during his visit to Mexico at the time of the Puebla conference, and again subsequently, he has consistently demanded the unequivocal freedom of the church in relation to the ideological conflict between capitalists and socialists, "while trying to bridge the gap between different viewpoints, without compromising on the central issues." In addressing the Puebla conference he avoided the use of the term "option for the poor," recognizing that for some it amounted to a Marxist class option. Others saw it as a concept with a firm basis in the Bible. The pope found another way around the problem by saying that the church is "prompted by an authentically evangelical commitment which, like that of Christ, is primarily a commitment to those most in need." The presence of the concept in the Puebla document is a clear indication of the conference's unequivocal stand in continuity with Medellin. On other occasions in Mexico the pope was more explicit: "Medellin was a call of hope showing 'preferential yet not exclusive love for the poor.' " "I feel solidarity with you because, being poor, you are entitled to my particular concern. I tell you the reason at once: the pope loves you because you are God's favourites."[13] Gutiérrez, in fact, argues that the pope's statements on the poor are in direct continuity with Puebla. Puebla had, he shows, by theological design affirmed an option for the poor which was preferential and not exclusive: "The gospel is not anyone's private property, to do with as one might wish. *Preference* for the poor is written into the gospel message itself. But this alleged exclusivity, if it gained the upper hand, would—paradoxically—deprive that very preference of its historical 'bite.' " The pope's rejection of an exclusive option for the poor is therefore in continuity with Puebla: "Thus the assertions of John Paul II to the effect that it is a matter of preference, not exclusivity, far from being a criticism, actually corroborates precisely what is clearest and sanest in recent Latin American theological experience and reflection."[14] Gregory Baum, in turn, writing on the pope's visit to Canada in 1984, identifies the pope's direct appeal for a restructuring of the capitalist economy "so that human needs will be put before mere financial gain." At least with regard to the Newfoundland fisheries dispute, the pope spoke of "the promotion of cooperatives of fishermen, collective agreements between workers and management, and some form of joint ownership or partnership." In so doing he gave concrete expression to what in *Laborem Exercens* he calls "the priority of labour over capital."[15]

Present and future developments in liberation theology are beyond the sphere of this introductory comment on the Medellin documents. It is perhaps helpful to draw attention to three dimensions of this development latent in the Medellin text. The first comes to expression most clearly in what Míguez Bonino refers to as the radical "monism" of liberation theology. He sees this occurring when love for God collapses without remainder into love for one's neighbor—when it becomes increasingly difficult to differentiate between liberation and salvation. To use Míguez Bonino's words, this occurs when "reference to the history of divine revelation is secondary, merely exemplary, or even dispensable." "If we carry that tendency," he continues, "to its ultimate conclusion, we will end up wittingly or unwittingly deifying history or humanity itself. . . . There can be no doubt that contemporary Latin American theology has no such intention. But we must ask ourselves whether the formulations we have worked out so far do enough to rule out that possibility."[16]

A second area of debate is given expression in what has recently been referred to as a shift in Latin American liberation theology.[17] Here a distinction is made between that brand of liberation theology done by "organic intellectuals" on behalf of the common people, charged with the responsibility to learn *how* oppressed people understand the popular faith, and what may be regarded as the theology *of* the poor. Acting against their own self-interest, the former have deliberately sought to articulate the concerns of the poor, while a certain amount of ideological suspicion has continued to prevail concerning their efforts. This, suggests Segundo, has given rise to a kind of theology which recognizes that conversion to the perspective of the poor demands a renunciation of the critical and creative resources of the intellectual in order to become an instrument of the poor.[18] Bluntly stated, the question is, who is it that is speaking for the poor and doing theology from the perspective of the poor? This locates the gap between First and Third World theologians, already referred to in identifying the shift from Vatican II to Medellin, within Latin American theology itself. Gutiérrez's latest book, *The Power of the Poor in History*, addresses the significance of the church of the poor, identifying the evangelical resources of the poor for the entire church.[19] In this way the history of the mission of the church has come full circle. The South is evangelizing the North, the poor the rich, and the weak the strong. Perhaps the question is rather whether the church has not been turned the right way up?

A third area of debate is raised in the document on liberation theology approved by Pope John Paul II.[20] This issue is Paul's identification of different emergent liberation theologies rather than one monolithic form of liberation theology. In this regard, he has raised questions concerning what are perceived as the "insufficiently critical" use of Marxism in some forms of liberation theology. A pertinent question in the liberation theology debate concerns the *extent* to which Marxist analysis ought to influence Christian theology. In many ways this debate has only just started.

The extent of the debate around liberation theology is itself indicative of its good health. The fact that the pope approved the declaration on liberation theology leaves no doubt on the acceptance of liberation by the Vatican. The broad-based appeal of this theology within Latin America and elsewhere makes it an enduring reality within the Christian quest for an authentic relationship between church and state.

NOTES

1. Enrique Dussel, *A History of the Church in Latin America* (Grand Rapids: Eerdmans, 1981), p. 139.
2. Donal Dorr, *Option for the Poor: A Hundred Years of Vatican Social Teaching* (Maryknoll, N.Y.: Orbis, 1983), p. 107. See also Dussel, p. 107.
3. For the full text of this declaration see M. E. Marty and D. G. Peerman, eds., *New Theology No. 6* (New York: Macmillan, 1972), pp. 243–54.
4. Dussel, pp. 140–44.
5. Dorr, p. 161.
6. Gustavo Gutiérrez, *A Theology of Liberation* (Maryknoll, N.Y.: Orbis, 1973), p. 134.
7. Ibid., p. 105.
8. See for example Dennis P. McCann, *Christian Realism and Liberation Theology* (Maryknoll, N.Y.: Orbis, 1981), p. 138. Gutiérrez, in turn, refers to "imperfections and lacunae," ibid., p. 135.
9. Dussel, p. 325.
10. Dom Helder Camara, *Spiral of Violence* (London: Sheed and Ward, 1971).
11. Gustavo Gutiérrez, *The Power of the Poor in History* (London: SCM, 1983), p. 126.
12. Dussel, p. 232.
13. Dorr, pp. 209–12. See also John Paul II, *John Paul II in Mexico: His Collected Speeches* (London: Collins, 1979).
14. Gutiérrez, *The Power of the Poor in History*, p. 129.
15. Gregory Baum, "The Labor Pope in Canada," *The Ecumenist*, 23 (Jan-Feb. 1985), 17–23.
16. José Míguez Bonino, "Historical Praxis and Christian Identity," in *Frontiers of Theology in Latin America*, ed. Rosino Gibellini (Maryknoll, N.Y.: Orbis, 1979), p. 263.
17. See J. L. Segundo, "The Shift Within Latin American Theology," *Journal of Theology for Southern Africa*, 52 (Sept. 1985).
18. Ibid.
19. Gutiérrez, *The Power of the Poor in History*, pp. 131–65.
20. "Instruction on Certain Aspects of the 'Theology of Liberation,' " Southern African Catholic Bishops' Conference Series, no. 38: *Pastoral Action* (Pretoria, 1984).

SELECT BIBLIOGRAPHY

Dorr, D. *Option for the Poor: A Hundred Years of Vatican Social Teaching*. Maryknoll, N.Y.: Orbis, 1983.

Dussel, E. *A History of the Church in Latin America*. Grand Rapids: Eerdmans, 1981.
Gibellini, R., ed. *Frontiers of Theology in Latin America*. Maryknoll, N.Y.: Orbis, 1979.
Gutiérrez, G. *A Theology of Liberation*. Maryknoll, N.Y.: Orbis, 1973.
———. *The Power of the Poor in History*. London: SCM, 1983.
John XXIII. *The Encyclicals and Other Messages of John XXIII*. Washington, D.C.: TPS Press, 1964.
John Paul II. *John Paul II in Mexico: His Collected Speeches*. London: Collins, 1979.
McCann, D. P. *Christian Realism and Liberation Theology*. Maryknoll, N.Y.: Orbis, 1981.
Míguez Bonino, J. *Doing Theology in a Revolutionary Situation*. Philadelphia: Fortress, 1975.
———. *Toward an Introduction to Christian Political Ethics*. Philadelphia: Fortress, 1983.
Second General Conference of Latin American Bishops. *The Church in the Present-Day Transformation of Latin America in the Light of the Council*. Washington, D.C.: United States Catholic Conference, 1973.

MEDELLIN CONFERENCE, 1968

1. JUSTICE

DOCTRINAL BASES

The Latin American Church has a message for all men on this continent who "hunger and thirst after justice". The very God who creates men in his image and likeness, creates the "earth and all that is in it for the use of all men and all nations, in such a way that created goods can reach all in a more just manner", and gives them power to transform and perfect the world in solidarity. It is the same God who, in the fullness of time, sends his Son in the flesh, so that He might come to liberate all men from the slavery to which sin has subjected them: hunger, misery, oppression and ignorance, in a word, that injustice and hatred which have their origin in human selfishness.

Thus, for our authentic liberation, all of us need a profound conversion so that "the kingdom of justice, love and peace", might come to us. The origin of all disdain for mankind, of all injustice, should be sought in the internal imbalance of human liberty, which will always need to be rectified in history. The uniqueness of the Christian message does not so much consist in the affirmation of the necessity for structural change, as it does in the insistence on the conversion of men which will in turn bring about this change. We will not have a new continent without new and reformed structures, but, above all, there will be no new continent without new men, who know how to be truly free and responsible according to the light of the Gospel.

Only by the light of Christ is the mystery of man made clear. In the economy of salvation the divine work is an action of integral human development and liberation, which has love for its sole motive. Man is "created in Christ Jesus", fashioned in Him as a "new creature". By faith and baptism he is transformed, filled with the gift of the Spirit, with a new dynamism, not of selfishness, but of love which compels him to seek out a new, more profound relationship with God, his fellow man, and created things.

Love, "the fundamental law of human perfection, and therefore of the transformation of the world", is not only the greatest commandment of the Lord; it is also the dynamism which ought to motivate Christians to realize justice in the world, having truth as a foundation and liberty as their sign.

This is how the Church desires to serve the world, radiating over it a light and life which heals and elevates the dignity of the human person, which consolidates the unity of society and gives a more profound reason and meaning to all human activity.

[Source: Second General Conference of Latin American Bishops, *The Church in the Present-Day Transformation of Latin America in the Light of the Council* (Washington, D.C.: United States Catholic Conference, 1973).]

Doubtless, for the Church, the fullness and perfection of the human vocation will be accomplished with the definitive inclusion of each man in the Passover or Triumph of Christ, but the hope of such a definitive realization, rather than lull, ought to "vivify the concern to perfect this earth. For here grows the body of the new human family, a body which even now is able to give some kind of foreshadowing of the new age". We do not confuse temporal progress and the Kingdom of Christ; nevertheless, the former, "to the extent that it can contribute to the better ordering of human society, is of vital concern to the Kingdom of God".

The Christian quest for justice is a demand arising from biblical teaching. All men are merely humble stewards of material goods. In the search for salvation we must avoid the dualism which separates temporal tasks from the work of sanctification. Although we are encompassed with imperfections, we are men of hope. We have faith that our love for Christ and our brethren will not only be the great force liberating us from injustice and oppression, but also the inspiration for social justice, understood as a whole of life and as an impulse toward the integral growth of our countries.

POLITICAL REFORM

Faced with the need for a total change of Latin American structures, we believe that change has political reform as its prerequisite.

The exercise of political authority and its decisions have as their only end the common good. In Latin America such authority and decision-making frequently seem to support systems which militate against the common good or which favor privileged groups. By means of legal norms, authority ought effectively and permanently to assure the rights and inalienable liberties of the citizens and the free functioning of intermediary structures.

Public authority has the duty of facilitating and supporting the creation of means of participation and legitimate representation of the people, or if necessary the creation of new ways to achieve it. We want to insist on the necessity of vitalizing and strengthening the municipal and communal organization, as a beginning of organizational efforts at the departmental, provincial, regional and national levels.

The lack of political consciousness in our countries makes the educational activity of the Church absolutely essential, for the purpose of bringing Christians to consider their participation in the political life of the nation as a matter of conscience and as the practice of charity in its most noble and meaningful sense for the life of the community.

We wish to affirm that it is indispensable to form a social conscience and a realistic perception of the problems of the community and of social structures. We must awaken the social conscience and communal customs in all strata of society and professional groups regarding such values as dialogue and community living within the same group and relations with wider social groups (workers, peasants, professionals, clergy, religious, administrators, etc.).

This task of "concientización" and social education ought to be integrated into joint Pastoral Action at various levels.

The sense of service and realism demands of today's hierarchy a greater social sensitivity and objectivity. In that regard there is a need for direct contact with the different social-professional groups in meetings which provide all with a more complete vision of social dynamics. Such encounters are to be regarded as instruments which can facilitate a collegial action on the part of the bishops, guaranteeing harmony of thought and activities in the midst of a changing society. . . .

The Church—the People of God—will lend its support to the down-trodden of every social class so that they might come to know their rights and how to make use of them.

2. PEACE

DOCTRINAL REFLECTION

The above mentioned Christian viewpoint on peace adds up to a negation of peace such as Christian tradition understands it.

Three factors characterize the Christian concept of peace:

a) Peace is, above all, a work of justice. It presupposes and requires the establishment of a just order in which men can fulfill themselves as men, where their dignity is respected, their legitimate aspirations satisfied, their access to truth recognized, their personal freedom guaranteed; an order where man is not an object, but an agent of his own history. Therefore, there will be attempts against peace where unjust inequalities among men and nations prevail.

Peace in Latin America, therefore, is not the simple absence of violence and bloodshed. Oppression by the power groups may give the impression of maintaining peace and order, but in truth it is nothing but the "continuous and inevitable seed of rebellion and war".

"Peace can only be obtained by creating a new order which carries with it a more perfect justice among men". It is in this sense that the integral development of man, the path to more human conditions, becomes the symbol of peace.

b) Secondly, peace is a permanent task. A community becomes a reality in time and is subject to a movement that implies constant change in structures, transformation of attitudes, and conversion of hearts.

The "tranquility of order", according to the Augustinian definition of peace, is neither passivity nor conformity. It is not something that is acquired once and for all. It is the result of continuous effort and adaptation to new circumstances, to new demands and challenges of a changing history. A static and apparent peace may be obtained with the use of force; an authentic peace implies struggle, creative abilities and permanent conquest.

Peace is not found, it is built. The Christian man is the artisan of peace. This task, given the above circumstances, has a special character in our continent; thus, the People of God in Latin America, following the example of Christ, must resist personal and collective injustice with unselfish courage and fearlessness.

c) Finally, peace is the fruit of love. It is the expression of true fraternity among men, a fraternity given by Christ, Prince of Peace, in reconciling all men with the Father. Human solidarity cannot truly take effect unless it is done in Christ, who gives Peace that the world cannot give. Love is the soul of justice. The Christian who works for social justice should always cultivate peace and love in his heart.

Peace with God is the basic foundation of internal and social peace. Therefore, where this social peace does not exist there will we find social, political, economic and cultural inequalities, there will we find the rejection of the peace of the Lord, and a rejection of the Lord Himself.

THE PROBLEM OF VIOLENCE

Violence constitutes one of the gravest problems in Latin America. A decision on which the future of the countries of the continent will depend should not be left to the impulses of emotion and passion. We would be failing in our pastoral duty if we were not to remind the conscience, caught in this dramatic dilemma, of the criteria derived from the Christian doctrine of evangelical love.

No one should be surprised if we forcefully re-affirm our faith in the productiveness of peace. This is our Christian ideal. "Violence is neither Christian nor evangelical". The Christian man is peaceful and not ashamed of it. He is not simply a pacifist, for he can fight, but he prefers peace to war. He knows that "violent changes in structures would be fallacious, ineffectual in themselves and not conforming to the dignity of man, which demands that the necessary changes take place from within, that is to say, through a fitting awakening of conscience, adequate preparation and effective participation of all, which the ignorance and often inhuman conditions of life make it impossible to assure at this time".

As the Christian believes in the productiveness of peace in order to achieve justice, he also believes that justice is a prerequisite for peace. He recognizes that in many instances Latin America finds itself faced with a situation of injustice that can be called institutionalized violence, when, because of a structural deficiency of industry and agriculture, of national and international economy, of cultural and political life, "whole towns lack necessities, live in such dependence as hinders all initiative and responsibility as well as every possibility for cultural promotion and participation in social and political life", thus violating fundamental rights. This situation demands all-embracing, courageous, urgent and profoundly renovating transformations. We should not be surprised, theretore, that the "temptation to violence" is surfacing in Latin America. One should not abuse the patience of a people that for years has borne a situation that would not be acceptable to any one with any degree of awareness of human rights.

Facing a situation which works so seriously against the dignity of man and against peace, we address ourselves, as pastors, to all the members of the Christian community, asking them to assume their responsibility in the promotion of peace in Latin America.

We would like to direct our call in the first place, to those who have a greater share of wealth, culture and power. We know that there are leaders in Latin America who are sensitive to the needs of the people and try to remedy them. They recognize that the privileged many times join together, and with all the means at their disposal pressure those who govern, thus obstructing necessary changes. In some instances, this pressure takes on drastic proportions which result in the destruction of life and property.

Therefore, we urge them not to take advantage of the pacifist position of the Church in order to oppose, either actively or passively, the profound transformations that are so necessary. If they jealously retain their privileges, and defend them through violence, they are responsible to history for provoking "explosive revolutions of despair". The peaceful future of the countries of Latin America depends to a large extent on their attitude.

Also responsible for injustice are those who remain passive for fear of the sacrifice and personal risk implied by any courageous and effective action. Justice, and therefore peace, conquer by means of a dynamic action of awakening (concientización) and organization of the popular sectors, which are capable of pressing public officials who are often impotent in their social projects without popular support.

We address ourselves, finally, to those who, in the face of injustice and illegitimate resistance to change, put their hopes in volence. With Paul VI we realize that their attitude "frequently finds its ultimate motivation in noble impulses of justice and solidarity. Let us not speak here of empty words which do not imply personal responsibility and which isolate from the fruitful non-violent actions that are immediately possible.

If it is true that revolutionary insurrection can be legitimate in the case of evident and prolonged "tyranny that seriously works against the fundamental rights of man, and which damages the common good of the country", whether it proceeds from one person or from clearly unjust structures, it is also certain that violence or "armed revolution" generally "generates new injustices, introduces new imbalances and causes new disasters; one cannot combat a real evil at the price of a greater evil".

If we consider, then, the totality of the circumstances of our countries, and if we take into account the Christian preference for peace, the enormous difficulty of a civil war, the logic of violence, the atrocities it engenders, the risk of provoking foreign intervention, illegitimate as it may be, the difficulty of building a regime of justice and freedom while participating in a process of violence, we earnestly desire that the dynamism of the awakened and organized community be put to the service of justice and peace.

Finally, we would like to make ours the words of our Holy Father to the newly ordained priests and deacons in Bogota, when he referred to all the suffering and said to them: "We will be able to understand their afflictions and change them, not into hate and violence, but into the strong and peaceful energy of constructive works".

PASTORAL CONCLUSIONS

In the face of the tensions which conspire against peace, and even present the temptation of violence; in the face of the Christian concept of peace which has been described, we believe that the Latin American Episcopate cannot avoid assuming very concrete responsibilities; because to create a just social order, without which peace is illusory, is an eminently Christian task.

To us, the Pastors of the Church, belongs the duty to educate the Christian conscience, to inspire, stimulate and help orient all of the initiatives that contribute to the formation of man. It is also up to us to denounce everything which, opposing justice, destroys peace.

In this spirit we feel it opportune to bring up the following pastoral points:

To awaken in individuals and communities, principally through mass media, a living awareness of justice, infusing in them a dynamic sense of responsibility and solidarity.

To defend the rights of the poor and oppressed according to the Gospel commandment, urging our governments and upper classes to eliminate anything which might destroy social peace: injustice, inertia, venality, insensibility.

To favor integration, energetically denouncing the abuses and unjust consequences of the excessive inequalities between poor and rich, weak and powerful.

To be certain that our preaching, liturgy and catechesis take into account the social and community dimensions of Christianity, forming men committed to world peace.

To achieve in our schools, seminaries and universities a healthy critical sense of the social situation and foster the vocation of service. We also consider very efficacious the diocesan and national compaigns that mobilize the faithful and social organizations, leading them to a similar reflection.

To invite various Christian and non-Christian communities to collaborate in this fundamental task of our times.

To encourage and favor the efforts of the people to create and develop their own grass-roots organizations for the redress and consolidation of their rights and the search for true justice.

To request the perfecting of the administration of justice, whose deficiencies often cause serious ills.

To urge a halt and revision in many of our countries of the arms race that at times constitutes a burden excessively disproportionate to the legitimate demands of the common good, to the detriment of desperate social necessities. The struggle against misery is the true war that our nations should face.

To invite the bishops, the leaders of different churches and all men of good will of the developed nations to promote in their respective spheres of influence, especially among the political and financial leaders, a consciousness of greater solidarity facing our underdeveloped nations, obtaining among other things, just prices for our raw materials.

On the occasion of the twentieth anniversary of the solemn declaration of Human Rights, to interest universities in Latin America to undertake investigations to verify the degree of its implementation in our countries.

To denounce the unjust action of world powers that works against self-determination of weaker nations who must suffer the bloody consequences of war and invasion, and to ask competent international organizations for effective and decisive procedures.

To encourage and praise the initiatives and works of all those who in the diverse areas of action contribute to the creation of a new order which will assure peace in our midst.

CHAPTER 8

THE BLACK CHURCH

"Blackness" is a distinctive theological symbol of the contemporary theology debate with a potency equal to that of any model of church-state relations in the Christian tradition. Yet as the Committee of Black Churchmen put it in 1969, "black theology is a black theology of *liberation*," and as such it must be considered in the larger context of liberation theology as practiced in Latin America and elsewhere.[1] This broader affinity has resulted in a vigorous debate between North American black and Latin American liberation theologians which has, in turn, contributed significantly to the precise identity of black theology.

Black theology is, of course, not unique to North America. It has been affirmed and articulated in various parts of the world—not least of all in South Africa. Each of these places has drawn on its own context of oppression in doing its black theology. Yet each of these manifestations of black theology has to a greater or lesser extent also been in dialogue with the vast and changing resources of black theology in the United States. For this reason attention is given here to North American black theology as a dominant model of black theology.

To understand this theology, it is necessary to understand its particular context. "Black theology," writes Gayraud Wilmore, "was the intellectual spark that flew from the anvil of oppression upon which the black religious groups were hammered into existence." "Black people have done theology out of their guts, out of individual and collective experiences of struggle." "From the beginning black theology and black history have been inseparable."[2] Given this unity, the origins of black theology in its embryonic forms must be traced back to the time of slavery in the United States. This is precisely what James Cone does in his *The Spirituals and the Blues* and what Benjamin Mays does in *The Negro's God*. The reflective and critical articulation of black theology as a discipline must, however, be traced back to the second half of the 1960s.[3]

This process is commonly said to have started with a group of black clergy who met in Harlem in July 1966 during the height of violence and urban rebellion. The meeting marked what Gayraud Wilmore has described as a break with Dr. Martin Luther King's interpretation of black power as "a nihilistic philosophy born out of the conviction that the Negro can't win."[4] These clergy had, however, realized that the extensiveness of white power required a different response—precisely in order so that blacks might win. From this historic meeting came the "Black Power Statement" of 1966. It marked a turning point in the history of the black church's involvement with the state. To quote from the statement: "Powerlessness breeds a race of beggars. We are faced now with a situation where conscienceless power meets powerless conscience, threatening the very foundations of our nation." James Cone, in his first major publication three years later, stated that "freedom is not a gift but a right worth dying for."[5] A new era in church-state relations had been inaugurated in the country. The black church was ready to celebrate its blackness like never before. There was a new commitment to be black and to confront the white power structures of both church and state. Integration and absorption were rejected. Self-identity and confrontation were seen as the prerequisites to a reconciliation of equals.

This led to a variety of responses to white racism from black theologians during the early years of black theology. More than any other black theologian, Albert Cleage identified the gospel with black nationalism, Joseph Washington spoke of the necessity of violence to attain black liberation, while James Cone identified "some correlation between Black Power and Christianity," although never fully allowing that black power *is* the gospel. Deotis Roberts, in turn, saw the need to differentiate between "the religion of Black Power" and black theology.[6] Out of those early days of continuing debate and internal critique, in spite of differences to be found within the ranks of black theology, there grew a consensus on the nature of black consciousness and theological grounding of the black quest for liberation. The two concluding essays, one by Gayraud Wilmore and the other by James Cone, in their authoritative *Black Theology: A Documentary History, 1966–1979*, as well as the discussion on the "Strengths and Weaknesses in the Early Development of Black Theology" in Cone's latest book, *For My People*, provide a helpful analysis of this development. What has not changed over the years is what black theologians have called the "particularity" of their way of doing theology, grounded in a contextual or situational struggle for liberation. In North America as in many other parts of the world, this particularity is in addition to all else a struggle against overt and insidious forms of white racism.

This emphasis is shown with no more clarity than in the "Theology in the Americas 1975" conference held in Detroit. Since those days, the tone of the debate between North and Latin American liberation theologies has changed. There is also evidence that both black and Latin American theologians have allowed their social analysis and theological methods to be substantially influenced by the debate. The Detroit conference did, however, provide a clarity of definition which has distinguished black theology from other liberation theologies. It has also clarified the unique contribution of black theology to church-state relations in the West. Herbert Edwards's contribution in particular made that point.[7] Black people in the United States are an oppressed minority divested of their spiritual and cultural identity, which means that even the structures from which they are excluded are white and therefore unacceptable. It is this struggle against white values and structures which provides black theology with its appeal in a vast number of colonial and neocolonial countries around the world, since it provides a theological grounding to the struggle of black people to realize their spiritual identity as people. Edwards's point is that black theology has authentically emerged from among those who have personally experienced this alienation and oppression, whereas in his opinion "both the women's liberation movement and the Latin American movement are spearheaded by those *concerned about* the suffering of the powerless and the poor; . . . all of black theology's spokesmen are *among* the powerless and oppressed." The validity of this statement need not be debated here, although certainly women would argue that their liberation movement is grounded in their own experience of oppression. What is important is the self-understanding of black theologians. At the same conference, James Cone, in debate with Hugo Assmann, argued similarly that there is a particularity about black theology which those who are not black can never fully understand. It is this, he argued, which provides blacks with a radical insight into the historical and sociological roots of oppression—especially racism—which is denied to many others.[8] This kind of emphasis has, of course, provided the radical emphasis on black consciousness well beyond the limits of the United States, an emphasis with which most white governments around the world have yet to come to terms.

The Detroit debate had many facets which cannot be considered here. Some of the more polemical exchanges do, however, identify the specific emphasis of black theology at issue in church-state relations. The concern of the Latin American delegates was the lack of Marxist analysis in black theology as a tool for understanding the nature of black oppression as a particular manifestation of a worldwide oppressive system. Black theologians, in turn, found the failure to place sufficient emphasis on white racism to be such a fundamental oversight that the more "universal" approach of the Latin Americans did not speak to their own particular situation. This point is provocatively made by Edwards: "My skepticism about the utilization of Marxism as a tool of analysis in our context is due simply to this: In our history in this country, whether one was Marxist, non-Marxist, pre-Marxist, or post-Marxist, if he was white, he was also racist; if he was black, he was also oppressed."[9]

An equally provocative contribution came from the other side of the debate: "What is the goal of black liberation and black theology? If the goal of black liberation is to become an American citizen equal to all others, I think that perhaps black theology is an American theology. Are blacks to be part of an imperial nation that is the oppressor of other nations? That is imperial theology."[10] This particular aspect of the debate was, perhaps accurately, summarized in this way: "Black theologians are suspicious that liberation theology is a white theology; in the same way theologians in Latin America are suspicious that black theology is more American than black."[11] Ultimately the difference between these liberation theologies is their respective contexts. Their different understanding of the nature of oppression, at least in the sixties and seventies, gave to Latin American liberation theology a less particular appeal, while black theology addressed white racism with the integrity that enabled black people throughout the world to make it their own.

Since the Detroit conference a great deal has happened in both black and Latin American theological debate. Gayraud Wilmore makes the point that while racism is still the particular concern of black theology, there has since Detroit, in subsequent meetings between black and Latin American liberation theologians, been "a less exclusive introspective obsession with the American race problem than was characteristic of the earliest development of Black Theology." After two further meetings between the two groups of theologians—in Mexico City in 1977 and in Matanzas, Cuba, in 1979—James Cone allowed that "for the first time the question of racism was faced head-on by Latin American liberation theologians." He further pointed to the fact that while Marxism as a tool of analysis was more directly relevant to Latin American liberation theology, "some Black theologians are beginning to introduce Marxism into Black Theology."[12] More recently Cone has become still more outspoken in his support of Marxist analysis: "The challenge of Marxism emerges out of Marx's critique of religion, but the necessity of Marxism arises out of his critique of capitalism." "Christians need to apply Marx's method of analysis not only to the doctrines and practices of their churches but also and especially to the public pronouncements and practices of their government."[13] Cornel West has, in turn, set a program for the future of black theology by identifying the fundamental similarity between the social intent of Marxism and that of Afro-American religious thought and promoting a "dialogical encounter between prophetic Afro-Christian thought and progressive Marxist analysis."[14]

The identity of black theology is clearly a changing one. There is also a significant difference between the theological methods of, for example, James Cone and Cornel West who feature among the best known black theologians in North America today. Yet equally clear is the common agenda which they share. It is to enlist oppressed black people in North America and beyond its borders in a struggle to overthrow all forms of oppression. If the structures of this oppression were once perceived by black theologians to be primarily racial structures, today these structures are seen to be inherently linked to economic forms of oppression. This point is more consistently made in Cornel West's writing, although it is not absent from Cone's latest writings.[15]

In December 1984 a group of black theologians and church leaders produced a statement of consensus "concerning a common expression of faith of the One, Holy, Catholic and Apostolic Church." It affirms "blackness" as "one of God's gifts for the realization of the unity of the church and humankind at this critical stage of history." "As the church of the poor and oppressed" it shares "the humanizing experience of suffering and joy in struggle with others who want to work for a world of justice and equality for all." This is an important document, prepared by Gayraud Wilmore, in many ways the doyen of black theology in North America, on the basis of a conference held in Richmond, Virginia, as a contribution to the World Council of Churches' Faith and Order study on a common expression of apostolic faith. It includes several new and emerging themes in black theology, and it seemed right to include this most recent statement on black theology in this anthology as a complement to the 1966 document which marked the beginning of black theology as a critical discipline.

Black theology is unabashedly and inherently political theology. As such, the debate on church-state relations is central to its agenda. The political significance of this agenda is attested to by the sustained attack which black theologians have been subjected to by a variety of governments and ideologically right-wing groups in many countries. Ready to translate theology into a political program of action in support of oppressed black people, black theology has been rejected by most white dominated societies around the world. According to the Richmond statement, what black Christians are asking for is merely an expression of the apostolic faith which "must be multi-racial and multi-cultural rather than captive to any one race." The problem is that dominant classes have never found that easy language to accept. That is what makes black theology both an affront to white elite groups and appealing to black Christians around the world.

NOTES

1. Gayraud S. Wilmore and James H. Cone, eds., *Black Theology: A Documentary History, 1966–1979* (Maryknoll, N.Y.: Orbis, 1979), p. 101.
2. Ibid., pp. 2, 3.
3. James H. Cone, *For My People* (Johannesburg: Skotaville, 1985), pp. 5–30; Wilmore and Cone, pp. 15–21.
4. Wilmore and Cone, p. 15.
5. James H. Cone, *Black Theology and Black Power* (New York: Seabury, 1969), p. 12.
6. For a useful summary of these different early emphases in black theology see Allan Boesak, *Farewell to Innocence* (Maryknoll, N.Y.: Orbis, 1977), pp. 72–80.
7. In Sergio Torres and John Eagleson, eds., *Theology in the Americas* (Maryknoll, N.Y.: Orbis, 1976), pp. 177–91.
8. Ibid., pp. 354–55.
9. Ibid., p. 355.
10. Ibid., p. 356.
11. Ibid.
12. Torres and Eagleson, pp. 453, 603.
13. Cone, *For My People*, pp. 184, 186.
14. Cornel West, *Prophesy Deliverance* (Philadelphia: Westminster, 1982), pp. 14, 95–127.
15. See Cone, *For My People*, especially the final section, "Where Do We Go From Here?"

SELECT BIBLIOGRAPHY

Boesak, A. A. *Farewell to Innocence*. Maryknoll, N.Y.: Orbis, 1977.

Cone, J. H. *A Black Theology of Liberation*. Philadelphia: Lippincott, 1970.

———. *For My People: Black Theology and the Black Church*. Maryknoll, N.Y.: Orbis, 1984.

———. *The Spirituals and the Blues*. New York: Seabury, 1972.

Torres, S., and J. Eagleson, eds. *Theology in the Americas*. Maryknoll, N.Y.: Orbis, 1976.

West, C. *Prophesy Deliverance: An Afro-American Revolutionary Christianity*. Philadelphia: Westminster, 1982.

Wilmore, G. S., and J. H. Cone, eds. *Black Theology: A Documentary History, 1966–1979*. Maryknoll, N.Y.: Orbis, 1979.

NATIONAL COMMITTEE OF NEGRO CHURCHMEN, JULY 31, 1966

BLACK POWER

We, an informal group of Negro churchmen in America, are deeply disturbed about the crisis brought upon our country by historic distortions of important human realities in the controversy about "black power." What we see shining through the variety of rhetoric is not anything new but the same old problem of power and race which has faced our beloved country since 1619.

We realize that neither the term "power" nor the term "Christian conscience" is an easy matter to talk about, especially in the context of race relations in America. The fundamental distortion facing us in the controversy about "black power" is rooted in a gross imbalance of power and conscience between Negroes and white Americans. It is this distortion, mainly, which is responsible for the widespread, though often inarticulate, assumption that white people are justified in getting what they want through the use of power, but that Negro Americans must, either by nature or by circumstance, make their appeal only through conscience. As a result, the power of white men and the conscience of black men have both been corrupted. The power of white men is corrupted because it meets little meaningful resistance from Negroes to temper it and keep white men from aping God. The conscience cf black men is corrupted because, having no power to implement the demands of conscience, the concern for justice is transmuted into a distorted form of love, which, in the absence of justice, becomes chaotic self-surrender. Powerlessness breeds a race of beggars. We are faced now with a situation where conscienceless power meets powerless conscience, threatening the very foundations of our nation.

Therefore, we are impelled by conscience to address at least four groups of people in areas where clarification of the controversy is of the most urgent necessity. We do not claim to present the final word. It is our hope, however, to communicate meanings from our experience regarding power and certain elements of conscience to help interpret more adequately the dilemma in which we are all involved.

I. TO THE LEADERS OF AMERICA: POWER AND FREEDOM

It is of critical importance that the leaders of this nation listen also to a voice which says that the principal source of the threat to our nation comes neither from the riots erupting in our big cities, nor from the disagreements among the leaders of the civil rights movement, nor even from mere raising of the cry for "black power." These events, we believe, are but the expression of the judgment

---

[Source: Gayraud S. Wilmore and James H. Cone, eds., *Black Theology: A Documentary History, 1966–1979* (Maryknoll, N.Y.: Orbis, 1979).]

of God upon our nation for its failure to use its abundant resources to serve the real well-being of people, at home and abroad.

We give our full support to all civil rights leaders as they seek for basically American goals, for we are not convinced that their mutual reinforcement of one another in the past is bound to end in the future. We would hope that the public power of our nation will be used to strengthen the civil rights movement and not to manipulate or further fracture it.

We deplore the overt violence of riots, but we believe it is more important to focus on the real sources of the eruptions. These sources may be abetted inside the ghetto, but their basic causes lie in the silent and covert violence which white middle-class America inflicts upon the victims of the inner city. The hidden, smooth and often smiling decisions of American leaders which tie a white noose of suburbia around their necks, and which pin the backs of the masses of Negroes against the steaming ghetto walls—without jobs in a booming economy; with dilapidated and segregated educational systems in the full view of unenforced laws against it; in short: the failure of American leaders to use American power to create equal opportunity *in life* as well as *in law*—this is the real problem and not the anguished cry for "black power."

From the point of view of the Christian faith, there is nothing necessarily wrong with concern for power. At the heart of the Protestant reformation is the belief that ultimate power belongs to God alone and that men become most inhuman when concentrations of power lead to the conviction—overt or covert—that any nation, race or organization can rival God in this regard. At issue in the relations between whites and Negroes in America is the problem of inequality of power. Out of this imbalance grows the disrespect of white men for the Negro personality and community, and the disrespect of Negroes for themselves. This is a fundamental root of human injustice in America. In one sense, the concept of "black power" reminds us of the need for and the possibility of authentic democracy in America.

We do *not* agree with those who say that we must cease expressing concern for the acquisition of power lest we endanger the "gains" already made by the civil rights movement. The fact of the matter is, there have been few substantive gains since about 1950 in this area. The gap has constantly widened between the incomes of non-whites relative to the whites. Since the Supreme Court decision of 1954, de facto segregation in every major city in our land has increased rather than decreased. Since the middle of the 1950s unemployment among Negroes has gone up rather than down while unemployment has decreased in the white community.

While there has been some progress in some areas for equality for Negroes, this progress has been limited mainly to middle-class Negroes who represent only a small minority of the larger Negro community.

These are the hard facts that we must all face together. Therefore we must not take the position that we can continue in the same old paths.

When American leaders decide to serve the real welfare of people instead of war and destruction; when American leaders are forced to make the rebuilding of our cities first priority on the nation's agenda; when American leaders are forced by the American people to quit misusing and abusing American power; then will the cry for "black power" become inaudible, for the framework in which all power in America operates would include the power and experience of black men as well as those of white men. In that way, the fear of the power of each group would be removed. America is our beloved homeland. But, America is not God. Only God can do everything. America and the other nations of the world must decide which among a number of alternatives they will choose.

II. TO WHITE CHURCHMEN: POWER AND LOVE

As black men who were long ago forced out of the white church to create and to wield "black power," we fail to understand the emotional quality of the outcry of some clergy against the use of the term today. It is not enough to answer that "integration" is the solution. For it is precisely the nature of the operation of power under some forms of integration which is being challenged. The Negro Church was created as a result of the refusal to submit to the indignities of a false kind of "integration" in which all power was in the hands of white people. A more equal sharing of power is precisely what is required as the precondition of authentic human interaction. We understand the growing demand of Negro and white youth for a more honest kind of integration; one which increases rather than decreases the capacity of the disinherited to participate with power in all of the structures of our common life. Without this capacity to *participate with power*—i.e., to have some organized political and economic strength to really influence people with whom one interacts—integration is not meaningful. For the issue is not one of racial balance but of honest interracial interaction.

For this kind of interaction to take place, all people need power, whether black or white. We regard as sheer hypocrisy or as a blind and dangerous illusion the view that opposes love to power. Love should be a controlling element in power, not power itself. So long as white churchmen continue to moralize and misinterpret Christian love, so long will justice continue to be subverted in this land.

III. TO NEGRO CITIZENS: POWER AND JUSTICE

Both the anguished cry for "black power" and the confused emotional response to it can be understood if the whole controversy is put in the context of American history. Especially must we understand the irony involved in the pride of Americans regarding their ability to act as individuals on the one hand, and their tendency to act as members of ethnic groups on the other hand. In the tensions of this part of our history is revealed both the tragedy and the hope of human redemption in America.

America has asked its Negro citizens to fight for opportunity *as individuals* whereas at certain points in our history what we have needed most has been opportunity for the whole group, not just for selected and approved Negroes. Thus in 1863, the slaves were made legally free, as individuals, but the real question regarding personal and group power to maintain that freedom was pushed aside. Power at that time for a mainly rural people meant land and tools to work the land. In the words of Thaddeus Stevens, power meant "40 acres and a mule." But this power was not made available to the slaves and we see the results today in the pushing of a landless peasantry off the farms into big cities where they come in search mainly of the power to be free. What they find are only the formalities of unenforced legal freedom. So we must ask, "What is the nature of the power which we seek and need today?" Power today is essentially organizational power. It is not a thing lying about in the streets to be fought over. It is a thing which, in some measure, already belongs to Negroes and which must be developed by Negroes in relationship with the great resources of this nation.

Getting power necessarily involves reconciliation. We must first be reconciled to ourselves lest we fail to recognize the resources we already have and upon which we can build. We must be reconciled to ourselves as persons and to ourselves as an historical group. This means we must find our way to a new self-image in which we can feel a normal sense of pride in self, including our variety of skin color and the manifold textures of our hair. As long as we are filled with hatred for ourselves we will be unable to respect others.

At the same time, if we are seriously concerned about power then we must build upon that which we already have. "Black power" is already present to some extent in the Negro church, in Negro fraternities and sororities, in our professional associations, and in the opportunities afforded to Negroes who make decisions in some of the integrated organizations of our society.

We understand the reasons by which these limited forms of "black power" have been rejected by some of our people. Too often the Negro church has stirred its members away from the reign of God in *this world* to a distorted and complacent view of *an otherworldly* conception of God's power. We commit ourselves as churchmen to make more meaningful in the life of our institution our conviction that Jesus Christ reigns in the "here" and "now" as well as in the future he brings in upon us. We shall, therefore, use more of the resources of our churches in working for human justice in the places of social change and upheaval where our Master is already at work.

At the same time, we would urge that Negro social and professional organizations develop new roles for engaging the problem of equal opportunity and put less time into the frivolity of idle chatter and social waste.

We must not apologize for the existence of this form of group power, for we have been oppressed as a group, not as individuals. We will not find our way out of that oppression until both we and America accept the need for Negro Americans as well as for Jews, Italians, Poles and white Anglo-Saxon Protestants, among others, to have and to wield group power.

However, if power is sought merely as an end in itself, it tends to turn upon those who seek it. Negroes need power in order to participate more effectively at all levels of the life of our nation. We are glad that none of those civil rights leaders who have asked for "black power" have suggested that it means a new form of isolationism or a foolish effort at domination. But we must be clear about why we need to be reconciled with the white majority. It is *not* because we are only one-tenth of the population in America; for we do not need to be reminded of the awesome power wielded by the 90% majority. We see and feel that power every day in the destructions heaped upon our families and upon the nation's cities. We do not need to be threatened by such cold and heartless statements. For we are men, not children, and we are growing out of our fear of that power, which can hardly hurt us any more in the future than it does in the present or has in the past. Moreover, those bare figures conceal the potential political strength which is ours if we organize properly in the big cities and establish effective alliances.

Neither must we rest our concern for reconciliation with our white brothers on the fear that failure to do so would damage gains already made by the civil rights movement. If those gains are in fact real, they will withstand the claims of our people for power and justice, not just for a few select Negroes here and there, but for the masses of our citizens. We must rather rest our concern for reconciliation on the firm ground that we and all other Americans *are* one. Our history and destiny are indissolubly linked. If the future is to belong to any of us, it must be prepared for all of us whatever our racial or religious background. For in the final analysis, we are *persons* and the power of all groups must be wielded to make visible our common humanity.

The future of America will belong to neither white nor black unless we Americans work together at the task of rebuilding our cities. We must organize not only among ourselves but with other groups in order that we can, together, gain power sufficient to change this nation's sense of what is *now* important and what must be done *now*. We must work with the remainder of the nation to organize whole cities for the task of making the rebuilding of our cities first priority in the use of our resources. This is more important than who gets to the moon first or the war in Vietnam.

To accomplish this task we cannot expend our energies in spastic or ill-tempered explosions without meaningful goals. We must move from the politics of philanthropy to the politics of metropolitan development for equal opportunity. We must relate all groups of the city together in new ways in order that the truth of our cities might be laid bare and in order that, together, we can lay claim to the great resources of our nation to make truth more human.

IV. TO THE MASS MEDIA: POWER AND TRUTH

The ability or inability of all people in America to understand the upheavals of our day depends greatly on the way power and truth operate in the mass media. During the Southern demonstrations for civil rights, you men of the communications industry performed an invaluable service for the entire country by revealing plainly to all ears and eyes, the ugly truth of a brutalizing system of overt discrimination and segregation. Many of you were mauled and injured, and it took courage for you to stick with the task. You were instruments of change and not merely purveyors of unrelated facts. You were able to do this by dint of personal courage and by reason of the power of national news agencies which supported you.

Today, however, your task and ours is more difficult. The truth that needs revealing today is not so clear-cut in its outlines, nor is there a national consensus to help you form relevant points of view. Therefore, nothing is now more important than that you look for a variety of sources of truth in order that the limited perspectives of all of us might be corrected. Just as you related to a broad spectrum of people in Mississippi instead of relying only on police records and establishment figures, so must you operate in New York City, Chicago and Cleveland.

The power to support you in this endeavor *is present* in our country. It must be searched out. We desire to use our limited influence to help relate you to the variety of experience in the Negro community so that limited controversies are not blown up into the final truth about us. The fate of this country is, to no small extent, dependent upon how you interpret the crises upon us, so that human truth is disclosed and human needs are met.

RICHMOND CONSULTATION, 1984

TOWARD A COMMON EXPRESSION OF FAITH: A BLACK NORTH AMERICAN PERSPECTIVE

INTRODUCTION

A special consultation on one common expression of the Apostolic faith from the perspective of Black Christians in the U.S. brought together representatives of several Black denominations at Virginia Union University in Richmond, Virginia, December 14-15, 1984. The consultation included representatives of the Black constituencies of several predominantly White denominations. In some cases the participants were delegated by denominational administrative headquarters; others were representatives of their communions without official appointment. The content of this document, therefore, stands upon the authority of the consultation alone and does not purport to convey the agreements of an ecclesiastical council of Black churches.

This document, moreover, does not pretend to be an exhaustive response to the Apostolic Faith Study or a formal statement of the major themes of the Black theology movement that has evolved in North America in recent years. The Richmond Consultation, sponsored by the Commission on Faith and Order of the National Council of Churches in the U.S.A., attempted to convey to the World Council of Churches and to other interested organizations what we, a group of Black theologians and church leaders from across the United States, perceive as a general consensus among us concerning a common expression of the faith of the One, Holy, Catholic and Apostolic Church. In the several working papers we discussed and in this report we seek to add to the worldwide ecumenical study of a common expression of Apostolic Faith the distinctive perceptions and insights that come out of the historic experience of Black Christians in North America.

As Black academics, denominational officials, pastors and lay leaders we speak out of more than two hundred years of suffering and struggle as "the stepchildren of church history" who have been ridiculed, ignored and scorned by the White churches of both Europe and North America. The truth of the gospel among our people, that some have sought to suppress or disregard, burns like fire in our bones. In any discussion of one common expression of faith we have no alternative other than to make certain clear affirmations to those churches that directly or indirectly participated in and benefited from the rape of Africa that resulted in the exploitation and oppression of an African Diaspora wherever Black people are found.

[Source: Statement by the Richmond Consultation of the Commission on Faith and Order of the National Council of Churches, December 1984.]

We speak, however, from our own particular locus in the so-called First World, where we are less than twelve percent of the population of what is the richest and most powerful nation in the world. But inasmuch as our churches and people have never truly shared that wealth and power, we speak as a marginated Black community with a unique understanding of White racism and with strong affinities with the so-called Third World.

In this document, from an historic consultation in Richmond, Virginia, we make bold to declare that God, our Creator, has condescended through Jesus Christ, our Liberator, by the power of the Holy Spirit, our Advocate and Comforter, to convey, preserve and enhance the faith of the Apostles among the despised and alienated African American people of the United States. We commend to all who may be concerned the fruit of our prayerful reflection on the themes of the Unity, Holiness, Catholicity and Apostolicity of the Church of Jesus Christ as we join with you in search of a common expression of the faith.

UNITY

We affirm that the unity of the Church not only expresses the unity of the Triune God, but is also a sign of the unity of humankind that holds together in one family the diversity of all races and cultures. In the economy of God each "tribe", each ethnic group and culture has its own vocation to bring its gift to the full household of faith. Notwithstanding the effort of some White Christians to disdain the contribution of Black folk to the faith and to its impact upon the institutions of the American Church and society, we declare that the meaning of Blackness as cultural and religious experience edifies and enriches the universal message of the Christian faith. Blackness, in the religions of the African Diaspora, is a profound and complex symbol of a diversified yet united experience: servitude and oppression, faithfulness through suffering, identification with the exclusion, martyrdom and exaltation of Jesus as the Oppressed One of God who triumphs over enemies, a passion for justice and liberation, the exuberance of Black faith and life, rejoicing in the Risen Lord in Pentecostal fervor and in service to the "least" of Christ's brothers and sisters.

White Christians have too often treated unity as if it were only a spiritual reality. We believe that unity must not be spiritualized, but manifested in concrete behavior, by doing justice and loving service to one another. The cost of unity in the Church is repentance and affirmative discipleship (i.e., action). We have, therefore, a profound hermeneutical suspicion about any movement for unity that is dominated by North Atlantic attitudes and assumptions. We have observed that when our White brothers and sisters speak of unity they often mean being together on terms that carefully maintain their political, economic and cultural hegemony. Unity is frequently confused with "Anglo-conformity"—strict adherence to premises and perspectives based upon the worldview and ethos of the North Atlantic community with its history of racial oppression. Christian unity is, however, based upon the worship of a common Creator who is no respecter of persons, obedience to a common lawgiver and Judge whose commandment to break every yoke is not abrogated by the gracious justification of sinners, and upon participation in the earthly mission of a common Redeemer, the sharing of whose suffering and ordeal makes us truly one, though of many races and cultures.

Blackness is one of God's gifts for the realization of the unity of the Church and humankind at this critical stage of history. It has been preserved by God as a cultural and religious inheritance of the Black churches of Africa, the Caribbean, and North and South America since the mission of the Ethiopian eunuch to the upper Nile Valley after his baptism by the Evangelist. It is rooted in the divine revelation to our African ancestors who lived before the Christian era. It has traditionally celebrated the goodness of the Almighty Sovereign God and the goodness of creation. It has emphasized the humanity of the historical Jesus, i.e., his earthly life, example, teaching, suffering, death and resurrection. It confesses belief in the humanity of Jesus together with the oneness with God, the Creator, and the Holy Spirit, but understands that humanity in non-sexist terms rather than being exclusively of the male gender. It identifies with the shadow of death that falls upon the Cross as a symbol of suffering and shame, yet crowned with light inexpressible in the victory of the resurrection.

Thus, the meaning of unity is related to the meaning of Blackness for the Afro-American Church and points to its vocation as a church of the poor and oppressed who claim liberation in the Black Messiah of God and want to share the humanizing experience of suffering and joy in struggle with others who want to work for a world of justice and equality for all. Unity is possible only when there is acceptance of suffering under Christ's work of liberation and when there is commitment to his mission.

HOLINESS

The Black churches of North America made a unique contribution to the Holiness and Pentecostal movements of world Christianity at the beginning of this century. The Black Pentecostal obsession with the text of Hebrews 12:14 "strive . . . for the holiness without which no one will see the Lord" (RSV), and Black leadership of the interracial Azusa Street Revival of 1906–1908 in Los Angeles created the groundwork for modern Pentecostalism—the most remarkable religious movement among the oppressed communities of the world since the Awakenings of the 18th and 19th centuries. Although most African American churches did not originate from Pentecostalism or the Azusa Street Revival most of them have been influenced by the Pentecostal emphasis upon the *ruach/pneuma* of God in their conception of the Person and Work of the Holy Ghost. Their understanding of holiness as a process of moral perfection is rooted in the necessity of a personal encounter with God that is manifested in both the ecstasy of congregational worship and the praxis of social justice.

Afro-American spirituality has to do with self-transcendence and is unembarrassed by displays of sincere emotion, but it is also related to faith and action in the world. The Holy Spirit moves, therefore, in the real world of everyday life, in the sanctuary and the realm of secular affairs. The Holy Spirit is not an abstraction of Trinitarian theology but participates dynamically in what it means to be a human being and to suffer and struggle with the assurance of victory in this world as in the world to come. The distinctiveness of the Black religious experience is that theology is experienced before it is thought. Moreover, holiness in the paradoxical sense of transcendence and existential involvement in the world, must accompany the act of "doing theology". Holiness is a criterion of the Church's theological authenticity. It creates a theology that is "hummed, sung and shouted" in Black churches, and contrary to White fundamentalism, has more to do with how Christians treat one another than how strictly they hold to Biblical literalism or ascetic life styles.

On the other hand, holiness in the Black Church is not coterminous, as in some expressions of White liberalism, with frenetic social activism. Personal encounter with God as a prerequisite of sanctification and commitment to social transformation are both necessary, but the obligation to "give glory to God," to "glorify the holiness of God" is an essential corollary of the obligation to be engaged in "building the Kingdom" that continues to be frustrated by racism and oppression. The Black Church is sustained by prayer and praise. It exists in and for the glory of God and not the glorification of human institutions. We know that to struggle in the midst of the world is to experience the glory of God that is thwarted by racism and oppression, but we also know that we need to praise God in the sanctuary in order to struggle! One of our Spirituals has the refrain: "Have you got good religion?" The response is, "Certainly, certainly, certainly Lord!". *Good* religion is, therefore, understood to make worldly things that were formerly dubious better, and *bad* religion ruins the best of all possible worlds where there is no acknowledgement of God's presence. Without holiness no one shall see the Lord.

Ultimately, the holiness of the Church is a work of the Holy Spirit. We affirm that the One, Holy Church cannot exist apart from ministries of justice and liberation. We also affirm that true liberation is inseparable from deep spirituality. The intimate involvement of Christians with the Holy Spirit is expressed first in worship that celebrates the manifest presence, goodness and glory of God and moves from the sanctuary to the streets where it empowers the world to goodness, transfigures its wretchedness and need, and creates the quality of life that is symbolized by the nimbus that encircles the throne of God.

CATHOLICITY

Although Afro-American Christians have customarily been denied equal partnership in the *koinonia* of Christ, we nevertheless affirm the universality of the Christian faith. Universality in the Black religious experience has to do with the particular reality of people in concrete situations that are dissimilar but inseparable. Afro-American churches share with all who confess Jesus Christ the conviction of the universality of God's love "from each to all in every place . . .". We recognize solidarity in creation, sin and redemption with all human beings and seek with them to make catholicity visible by overcoming humanly erected barriers between people.

We deplore the fact that the profession of universality has actually meant that the norms of what is considered acceptable to the Church had to originate in the West. For years anything that White Christians in Europe and North America did not interpret as catholic lay outside the realm of true faith and proper order. Such assumptions distorted the truth about Jesus Christ and permitted the gospel to be used to divide people rather than free them to express the fullness of the faith in their own cultural styles and traditions. It also robbed the White churches of the opportunity to correct their own deficiencies.

In the late 18th and early 19th centuries, Black preachers were refused ordination and their congregations were not considered in good order. Not until rebellious White Methodist and separatist Baptist clergy defied custom and accepted them as duly constituted ministers and churches did Black Christianity become legitimate in the eyes of Whites. To this day Black churches have protested any semblance of alienation or exclusion on account of race, class or discriminatory educational qualifications. Unfortunately the struggle for sexual equality has lagged behind in many Black churches and Black women need greater support in their resistance to subordination.

From the perspective of the Richmond consultation, catholicity has to do with faith in Jesus Christ, baptism, and continuing in "the apostles' teaching and fellowship" and in "the breaking of bread and the prayers" (Acts 2:42). No person, group or institution that meets these requirements should be excluded from the visible Church or relegated to an inferior status by human authority, ecclesiastical or secular. The sin of racism, sexism and classism that refuses or discourages the fellowship of African Independent church or Black Holiness and Pentecostal denominations, among others in various parts of the world, must be repudiated as denying the catholicity of the Body of Christ.

Catholicity, in our view, also demands a persistent critique of and challenge to the economic and political status quo; for those churches that benefit from the existing international order too easily assume its normative character and become self-appointed guardians of what is supposedly good for all. Thus, many North American conservatives and fundamentalists speak of American democracy as "Christian" and oppose Christian socialists as irregular at best and heretical at worst. Similarly, the "Moral Majority" in the U.S. supports "constructive engagement" with apartheid in South Africa as consistent with universal reason and the welfare of "all people of good will". In this view anti-communism becomes the test of universal Christian ethics and those who do not fall into line are considered sectarian, ignorant and contrary to the mainstream White American tradition which is regarded as the universal faith of the Church.

Jesus Christ challenged the assumption that faith in God or salvation was limited to the scribes and the Pharisees, or the rich and powerful. Instead he empowered sinners, the poor, strangers and women. His demonstration of catholicity was to open his arms to all who would be saved. His Church today can do no more or less.

APOSTOLICITY

We affirm the Apostolic tradition that recognizes the transmission of authentic faith down the centuries by all those who have faithfully lived it, whether or not they have been officially designated as apostles. We believe that, "What does not teach Christ is not Apostolic, even if it was taught by Peter or Paul; again what preaches Christ, this is Apostolic, even when preached by Judas, Annas, Pilate and Herod." We recognize, therefore, the apostolicity of what we have received from our slave ancestors who, though "unlearned and ignorant" men and women, reinterpreted the distorted Christianity they received from the slavemasters and passed down to succeeding generations of Black believers the story of Jesus who was "the strong Deliverer", "the rose of Sharon, the bright and morning star", "the king who rides on a milk-white horse", "the dying lamb", "the Lord who's done just what he said", "the Balm in Gilead", and "the help of the poor and needy, in this lan' . . .". But we acknowledge the importance of the Apostolic tradition being engaged and not merely passed on. Apostolicity must be lived out in the context of contemporary events. It is not the recitation of past formulations, but the living of the present commandments of the Risen Lord.

In the final analysis the test of apostolicity is the experiencing of the life, death and resurrection of Jesus Christ in our daily struggle against demonic powers that seek to rob us of our inheritance as children of God redeemed by the blood of Jesus Christ. Our deeds, more than our creeds, determine whether we have fully received and acted upon the faith of the apostles.

Jesus said, "If you continue in my word, you are truly my disciples, and you will know the truth, and the truth will make you free" (John 8:31, 32). Afro-American Christians look to the words and acts of the Jesus of history for the Apostolic teaching as well as to the mystery of the Christ of faith. We take seriously the life, ministry and teaching of Jesus as the One who identified with the marginated of society and continues to identify with them. It is in the Black Church's historic identification with marginality that Jesus is appropriated as the Black Messiah, the paradigm of our existential reality as an oppressed people and the affirmation of our survival and liberation.

Finally, for Black Christians, the search for an expression of the Apostolic faith must be multi-racial and multi-cultural rather than captive to any one race, sex, class or political ideology. The Church and the ecumenical movement must no longer submit to domination by social, economic or intellectual elites. The faith once delivered to the apostles by Jesus Christ is for the whole world and must be capable of being transmitted and responded to by all.

CONCLUSION AND RECOMMENDATIONS

1. The Afro-American Christian tradition, embodied particularly in Black Baptist, Methodist and Pentecostal Churches, but continuing also in other Black-led Protestant and Roman Catholic congregations, has been and continues to be an indigenous expression of the faith of the apostles in North America.

2. The Richmond Consultation affirms the World Council of Churches study "Towards the Common Expression of the Apostolic Faith Today" and is committed to work with the WCC and other ecumenical bodies toward the unity we seek.

3. We invite the other churches participating in the Faith and Order move-

ment to give greater study and recognition to how God has maintained the continuity of the Apostolic Faith primarily through the oral character and noncreedal styles of the African American tradition expressed in worship, witness and social struggle.

4. We urge the other member churches of the National and World Council Commissions on Faith and Order to take note of the unity of faith and practice that the Black Church has historically emphasized and to engage the Faith and Order movement in greater involvement in the struggle against racism and all forms of oppression as an essential element of the Apostolic confession.

5. We call upon Black churches in North America, the Caribbean and in Africa to confess boldly the faith we received from the Apostles, despite every effort made to distort and falsify it, and joining with us who were a part of this historic consultation in Richmond, to intensify their involvement in the Faith and Order movement by sharing the "gift of Blackness" with those of other traditions.

6. Finally, we urge that this report be published and widely disseminated by the Commission on Faith and Order of the WCC as a study document and that Black Christians all over the world be encouraged to initiate interracial discussion groups for the consideration of its content and implications for the ecumenical movement; and that the result of such dissemination and discussion be reported back to the Commission on Faith and Order by cooperating national councils.

CHAPTER 9

THE CHURCH IN AFRICA

The African church has always been both divided and united. Its division is a reflection of the divided church which sent missionaries to Africa. Its unity is grounded in "the social ties binding the African Christian to his extended family and clan [which] have always been stronger than the forces of separation that arise from membership in different denominations . . . a unity that [has] roots in the traditional past."[1] It is this reality which motivates Gabriel Setiloane to say: "Perhaps this is the reason for the lack of fervour for so-called 'organic unity.' There are other forces at work in the African soul that continue to reduce the dividedness of the church as planted in Africa from abroad."[2] It is this division and unity which have influenced church-state relations in Africa over the years and which have been manifested, from the time of its inception, in the hopes and the fears of the All Africa Conference of Churches (AACC) regarding the prophetic role of the church in relation to African nationalism.

The planting of the church in Africa started quietly enough with the Ethiopian Orthodox Church in the fourth century. The major thrust of mission activity was, however, to coincide with the hunger for empires, the termination of slavery, and the "scramble for Africa" following the discovery of precious metals and other natural resources. Throughout this period the churches in Africa were the colonial outposts of churches in Europe, Britain, the United States, and elsewhere. The identity of the African churches was provided by foreign missionaries, while what M'Timkulu calls the "quiet intrusions of African culture, nibbling away at the new institutions of change," was always a feature of the African church.[3] At the same time, by the end of the last century African independent churches were beginning to emerge in protest against the foreign identity of the mission churches throughout the continent.

In time the foreign missions became churches, although often still dominated by and certainly financially dependent on foreign church bodies. National church councils were established in Ghana in 1929, Kenya in 1942, and what was Northern Rhodesia in 1944. Continentwide consultation was, however, almost nonexistent. When the International Missionary Council (IMC) met in

Jerusalem in 1928, only five African countries were represented. Two of the delegates were African, and both were laymen. Even when a special conference on Africa was called two years earlier in Belgium only seven of the seventy-nine delegates were African. At the IMC Tambaram Conference in 1938, priority was given to the participation of "people from the younger churches," and although seventeen African countries were represented by seventeen African delegates, there were also eighteen white missionaries in the African delegation. When therefore the first All Africa Christian Conference met in Ibadan in January 1958, it could claim to be "a much more widely representative gathering of Africans than had ever before come together for any purpose." It had brought together representatives from all the major Protestant churches from twenty-five countries, and 96 of the 144 delegates were African.[4] "Here for the first time the Church in Africa found its voice."[5] The conference appointed a provisional committee to create an African regional ecumenical body. "The days of 'Christianity by proxy' were over."[6] At the same time the political "winds of change" were blowing across the continent, the spirit of African nationalism was being experienced in every capital, and Pan-Africanism was being affirmed as an ideology to counter imperialism.

In this milieu the first assembly of the AACC met in Kampala in April 1963. High on the agenda were the issues of colonialism, African religiosity, independence, cultural identity, unity, the church's prophetic task, and nationalism. A statement formulated from addresses delivered by Richard Andriamanjato of Madagascar and Ndabaningi Sithole of Southern Rhodesia and the report of the assembly on "The Church and Nationalism"—both of which are appended—capture the milieu of the assembly as well as the commitment of the African church to political responsibility. The independence process and democracy were affirmed as the "only outcome of that long and laborious process in which God has often intervened to permit man to achieve a greater liberty and a greater enlightenment." Nationalism was identified as "a necessary phase" to the awakening of a people and "indispensable in constructing a new country and a new continent." Violent and nonviolent protest against civil authority were seen as "sure symptoms of an evil social order." "People do not embark on . . . [such] campaigns for the sheer joy of it," said Andriamanjato. "If the powers-that-be have no moral conscience to which non-violence can appeal, it would be unrealistic to expect people to continue to use non-violence as a political weapon." The report of the assembly, however, condemned "the indiscriminate use of violence." Looking beyond the independence process, the assembly recognized that "in the interests of cohesion and national unity, the one-party system might be acceptable," but warned against "the inherent danger of dictatorship." The political obligation of the church was stated to be "the Watchman in the midst of the nation."

The theme of the assembly was itself indicative of the African church's priorities: "Freedom and Unity in Christ." The cry of the times was for freedom from both external control and internal submission. M'Timkulu, the South African educator and first general secretary of the AACC, who did so much to articulate the goals of the conference in its early years, said precisely this in reporting on the need to be engaged "not in mere criticism of the past performance of the white missionaries but in a soul-searching self-examination of African Christians themselves."[7] The postcolonial period, in turn, demanded a sense of unity which had been so severely disrupted by divisive missionary policy, imperialist rivalry, and internal political divisions.[8] This was a unity which was demanded beyond the structures of the church. For this the colonial-missionary phase of the church had not made adequate preparation. To quote Adrian Hastings: "A large number of missionaries and African Christians doubtless believed that there was little or no connecting link between their religious concerns and the present political state or future constitutional prospects of the lands where they lived and worked."[9] "African Christians," warned M'Timkulu, ". . . are growing impatient with so-called non-participation in politics or political neutrality of Protestant churches and missions." "Freedom from colonialism thus means the freedom and obligation of all nationals to participate in the nation's political life." For him, a commitment to unity had to do with national self-identity and nation building. It meant sharing in the birth pangs of the new nations of Africa. It meant being "involved on the ground floor in the task of nation-building."[10] For Rev. A. Adegbola, then principal of the Immanuel Theological College in Ibadan, "the African revolution is a triumph of Christian ideals, which have been taught and preached, worked for and fought for."[11] This commitment to the liberation process in Africa was, however, never blind submission. Again M'Timkulu places this commitment in perspective:

> In its relationship with the nation, the Church has a positive function which is far more important than its negative one of rejecting certain actions of the State. The main duty of the Church is not to say "No" when the occasion demands it: its objective must always be to create conditions within the State under which the need to say "No" would never arise. . . . This means further that when the Church must protest against some action as being un-Christian it would be more seemly to adopt the attitude not of a judge on the bench, but one of identification with the culprit in the dock, because the entire Church membership is included in the nation whose action the Church condemns.
>
> But while the main function of the Church is clear and is not disputed, it still has the negative duty of saying "No" to certain proposals made by the State.[12]

Clearly there is also evidence that the African church has often lived up to this position while at other times it has become entrapped in the morass of political intrigue.[13] It must suffice to cite only two of the better known events of church-state confrontation: Kwame Nkrumah's claim to be Saviour, in appropriating the term *Osajefu*, was rejected as outright heresy, while Idi Amin was confronted with a team of churchmen who went "to speak the prophetic truth of God" to him.[14] The AACC has also addressed itself to the continuing liberation struggle in Africa. Canon Burgess Carr, the general secretary of the AACC in 1974, caused a stir in many church circles around the world when, in arguing that "any outright rejection of violence is an untenable alternative for African Christians," he submitted that "in accepting the violence of the cross, God, in Jesus Christ, sanctified violence into a redemptive instrument for bringing a fuller human life." In the same speech he made an important distinction between what he called "selective violence" employed by the liberation movements fighting minority regimes in southern Africa, and the "collective vengeance" employed by these regimes against the oppressed people of the region. The relevant sections of this speech are reprinted below. Today it is more common to talk of "institutional violence" and "counter violence," but Burgess Carr forced Christians in the southern African region to address the problem of violence in a decisive manner. African Christians have always understood the Programme to Combat Racism of the World Council of Churches, and especially the decision of this program to supply humanitarian aid to liberation movements, in a way that First World churches have never understood it. It was the solid support for this program by the African churches, after the Nairobi Assembly of the WCC heard strong criticism of the aid to these movements, which gave it a new lease on life in the face of sustained attacks from some European, American, and South African churches. The AACC has also been involved in negotiations to end the Nigeria-Biafra civil war, in pre- and post-independent Zimbabwe, in the Horn of Africa, and elsewhere. The difficulties facing a people's church committed to both sharing in the revolution and nation building while exercising an incisive prophetic ministry are, however, at times almost impossible to cope with. At times it takes an extraordinary effort to distance oneself sufficiently from one's own people in order to speak the decisive word and engage in the creative action which can bring life and hope to a situation which needs renewal, while its leaders cannot politically afford to admit it.

On occasions, a church which understands itself to be theologically obliged to be intimately involved in the affairs of its people becomes actively involved in the failure of the state. On other occasions it becomes so embroiled in its own internal affairs, arguing that this is the best contribution it can make to national unity, that it neglects its prophetic task in relation to the state. And simply because the church is composed of fragile human beings who are not exempt from any of the temptations or anxieties which hold others captive, it more often than not simply fails in its duty. In such a case the church itself needs a prophet, and Desmond Tutu is on record as having reminded this church of its obligation to address itself to the violation of human rights in Africa.[15]

The church of Africa, like the church elsewhere, has failed to achieve all that it has sought to accomplish. There are inherent difficulties involved in being both pastor and prophet to a young nation—not least of all when such a nation is part of a continent that has until very recently existed not for itself, but for the benefit of other nations who saw Africa as no more than a repository of raw materials. The debate on the function of the church in independent Africa is no more than a few decades old. There is no specific model for church-state relations in Africa, and many of the traditional doctrines of church and state considered in this volume continue to function in Africa through the persistence of different denominations and Western traditions. There is only the beginning of a quest for an authentic doctrine of church and state applicable to the African continent.[16] This freshness at once gives to this quest a vibrancy which is lacking from the centuries old debate in Europe and elsewhere while it also means that there are presumably mistakes to be made and lessons to be learned. The history of the

Christian church shows, however, that time is no adequate inoculation against errors and failure. The struggle for theological integrity in relationship between what Míguez Bonino calls identification and truth, or what could be regarded as nation-building and prophetic distance, is something that each church in each new generation is obliged to work out for itself.[17] Karl Barth would argue that the prophetic ministry of the church is ultimately, even when it is not readily apparent, the most significant contribution which the church can make to nation-building.

NOTES

1. D. M'Timkulu, *Beyond Independence* (New York: Friendship Press, 1971), p. 22.
2. G. Setiloane, "The Ecumenical Movement in Africa: From Mission Church to Moratorium," in Charles Villa-Vicencio and John W. de Gruchy, eds., *Resistance and Hope: South African Essays in Honour of Beyers Naudé* (Grand Rapids: Eerdmans, 1985), p. 147.
3. M'Timkulu, p. 23.
4. T. A. Beetham, *Christianity and the New Africa* (London: Pall Mall Press, 1967), pp. 171–72.
5. *Drumbeats From Kampala. Report of the First Assembly of the* AACC (London: Lutterworth, 1963), p. 5.
6. Setiloane, p. 140.
7. D. M'Timkulu, *Africa in Transition: The Challenge and the Christian Response* (Geneva: AACC and WCC, 1962), p. 19.
8. O. U. Kalu, "Church Unity and Religious Change in Africa," in E. Fashde-Luke, R. Gray, A. Hastings, and T. Tasie, eds., *Christianity in Independent Africa* (London: Rex Collings, 1978), pp. 164–75.
9. A. Hastings, A *History of African Christianity: 1950–1975* (Cambridge: Cambridge University Press, 1979), p. 21.
10. M'Timkulu, *Africa in Transition*, pp. 15–27.
11. See "A Christian Interpretation of the African Revolution," AACC *Bulletin*, June 1965, pp. 111–22.
12. M'Timkulu, *Africa in Transition*, p. 25.
13. Hastings, pp. 86–107; 131–158.
14. Setiloane, p. 143.
15. Bishop Tutu spoke this message to African church delegates at the Vancouver Assembly of the WCC in 1984 and again on a recent visit to African countries.
16. See among others Kofi Appiah-Kubi and Sergio Torres, eds., *African Theology En Route* (Maryknoll, N.Y.: Orbis, 1979). For an interesting comment on the political quest for an African model of independence see Aaron Tolen's "Political Ethics in Africa," in K. Srisang, *Perspectives on Political Ethics* (Geneva: WCC, 1983), pp. 45–49.
17. José Míguez Bonino, *Doing Theology in a Revolutionary Situation* (Philadelphia: Fortress, 1975), p. 145.

SELECT BIBLIOGRAPHY

Appiah-Kubi, K., and S. Torres, eds. *African Theology En Route.* Maryknoll, N.Y.: Orbis, 1974.

Fashde-Luke, E., R. Gray, A. Hastings, and G. Tasie, eds. *Christianity in Independent Africa*. London: Rex Collings, 1978.

Hastings, A. A *History of African Christianity: 1950–1975*. Cambridge: Cambridge University Press, 1979.

Rotbert, R. I., and Ali A. Mazrui, eds. *Protest and Power in Black Africa*. New York: Oxford University Press, 1970.

Shorten, A. *African Culture and the Christian Church*. London: Geoffrey Chapman, 1973.

THE KAMPALA ASSEMBLY OF THE ALL AFRICA CONFERENCE OF CHURCHES, 1963

FREEDOM AND UNITY IN THE NATION

LIBERTY AND ANARCHY IN THE COLONIAL ERA

Liberation is always an anarchical action in regard to the established authority. Liberation is first negative before becoming constructive. The greatest problem of the passage from liberation to liberty consists precisely in how to get through the anarchic situation of liberation to arrive at a new order where the liberty that has been acquired might reign.

We must recognize that political independence is not simply a judicial framework that favours the practice of liberty but that it can become a new form of oppression of one part of the population by another part. Political independence, which in judicial terms means the end of thc colonial regime, does not necessarily mean the death of all the pernicious forces which had acted throughout the colonial period. The presence of these forces under a number of forms, especially cultural and economic ones, within Africa, changes the state of liberty into a state of anarchy, meaning a state in which there is a continuous denial of the authority in power and of established order. This manifests itself in two ways. If the authorities in power try to install a truly democratic system that is different from the preceding colonial system, those who have been used to the previous system are not going to admit that they have been won over, and they are going to look for all possible ways to sow disorder and anarchy in the country in order to make their own hegemony last longer.

If the authorities in power do nothing but continue the habits created during the colonial period and have only changed the colour of these in places of responsibility (putting a docile black man in the place of a white man), the false independence which results from this can only stir up opposing forces that would try to bring about a real independence.

If we go back a bit into the colonial period, what do we notice? Colonialization was a revolution in that it was a radical change of relationship among individuals and especially a radical change in the scale of values. The black man was initiated into the western notions of liberty and justice but he was made to feel that that liberty and that justice were not for him. He was taught how to distinguish the truth. But the truth about himself as a black man, the truth of his everyday life, was never accepted by the standard imported from the outside. The colonial state is a profoundly anarchical thing for each individual in his human relationships. Individuals, who found themselves faced with the fundamental rupture introduced by colonialism, and who now existed on a social basis that had the cohesion and traditional organization of African society sapped from it,

---

[Source: *Drumbeats from Kampala: Report of the First Assembly of the* AACC (London: Lutterworth, 1963). This text was prepared by the Assembly on the basis of addresses delivered by Richard Andriamanjato and Ndabaningi Sithole.]

began degenerating into poor opportunists grasping for gain and detaching themselves little by little from their roots in the African nation to become unadapted persons who were more or less happy.

The large mass of the African population became conscious of the fact that they were made up of extremely unhappy unadapted persons, and they went ahead to create a new order, a new force, an anticolonialist force. Nationalism won the popular feeling more and more. With the aid of certain leaders who made themselves the interpreters of the will of the mass of the people for liberty, nationalism took on that form we have all known, which is the struggle against all foreign domination, struggle for the right of people to decide their own affairs. African nationalism is characterized essentially as a liberation from colonialism. Its logical end will be national independence and after that the liquidation of the vestiges of colonialism. Nationalism presents itself thus as a liberating force opposing the anarchy of consciences. In the face of colonial despotism it is a unifying force that requires a certain amount of discipline from each individual in order to get satisfaction for its claims.

DEMOCRACY IN AFRICA

Democracy appears in the history of humanity as the liberation of men from certain other categories of individuals among them who abused their social position and strength to exploit unjustly the mass of people in general. Quite naturally the democratic revolution does not always and in all places appear the same—each country in its own history has gone through the experience of democratic evolution. But democracy requires a fairly well-advanced intellectual, civic and moral evolution in order to be true, real and efficient. The rule of everyone is not necessarily the rule of each individual. If despotism was able to maintain its rule by force, democracy demands a higher type of discipline which amounts to each individual facing up to his responsibility.

It is precisely at this point that the democratic situation becomes problematic on a continent such as Africa. This does not mean that Africans are incapable of living in a democracy or of organizing a democratically coherent nation, but in the difficulties in which some of our leaders now find themselves enmeshed, certain of our governments have a tendency to establish a democracy by force rather than by a free adherence of the population to the national objectives. From this fact democracy risks becoming profoundly degraded before it is fulfilled.

We often see a glaring contradiction between the luxury which some leaders provide for themselves and the misery suffered by their people. This contradiction itself looks anti-democratic to the simplest peasant. And besides, we must add that some of those who govern have consciences that are little touched by concern for public matters or by an honesty required in the administration of the public affairs of a democracy. Is it not significant that some of our government leaders tackle the hard task of the decolonization of people's minds by trying to have them practise a policy of austerity? Thus a man such as Mr. Dialle Saifoulaye was able to say when he was president of the National Assembly in Guinea: "We must put an end to corruption and the race for personal enrichment of our leaders". Thus also President Senghor of Senegal started again on a policy of breaking down the system of privileges that had existed until then for civil servants.

We must recognize that in some of our countries the independence which they have recovered has not measured up to the hopes that moved the people to fight for their liberty. For many, liberation had no other significance than the end of a sordid exploitation of man by man. Unfortunately, in some of our countries, the colour of the man responsible for the destiny of the nation changed; but his method did not. The building of our different democracies does not always appear to be based upon a sharpened and enlightened sensitiveness to the masses of our population.

THE GOSPEL IS REVOLUTIONARY

For most of the time in most of our countries, the history of the Church follows the same plan as the history of colonization, and the question we have the right to ask is this: has it always been faithful to its calling, to its reason for being, to the Gospel which it had to preach and which it must always preach?

We wonder if even in the preparation of its own native leaders the Church did not fall in step with the colonial power. It contented itself hastily to train preachers who were to take the echo of the "good news" from village to village without giving them a sufficient intellectual and spiritual training so they could question for themselves. Are we not at this very time witnessing the disquieting results of such an action? Because at a moment when the African Church is, so to speak, called upon to fly with its own wings, we see a lack of trained leadership in the religious domain that is just as important as that in the public domain. We would ask ourselves the reason for this deficiency, and the least answer we can give is this: The Church did not know how to disengage itself from the embrace of colonialism, and sometimes it betrayed its mission by being too preoccupied with making that mission succeed.

Should we not remind ourselves that the Church ought to present itself to the world as the messenger and the witness of that revolution which began in accomplishing that supreme act which reconciled man to God. This revolution penetrates all levels of society: in all aspects of our life as men, in every dimension, individual, family, national, international. Christ upset all the traditional ideas that had congealed the Judaic church into a state of inconsequential immobility, and not unite in the same salvation and under one grace all men, whatever might be their colour, their station in life or their social rank.

It seems to us that democracy is only the outcome of that long and laborious process in which God has often intervened to permit man to achieve a greater liberty and a greater enlightenment. If our democracy remains imperfect because it is human, nevertheless do we not see in it certain principles which agree in quite a striking and logical fashion with that glory and honour which God wanted to give to man in regenerating him?

Without going further, let us simply accept the fact that democracy appears in the history of mankind as a favourable framework for the preaching of the Gospel because it emphasizes equality, the dignity of man, and his right to pursue happiness. These are notions which we find in other forms in the Christian conception of man, notions that are based on one foundation, which is love. But the Church, in the difficulties which it has often encountered, has not always been able to remain faithful. The deliberate refusal of certain colonial administrators, who were supposedly Christian, to recognize the real foundation and root of the Christian religion, ended by sowing an opaque mistiness in the mind of the native, a mistiness which many missionaries have been tempted not to dispel. We have already said that the Christian religion is in itself a revolution, and also that it is for fear that the black man would become aware of his value and his place in the world that the supporters of the colonial order invented a theology of colonization based, not on submission, but servitude. They were not afraid to quote the Epistles of Paul where he speaks of servants and masters or of governors and those who are governed, but they did not get to the root of the matter in understanding that love which effectively disperses all differences of the human condition.

If a preacher, pastor or priest who had especially deepened his religious faith, was moved by the Holy Spirit to give himself to a truly sincere witness for truth, for justice among men and for love of neighbour, he was always considered as a dangerous man, as a revolutionary. The colonial power tried to silence him by any means it could. There is nothing astonishing in this, for a true witness of Christ will always remember the words of the Master: "Behold I sent you out as sheep in the midst of wolves; so be wise as serpents and innocent as doves. Beware of men; for they will deliver you up to councils and flog you in their synagogues, and you will be dragged before governors and kings for my sake, to bear testimony before them and the Gentiles." (Matt. 10:16-18) Moreover, did not the apostles live in their own flesh the suffering of those who know the truth? They, by love of their neighbour, wanting at any cost to communicate that truth to others, encountered incomprehension, malice, perfidy, prison, torture, and even martyrdom.

The unfortunate thing for the Church is that it did not witness enough. It did not work closely enough with those civil servants who still thought themselves to be at least to a certain extent Christian. It did not know how to remind them of the limits of their power and of the danger of their abuses, not only for them but also for the civilization of which they were the representatives and for the Church of which they were members.

The nationalistic phase is a necessary phase, otherwise, how can we awaken the people where they are to an enthusiasm that is indispensable in constructing a new country or a new continent?

However, the Church is afraid that the democracy we are talking about will implant an idea of humanity that will replace God. And with a conservative reaction that is a human tendency, the Church prefers to remain in a state of meaningless quiescence, and that quiescence can only be betrayal in the face of the living word that has been entrusted to it. We can always advance a possible justification of the Church, that the Church is caught between two completely opposite ideas. It is aware, on the one hand, that democracy can be a form of government favourable to the development of man in liberty, equality and love.

On the other hand, it realizes how imperfect human democracy is and how incapable it is of respecting effectively the principles on which it is based. Thus the hesitation of the Church that can neither feel completely at ease in the company of democracy nor bring itself to preach any other form of government. And yet, is not that the commitment that is waiting for the Church?

Democracy, in order to succeed, calls for greater honesty, greater scrupulousness, on the part of its citizens and all those responsible for the destiny of the nation. And to come to the point where Christian conscience is forced to exert itself, democracy can only completely succeed when it is based on the love of neighbour which necessitates the conception and construction of a society where men no longer exploit men by their covetousness, their ruthlessness in the grasp of money, their unconscious murder of those who are not helped in the midst of their need and misery.

THE PARTY SYSTEM

An important point which we cannot ignore when we speak of democracy is the insistence on a party or parties and their role in the nation. In speaking of this, one cannot generalize, knowing full well that the party systems of the different nations are not alike. In one case it is considered wise, or even indispensable, to impose a single party or a unified party; in another case, it has been thought wise to let several parties coexist. It is not a matter of resolving the question of the advisability of a single party. What we want to examine is the phenomenon of the creation of parties in that progression toward a democracy which becomes gradually more genuine and more important. A party must not be conceived merely as an instrument taking over power. The party must exist and function in the interests of the nation. In a democratic order, we have said, a greater awareness and a stricter discipline are required of every citizen. The party is thus only a school for leaders, a school of civic education. Thus, given the complexity of our contemporary situation and the influence of so many factors in the evolution of the nations, it is inevitable but necessary to have a national structure based upon one or more parties. But people must know that the party is only a school. Discipline is essential in every school, and a programme is even more necessary. Those who attend must be willing to set aside their prejudices and their conceits in order to accept humbly those new ideas which are favourable to the development of a country.

It is natural for a Christian to ask himself questions about parties. As is true in the party, he too, in the interest of discipline, is obliged to accept decisions that are not always compatible with his deep convictions. This fact has often motivated the Christian to steer clear of politics, considered as dishonest or even Satanic. But if the Christian refrains from engaging in this unceasing struggle toward a better existence and a greater liberty, who will engage in it? If Christians are afraid to soil their hands, have they forgotten that Christ was not afraid to contaminate Himself in the eyes of his contemporaries by eating with tax-collectors, free women and others considered to be in a permanent state of sin by the Jewish doctors? Sin, permeating the world, won over every realm of man's life, including the political realm. Christ in His great desire to save the world broke through every sphere of life, including the political sphere, in order to announce liberation and liberty. The Christian's hesitation is, in reality, the visible sign of the irrelevance of his faith. For, if his faith were really strong he would have the courage to witness in every realm, even in political parties. It is the Christian's duty to be the "salt of the earth". His participation in the various political organizations must be a witness, and that witness is to Christ himself, Christ the conqueror of the world, the loving Christ who draws all men unto Himself.

VIOLENCE AND NON-VIOLENCE

The clash between African nationalism and Christianity comes in the area of methods used in the struggle for the liberation of the African people. Christianity has tended to advocate non-violence whereas African nationalism has tended to espouse violence. Because African nationalism has upheld violence as a method of bringing about the new social order for which millions of people yearn, the supporters of Christianity have not hesitated to brand it as an evil force. Some have actually called it a "satanic manifestation". In retaliation, the supporters of African nationalism have described Christianity as the white man's religion, the deeper meaning being that it oppresses the African, and therefore no African should have anything to do with it. Since this sharp difference is due to the method of bringing about better conditions, it is important that we take a more realistic view with regard to each of these methods.

There are, broadly speaking, two methods through which African nationalism can realize itself. One is the way of non-violence and the other is the way of violence. The former presupposes that peaceful and non-violent demonstrations and protest marches can appeal to the moral conscience of the powers-that-be, and hence bring about a desirable social order. Violence, on the other hand, takes over where non-violence fails. If the powers-that-be have no moral conscience to which non-violence can appeal, it would be unrealistic to expect people to continue to use non-violence as a political weapon. Human nature tends to use only that which produces desired results. It should be noted that both non-violence and violence aim at one and the same thing, a just social order. Too often Christians, by their silence on the burning issue of social justice, and by their active support of a social order that denies millions of people their birthright, have helped the seeds of violence to spread, and have hindered the course of non-violence. Both violence and non-violence are sure symptoms of an evil social order which requires improvement.

The history of African nationalism is marked with violence in varying degrees, and this violence comes at the point where common sense has failed. The history of Christianity also shows violence from the first to the twentieth century. In this respect, Christianity cannot boast over African nationalism. The two are equally guilty of violence. People do not embark on non-violence and violence campaigns for the sheer joy of it, but do so seriously in order to remove social injustice. This, basically, is the essence of both non-violence and violence.

Those who live in Central Africa have witnessed the burning of churches by some desperate supporters of African nationalism. Does this burning down of these churches prove that the African people as such are against Christianity? In some cases school buildings have also been burned down. Does this mean that Africans are against education as such? Beerhalls have also been attacked. Does this mean that Africans do not like beer? It would appear that these acts prove only one thing, and that is the desperation of the perpetrators rather than their dislike for these things. When the Israelis blew up bridges on what has become known as "the night of the bridges", this did not suggest that they did not like bridges, but that they did not like their subject status. Who knows whether these acts against church buildings were in fact an effort to remind the Church to speak up and stop supporting an unjust social order?

THE KAMPALA ASSEMBLY OF THE ALL AFRICA CONFERENCE OF CHURCHES, 1963

THE CHURCH AND NATIONALISM

Nationalism cannot be defined only in terms of opposition to foreign domination; it is present in countries even where self-rule has been achieved. Nationalism should rather be defined as the common desire of a people to work together for their emancipation from any form of bondage, whether colonial, economic, social or racial.

Four forms of nationalism can be distinguished:

(1) Nationalism working towards freedom and independence, as, for example, in those countries still subject to colonial rule, or the rule of a minority group.

(2) Nationalism working towards the creation of national cohesion (particularly important in newly independent nations).

(3) Nationalism of older nations which, even when repudiated, manifests itself through the attempt to conserve the traditional way of life.

(4) Nationalism which evolves into an ideology of totalitarian character, e.g. National Socialism.

From this brief analysis it appears that two factors play an essential role in the understanding of nationalism: the notion of history as a past to preserve, or a task to undertake; and the concept of authority as the goal of emancipation and the responsibility of nationhood. These two notions are also essential in Christian theology: history is the object of God's rule and the place of our obedience; authority is exercised by God over men and nations and entrusted to men within the nations. Historical movements such as nationalism can be the instrument of the Divine Rule or the manifestation of the human revolt against that rule. It is therefore necessary to define the limits within which nationalism may be a form of Christian obedience and beyond which it may become demonic.

Nationalism must aim at the establishment of freedom and concern for power for its own sake. It must work for the unity and cohesion of the nation instead of serving the power of one group at the expense of others. This does not mean the exclusion of a strong authority, but it does mean that the strong authority must not work for the exclusive benefit of one group of the community. Nationalism should be open to, and concerned for the establishment of international solidarity instead of expressing the will to dominate other nations.

THE QUESTION OF THE USE OF FORCE

One of the essential and urgent issues raised for Christians in relation to nationalism is the use of violence. Several different convictions were expressed. Some believe that Christians should refuse violence under all circumstances, and witness

---

[Source: *Drumbeats from Kampala: Report of the First Assembly of the* AACC (London: Lutterworth, 1963).]

only through suffering. Some believe that the use of violence as an ultimate course of action is legitimate when the established authorities are instruments of injustice and oppression, and provided that such violence is exercised in an organized fashion and is likely to lead to the establishment of a better order of justice and freedom. All agreed that the indiscriminate use of violence for the achievement of collective vengeance or personal ends is never justified.

THE QUESTION OF THE POLITICAL PARTY

There was general agreement that the Christian should share the national aspirations of his people. For this he should be involved in the struggle for their emancipation. But this involvement should always be enlightened and informed by a Christian conscience. The political party is the instrument by which national aspirations are expressed. The political party should be the place where the dialogue between those in authority and the people can be effectively engaged. We recognize that in the interests of cohesion and national unity the one-party system might be acceptable; but the inherent danger of dictatorship must be guarded against.

THE TASK OF THE CHURCH

In the face of nationalism we see the task of the Church as three-fold:

(1) The Church is called to be a "Watchman" in the midst of a nation, prophetically witnessing to the Divine demands for truth, justice and peace, and against all forms of oppression, discrimination, injustice and corruption. For this prophetic task the Church has a duty to be well-informed of what is happening in the nation.

(2) The Church is called to witness to the reconciliation which is in Jesus Christ in the midst of those situations where political leaders, parties, nations, and power blocs, are in conflict.

(3) The Church is called to witness by her own life and example the love and peace which she commends to the nations. Herein is the challenge to the Church to take seriously the problem of her own disunity.

BURGESS CARR

ON VIOLENCE

I believe that the distinction made . . . between "violence" and "collective vengeance" is still valid, and offers a framework for determining our attitude to the struggle of the liberation movements. The selective violence employed by the liberation movements is in sharp contrast to "collective vengeance" perpetrated by the South African, Rhodesian and Portuguese regimes in Africa. Thus, any outright rejection of violence is an untenable alternative for African Christians.

If for no other reasons, we must give our unequivocal support to the liberation movements, because they have helped the Church to rediscover a new and radical appreciation of the Cross. In accepting the violence of the cross, God, in Jesus Christ, sanctified violence into a redemptive instrument for bringing into being a fuller human life.

Moreover, the truth of the claim made by the liberation movements that their struggle is not only to free the Black man, but especially the White man, has been borne out by recent developments in Portugal. The Portuguese themselves have been the first to benefit from the fruits of a decade of armed struggle. . . .

It remains to be seen whether and to what extent Africans in Mozambique, Angola and Guinea Bissau will reap the fruits of the enormous toll in human life going back five centuries. One thing is certain. No arrangement short of full and complete freedom from Portuguese political domination and economic exploitation can be an alternative to continuing the armed liberation struggle.

[Source: excerpt from an address delivered in Lusaka, May 14, 1974.]

CHAPTER 10

THE EASTERN ORTHODOX CHURCH

For Eastern Orthodoxy, worship, being the mystical union between Christ and his church, is "the centre of the life of the church, but it should also determine the whole life of every Christian. 'Every tree that does not bear good fruit is cut down and thrown into the fire. Thus you will know them by their fruits. Not everyone who says to me "Lord, Lord" shall enter the kingdom of heaven' (Matt. 7:20-23)."[1] For the Orthodox church, witness and worship are an inherent unity. "Two inseparable movements take place in the action of liturgy, which in fact constitute the rhythm of mission: the gathering and the sending forth."[2]

For me, this rhythm was passionately witnessed at a gathering of South African, American, and Middle East theologians in Beirut in December 1980. While we shared in a final meal together, one of the persons who had helped prepare the food was shot in a street of that city. Metropolitan George Khodre of Mount Lebanon, who presided at the meal, spoke these memorable words: "Gentlemen, before we depart I must inform you that we today did indeed eat the body of Christ and drink his blood, because one who prepared this meal lies dead. Let us now depart and join the higher liturgy of the poor in the streets." It is this theological unity between what the West so easily separates—the sacred and secular—which surely constitutes the most profound challenge of the East to the church-state debate in the West.

To understand this emphasis in worship is to understand the Orthodox attitude to life in all its complexities, including church-state relations. The centrality of worship with a spirituality related to the social events of life and the theological grounding of the Christian witness in liturgy has in recent decades reawakened the interest of Western Christians in Eastern Orthodoxy. Worship in the Orthodox tradition is an all-inclusive activity that engages a person "in spiritual poetry, in church music, in iconography, with body and soul," an "involvement of the entire human nature—and not only of reason—in glorifying God." It "reaches not only man as an individual, but his entire environment." "The reverse is also true; one should take account of the fact that each Christian who actively participates in worship may bring into it cultural heritage and personal creativity." With this the concerns and contributions of a particular community are integrated into the life and worship of the church. Worship is also the act of integrating the present generation of the church into the life of past generations as recalled in the Christian tradition. This is, however, always more than "simply a memorial"; it is "a living reality."[3] In this sense, it is in liturgy that the Orthodox Christian quite literally lives, moves, and has his or her being. All of life is worship. It is the *raison d'etre* of the church.

Orthodoxy can be understood as a community of faith which deals with the question of the presence of God iconographically; that is to say, an icon is a symbol which mediates the presence of God by way of suggestion and hint but not by way of analysis and rationalistic definition. Icons are the signs of the mystery of divine presence and not explanations for it. This iconographic way of thinking and responding helps explain the nature of all of life as an act of worship of the divine presence symbolized in the iconographic foci of the liturgy. Aesthetic sensitivity is therefore as much a part of the practice of worship as rational deduction. Hence, the importance of human imagination.

From this flows an important dimension of the Orthodox social witness. Metropolitan Khodre, already mentioned, has stressed the need to put aside "the dizzy impatience for effectiveness." There is an explicit rejection of "any attempt at amalgamating Christianity with any ideology that gives Christianity a systematized character and prevents it from being a foretaste of the Kingdom." Metropolitan Emilianos Timiadis of Sylibria has, in turn, identified the essence of the Christian witness to the world to be the monk as the "permanent dissident, a living reminder of the demands of God, master of the world, and herald of the finality of the world, the parousia."[4] Yet, to quote Sergius Bulgakov, "side by side with heroes of monastic asceticism we find day-labourers, pious soldiers, kings and princes, mothers and wives; here is direct testimony to the almost equal value of diverse ways. Each should be monk and ascetic in his heart. . . . [This] makes impossible the excessive attachment to this world."[5] The apparent contradiction, at least from a Western perspective, between the Christian ideal of dissidence and being a soldier or a king is partly resolved in the Orthodox category of "interior renunciation." To this we must return, but first it is necessary to understand this emphasis within the socio-political context of the history of the Orthodox church.

In 324, a little more than a decade after the Edict of Milan granted tolerance to the Christian church, Constantine decided to move the capital of the Roman Empire to the site of the Greek city, Byzantium, which was renamed Constantinople. As time passed, the wealth and power of Constantinople grew as the influence of Rome declined. It became the center of Greek culture and a major center of the Christian church, although Rome would continue to enjoy primacy of honor among the ancient sees. By the year 700, Christianity was in the process of losing to Islam large areas which had been "Christian" for hundreds of years. The patriarchates of Alexandria, Antioch, and Jerusalem lost immediate access to the rest of the church, with Rome and Constantinople sharing what was left between them. The effect of this loss was initially to draw these two rival centers together, resulting in a form of unity—but one that could not overshadow the dominant forces of schism: divergent customs and cultures, political separation, and doctrinal differences. In 1054 came the Great Schism which marked the separation of the Orthodox church in the East from the Roman Catholic church in the West.

Any possibility of healing this schism came to an end with the capture of Constantinople during the fifth Crusade in 1204. The breach was complete. Then in 1453 Constantinople fell to the Turks, and the Church of the Holy Wisdom became a mosque. The Byzantine Empire had come to an end, but not the Orthodox faith. In the meantime the political influence of the Russian Tsar was growing rapidly. With the fall of Constantinople he came to be regarded by some as the direct successor to the Orthodox emperor, and Moscow soon became the center of the Orthodox faith. Eventually the Russian Empire would collapse and Russian Orthodoxy (like Greek Orthodoxy at the fall of Byzantium) would need to redefine its identity, while never losing sight of its sense of continuity with the church of the past.

To do justice to a discussion on church-state relations in Orthodoxy, it would be necessary to consider these relations within several chronological periods, in much the same way as we have done with the Western history of church-state relations. Several obvious divisions suggest themselves: the Byzantine period, the Ottoman Empire, the Russian Empire, the period of the nation-states of the nineteenth century, Orthodoxy in Marxist countries, and the contemporary forms of Orthodoxy in the West. But such an exercise is beyond the confines of an essay of this kind, and we will therefore focus our attention on some contemporary Orthodox perspectives and statements.

At no time in its history had Orthodoxy regarded itself as subordinate to the state, but neither had there been a distinct separation of church and state. At the level of theory at least, the one had not sought to gain absolute control over the other. This is generally known as the "principle of synergy." Fotios Litsas defines this concept as follows: "It is to be distinguished from a sharp division of church and state, on the one hand, and a total fusion of church and state on the other hand. It recognizes and espouses a clear demarcation between church and state, while calling for a co-operative relationship between the two." He continues, "in the practical area of political life, it is nearly always impossible fully to realize the principle of synergy, but the church has supported a range of attitudes which allow it to become involved in the political process on the one hand, while retaining its clear distinction from and transcendence to it, on the other."[6] Bulgakov, in turn, suggests that the fall of the Russian Empire in fact showed the extent to which the emperor had influenced the church, recognizing how vulnerable all theories of church-state relations are, including the principle of synergism, to the power of the totalitarian state: "The Orthodox Church has twice lost its Orthodox Emperor, once by the fall of the Byzantine and again, in our day, by the fall of the Russian Empire. Under these circumstances it has returned to the state of things which existed before Constantine."[7] What must be conceded is that in contrast to its former position of official prominence, the church had returned to a minority and politically powerless situation, which was in some ways reminiscent of the pre-Constantinian period.

With the Russian Revolution, the political function of the church, grounded in worship and permanent dissidence in the form of an interior renunciation of the existing social order, came to be reaffirmed in a new and decisive manner. Orthodox Christians were forced to see themselves as a minority in a non-Christian environment. Meyendorff, in fact, shows that the process of ecclesiastical renewal and separation from state control had already been underway for more than a decade by the time of the Bolshevik Revolution in 1917. "Thus, far from seeming to uphold the *ancien regime,*" the Orthodox church, he argues, "boldly asserted its right to independence from the state." At the same time, "the Church had reformed itself internally, but its attitude toward the various phases of the Russian Revolution was determined pragmatically by the mental outlook and conscience of its rulers."[8] This was no match for the intense and disciplined activity of the Communist party, which persecuted the popular clergy and the mass of believers who did not identify with the cause of the revolution. It was this that "succeeded in transforming the Orthodox Church into a martyred Church."[9] In time, suggests Meyendorff, both the party and the church opted for an unstable form of coexistence, each looking to the future rather than the present as its time for victory. The party waited for religion to wither away as the process of communist re-education took its toll, while the church waited in anticipation for the coming kingdom.[10]

In this situation Orthodox ecclesiology, certainly in the Eastern bloc countries, but also in parts of the Middle East and elsewhere, acquired a new emphasis. Conscious of its limited temporal power, the major function of the church was survival and an affirmation of the historic Christian faith. This witness to the truth was, in turn, seen as the source of the renewal of the nation itself. " 'Mission' is identified with tradition and appeals to history, the continuity of the Church in time, the transmission of the faith from age to age and from one generation to the next. The object of Orthodox mission has been not so much to conquer new geographical frontiers at all costs, but rather to hold people to the faith in a permanent historic continuity."[11] In so doing the church discovers its true identity; "living fully the mystery of incarnation and divinization in all its dimensions,"[12] it "stands on the power of the Holy Spirit as an 'ikon' of the Kingdom in history."[13] For Freda Haddad, "God is ever incarnate in the very flesh of human history." She quotes St. John of Damascus: "Just as charcoal burns not of itself but through the fire with which it is impregnated . . . I am but black cold charcoal. In order to be set ablaze by the fire of Pentecost I want the bread of God which is the flesh of Christ of the seed of David, and I want to drink His blood which is love incorruptible." Writing from within her context in Lebanon, the church is, for her, the impregnated and incarnated presence of God in the world, obliged to share in "the depth of the cup of bitterness," and yet this it does conscious that "ours is the night of expectation."[14] "Reconciled in the very depths of his being, the Christian seeks not so much merely to speak of the Gospel as rather to proclaim the Risen Christ to his fellow human beings by his whole life." "Acquire a spirit of peace," said St. Seraphin of Sarov, "and thousands will find salvation in your company."[15] "Orthodoxy does not persuade or try to compel; it charms and attracts; such is its method of working in the world."[16] To quote Vitaly Borovoi, from the Leningrad Theological Seminary, "All human alienation and exclusiveness are eliminated in the Eucharist. Believers become 'co-members' in Christ, and by means of this—co-members to each other. A new catholic humanity is created—a new family of human kind. St. Simeon teaches: 'All are the One Christ, as one body of many members.' "[17] The primary task of the Orthodox church is seen to be the establishment of this new humanity, with prophecy taking the form of a substantive witness from within by way of example rather than a statement of judgment and coercion. It is to identify with the victim rather than to condemn the offender.

The stated goals of the Orthodox witness in relation to socio-economic and political demands of the time as seen in the appended texts are essentially the same as those of the church in the West as illustrated elsewhere in this volume. The Orthodox contribution to the Melbourne conference on mission clearly identifies "racism, money, chauvinism, ideologies, robotization, and the exploitation of man" as the demons to be exorcised from society by the church. But this document also identifies the particular approach of Orthodoxy to these problems. That approach does not involve direct political action. "In speaking of poverty the Church does not identify its message with the political and social programmes of our time." Yet there is a quest for a form of solidarity with the poor and a manifestation of compassion which is identified as "a sacred liturgy." In the 1982 Kiev document on "Just Development" a similar emphasis is found: "The way of the Gospel is not . . . the violent overturn or change of existing economic, social or political structures. But the Church is in the world to be a blessing, a light and an inspiration. While continuing in prayer and thanksgiving, the Church has to offer herself, her individual members, but also her structures and corporate life, as an example of justice, participation and flowering of life."

Fiotis Litsas's *A Companion to the Greek Orthodox Church* states that in keeping with the principle of synergy the stance of Orthodoxy is one of "general non-partisanship" in political affairs. Regardless of the political system of the nation and government, the church is prepared to pray for the leader. Where officials impose heretical teachings on the church or persecute the church they are condemned, yet here too with hesitation. The church, it is argued, needs to be involved in politics not directly as an institution, but through its laity. The basic task of the government is justice, and "there is nothing in the tradition which would reject out of hand revolutions which are motivated by a sense of unbearably oppressive injustice. . . . Such concerns as embodied in modern day 'liberation theology' movements have their antecedents in the writing of Church fathers such as St. John Chrysostom who railed against the exploitation of the poor by the rich."[18]

If the aims of the church in the East and West are similar, the proposed methods of getting there are, generally speaking, not the same. The point has already been made. The Orthodox method is one of quiet witness from within by way of example and the acceptance of suffering rather than judgment and rebuke. This became apparent at the Vancouver Assembly of the WCC in 1983. The assembly voted in support of a resolution strongly condemning South Africa, but was prevented from passing a similar resolution in condemnation of the Soviet invasion of Afghanistan—by the vote of the Eastern Orthodox delegates. A leading and outspoken black opponent of apartheid in the South African delegation responded in desperation: "It is people like them who make our task so difficult back home!" In addition to all else that was involved in those two votes—and it would be wrong to judge Orthodox church-state doctrine on the basis of this one vote—there were also two different theological perceptions of a viable relationship between church and state. Extra-theological factors are always operative in such voting, and some observers of the vote insisted that the Eastern bloc delegates were not free to oppose the policy of the Kremlin. Equally important is the fact that South African delegates who voted in condemnation of South Africa also had to pay a price for their protest.

The contribution of the Eastern Orthodox church to ecumenical debate on church-state relations, at least from the perspective of the West and especially from the perspective of the mainline Protestant churches in the West, clearly includes the place of authentic worship in the witness of the church to the state. The classical division in the Western church is between those who emphasize social action—sometimes to the neglect of spiritual devotion and worship—and those who emphasize piety and devotion—sometimes to the neglect of social responsibility. At its best Orthodox theology knows no separation between the two. The encounter with the East, a rediscovery of the spiritual resources of the Western tradition, and not least of all the place of what Latin American liberation theologians as well as black and other Third World Christians call the "spirituality of liberation" have led to a new interest in worship as a formative Christian resource in the struggle for a just society.

Certain instinctive questions concerning church-state relations in Eastern Orthodoxy come to the mind of Christians who stand in the Western tradition of the church. Not least of all is the explicit refusal of Orthodoxy, as expressed in the Kiev document, to become involved in direct action leading to the change of "existing social, economic or political structures." Orthodox theologians, in turn, have numerous questions to ask of Western theologians with regard to the use of the church for ideological ends. The purpose of this essay is to introduce the significance of Orthodoxy into the Western debate on church-state relations. Western Christians can only be humbled by the witness of Orthodox Christians in conflict situations in the Middle East and elsewhere, Christians who in obedience to their understanding of mission have in a quiet but courageous manner contributed to the struggle for justice in often very difficult situations.

NOTES

1. See the findings of the WCC consultation on "Confessing Christ Today" held in Bucharest in June 1974, in G. Tsetsis, ed., *Orthodox Thought* (Geneva: WCC, 1983), pp. 3–8.
2. I. Bria, ed., *Martyria/Mission* (Geneva: WCC, 1980), p. 9.
3. Tsetsis, pp. 3–8.
4. Bria, pp. 37, 42.
5. S. Bulgakov, *The Orthodox Church* (London: The Centenary Press, 1935), p. 178.
6. Fiotis K. Litsas, *A Companion to the Greek Orthodox Church* (New York: Department

of Communication, Greek Orthodox Archdiocese on North and South America, 1984), p. 226.
7. Bulgakov, p. 184.
8. J. Meyendorff, *The Orthodox Church* (New York: St. Vladimir's Seminary Press, 1981), p. 123. Also J. M. Cunningham, *A Vanquished Hope: The Movement for Church Renewal in Russia, 1905–1906* (Crestwood, N.Y.: St. Vladimir's Seminary Press, 1981).
9. Meyendorff, p. 125.
10. Ibid, pp. 125, 140.
11. Bria, p. 4.
12. Tsetsis, p. 6.
13. Bria, p. 8.
14. Freda Haddad, "Life Confronting and Overcoming Death," *Journal of Theology for Southern Africa*, 45 (Dec. 1983).
15. Tsetsis, p. 8.
16. Bulgakov, p. 179.
17. Vitaly Borovoi, "Life in Unity," *Journal of Theology for Southern Africa*, 45 (Dec. 1983).
18. Litsas, p. 229.

SELECT BIBLIOGRAPHY

Bria, I., ed. *Martyria/Mission: The Witness of the Orthodox Churches Today.* Geneva: WCC, 1980.

Bulgakov, S. *The Orthodox Church.* London: The Centenary Press, 1935.

Cunningham, J. M. *A Vanquished Hope: The Movement for Church Renewal in Russia, 1905–1906.* Crestwood, N.Y.: St. Vladimir's Seminary Press, 1981.

Litsas, F. K., ed. *A Companion to the Greek Orthodox Church.* New York: Department of Communication, Greek Orthodox Archdiocese of North and South America, 1984.

Meyendorff, J. *Byzantine Legacy in the Orthodox Church.* Crestwood, N.Y.: St. Vladimir's Seminary Press, 1982.

———. *Byzantine Theology: Historical Trends and Doctrinal Themes.* Crestwood, N.Y.: St. Vladimir's Seminary Press, 1985.

———. *The Orthodox Church: Its Past and Its Role in the World Today.* Crestwood, N.Y.: St. Vladimir's Seminary Press, 1981.

Tsetsis, G., ed. *Orthodox Thought: Reports of Orthodox Consultations by the World Council of Churches, 1975–1982.* Geneva: WCC, 1983.

WCC COMMISSION ON WORLD MISSION AND EVANGELISM, MELBOURNE, 1980

THY KINGDOM COME: THE ORTHODOX CONTRIBUTION

THE LITURGY AS DYNAMIC OF THE REIGN OF GOD

Defaulters that we are, how are we to experience the Kingdom so as to become what we are called to be, namely, the Church of the Lord? How are we to fulfill our mission and to appear before the world—not as a hypocritical and piously disguised copy of the society to which we belong but as the Bride of Christ "without spot or blemish", an image and an anticipation of the Kingdom?

It is the role of the eucharistic liturgy to initiate us into the Kingdom, to enable us to "taste . . . and see that the Lord is good" (Ps. 34:8, quoted by 1 Pet. 2:3). It is the function of the liturgy to transform us as individuals into "living stones" of the Church and as a community into an authentic image of the Kingdom.

The Divine Liturgy—divine because, though celebrated by human beings, it is essentially the work of God—therefore with a cry of joy and gratitude: "Blessed is the Kingdom of the Father, Son and Holy Ghost". The entire eucharistic liturgy unfolds within the horizon of the Kingdom which is its raison d'être and its goal.

This Kingdom is a dynamic reality: it has come and it is coming, because Christ has come and Christ is coming. The mission of the Church will therefore be to summon people of all nations and of all ages to become a pilgrim people. The liturgy is an invitation to enlist with the Lord and to travel with him. This appears at the beginning of the Orthodox liturgies in the Little Entrance with the Gospel and in the Great Entrance with the offering of bread and wine: "In thy Kingdom, Remember us, O Lord, when thou comest in thy Kingdom. . . . May the Lord God remember us all in his Kingdom. . . ." This movement of the liturgy carries us along with Christ towards the Promised Land.

The Kingdom, prepared for us before the creation of the world (Mt. 25:34) and proclaimed to men in the whole of Christ's preaching, was given to the world by the Lamb of God offering himself on the cross and by his rising again from the dead. In its liturgy, the Church gives thanks, makes eucharist, for this gift, in the words: "Thou . . . hast left nought undone till thou hadst brought us unto heaven and bestowed upon us thy Kingdom for to come". By its thanksgiving, by its eucharist, the Church receives the gift of the Kingdom.

This gift donated by the Son in his self-offering on the cross is communicated to the people of all ages by the Holy Spirit who receives what belongs to the Son and communicates it to us (cf. Jn. 16:14). When the Holy Spirit is

---

[Source: G. Tsetsis, ed., *Orthodox Thought: Reports of Orthodox Consultations by the World Council of Churches, 1975–1982* (Geneva: WCC, 1983).]

invoked in the prayer of epiclesis, the celebrant prays: "that thy Holy Spirit may come upon us and upon these gifts . . . that they may be to them that partake thereof unto sobriety of soul, the remission of sins, the participation of thy Holy Spirit, the fulfilment of the Kingdom of heaven. . . ." In the course of the liturgy, the radiance of the Holy Spirit projects onto the Church gathered together by Him the full image of the Kingdom. The liturgy is the continuation of Pentecost. When all the faithful come to communicate, they enter into the splendour of the Kingdom.

Immediately after they have in this way met with Him, who has come but whom they also expect to come again, they cry out: "Grant that we may partake of thee more truly, in that day of thy Kingdom which shall have no night". Everything is given to us in this communion yet everything is not yet accomplished. The efficacy of the Church's missionary witness depends on the authenticity of our communion. Our ability to present the Light of the Kingdom to the world is proportionate to the degree in which we receive it in the eucharistic mystery.

HOLINESS, PROPHETIC SIGN OF THE COMING OF THE KINGDOM

The liturgy does not end when the eucharistic assembly disperses. "Let us go forth in peace"; the dismissal is a sending off of every believer to mission in the world where he or she lives and works, and of the whole community into the world, to witness by what they are that the Kingdom is coming. Christians who have heard the Word and received the Bread of Life should henceforth be living prophetic signs of the coming Kingdom. Having been sanctified, for they have become temples of the Holy Spirit, and deified, because they have been kindled by the fire descended from heaven, they hear the exhortation: "Heal the sick . . . and say, 'The Kingdom of God has come close to you . . . And now you see that I have given you the power to tread underfoot . . . all the forces of the Enemy' " (Lk. 10:9-19). Every Christian is called to proclaim the Kingdom and to demonstrate its power. Hence a twofold function:

The exorcism of the demons: the struggle against the idols, racism, money, chauvinism, ideologies, the robotization and exploitation of man.

The healing of the sick: the Church exercises this function not only in the sacraments of penance and the anointing of the sick but also by tackling all the ills and disorders of man and society. It does this in the power of the cross: self-effacing service of the sick and prisoners, solidarity with the tortured and the oppressed, especially those who suffer for their opinions. As the voice of the voiceless, the Church will in the discharge of its calling, teach and practise respect for every human being, with the aim of restoring the divine image in each individual and communion among all. It will encourage respect for the whole of creation and everything in nature: a kingdom of priests, it will offer up the whole creation—obedient to Christ and renewed by his Spirit—to God the Father.

Those who practise a "Christian maximalism", renewal groups, religious orders, set us an example of mission. A joyful asceticism whereby the old man is crucified with Christ so that the new man may rise with him and live for God (Rom. 6:5-11) carries the cross and resurrection of Christ into daily life; it develops all the potentialities of baptism and constitutes an essential sign of the coming Kingdom.

Voluntarily accepted poverty in demonstration of solidarity with the Poor King (cf. Zech. 9:9), fasting with Him who said that "man does not live by bread alone", "for the Kingdom of God is not eating and drinking, but justice, peace and joy, inspired by the Holy Spirit" (Rom. 14:17) and identification with all those who go hungry, chastity not only in monastic life but also in conjugal love and procreation; revaluation of the humility which makes it possible for the other person to be renewed; mutual submission (Eph. 5:21) in listening to the Spirit who speaks through the Church; a liberty which refuses to let itself be intimidated by threats or taken in by false promises; constant interior prayer throughout all the vicissitudes of daily life—all these are many aspects of a life based on an eschatological vision of existence, on an evangelical life worthy of the children of the Kingdom.

MISSION AS WORK OF THE SPIRIT AND GIFT OF THE TRUTH

The proclamation of the Kingdom of God lies at the very heart of the Church's vocation in the world. Without mission there is no Church, for the Church continues the work of mankind's salvation revealed and achieved by Jesus Christ our Saviour. Only by the Pentecostal outpouring of the Holy Spirit is the mission of the Church possible and the apostolic community endowed with the power of the Spirit for the announcement of the Gospel of the Christ who died and rose again for our salvation. The coming of the Holy Spirit in the Church is not an isolated historic event in the past but a permanent gift which gives life to the Church, ensuring its existence in the history of humanity, making possible its witness to the inaugurated Kingdom of God. The Holy Spirit is the divine power whereby the Church is able to obey the command of the Risen Lord: "Go forth then and make all nations my disciples" (Mt. 28:19); "Go forth to every part of the world and proclaim the Good News to the whole creation" (Mk. 16:15; cf. Lk. 24:47 and Acts 1:8). This permanent Pentecostal outpouring of the Spirit on the Church is a reality in the Church's worship, in its public prayer, in the Sunday celebration of the Eucharist, but it overflows the limits of ecclesial worship and constitutes the inner dynamic which gives character to all expressions of, and all activities in the life of the Church.

Neither the Church nor its worship or mission can be defined exclusively as forms of the existence and activity of the human beings gathered together in the name of Jesus Christ. The Church is above all the true manifestation of the divine presence in the history of the world, the sign of the constant intervention of the Love of God in the existence of human society, in and through the most concrete everyday conditions of human life, in its most diverse and even profane activities. The coming of the Spirit of the Risen Christ into the world and His presence in the world moves inexorably in the direction of the abolition of the frontiers between a sacred spiritual world, receptive to the divine grace, and a profane material world which is thought to exist only in accordance with its own internal laws. In face of the contemporary world it cannot be too strongly insisted that human existence in all its aspects is subject to the proclamation of the Gospel and that the fundamental principles of the spiritual life of the human person (pardon, mercy, justice) must permeate all aspects of the social and political life of human society.

If the missionary proclamation of the Gospel of the Kingdom is to reach human hearts, there must be a palpable and real correspondence between the Word preached in the power and joy of the Holy Spirit and the actual life of the preacher and of the Christian community. The gap between the message and the life of the historical Church and its members constitutes the most massive obstacle to the credibility of the Gospel for our contemporaries. "See how these Christians love one another"—declared an ancient Christian apologist. The love of Christians is the very substance as well as the radiance of the Gospel. In the apostolic community of Jerusalem as well as in the communities founded by St. Paul, the sharing of material things and concern for the poor became the spontaneous and necessary expression of their experience of the Trinitarian love which is disclosed in the life of the Church. The sharing of material things and of life itself thus flows from eucharistic communion and constitutes one of its radical requirements. When the Church identifies itself with the prayer of its Saviour, "Your Kingdom Come!", it must above all ask itself in a spirit of penitence how far the unworthiness of Christians acts as a screen hindering the radiance of Christ Himself from shining through.

The dynamic of the Church's mission springs from a deep awareness of the suffering of a human race steeped in ignorance of God, torn apart by hatred and conflict of every sort, alienated by material and spiritual poverty in all its forms. Together with the whole of creation man experiences a profound nostalgia for a paradise lost, in which justice, well-being and peace would prevail. The Church's responsibility is to bring to this tormented and enslaved world the vigorous response of God to its questionings and rebellions. This response is the living Truth of Christ which reaches down into the very depths of man's being and liberates him. It is also the gift of the infinite love and compassion of God who ignores no human suffering and distress, and towards whom the blood and tears of the oppressed arise in mute appeal.

We are convinced that the sacred deposit of the Truth and Love of its divine Founder, of which the Church's faith is the expression and of which the Church has been the channel throughout the centuries, is the living response which is needed to the quest of man in all ages. The infinite love of the divine Trinity is communicated to us by Christ, true God and true man, in the power of the Holy Spirit. The doctrine and preaching of the Church should be nothing other than an education in this living love of God, a visible manifestation of the presence of Christ in our lives. "Dear children—for my children you are, and I am in travail with you over again until you take the shape of Christ" (Gal. 4:19). The only goal of the Church's mission, in the last analysis, is to manifest the presence of Christ and his love in the life of Christians both individually and in their love for one another, as well as in their witness in the world by their life, actions, and love.

THE LIFE OF THE CHRISTIAN AS PROPHETIC WITNESS OF THE KINGDOM OF GOD

Although the mission of the Church and the proclamation of the Kingdom are above all the work of the Holy Spirit who manifests in power and truth the intervention of God Himself in history, it is also important to remember that man is called to cooperate in the divine plan for the salvation of the world.

"We are God's fellow-workers", declares St. Paul (1 Cor. 3:9). Through human voices and human lives, Christ's call to follow him reverberates throughout the centuries. For those who take it seriously and at cost, this 'service' of the divine Word and the divine Love entails a deep and permanent surrender of their lives. The Christian who obeys the word of his Lord must resist the temptation to overrate his own importance and to come between God and His children. The service of God and His Word demands a radical exercise in self-renunciation and spiritual poverty, the better to be able to serve God and one's brothers and sisters. What St. John the Baptist said of himself in relation to Christ must also be true of us: "He must increase, I must decrease" (Jn. 3:30). This way of voluntary impoverishment following the pattern of the 'Poor Man' thus helps to 'liberate' the inner man and to make him capable of receiving the diverse charisma of the Holy Spirit so that through his sanctification, community and communion is strengthened and developed among human beings. "Acquire a spirit of peace", St. Seraphim of Sarov (early 19th cent.) used to say, "and thousands around you will find salvation".

That is the basis of the Orthodox theology of mission: to acquire the dynamic, the power of the Spirit of Christ. It is He who creates the languages, forms and methods of mission . . .

The efficacy of missionary witness will be directly proportionate to the Christian experience of the love of Christ. This love, says St. Paul, "constrains us" (2 Cor. 5:14).

Once this flame of love sets a man's heart ablaze, it prevents him from isolating himself comfortably in his own personal existence or that of his community. The dismissal of the faithful at the end of the liturgy with the words "Go forth in peace!" does not mean that the liturgy is 'over' but that it is transposed into another form in which it continues, in the inner worship of the heart, in a life immersed in the daily life of human society. It is high time we overcame the very real temptation to make an absolute distinction between a spiritual life and a secular life. All human existence is sacred and remains within God's sight. It is within that existence that Christ's sovereignty purposes to be installed, so that no realm or aspect of human life may be abandoned to the forces of evil.

The Christian thus experiences in his own flesh and blood the inevitable tension between existence in the world and not belonging to the world. It is precisely because of the Christian's heavenly citizenship (Heb. 13:14) that he is able to enter fully into the whole life of human society and to bring the light of Christ to bear on that life.

In every area of human activity there needs to be a constant reminder, in season and out of season, of the meaning of human dignity, of the unique and intrinsic value of the human person who cannot be reduced to a mere cog in the social machine.

The Church of Christ cannot shut its eyes to, or rest content with merely pious words about the deeply ingrained defects which disfigure modern society, nor ignore the inequalities in the distribution, use and management of the material riches of the earth of which man is meant to be the steward. Nor can it be indifferent to the hunger and destitution of a large proportion of humankind. Is real solidarity still possible within the vast community of Christ's disciples in face of the ocean of suffering and poverty, especially in the Third World, around us? We should not forget the social preaching of a St. John Chrysostom who reminded the rich and powerful of his time (4th cent.) that compassion to the poor is also a sacred liturgy in which man is the priest and which in God's sight has an incomparable dignity.

In speaking of poverty the Church does not identify its message with the political and social programmes of our time. Yet the Church cannot turn a blind eye to the fact of human poverty by which a great part of humanity is burdened today. Poverty and its consequences are themselves only the fruit of a deep disorder from which humanity has suffered since the fall of Adam. None of the social programmes and efforts to achieve prosperity and justice are able to bring mankind healing for its deepest ills, its sin, its hatred, egotism, pride. It is when man becomes the slave of his spiritual and physical passions that he succumbs to poverty in its most real form, especially when he fails to realize it.

The Gospel of Christ is a message of life and healing addressed to all who are poor on this human earth. From all, the Gospel demands thorough conversion, the abandonment of human glory and the abjuring of the idols we have made of money, political and economic power, ideologies, racism . . . The Gospel alone brings to all men, whatever their racial, social or political origin, true liberation and life.

This radical conversion of the heart is the principal fruit of the invisible action of the Holy Spirit within us, fashioning us in the image and likeness of Him who though "he was rich, yet for your sake . . . became poor, so that through his poverty you might become rich" (2 Cor. 8:9). The disciples of Christ are called to a voluntary poverty which makes it possible for them, on the one hand, to become available for the inauguration of the Reign of Christ in our human life and, on the other hand, to serve their own apprenticeship to love and complete sharing, and to communicate it to others.

The Church in our time should resist the temptation to insure itself, and even to enter into partnership with the authorities and powers of this world, lest it betray the most precious gift of the Spirit, namely, the liberty of the children of God. In all the struggles and conflicts which rend asunder the extended human family, the Church should seek to reflect the sufferings, injustices and forms of violence (open or concealed), to reverberate the cries and appeals of all those—Christians and non-Christians—who are persecuted for their faith, brutally treated in violation of human dignity and the basic principles of justice.

WCC COMMISSION ON THE CHURCHES' PARTICIPATION IN DEVELOPMENT, KIEV, 1982

JUST DEVELOPMENT FOR FULLNESS OF LIFE: AN ORTHODOX APPROACH

THEOLOGICAL REFLECTIONS ON DEVELOPMENT

Orthodoxy values life because:

—it is a gift of God to us,

—it is a gift which we, while on this Earth, may commit to God,

—it is a gift that we can offer to our fellow Christians and our fellow human beings every day.

However, mere survival can have no meaning in itself, nor life lived for its own sake alone. It must be lived for the sake of others.

Because human beings are created in God's image and are stewards of His creation, they are co-workers with God, which means that human beings are agents of their own development and of the development of others.

In the Old Testament believers in God were called by the prophets bearers and performers of righteousness. This call was necessary because human nature is fallen and has been overtaken by injustice. The early Church also was aware of the power of injustice. For instance, when members of the Apostolic community complained of unjust distribution, the Church created a new ministry, the Diaconate, to study the problem. The Triune God, who has always revealed Himself as Agape, also reveals Himself as a God who demands justice among His people, showing that agape and justice are indissolubly linked to each other.

For Christians, in addition, fullness of life requires that we continuously die with Christ for the sake of others, and rise with Christ into a new life. Fullness of human life on Earth reflects the life of the Holy Trinity.

The Church is concerned on many levels with the different kinds of human and social development, though there can be no full and complete development for humanity unless we are reborn inwardly. Development begins with meeting the most basic requirements of life, to which every person in every society is justly entitled. It continues with progress towards the affirmation of human dignity, achievement of freedom, fulfilment of just social goals, and realization of human potentialities which at the same time are included in, and transcend this world.

The Church addresses its message to all. Those who do not believe in God, and yet seek a meaning to life, are asked to consider that by having life, they have something to offer to their fellow human beings. Our Christian experience is

---

[Source: G. Tsetsis, ed., *Orthodox Thought: Reports of Orthodox Consultations by the World Council of Churches, 1975–1982* (Geneva: WCC, 1983).]

that, in as much as we sacrifice our lives daily in the service of our fellow human beings, this sacrifice is returned to us incomparably fuller and richer.

Addressing those who have much, the Church reminds them in words and deeds of Christ's judgment on the rich. The Gospel teaches a way of life that strives to minimize selfish and superfluous consumption in order to promote a more human life for oneself and for others.

Addressing those who have little or nothing of the world's riches, the Church reminds them of Christ's blessing of the poor. The awareness that they possess the dignity of the children of God should become for them a source of inspiration in creativity for their own development, in imitation of God's creative will.

Those in authority should be reminded unceasingly in word and deed of their responsibility to work for a more just, participatory and sustainable society, a responsibility which ultimately belongs to all of us as citizens. Tolerating and perpetuating the structures of injustice not only inhibits development, but also encourages and provokes regress. Justice is a divine demand and we have the duty to seek it for all in our own time.

The way of the Gospel is not, of course, the violent overturn or change of existing economic, social or political structures. But the Church is in the world to be a blessing, a light and an inspiration. While continuing in prayer and thanksgiving, the Church has to offer herself, her individual members, but also her structures and corporate life, as an example of justice, participation and flowering of life.

Further, the Church has to be an untiring preacher and worker for peace through justice as a primary pre-condition for the wholesome development of humanity, that is, a development which is both spiritual and material, individual and social.

It is both spiritual and material because it was the good will of God to create human beings as a bond between spirit and matter, endowing them with the Divine image.

It is both individual and social because we have been created in the image of God who is a communion of persons: the Holy Trinity.

Throughout the ages, the witness to this faith has been expressed through service, or DIACONIA, to the neighbour and to the world.

MACRODIACONIA

In defining the terms 'Microdiaconia' and 'Macrodiaconia', the Orthodox recognize the danger of over-emphasizing the difference between these two concepts. In reality, there exists only one diaconia in the Church under two different forms: 'Microdiaconia' by and to individual members, 'Macrodiaconia' as service to societies and their structures. The basis for both forms of service is agape or love for God and humanity. Both Diaconias are extensions of the Eucharistic Service. Both are a liturgy after the Liturgy. Both express the missionary task of the Church.

In different countries and societies there may exist different forms of service. In some cases the Church's influence can extend to all aspects of society: social, economic, cultural, and political life. Each Church is an agent of development in the context in which it lives and witnesses. In some situations, the Church can be directly involved in the public and economic life of the nation. Thus, for example, in the Middle East the local Churches and the WCC are giving support to the suffering people of the region, providing financial assistance, building homes and hospitals for refugees, etc. In other contexts, the Churches are able to serve the people by keeping homes for the aged, hospitals, educational institutions, etc. The Church can and must contribute to the cultural life of the society. National Churches can be greatly enriched, for instance, by different forms of ecclesiastical art such as Church architecture, iconography, hymnography and Church music.

It must be emphasized that the Churches should continue to exert their constructive influence on the social, public and cultural life of nations. In such circumstances when the Christians cannot have direct influence, individual Christians can be the voice of the Church.

The Churches have a special God-given duty to work for the realization of justice and peace, for the development of peoples and nations. The Churches should be ready to defend human rights (freedom of conscience, freedom of speech, of belief) and condemn their violations.

One of the noble tasks of the Church today is to work for the preservation of peace on Earth. It is important to recognize that in its Christian sense, peace does not mean merely the absence of violence or open conflicts. It means peace within the heart of each human being, peace with neighbours, peace in society and in the whole creation. The foundation of this kind of peace is to be found in the reconciliation of man with Jesus Christ. It is important to recognize that Christians are not necessarily seeking peace at any price. Rather, they seek only that peace which is based on justice and on the realization of human rights. However, when conflicts arise, they are to be solved by peaceful means and not by violence.

For Orthodox Christians and for Orthodox mission today, it is essential that our faith be expressed in everyday life as 'Orthopraxia'. It is our duty to participate in all aspects of society, contributing to just development of life. However, it is very important to remember that the salvation of human beings and that of the world is the ultimate mission of the Church. All our development expresses in an incomplete way our striving towards the Kingdom of God, which can never be fully realized in this world, but only in the Eschaton, the age to come.

MICRODIACONIA

The Church in its service to the world has flourished when the other aspects of full Church life have also flourished: liturgical, theological, spiritual. No one aspect of Christian life can be fully developed without the others. Spiritual renewal stands at the heart of renewed commitment to one's fellow human beings and their salvation.

Fundamental social change, meaning a deep change in the relationships among persons, can never be imposed as a system or structure from without. It comes about only through a radical change of heart. It is this kind of social change which Christians seek, a model of which life of the Kingdom is to be found in the perfecting of personal relationships both within and outside the life of the Church. When we acquire the sense that we are members one of another, that we bear one another's burdens, we are led to bring forth fruit in more perfect Christian service to our neighbour, i.e. 'Microdiaconia'.

Each parish and each Christian is to be an imitator of Christ, who came to serve and not to be served. Some areas where the potential for 'Microdiaconia' is greatest may be noted. Parents must practise 'Microdiaconia' and justice if the children are to emulate Christ through their example. Orthodox parishes must become sources of service to their flocks, and to the communities in which they live. As did the early Church, parishes and Christians should respond to the cries of suffering people in all corners of the world, and in particular to the members of the household of faith. Churches must develop resources and train pastors and laity for carrying out the many and varied tasks of 'Microdiaconia'. Special attention should be paid to developing the 'Microdiaconia' of the laity. In recent years, though the theological importance of the laity has been recognized, the Church has not sufficiently tapped the potential contribution of the laity.

We live in changing times which challenge the Church to continue in new forms its traditional service of love. For example, the phenomenon of urbanization often isolates parishioners from their neighbours, the young from the old, the healthy from the infirm. The Church should become sensitive to this and other similar problems and seek creative pastoral responses to them. For instance, the ancient service roles of the deacons and deaconesses could be revived.

'Microdiaconia' can also contribute to the healthy development of ecumenism. Our world is a divided world, and division is real not only among nations, but among Christians as well. Words alone are no longer adequate means to achieve unity, but deeds are needed to foster visible and concrete progress along the path towards unity. When Christians from different Churches work together to serve fellow humans in need, their love and their concern for justice may serve to draw them together. 'Microdiaconia' in ecumenical form can become an effective element in healing the division among Christians.

PART THREE

THE SOUTH AFRICAN CONTEXT

CHAPTER 11

THE CHURCH IN SOUTH AFRICA

The history of church-state relations in South Africa is in direct continuity with the classical and contemporary history of those relations as introduced in the preceding two sections.

This continuity has not, however, distracted from the agony and pathos inherent in being the church of Jesus Christ among the divided people of this land. Indeed those who have remained faithful to the prophetic tradition of the church have been condemned by those who have deviated from this tradition. A rueful consequence of this is a church which is prepared theoretically to affirm a particular church-state doctrine—and in its more triumphalist moments, even to celebrate it—while condemning those who put this doctrine into practice in more critical times. In so doing the most sincere, courageous, and obedient sons and daughters of the church are alienated from the very institution whose theological *raison d'etre* they affirm. The result is a church with a yawning gap between what it *says* is theologically true, and what it actually *does*—and in practice even hinders. The truth of the matter is that prophets are never easy people to live with, and it is usually the case that they are without honor among their own. At least some of the documents reprinted below originate from prophetic people and groupings in the church in South Africa. That church continues to struggle to know precisely how to respond to these declarations and repeatedly falls short of its own finest confessions of faith.

For a person to be both a citizen of the state and an obedient disciple of Jesus Christ is never easy, and when a political crisis leaves people unable to hold these two responsibilities in creative unity, the consequences become far-reaching. In fact, such is the intensity of church-state relations in South Africa that the political history of this land cannot be understood without reference to the interaction between these two institutions. What is most significant is that while many of the major churches in this country have at various stages of their history found themselves in different relations to the state—at times the church of the government and at times the voice of opposition—they have generally all affirmed a similar doctrinal perspective on church-state relations: the need for legitimate government capable of instituting justice and good order; the obligation of the church to exercise a prophetic ministry in relation to the state; and in certain circumstances the possibility of conscientious disobedience to the laws of the state. The specific political and social context within which a particular church has found itself at a given time has influenced which of these doctrinal perspectives was given prominence, resulting in divisions both *within* and *between* these churches.

THE PERIOD OF ALIGNMENT

The history of Christianity in South Africa tells of both confrontation and cooperation between church and state from the time of the first white settlers and through the early missionary period. Our focus, however, is on the modern period from the close of the Anglo-Boer War to about 1960. This was, loosely speaking, a period of alignment, as the Afrikaans and the English-speaking churches aligned themselves, with some important exceptions, over against each other. Two events starkly illustrate this alignment.

The English-speaking churches emerged from the Anglo-Boer War with a semblance of unity, although there is clear evidence that behind the imperialistic facade presented by these churches there were English-speaking clergy, both in South Africa and in Britain, who showed great sympathy for the Boers, especially during the early part of the war.[1] The Afrikaans churches, on the other hand, were less compromising in their support for the Boer cause. Leonard Thompson has, for example, defined the Dutch Reformed church as "the most powerful Afrikaner institution which survived the war intact."[2] This was, however, a unity that was short-lived. Less than three years after the union of the Cape Colony, Natal, and the two former Boer republics in the Transvaal and the Orange Free State was declared in May 1910, it was torn to near breaking point by the decision of the government, under the former Boer general, Louis Botha, to enter World War I on the side of Great Britain.

Some Afrikaners, never fully satisfied with the negotiated union under the British crown, saw this as the right time to regain the independence of the former Boer republics. Several former Boer generals led a rebellion against the Botha regime. A state of emergency was declared, the rebellion was suppressed, and some leading figures in the rebellion were killed. General J. H. de la Rey was killed by a ricochet police bullet in an incident not directly related to the rebellion, General Christiaan Beyers drowned in the Vaal River while trying to escape the government forces, and Commandant Jopie Fourie was shot by a firing squad on December 20, 1914. The scene was set for a split within the Afrikaner churches. The division was a penetrating one, although every effort was made to maintain Afrikaner national unity within the churches, as Carel Borchardt has made clear.[3] A special sitting of the *Raad Der Ned. Ger. Kerken in Zuid Afrika*—the Council of the Nederduitse Gereformeerde Kerk (the NGK)—was called in Bloemfontein in January 1915, and several resolutions, some of them reprinted below, were finally adopted and referred to the synods of the three Dutch Reformed churches.[4] The council was not prepared ultimately or explicitly to condemn the 1914–15 rebellion. It rather allowed, in principle, that in certain exceptional circumstances the legal authority of the state may be disobeyed, assuming that such behavior was justified by God's Word. The council was not, however, prepared to apply this principle to a specific situation. No one was prepared to indicate in what sense the rebellion was such an exceptional instance, but neither were the rebels condemned. In fact, at a certain point the meeting explicitly refused to accept a proposal in which obedience to the state was expressly demanded.[5] To quote Borchardt, the council "allowed that it is only permissible to resist the state should the state act in contradiction to God's law." No one argued in the synods that followed that the declaration of war against Germany was such an instance, but neither did "the churches tell those of their members who took up arms against a democratically elected government that they were wrong."[6]

The lengthy debate in the council, only a small part of which is appended below, has a strangely contemporary dimension to it. The council warned that if the rebellion was merely responded to with force the situation in the country would not be adequately addressed, there could be no national unity, and the political problems of the day would remain unsolved. An appeal was therefore made for a nonpartisan inquiry into the "real motives and purposes of this resistance," recognizing that it was only in this way that peace could be restored. Today different churches and different organizations are making almost identical pleas concerning the present response of black people to the political oppression in South Africa. What the council did in 1915, almost in spite of its agonizing debate, was to reiterate the traditional obligation of Christians, in certain circumstances, to entertain the possibility of disobedience to the state in obedience to God's Word. The resolutions of the council make this point clearly: Christians, it was emphasized, may not engage in resistance against lawful government, "other than for very weighty and sound reasons, which are confirmed by God's Word, and by a conscience which has been enlightened by the Word of God."

Forty-two years later the English-speaking churches found it necessary to affirm a similar principle of civil disobedience. In 1957 the Native Laws Amendment Bill was promulgated under the direction of Dr. Hendrick Verwoerd, the architect of the legal edifice of apartheid and at that time minister of native affairs. The law was designed, among other things, to make it virtually impossible for black people to worship in churches located in so-called white areas. Opposition to what soon became known as the "church clause" from the leadership of English-speaking churches was extensive, and the Federal Council of the progovernment Dutch Reformed churches counseled the government to rephrase the wording of the legislation to ensure that "all possible misunderstanding" was eliminated, while assuring its members that the law was not intended to interfere with the freedom of worship.[7] It was this legislation, ultimately passed by parliament in a slightly modified form (allowing the minister to prevent blacks from worshipping with white Christians if they were a "nuisance" or worshipped in "excessive numbers"), which precipitated the letter from the archbishop of Cape Town to the prime minister included below. The bishops with whom Archbishop Geoffrey Clayton had consulted were of a common mind: clause 29 (c) of the proposed legislation could not be obeyed. Other English-speaking churches responded similarly, while the Roman Catholic church in the same year made an unprecedented statement rejecting "apartheid as something intrinsically evil."

There has never been unqualified support for the hierarchical decisions of any of the churches, and certainly the praxis of the English-speaking churches has often denied the resistance of both church conferences and leaders such as Clayton. Moreover, the Dutch Reformed churches have had their dissident voices throughout their history. By and large, however, the white Dutch Reformed churches as institutions have aligned themselves on the side of the present political establishment in South Africa while the English-speaking churches, with their predominant black membership, have at least in their official policy stood against the government.[8]

THE PERIOD OF RESISTANCE

The next phase of church-state relations in South Africa came as a direct result of the Sharpeville shootings in 1960. The WCC called the South African member churches, which at the time included the NGK of the Cape Province and the Transvaal, to a consultation at Cottesloe, outside of Johannesburg. The findings of the consultation amounted to the rejection of some of the central emphases of the apartheid policy of the time. By today's standards the findings were mild, even reactionary. Yet in South Africa, a conclusion which stated "we recognize that all racial groups who permanently inhabit our country are a part of our total population, and we regard them as indigenous" was a fundamental rejection of the apartheid ideology with which the present government has not yet come to grips. In a similar vein, the affirmation that "no one who believes in Jesus Christ may be excluded from any church on the grounds of his colour or race" continues to cause major division within the Dutch Reformed churches. Verwoerd, who was prime minister by that time, reprimanded the Dutch Reformed delegates, accusing them of allowing themselves to be influenced by the WCC and forgetting their responsibility with regard to the "high purpose of apartheid."[9]

A new phase of resistance had developed for the churches. The Christian Council, which changed its name to the South African Council of Churches (SACC) in 1968, was expanding its program. The Christian Institute under the leadership of Beyers Naudé was established in 1963. These are stories which are told elsewhere.[10] Then came the WCC's 1966 Conference on Church and Society held in Geneva, which would pave the way for the Program to Combat Racism (PCR). Bishop Bill Burnett, general secretary of the Christian Council, and Beyers Naudé, director of the Christian Institute, returned home from Geneva to organize a series of regional meetings to explore the significance of the Geneva recommendations for South Africa. During this period the council appointed a commission "to consider what obedience to God requires of the church in her witness to her unity in Christ in South Africa." The outcome was the "Message to the People of South Africa," published in 1968, which rejected apartheid as a "pseudo-gospel" and called Christians to obey God rather than man. The reaction from the English-speaking churches showed the division within these churches. Prime Minister John Vorster warned those "who wish to disrupt the order in South Africa under the cloak of religion." Ultimately, however, the English-speaking churches stood by the document. These churches had stated the need to resist the ideology of apartheid as being in fundamental contradiction to the gospel.

Such resistance was neither easy nor was it without its cost. The appointment of the Schlebusch Parliamentary Commission of Inquiry in 1974, a commission charged with investigating several church and other organizations, was but one instance of the state's attack on the churches. The story of this confrontation between church and state is also told elsewhere.[11] The leadership of the Christian Institute refused to give evidence before the commission, arguing that because the inquiry was not of a judicial nature, conducted according to standard legal procedure, it would be wrong for a Christian to give evidence before it. Evidence from such proceedings, it was argued, could implicate others without allowing them the opportunity to refute any allegations which might be derived by the commission. This refusal to testify led to a series of court cases, including the trial of Beyers Naudé, documented in a publication by the International Commission of Jurists.[12] Among the most significant of the submissions from the perspective of church-state relations was the statement signed by Theo Kotzé (director of the Cape Town region of the Christian Institute), Roelf Meyer (editor of the Christian Institute's official journal *Pro Veritate*), and Beyers Naudé. Their statement clearly placed them within what they regarded as the Reformed theological tradition.

Having resigned from the WCC after the Cottesloe Consultation and under increasing pressure to define its position in relation to the government's apartheid policy, the NGK appointed a commission to prepare a statement on race relations. After deleting some of the more progressive findings of the commission, the 1974 synod adopted the report entitled "Ras, Volk en Nasie en Volkereverhoudings in die Lig van die Skrif," later translated as "Human Relations and the South African Scene in the Light of Scripture." The report was distributed worldwide as the official position of this church on race relations. This document, providing what the church regards as the biblical justification for apartheid, has been extensively discussed elsewhere.[13] It led directly to the declaration by the World Alliance of Reformed Churches (WARC) in 1982 that apartheid is a heresy and to the suspension of the membership of the NGK from the WARC. In spite of the theological support for apartheid which is the dominant theme of the document, the results of the investigation of church-state relations recorded in the document are in continuity with the dominant emphases of classical church-state relations in the history of the church. While recognizing the state as a God-given institution "for the sake of public order, to combat evil and to preserve justice," the document makes it clear that the church has an obligation "to preach the Word of God to the authorities, in particular the norms of the Bible in respect of mutual relationships and social justice, and the duties of the authorities in this connection." It warns that justice and love are "sufficient to preserve the state from revolutionary chaos and political absolutism and tyranny," affirming the need for the church to submit to the state, "provided the legal order does not conflict with the Word of God." The social situation in which this church finds itself is, however, such that the oppressive legislation of the present government is not weighed against the Word of God, but rather justified in terms of a brand of theology which almost every major church body inside and outside the country has rejected as heretical.

The document then goes further to justify, on biblical grounds, what it calls "autogenous separate development" or apartheid. As it had at the time of the 1914–15 rebellion, the church again found itself allowing political ideology to influence its theological findings. This time it went further to use theology to substantiate a political ideology.[14] Borchardt's words on the response of the Afrikaans churches to the rebellion seem appropriate here, too: "The Afrikaans churches have indeed sought to speak to the heart of the Afrikaner people, but in so doing have been unfaithful to the Church of Jesus Christ."[15] Nationalism and ideological persuasion makes it extremely difficult for a church to judge whether a particular political dispensation is in accordance with God's Word.

Such unity as existed in the English-speaking churches was tested by the 1974 SACC national conference's conscientious objection debate, in a way not dissimilar from the manner in which the unity of the Afrikaans churches was tested in 1914–15.[16] Frelimo had come to power in Mozambique after a long war of independence; the Angolan civil war was at its height with South African troops heavily involved in that region, although this was unknown to most South Africans; the independence war in what was then known as Rhodesia was escalating; and the South African army build-up in Namibia had reached new heights. At the same time the WCC member churches in South Africa had, under pressure from the state and their white membership, distanced themselves from the decision of the WCC to fund liberation movements for humanitarian purposes through the PCR. The dilemma facing the English-speaking churches was obvious. How could these churches, given their black majority membership, allow their white members to fight in the army of a white minority government without censure when they had already declared themselves to be against all forms of violence, even to the point of refusing to provide humanitarian aid to liberation movements which had resorted to armed combat? The conscientious objection resolution proposed by a Presbyterian minister, Douglas Bax, and seconded by Beyers Naudé stated that "the Republic of South Africa is at present a fundamentally unjust and discriminatory society" and that "the military forces of our country are being prepared to defend this unjust and discriminatory society," and it called on Christians to obey God rather than man. The government responded with even more severe legislation against conscientious objectors and those who counseled conscientious objection. White members of the English-speaking churches were compelled to question the nature of their allegiance to both state and church as never before, with military conscription and the provision of military chaplains in the uniform of the South African armed forces being among the most divisive issues in the English-speaking churches still today. The South African Catholic Bishops' Conference (SACBC), which has consistently affirmed the conscientious right to object to military service, issued a statement in 1985 calling for an end to conscription, which is included in the appended documents.

THE PERIOD OF INITIATIVE

The mid-seventies, which saw the 1976 Soweto riots spread throughout the country in renewed acts of resistance, ushered in a new phase of the church's response to the state. Black people were taking the initiative in the churches. Desmond Tutu was elected general secretary of the SACC in 1978, an increasing number of black people were being elected to leadership positions in the SACC member churches, and in 1982 Allan Boesak was elected president of the WARC. The state was on the defensive. Desmond Tutu's letter to the prime minister on May 6, 1976, illustrates the shift in initiative—the black dean of Johannesburg is offering the white prime minister his counsel. Three years later, having been warned by the minister of justice because of an address delivered to the SACC national conference, Allan Boesak felt obliged to respond to this threat in a letter to the minister, affirming the long prophetic tradition of the church.

It was, however, the decision of the WARC in 1982 to declare apartheid to be a heresy that gave the churches opposed to the government a new sense of initiative. Similar resolutions were adopted by most of the SACC member churches in South Africa in response to the WARC resolution. The NG Sendingkerk (NG Mission Church) declared apartheid to constitute a *status confessionis,* a condition in which the very truth of the gospel is at stake, and adopted a "Confession of Faith" which has been referred to local congregations as a basis for Christian living.

It would be quite wrong, however, to imply that those churches opposed to apartheid failed to address the instances of apartheid in their own situations. The Catholic church in particular addressed itself to the need for reconciliation within its own ranks through an important "Declaration of Commitment" in 1977, which identified the forms of racism, paternalism, and exploitation within its own ranks in a frank and revealing manner. This document is included here as representative of the kind of admission of guilt which some churches were compelled to make as they confronted the state in prophetic judgment and reconciliation.

Among other significant documents of recent times has been "A Theological Rationale and a Call to Prayer for the End to Unjust Rule," written by an ecumenical working group in response to a decision by the 1984 SACC national conference to pray for the end to unjust rule in the country. The document calls specifically for prayer "that God will replace the present structures of oppression with ones that are just, and remove from power those who persist in defying his laws, installing in their place leaders who will govern with justice and mercy." This is a document that again shows the church-state struggle in South Africa to be in direct continuity with the theological tradition already identified in this volume. As such, it summarizes much that has been documented in this book. The uncompromising attack on this statement by the state-controlled media, the newspapers favoring the present regime, and many powerful influences within the churches reemphasizes the awareness of those who benefit from the existing order of the latent power for political change within such theological attacks on the state.[17] It is this that makes the debate of church-state doctrine such a poignant one.

The Kairos document is a biblical and theological comment on the political crisis in South Africa, initiated in Soweto and worked out in dialogue with a number of concerned Christians from other parts of the country in a reflection on what is called in its preface "the situation of death." It arises out of the struggle to discover how to respond as Christians to the intensifying civil war in South Africa. The document is critical of the many "church theology" statements which have emerged in criticism of apartheid, some of which appear in this volume. The document challenges the uncritical affirmation of "a few stock ideas derived from Christian tradition" which are repeatedly affirmed within these church statements: reconciliation, justice, and nonviolence. In so doing it shows how even the most orthodox and pious Christian critique of oppression can be no more than a liberal conscious-salving exercise, while allowing oppression to persist. "Prophetic theology" as defined in the Kairos document is a theology both *for* the church and *against* the church. It is a call to renewal of church and state. It is group theology, open-ended and not to be regarded as a final statement. It is an invitation to critical thought and a challenge to action.

The response to the Kairos document has only begun to become public, but if it is taken as seriously as it deserves, this document could become one of the seminal documents in contemporary South African church history. British historian Robin Hallett suggests that the prophetic theology of the Kairos document "presents the apartheid regime with an ideological threat infinitely more powerful than any form of communism is ever likely to do, for South Africa is still a deeply Christian country."[18] The question is whether it can become a basis for breaking the impasse between church and state in South Africa. Its call is for Christian action against a state which has "no moral legitimacy" and has become "an enemy of the common good." Herein is both its strength and weakness—its strength because it could be the basis for motivating Christians to resist the forces of oppression within the country as a whole and the tyranny of the state in particular, and its weakness because the church has never succeeded in translating its noblest ideals into practice.

Most critics of the Kairos document respond from a traditional, Western perspective of what constitutes theology. Even friendly critics do this. One such commentator allows that "prophecy always oversimplifies. . . . But in a document that claims to be serious theological analysis of a critical situation, such oversimplification is to be avoided." A pertinent question is whether prophecy is necessarily precluded from being theology. Such theoretical discussions aside, the question is whether anything is to be gained by schooled theologians (and no few pretenders) judging, on the basis of certain preconditioned theological presuppositions, a document which emerges from the cauldron of black Christian reflection. Is it not more profitable at times to bracket one's own sensitivities and *hear* what a significant group of people are saying? If we miss this rare word, we miss a message. In so doing we have used our academic sophistication against ourselves.

The Kairos document uses the strongest possible language to reject the present regime as the antithesis of what it claims to be. The authors do not see South Africa as a country living "in humble submission to Almighty God"—as its constitution proclaims—but as the anti-Christ. Such apocalyptic language has been used often in the past—not least of all by many a zealous Afrikaner nationalist. Its function is to draw a distinction between the "good guys" who tend to be divinized and the "bad guys" who are demonized. This all too often promotes little more than blind fury as the latter are declared worthy only of damnation. Rational analysis is the first casualty. The outcome is political obscurantism. The Kairos document does not allow itself to fall into this impasse. It concerns itself quite explicitly with an analysis of the prevailing socio-economic order, endeavoring to show that the nature of this order is such that it cannot be reformed—it must be destroyed. This is where the Kairos theologians and the English-speaking churches are both in agreement and in conflict. They agree not only that the existing order must change but also that any attempt by the church to defend it is *heresy*. However, the churches have made no serious attempt to move beyond rhetoric. They remain trapped in their own ambiguity.

The burning question facing the English-speaking churches is whether they have fully faced the consequences of their call for the destruction of apartheid. This cannot be done without striking at the heart of the capitalist system, which in this country is built and maintained by racist legislation. The divide concerning questions of economics and the tough political implications of what Christians mean by reconciliation, the pursuit of justice, and the place of violence is still ahead of the churches. The publication of the Kairos document has anticipated this division.

Many of the documents pertinent to the discussion on church-state relations are included in this section of the book. In some instances, the portions we have reprinted are excerpts from longer publications. This is the case with the extract from the minutes of the council of the NGK which met in response to the 1914–15 rebellion, the extract from the NGK publication "Human Relations and the South African Scene in the Light of Scripture," and the extract from the Beyers Naudé trial. The "authorized summary" of the "Message to the People of South Africa" is provided; the full text is printed in *Apartheid Is a Heresy*, cited in the notes. Allan Boesak's letter to the minister of justice is a slightly reduced English translation of the Afrikaans text which was sent to the minister. The remaining documents are reprinted in full.

NOTES

1. T. N. Hanekom, *Kerk en Volk* (Cape Town: NG Kerk Boekhandel), pp. 59–60.
2. Leonard M. Thompson, *The Unification of South Africa 1902–1910* (Oxford: Oxford University Press, 1961), p. 17.
3. Carel F. A. Borchardt, "Die Afrikaner Kerke en die Rebellie," in I. Eybers, A. Konig, and C. Borchardt, eds., *Teologie en Vernuwing* (Pretoria: University of South Africa, 1975), pp. 85–116.
4. *Handelingen van eene Buitengewone vergadering van den Raad van der Ned. Geref. Kerken*, Jan. 27, 1915.
5. Borchardt, p. 97.
6. Ibid., pp. 113, 115.

7. Alan Paton, *Apartheid and the Archbishop: The Life and Times of Geoffrey Clayton* (Cape Town: David Philip, 1973), pp. 275–88.
8. For a more complete discussion on this alignment see my essay "An All-Pervading Heresy: Racism and the 'English-Speaking Churches,' " in John W. de Gruchy and Charles Villa-Vicencio, eds., *Apartheid is a Heresy* (Grand Rapids: Eerdmans, 1983).
9. See A. H. Luckhoff, *Cottesloe* (Cape Town: Tafelberg, 1978); see also W. A. de Klerk, *The Puritans in Africa* (London: Collins, 1975), pp. 250f.
10. See John de Gruchy, *The Church Struggle in South Africa* (Grand Rapids: Eerdmans, 1979); P. Walshe, *Church Versus State in South Africa: The Case of the Cristian Institute* (Maryknoll, N.Y.: Orbis, 1983); Charles Villa-Vicencio and John W. de Gruchy, eds., *Resistance and Hope: South African Essays in Honour of Beyers Naudé* (Grand Rapids: Eerdmans, 1985).
11. de Gruchy, *Church Struggle*, pp. 109–15.
12. International Commission of Jurists, *The Trial of Beyers Naudé* (Johannesburg: Ravan Press, 1975).
13. See the articles by Willem Vorster and Douglas Bax in de Gruchy and Villa-Vicencio, *Apartheid is a Heresy*.
14. See de Gruchy and Villa-Vicencio, *Apartheid is a Heresy*.
15. Borchardt, p. 116.
16. For a discussion on this debate see de Gruchy, *Church Struggle*, pp. 138–47.
17. Allen Boesak and Charles Villa-Vicencio, eds., *When Prayer Makes News* (Philadelphia: Westminster, 1986).
18. Robin Hallett, *Cape Times*, December 28, 1985.

BIBLIOGRAPHY

Boesak, A. *Black and Reformed: Apartheid, Liberation and the Calvinist Tradition*. Maryknoll, N.Y.: Orbis, 1984.

Boesak, A., and C. Villa-Vicencio. *When Prayer Makes News*. Philadelphia: Westminster, 1986.

Cloete, G. D., and D. J. Smith, eds. *A Moment of Truth: The Confession of the Dutch Reformed Mission Church, 1982*. Grand Rapids: Eerdmans, 1984.

de Gruchy, J. W. *The Church Struggle in South Africa*. Grand Rapids: Eerdmans, 1979.

de Gruchy, J. W., and C. Villa-Vicencio, eds. *Apartheid is a Heresy*. Grand Rapids: Eerdmans, 1983.

Leatt, J., T. Kniefel, and K. Nürnberger, eds. *Contending Ideologies in South Africa*. Grand Rapids: Eerdmans, 1986.

Prior, A., ed. *Catholics in Apartheid Society*. Cape Town: David Philip, 1982.

Tutu, D. *Hope and Suffering*. Grand Rapids: Eerdmans, 1984.

Villa-Vicencio, C., and J. W. de Gruchy, eds. *Resistance and Hope: South African Essays in Honour of Beyers Naudé*. Grand Rapids: Eerdmans, 1985.

COUNCIL OF THE NEDERDUITSE GEREFORMEERDE KERK IN ZUID AFRIKA, 1915

A RESPONSE TO THE 1914–15 REBELLION

POLITICAL SITUATION

The ministers of the Federated Churches from the four provinces of the Union meeting in Conference at the invitation of the Council of Churches [Raad der Ned. Ger. Kerken in Zuid Afrika] wish to express their deep pain at the serious political division which has recently emerged in the Afrikaner [Hollandsch-Afrikaansche] Community. We are concerned about the serious situation of mutual mistrust and bitterness that has resulted from this division, and especially about the armed struggle and shedding of blood among kinsmen who are bound to each other by blood and faith.

We are, however, aware of the hand of God in our people's history and of His wonderful guidance in the past, especially in times of extreme trial and suffering. We wish further to give expression to the unwavering faith to which we hold, and the strong trust that we have seen anew among our people, namely, that the God whom our fathers trusted, and who helped them, is also our God. He will not desert us in this darkest hour of the history of our people.

In earnestness we wish to arouse our people humbly to pray that God may powerfully use this testing of our people to improve their spiritual well-being. This will awaken a deeper realization of sin, the necessity of conversion and the sanctifying of this life, with a view to strengthening our awareness that we are called in our social and political lives to acknowledge and serve God.

POSITION OF THE CHURCH

[The following resolution was proposed by J. D. Kestall and seconded by J. M. Louw.]

(a) Concerning the Government: The Conference wishes clearly to state that according to God's Word the Government is ordained of God. The Church must, therefore, always recognize and teach that it is a Christian responsibility that law and order—in the state as well as the Church and family life—be honoured and maintained. Resistance by reason of conscience may not therefore be undertaken against lawful government, other than for very weighty and sound reasons.

(b) Concerning People's Movements: The Conference further wishes emphatically to declare its serious conviction that, when one takes the wider considerations into account, genuine peace and lasting unity in the country will not

---

[Source: *Handelingen van eene Buitengewone vergadering van den Raad van der Ned. Geref. Kerken*, Jan. 27, 1915.]

return, and cannot exist if resistance against the government is countered with violence alone. Only when the government and the people are inclined, in a serious and non-partisan way, to enquire into the real motives and purposes of this resistance, giving due consideration to all the factors that have contributed to the creation of this extremely tragic situation, whether these factors be real or reputed, will peace return. For this to happen negotiations on the basis of this investigation, must take place in the spirit of justice and with a willingness to satisfy the will of the people.

[After extensive debate the motion was amended as follows]:

(i) In section (a) the words "by reason of conscience" be deleted.

(ii) At the conclusion of this section the following words be added, "which are confirmed by God's Word and by a conscience which has been enlightened by the Word of God".*

THE CALLING OF THE CHURCH

With a view to the participation of the Church and her officers in the public life of the people, it is the Conference's opinion that the following two principles must be kept in mind:

1. That our Church, apart from its general calling as a Christian Church, has also received from God a more specific calling with regard to the Dutch-speaking Afrikaner people to whose existence she is intimately bound. It must therefore always be regarded as her responsibility to be a national Church, to watch over our particular national interests, and to teach our people to see God's hand in their own history and origin. It is further to keep alive among the Afrikaner people an awareness of national calling and destiny, wherein lies the spiritual, moral and physical progress of a people.
2. That our Church will best be able to fulfil both her task regarding God's Kingdom, and regarding our Afrikaner existence as a people, when the Church, and her preachers in their official positions, remain strictly outside of the party political struggle, unless religious or moral principles are at stake, or the concerns of the Kingdom of God explicitly justify such actions.

---

*The proposal as amended was adopted by a majority vote, while an alternative resolution which, quoting from the Netherlands Confession of Faith, demanded explicit obedience to the state, was defeated. C. F. A. Borchardt makes a significant comment regarding this decision: "From the proposal which was adopted, it would appear that the conference affirmed a general principle, but refused to apply it in a specific situation. While no one tried to indicate in what sense the rebellion was 'for weighty and sound reasons which are confirmed by God's Word,' neither was the situation of the rebels addressed. Alternatively it would appear that the meeting was not prepared to adopt a resolution in which a part of the Netherlands Confession of Faith is quoted, and in which obedience to the state is emphatically demanded." See C. F. A. Borchardt, "Die Afrikaanse Kerke en die Rebellie, 1914–15," in I. Eybers, A. König, and C. Borchardt, eds., *Teologie en Vernuwing* (Pretoria: University of South Africa, 1975), p. 97.

GEOFFREY CLAYTON

A LETTER FROM THE RIGHT REVEREND GEOFFREY CLAYTON, ARCHBISHOP OF CAPE TOWN MARCH 6, 1957

Dear Mr. Prime Minister,

We, Bishops of the Church of the Province of South Africa, are approaching you rather than the Minister of Native Affairs because we believe that the issues raised in Clause 29 (c) of the Native Laws Amendment Bill cannot be regarded merely as Native affairs. It appears to us that as far as the Anglican Church is concerned, churches and congregations in every urban area within the Union, even those mainly attended by Europeans, will be affected by this clause. Further, it is our belief that the Clause raises the issue of religious freedom and more particularly that of freedom of worship, and we venture to submit that this is a wider issue than that of Native Affairs only.

We desire to state that we regard the above-mentioned clause as an infringement of religious freedom in that it makes conditional on the permission of the Minister of Native Affairs

(a) The continuance in existence of any church or parish constituted after January 1st 1938 in an urban area except in a location which does not exclude Native Africans from public worship;

(b) the holding of any service in any church in an urban area except in a location to which a Native African would be admitted if he presented himself;

(c) the attendance of any Native African at any synod or church assembly held in an urban area outside a location.

The Church cannot recognise the right of an official of a secular government to determine whether or where a member of the Church of any race (who is not serving a sentence which restricts his freedom of movement) shall discharge his religious duty of participation in public worship or to give instructions to the minister of any congregation as to whom he shall admit to membership of that congregation.

Further, the Constitution of the Church of the Province of South Africa provides for the synodical government of the Church. In such synods, bishops, priests and laymen are represented without distinction of race or colour. Clause 29 (c) makes the holding of such synods dependent upon the permission of the Minister of Native Affairs.

We recognise the great gravity of disobedience to the law of the land. We believe that obedience to secular authority, even in matters about which we differ in opinion, is a command laid upon us by God. But we are commanded to render

---

[Source: Alan Paton, *Apartheid and the Archbishop: The Life and Times of Geoffrey Clayton* (Cape Town: David Philip, 1973).]

unto Caesar the things which be Caesar's, and to God the things that are God's. There are therefore some matters which are God's and not Caesar's, and we believe that the matters dealt with in Clause 29 (c) are among them.

It is because we believe this that we feel bound to state that if the Bill were to become law in its present form we should ourselves be unable to obey it or to counsel our clergy and people to do so.

We therefore appeal to you, Sir, not to put us in a position in which we have to choose between obeying our conscience and obeying the law of the land.

We have the honour to remain, Sir,

Yours faithfully,
(signed on behalf of the Bishops of the
Church of the Province of South Africa)
✠GEOFFREY CAPETOWN
Archbishop & Metropolitan

THE COTTESLOE CONSULTATION STATEMENT, 1961

I

We have met as delegates from the member churches in South Africa of the World Council of Churches, together with representatives of the World Council itself, to seek under the guidance of the Holy Spirit to understand the complex problems of human relationships in this country, and to consult with one another on our common task and responsibility in the light of the Word of God. Our worship, Bible study, discussion and personal contacts have led us to a heightened appreciation of one another's convictions and actions. Our next task will be to report to our several Churches, realizing that the ultimate significance of our meeting will consist in the witness and decisions of the Churches themselves in consequence of these consultations.

The general theme of our seven days together has been the Christian attitude towards race relations. We are united in rejecting all unjust discrimination. Nevertheless, widely divergent convictions have been expressed on the basic issues of apartheid. They range on the one hand from the judgment that it is unacceptable in principle, contrary to the Christian calling and unworkable in practice, to the conviction on the other hand that a policy of differentiation can be defended from the Christian point of view, that it provides the only realistic solution to the problems of race relations and is therefore in the best interests of the various population groups.

Although proceeding from these divergent views, we are nevertheless able to make the following affirmations concerning human need and justice, as they affect relations among the races of this country. In the nature of the case the agreements here recorded do not—and we do not pretend that they do—represent in full the convictions of the member Churches.

The Church of Jesus Christ, by its nature and calling, is deeply concerned with the welfare of all people, both as individuals and as members of social groups. It is called to minister to human need in whatever circumstances and forms it appears, and to insist that all be done with justice. In its social witness the Church must take cognizance of all attitudes, forces, policies and laws which affect the life of a people; but the Church must proclaim that the final criterion of all social and political action is the principles of Scripture regarding the realization of all men of a life worthy of their God-given vocation.

We make bold therefore to address this appeal to our Churches and to all Christians, calling on them to consider every point where they may unite their ministry on behalf of human beings in the spirit of equity.

[Source: South African Council of Churches.]

II

1. We recognize that all racial groups who permanently inhabit our country are a part of our total population, and we regard them as indigenous. Members of all these groups have an equal right to make their contribution towards the enrichment of the life of their country and to share in the ensuing responsibilities, rewards and privileges.

2. The present tension in South Africa is the result of a long historical development and all groups bear responsibility for it. This must also be seen in relation to events in other parts of the world. The South African scene is radically affected by the decline of the power of the West and by the desire for self-determination among the peoples of the African continent.

3. The Church has a duty to bear witness to the hope which is in Christianity both to white South Africans in their uncertainty and to non-white South Africans in their frustration.

4. In a period of rapid social change the Church has a special responsibility for fearless witness within society.

5. The Church as the body of Christ is a unity and within this unity the natural diversity among men is not annulled but sanctified.

6. No one who believes in Jesus Christ may be excluded from any Church on the grounds of his colour or race. The spiritual unity among all men who are in Christ must find visible expression in acts of common worship and witness, and in fellowship and consultation on matters of common concern.

7. We regard with deep concern the revival in many areas of African society of heathen tribal customs incompatible with Christian beliefs and practice. We believe this reaction is partly the result of a deep sense of frustration and a loss of faith in Western civilization.

8. The whole Church must participate in the tremendous missionary task which has to be done in South Africa, and which demands a common strategy.

9. Our discussions have revealed that there is not sufficient consultation and communication between the various racial groups which make up our population. There is a special need that a more effective consultation between the Government and leaders accepted by the non-white people of South Africa should be devised. The segregation of racial groups carried through without effective consultation and involving discrimination leads to hardship for members of the groups affected.

10. There are no Scriptural grounds for the prohibition of mixed marriages. The well-being of the community and pastoral responsibility require, however, that due consideration should be given to certain factors which may make such marriages inadvisable.

11. We call attention once again to the disintegrating effects of migrant labour on African life. No stable society is possible unless the cardinal importance of family life is recognized, and, from the Christian standpoint, it is imperative that the integrity of the family be safeguarded.

12. It is now widely recognized that the wages received by the vast majority of the non-white people oblige them to exist well below the generally accepted

minimum standard for healthy living. Concerted action is required to remedy this grave situation.

13. The present system of job reservation must give way to a more equitable system of labour which safeguards the interests of all concerned.

14. Opportunities must be provided for the inhabitants of the Bantu races to live in conformity with human dignity.

15. It is our conviction that the right to own land wherever he is domiciled, and to partake in the government of his country, is part of the dignity of the adult man, and for this reason a policy which permanently denies to non-white people the right of collaboration in the government of the country of which they are citizens cannot be justified.

16. (a) It is our conviction that there can be no objection in principle to the direct representation of coloured people in Parliament. (b) We express the hope that consideration will be given to the application of this principle in the foreseeable future.

17. In so far as nationalism grows out of a desire for self-realization, Christians should understand and respect it. The danger of nationalism is, however, that it may seek to fulfil its aim at the expense of the interests of others and that it can make the nation an absolute value which takes the place of God. The role of the Church must therefore be to help to direct national movements towards just and worthy ends.

SOUTH AFRICAN COUNCIL OF CHURCHES

A MESSAGE TO THE PEOPLE OF SOUTH AFRICA, 1968

THE AUTHORISED SUMMARY

In the name of Jesus Christ.

We are under an obligation to confess anew our commitment to the universal faith of Christians, the eternal Gospel of salvation and security in Christ Jesus alone.

The Gospel of Jesus Christ is the good news that in Christ God has broken down the walls of division between God and man, and between man and man.

The Gospel of Jesus Christ declares that Christ is the truth who sets men free from all false hopes of freedom and security.

The Gospel of Jesus Christ declares that God has shown himself as the conqueror of all the forces that threaten to separate and isolate and destroy us.

The Gospel of Jesus Christ declares that God is reconciling us to himself and to each other; and that therefore such barriers as race and nationality have no rightful place in the inclusive brotherhood of Christian disciples.

The Gospel of Jesus Christ declares that God is the master of this world, and that it is to him alone that we owe our primary commitment.

The Gospel of Jesus Christ declares that the Kingdom of God is already present in Christ, demanding our obedience and our faith now.

The Gospel of Jesus Christ offers hope and security for the whole life of man, not just in man's spiritual and ecclesiastic relationships, but for human existence in its entirety. Consequently, we are called to witness to the meaning of the Gospel in the particular circumstances of time and place in which we find ourselves. In South Africa, at this time, we find ourselves in a situation where a policy of racial separation is being deliberately effected with increasing rigidity. The doctrine of racial separation is being seen by many not merely as a temporary political policy but as a necessary and permanent expression of the will of God, and as the genuine form of Christian obedience for this country. It is holding out to men a security built not on Christ but on the theory of separation and the preservation of racial identity; it is presenting the separate development of our race groups as the way for the people of South Africa to save themselves. And this claim is being made to us in the name of Christianity.

We believe that this doctrine of separation is a false faith, a novel gospel; it inevitably is in conflict with the Gospel of Jesus Christ, which offers salvation, both individual and social, through faith in Christ alone. It is keeping people away from the real knowledge of Christ; therefore it is the Church's duty to enable

---

[Source: South African Council of Churches.]

our people to distinguish between the demands of the South African state and the demands of Christian discipleship.

The Christian Gospel requires us to assert the truth proclaimed by the first Christians, who discovered that God was creating a new community in which differences of race, language, nation, culture, and tradition no longer had power to separate man from man. The most important features of a man are not the details of his racial group, but the nature which he has in common with all men and also the gifts and abilities which are given to him as a unique individual by the grace of God; to insist that racial characteristics are more important than these is to reject what is most significant about our own humanity as well as the humanity of others.

But, in South Africa, everyone is expected to believe that a man's racial identity is the most important thing about him: only when it is clearly settled can any significant decisions be made about him. Those whose racial classification is in doubt are tragically insecure and helpless. Without racial identity, it seems, we can do nothing; he who has it, has life; he who has not racial identity has not life. This belief in the supreme importance of racial identity amounts to a denial of the central statements of the Christian Gospel. In practice, it severely restricts the ability of Christian brothers to serve and know each other, and even to give each other simple hospitality; it limits the ability of a person to obey Christ's command to love his neighbour as himself. For, according to the Christian Gospel, our brothers are not merely the members of our own race group. Our brother is the person whom God gives to us. To dissociate from our brother on the grounds of natural distinction is to despise God's gift and to reject Christ.

Where different groups of people are hostile to each other, this is due to human sin, not to the plan of the Creator. The Scriptures do not require such groups to be kept separate from each other; on the contrary, the Gospel requires us to believe in and to act on the reconciliation made for us in Christ. A policy of separation is a demonstration of unbelief in the power of the Gospel; any demonstration of the reality of reconciliation would endanger this policy. Therefore, the advocates of this policy inevitably find themselves opposed to the Church if it seeks to live according to the Gospel and to show that God's grace has overcome our hostilities. A thorough policy of racial separation must ultimately require that the Church should cease to be the Church.

The Gospel of Jesus Christ declares that God is love; separation is the opposite force of love. The Christian Gospel declares that separation is the supreme threat and danger, but that in Christ it has been overcome; it is in association with Christ and with each other that we find our true identity. But apartheid is a view of life and of man which insists that we find our identity in dissociation and distinction from each other; it rejects as undesirable the reconciliation which God is giving to us by his Son; it reinforces distinctions which the Holy Spirit is calling the people of God to overcome; it calls good evil. This policy is, therefore, a form of resistance to the Holy Spirit.

The Gospel of Jesus Christ declares that Christ is our master, and that to him all authority is given. Christians betray their calling if they give their highest loyalty, which is due to Christ alone, to one group or tradition, especially where that group is demanding self-expression at the expense of other groups. God judges us, not by our loyalty to a sectional group but by our willingness to be made new in the community of Christ. Christ is inevitably a threat to much that is called 'the South African way of life'; many features of our social order will have to pass away if the lordship of Christ is to be truly acknowledged and if the peace of Christ is to be revealed as the destroyer of our fear.

And Christ is master of the Church also. If the Church fails to witness to the true Gospel of Jesus Christ it will find itself witnessing to a false gospel. If we seek to reconcile Christianity with the so-called 'South African way of life' we shall find that we have allowed an idol to take the place of Christ. Where the Church abandons its obedience to Jesus Christ, it ceases to be the Church; it breaks the links between itself and the Kingdom of God. The task of the Church is to enable people to see the power of God at work, changing hostility into love of the brethren, and to express God's reconciliation here and now. For we are not required to wait for a distant 'heaven' where all problems will have been solved. What Christ has done, he has done already. We can accept his work or reject it; we can hide from it or seek to live by it. But we cannot postpone it, for it is already achieved; and we cannot destroy it, for it is the work of the eternal God.

We believe that Christ is Lord, and that South Africa is part of his world. We believe that his Kingdom and its righteousness have power to cast out all that opposes his purposes and keeps men in darkness. We believe that the word of God is not bound, and that it will move with power in these days, whether men hear or whether they refuse to hear. And so, we wish to put to every Christian person in the country the question which we ourselves face each day; to whom, or to what, are you giving your first loyalty, your primary commitment? Is it to a subsection of mankind, an ethnic group, a human tradition, a political idea: or to Christ?

May God enable us to be faithful to the Gospel of Jesus Christ, and to be committed to Christ alone!

THE CHRISTIAN INSTITUTE ON TRIAL

DIVINE OR CIVIL OBEDIENCE, 1973

THE RIGHT AND THE DUTY TO RESIST UNCHRISTIAN GOVERNMENTAL AUTHORITY IN THE NAME OF CHRIST

The believer in Christ not only has the right, but the responsibility to hearken to the Word of God and his righteousness rather than to the Government, should the Government deviate from God's will. Does not the responsibility lie with the Christian not to co-operate with the Government in a matter which is in conflict with the Gospel? By doing so is he not witnessing to Christ and his righteousness?

Civil disobedience is an act of protest by the Christian on the grounds of Christian conscience. It is only permissible when authority expects of him an un-Christian deed and pleas for a return to observance of the Gospel have not availed. 'The right of passive resistance can only be applied if it becomes apparent that no other method can overcome the emergency situation and restore righteousness' (*Die Stryd om die Ordes*, Prof. H. G. Stoker, p. 243). The State and its Commissions do have authority over the citizens, but in a moral sense the individual has a personal right towards the State for inasmuch as the citizen is part of the structure of the State, he is subject to the authority of the State; as a person before God even within the structures of the State he is, however, totally subject to God. 'In the last instance the Christian may not be bound by the State's authority because it is not the final dominion of God and therefore belongs to the being of the historical world which passes' (*Glaube in politischen Entscheidung*, Dr A. Rich, p. 161). Man never belongs totally to the State. He cannot be degraded into being a pawn of the State; the State exists for the benefit of man, not man for the benefit of the State.

Is it possible that the powers granted to this Commission by the Government and the results flowing from it reveal a totalitarian tendency? A totalitarian State usually wants complete control over its subjects. 'Its conflict with the Church is therefore not a coincidence, but is inevitable for as long as the Church remains a Church which knows the absolute necessity of its inner independence. Such a State can tolerate the inner independence of the Church even less than its outward independence, because it wants to control the soul of man. It is the soul that it wishes to control and shape after its own image' (*Gerechtigheit*, Prof. E. Brunner, p. 216).

It must be remembered that the most important matter for the citizens of a democratic state is not blind *obedience* and servile *submissiveness* to the Government, but joint responsibility for the concerns of State in the sight of God. 'Democracy strives to curtail the freedom of the individual as little as possible

---

[Source: International Commission of Jurists, *The Trial of Beyers Naudé* (Johannesburg: Ravan Press, 1975).]

but that freedom must result in maintaining the joint responsibility' (Wessler, *op. cit.*, p. 142). Cf. also Wolfgang Trillhaas: 'Accordingly obedience is no longer the predominant problem of the citizen. Much more is it the responsibility (or the joint responsibility) for the success of the State in the political life' (*Ethik*, Wolfgang Trillhaas, p. 373).

It must also be remembered what Reinhold Niebuhr said about the Christian motivation of democracy, namely, that human strivings towards justice make democracy possible, but the human inclination towards injustice makes democracy *essential*.

It may be that this type of action on the part of the Government reveals tendencies towards fascism, and such a Government then no longer *serves* but *dominates*. In such a situation the tendency is to govern by means of arbitrary power and to control by force. Government becomes primarily a power structure. If such a Government continues in this headlong way, the logical outcome is that it becomes idolatrous because everything has to flow out of, through and towards the National State (cf. Revelation 13). The Government's task is *not* to create arbitrary law. Its task is to reduce to writing in the form of legislation the substantive will of God as revealed in the Gospel. A Government with fascist leanings, however, creates its own justice which it enforces by way of penal sanctions. Anything opposed to the will or policy of such a Government is then regarded as subversive or as dangerous to the State. Freedom is regarded as a concession from the Government and not the normal way of life. In this the Government as well as the Commission will have to answer to God in regard to the bannings and also in regard to punishment which may possibly follow for those who refuse on grounds of conscience to testify before the Commission.

The power of a State such as this is not only territorial and military but also moral. As a result everything has to be subjected to the authoritarian, co-operative State—nothing is outside its power and authority and it determines the norms, even in relation to conscience. As a result a person may be led to violate his conscience, make it comformable and sacrifice it to the State. 'The more sensitive such a conscience is and the more receptive to the will of God, the more dangerous it is to offer it in sacrifice. He who is more obedient to man than to God against his better judgment and his conscience, destroys the integrity of his being, his unity within himself, and sooner or later he falls victim to schizophrenia' (*Freiheit und Bindung des Christen in der Politik*, T. Ellwyn, p. 27).

In this kind of State the real issue at stake is not whether the Government is *right or wrong, good or bad*, but whether the order, the policy and the will of the State, *fails or succeeds*.

If the present Government, as shown incidentally by the appointment of this Commission, reveals the above-mentioned traits, should it not be called back to the Gospel of Christ? If we too are guilty, the same applies to us. If such a call is ineffectual '. . . it becomes a matter of a clash between religious belief and Government, a clash in which man should be obedient to God rather than to the person in authority . . .' (Prof. H. G. Stoker, *op. cit.*, p. 213). The believer can, however, only act outside the law and refuse to co-operate if he acts according to God's will which is being violated by authority. 'Without justification nobody should claim the "right" to offer resistance against the authorities. This justification should, in my opinion, include the responsibility of resistance and must be included with the "Higher Authority" in whose name you are acting' (*Ethik*, Wolfgang Trillhaas, p. 373).

When reading Romans 13:1, 'Let every person be subject to the governing authorities . . . ,' it must be remembered that the Government does not have authority and power just because it is the Government as such, but because it is 'God's servant' (verse 4). 'The problem about the right to resist . . . is in fact contained in Romans 13. We ought to consider whether the term "God's servant" does not include the right to resist when the authorities exceed their God-given mandate and turn away from the clearly articulated commandments of God' (W. Schulze, quoted in *Politik zwischen Dämon und Gott*, Dr W. Kunneth, p. 301). Authority is only legitimate when it does not act contrary to God's will.

The same thought was expressed in the 1973 *Studies of the Christian Institute* as follows: '. . . the concept of the Government of a country as a creation and system of God in itself, is false and a Government is always subject to the righteousness of the Gospel. "It is exegetically no longer possible to base obedience to Governments on some peculiar character in them" (H. W. Bartsch).

'1 Peter 2:13, "Be submitted to every human ordinance because of the Lord," must be correctly translated as "Be subject to everyone (every human creature) for the Lord's sake" ' (H. W. Bartsch).

'The words in Romans 13: "The Government is ordained by God" and "they are servants (ministers) of God" do not refer to a peculiar commission or dignity of the Government but to what it in fact is, whether it accepts Romans 13 or not. God did not give special commission to the Government as such. The trend, therefore, is to *debunk the false concept of Governments*' (*Poverty in Abundance or Abundance in Poverty?*, Roelf Meyer, p. 13).

Where such deviation from the Gospel occurs, it is therefore not only the right of the Christian to resist authority, but his duty to offer passive resistance in obedience to the Gospel, even if in so doing he has to disobey the Government. If a Government violates the Gospel, it loses its authority to be obeyed in its office as ruler. 'The Government loses its essential office because of its contradictory attitude towards God' (W. Kunneth, *op. cit.*, p. 294). And: 'As an extension of these thoughts the right, even the duty can be imposed on the subject to resist the tyrant who commits an act of violence against a private person by the misuse of his office' (W. Kunneth, *op. cit.*, p. 295).

Therefore one can only speak of Government and its authority '. . . as long as it is said that it possesses the intention and the capability to accept responsibility for justice and righteousness. If this governmental function is distorted, however, then that Government has dissolved itself, its authority is no longer from God, and it is plainly in conflict with God. As a result of this, according to Romans 13, the Christian is no longer required to be obedient to the guilty (Government), but to a much greater extent obliged to resist such a Government which has degenerated' (W. Kunneth, *op. cit.*, p. 301).

The Calvinist John Knox also advocates the same idea. In his '. . . conversations with Queen Mary he had declared not only the right of the nobility to resist in defence of the people but the right of the subject to disobey where the ruler contravenes the law of God' (*Calvinism and the Political Order*, G. L. Hunt, p. 14). Calvin championed this same truth in vigorous language: 'Because earthly princes forfeit all their power when they revolt against God . . . We should resist them rather than obey . . .' (*Lecture* XIII).

The authority of the Government and State as such is not rejected in general by these ideas but maintained, because it is still *de facto* the Government, even if it deviates in essential points from the Gospel and then it has to be resisted. 'Even a distorted governmental system still retains the remnants and elements of the stable order of God' (W. Kunneth, *op. cit.*, p. 302).

A step such as this of disobeying the Government, must be taken on grounds of Christian conscience. The Christian's conscience is that God-given ability to distinguish between right and wrong according to the criterion of the Gospel, which inwardly compels him to follow the right course. '. . . Conscience also has the remarkable result that it can suddenly initiate resistance against the Government; an inner distress can also make itself felt when he allows the Government to force him to commit acts which he knows to be wrong.' Paul experiences a similar distress in Romans 9:1, 2 (*Christelijke Enzyclopedie*, Deel III, Prof. H. Schippers, p. 218). Conscience is the inner will that urges one to respond to the conscious norms, and the Christian conscience is bound up with the Gospel.

When the Government deviates from the Gospel, the Christian is bound by his conscience to resist it. Even if this results in breaking the law, it has to be done because God's will must be maintained above the law of man (Acts 4). The Government is God's servant and this means that it cannot arbitrarily place itself above the rule of law without impinging on the highest authority. If it does it, it becomes the evil-doer, (Romans 13) which must be resisted in obedience to God.

CHRISTIANS MAY IN PRAYERFUL ANTICIPATION HOPE

Christians may in prayerful anticipation hope that a Government which does not conform to the Gospel with regard to a particular matter may be brought to 're-think' its attitude. They hope for even more; namely, that God's righteousness may become the criterion in every facet of their lives, and particularly in their political life in South Africa. For this they work and pray.

If, however, the Government persecutes a Christian who finds it impossible to co-operate when departure from the Gospel occurs, the pertinent question must be asked: What is the crime against Christ for which he has to be punished? For this the Government would have to supply an answer to God and to South Africa. The Government, already persecuting and punishing people in an un-Christian manner, must remember that when Saul persecuted some believers, Christ asked him: 'Saul, Saul, why do you persecute *Me*?' (Acts 9:4). Is it not the duty of a Christian in such a situation constantly and in deep humility to call his fellow men to the same obedience in the light of the Gospel? And should a Christian not appeal to the Government in terms of the Gospel to turn away from its wrong course? 'Repent . . . even now the axe is laid to the root of the trees;

every tree therefore that does not bear good fruit is cut down and thrown into the fire' (Matthew 3).

In conclusion we wish to repeat that we have nothing to hide and that, if an inquiry is necessary (which we do not believe), we are willing to give evidence before a public, impartial, judicial tribunal and to co-operate. We do not wish to make ourselves heroes or martyrs as the Afrikaans press has implied; to us it is not a matter of martyrdom or heroism but a matter of obedience to Christ, the highest authority.

Through the Grace of God, we only want to remain obedient to Christ, the Word of God, because:

Verbum Dei manet in aeternum.

Signed: *Theo Kotzé, Roelf Meyer, Beyers Naudé.*

NEDERDUITSE GEREFORMEERDE KERK

HUMAN RELATIONS AND THE SOUTH AFRICAN SCENE IN THE LIGHT OF SCRIPTURE, 1974

THE CHURCH AND SOCIAL JUSTICE: POLITICAL ASPECTS

Our study of the data contained in the Bible has led us to the following conclusion with regard to state and church as separate institutions and instruments of God, each with its own authority, structure and functions, and the relationship between them.

Task of the church. In the first instance, it is the function of the church to preach to its adherents the gospel of personal salvation in Christ in order to strengthen them in holy faith and to prepare them for their service in the broad sphere of the church as organism (Eph. 4:11-16). This aspect of the church's function is of the utmost importance, because through the life and testimony of its spiritually equipped members the church fulfils its calling to be the salt of the earth and the light of the world, to see that justice is done in all spheres of life (Col. 4:1), to carry the norm of God's Word into all spheres of human endeavour, including that of the central authorities charged with the complex and demanding function of governing a multinational and multiracial society. The church also has an external function—to preach the Word of God in all spheres of life and, consequently, also to the authorities. This aspect of the church's task is not set out in so many words in the New Testament, but it is part and parcel of the essential being of the church, i.e. as aspect and instrument of the kingdom of God, on the basis of which it is called upon to preach the supremacy of Christ in all spheres of life, including that of the state.

In a multinational situation the calling of the church vis-à-vis the state is two-fold: it must preach the norms of God's Word for the mutual relationships of various groups of people and for the duties of the authorities in this situation, *and* it must warn when injustice is being done in the implementation of national policy and the application of laws.

The church must be both bold and cautious in the fulfilment of these functions. The manner in which the church addresses itself to the central authorities is determined by the following considerations: recognition of the fact that the authorities are an institution of God and have competency in their own sphere (Rom. 13:1-7). The actions of the church vis-à-vis the authorities are therefore circumscribed by the fact that the church shall honour and acknowledge the

---

[Source: *Human Relations and the South African Scene in the Light of Scripture* (Cape Town: Dutch Reformed Church, 1976).]

different character and competency of the authorities: acknowledgement of the believer's function in the sphere of the state; the fact that it is not part of the church's calling to dictate to the authorities, for instance, exactly how they should regulate the intercourse and relationships between the various groups in a multinational or multiracial situation, precisely because the Bible does not provide a clear indication on the nature of the structures by which the mutual relationships should be regulated; the nature of the church's contact with the authorities which should preferably be established and maintained through the various official church bodies; acknowledgement that in its dealings with the authorities the church should be sure of two things: the accuracy and the expertise of its facts; and that, in each case, it is indeed giving expression to the demands of the Word of God. The church not only has a preaching, but also an intercessionary function, with a view to the coming of the kingdom of God (according to 1 Tim. 2:1-4).

Function of the state. It is the duty of the state to preserve public order within its own particular area of jurisdiction, to reconcile and regulate the legal interests of the various groups for the sake of public order, to combat evil and to preserve justice. For without this, an orderly society is not possible (cf. 1 Tim. 2:2-4). In all this the state should act in accordance with Biblical norms, i.e. love of God and neighbour as guide-line for the public administration of justice (cf. 2 Chron. 19:6). The state may use institutions of power and even the sword to keep in check the pervasive influence of sin (Rom. 13:4). While this system of authority is essential for the regulation of various aspects of everyday life, it may never degenerate into a totalitarian system in which the state usurps the sovereignty of other institutions in their own particular fields in order to regulate all aspects of human existence. The golden rule of sovereignty for each institution in its own sphere, of justice and of love, should be sufficient to preserve the state from revolutionary chaos and political absolutism and tyranny.

Limited responsibility of the state. Because the state alone does not regulate the internal activities of all institutions of society, it cannot be held solely responsible for all abuses resulting from a given political system. Industry is a separate sphere of human endeavour in our modern society. The manner in which it organises and utilises its labour and capital should also be tested by the norms of the Bible and should, in terms thereof, be called to account for its Christian bias so that it may realise the norms of justice within its own sphere.

Conduct of church vis-à-vis state. As institution the church submits itself to the authority and law of the state, as far as its participation in the normal processes of justice and the exercising of its civil rights are concerned, provided the legal order does not conflict with the Word of God (Church order 65.2). It is the duty of the church to preach the Word of God to the authorities, in particular the norms of the Bible in respect of mutual relationships and social justice, and the duties of the authorities in this connection.

Human rights. We cannot accept, purely according to the teaching of the Bible, that man has rights in the sense of claims on the basis of his own merits, as the term is generally understood today. Human rights are those rights which God has bestowed upon man as the bearer of his image so that he may be able to fulfil his duties and calling as a human being. In order to be able to fulfil his calling as a human being, man has a right to life and the propagation thereof through marriage and the creation of communities and associations, to property and to freedom of religious practice and of conscience. It is self-evident that the exercise of these rights can never be divorced from the community in which the individual lives his life. For, as an association of people, the community has collective rights on the basis of which it must fulfil its divine calling. When it comes to the acknowledgement of rights, privileges must at all times be accompanied by responsibility. Rights and privileges may not be withheld when the claim is just.

Autogenous separate development. A political system based on the autogenous or separate development of various population groups can be justified from the Bible, but the commandment to love one's neighbour must at all times be the ethical norm towards establishing sound inter-people relations.

The Christian and politics. Since the Christian must apply the principles of the kingdom of God in the sphere of politics as well, he must enjoy the freedom of political thought and action, exercised in a responsible manner under the guidance of the Word and Spirit of God. The message of reconciliation of the Bible implies that there should at all times be channels for effective communication and consultation in a multinational situation.

The Christian must at all times seek to ensure that his political thinking and actions are based on justice and righteousness.

SOUTH AFRICAN COUNCIL OF CHURCHES

CONSCIENTIOUS OBJECTION

A RESOLUTION OF THE SACC NATIONAL CONFERENCE, JULY 31–AUGUST 2, 1974

The National Conference of the SACC acknowledges as the one and only God Him who mightily delivered the people of Israel from their bondage in Egypt and who in Jesus Christ still proclaims that He will "set at liberty those who are oppressed" (Luke 4:18). He alone is supreme Lord and Saviour and to Him alone we owe ultimate obedience. Therefore "we must obey God rather than men" in those areas where the Government fails to fulfil its calling to be "God's servant for good" rather than for evil and for oppression (Acts 5:29; Romans 13:4).

In the light of this the Conference:

1) Maintains that Christians are called to strive for justice and the true peace which can be founded only on justice;

2) does not accept that it is automatically the duty of those who follow Christ, the Prince of Peace, to engage in violence and war, or to prepare to engage in violence and war, whenever the State demands it;

3) reminds its member Churches that both Catholic and Reformation theology has regarded the taking up of arms as justifiable, if at all, only in order to fight a "just war";

4) points out that the theological definition of a "just war" excludes war in defense of a basically unjust and discriminatory society;

5) points out that the Republic of South Africa is at present a fundamentally unjust and discriminatory society and that this injustice and discrimination constitutes the primary, institutionalised violence which has provoked the counter-violence of the terrorists or freedom fighters;

6) points out that the military forces of our country are being prepared to defend this unjust and discriminatory society and that the threat of military force is in fact already used to defend that status quo against moves for radical change from outside the white electorate;

7) maintains that it is hypocritical to deplore the violence of terrorists or freedom fighters while we ourselves prepare to defend our society with its primary, institutionalised violence by means of yet more violence;

8) points out further that the injustice and oppression under which the black peoples of South Africa labour is far worse than that against which Afrikaners waged their First and Second Wars of Independence and that if we have justified the Afrikaners' resort to violence (or the violence of the imperialism of the English) or claimed that God was on their side, it is hypocritical to deny that the same applies to the black people in their struggle today;

9) questions the basis upon which chaplains are seconded to the military

forces lest their presence indicate moral support for the defence of our unjust and discriminatory society.

The Conference therefore:

1. Deplores violence as a means to solve problems;

2. calls on its member Churches to challenge all their members to consider in view of the above whether Christ's call to take up the Cross and follow Him in identifying with the oppressed does not, in our situation, involve becoming conscientious objectors;

3. calls on those of its member Churches who have chaplains in the military forces to reconsider the basis on which they are appointed and to investigate the state of pastoral care available to the communicants at present in exile or under arms beyond our borders and to seek ways and means of ensuring that such pastoral care may be properly exercised;

4. commends the courage and witness of those who have been willing to go to jail in protest against unjust laws and policies in our land, and who challenge all of us by their example;

5. requests the SACC's task force on Violence and Non-violence to study methods of non-violent action for change which can be recommended to its member Churches;

6. prays for the Government and people of our land and urgently calls on them to make rapid strides towards radical and peaceful change in our society so that the violence and war to which our social, economic and political policies are leading us may be avoided.

DESMOND TUTU

OPEN LETTER TO MR. JOHN VORSTER

The Hon. Prime Minister Mr John Vorster
House of Assembly
CAPE TOWN
8000

6 May 1976

Dear Mr Prime Minister
This will be my second letter ever to you. In 1972 after I had been refused a passport to take up a post as Associate Director of the Theological Education Fund, I appealed to you to intervene on my behalf with the appropriate authorities. Your intervention was successful because, soon thereafter, the then Minister of the Interior changed his mind and granted me and my family our passports. I am writing, therefore, optimistically in the hope that this letter will have similar happy results for all of us.

I am writing to you, Sir, in all deep humility and courtesy in my capacity as Anglican Dean of Johannesburg and, therefore, as leader of several thousand Christians of all races in the Diocese of Johannesburg. I am writing to you as one who has come to be accepted by some Blacks (i.e. Africans, Indians and Coloureds) as one of their spokesmen articulating their deepest aspirations, as one who shares them with equal steadfastness. I am writing to you, Sir, because I know you to be a loving and caring father and husband, a doting grandfather who has experienced the joys and anguish of family life, its laughter and gaiety, its sorrows and pangs. I am writing to you, Sir, as one who is passionately devoted to a happy and stable family life as the indispensable foundation of a sound and healthy society. You have flung out your arms to embrace and hug your children and your grandchildren, to smother them with your kisses, you have loved, you have wept, you have watched by the bed of a sick one whom you loved, you have watched by the deathbed of a beloved relative, you have been a proud father at the wedding of your children, you have shed tears by the graveside of one for whom your heart has been broken. In short, I am writing to you as one human person to another human person, gloriously created in the image of the selfsame God, redeemed by the selfsame Son of God who for all our sakes died on the Cross and rose triumphant from the dead and reigns in glory now at the right hand of the Father; sanctified by the selfsame Holy Spirit who works inwardly in all of us to change our hearts of stone into hearts of flesh. I am, therefore, writing to you, Sir, as one Christian to another, for through our common baptism we have been made members of and are united in the Body of our dear Lord and Saviour, Jesus Christ. This Jesus Christ, whatever we may have done, has broken

---

[Source: Desmond Tutu, *Hope and Suffering* (Grand Rapids: Eerdmans, 1984), pp. 28–36.]

down all that separates us irrelevantly—such as race, sex, culture, status, etc. In this Jesus Christ we are forever bound together as one redeemed humanity, Black and White together.

I am writing to you, Sir, as one who is a member of a race that has known what it has meant in frustrations and hurts, in agony and humiliation, to be a subject people. The history of your own race speaks eloquently of how utterly impossible it is, when once the desire for freedom and self-determination is awakened in a people, for it to be quenched or to be satisfied with anything less than freedom and that self-determination. Your people against tremendous odds braved the unknown and faced up to daunting challenges and countless dangers rather than be held down as a subjugated people. And in the end they emerged victorious. Your people more than any other section of the White community must surely know in the very core of their beings, if they were unaware of the lessons of history both ancient and modern, that absolutely nothing will stop a people from attaining their freedom to be a people who can hold their heads high, whose dignity to be human persons is respected, who can assume the responsibilities and obligations that are the necessary concomitants of the freedom they yearn for with all their being. For most Blacks this can never be in the homelands because they believe they have contributed substantially to the prosperity of an undivided South Africa. Blacks find it hard to understand why the Whites are said to form one nation when they are made up of Greeks, Italians, Portuguese, Afrikaners, French, Germans, English etc., etc.; and then by some tour de force Blacks are said to form several nations—Xhosas, Zulus, Tswanas etc. The Xhosas and the Zulus, for example, are much closer to one another ethnically than, say, the Italians and the Germans in the White community. We all, Black and White together, belong to South Africa against a visiting Argentinian side. The South African team won hands down and perhaps for the first time in our sporting history South Africans of all races found themselves supporting vociferiously the same side against a common adversary. The heavens did not fall down. Is it fanciful to see this as a parable of what will happen when all South Africans together are given a stake in their country so that they will be ready to defend it against a common foe and struggle for its prosperity vigorously and enthusiastically?

I write to you, Sir, because our Ambassador to the United Nations, Mr Botha, declared that South Africa was moving away from discrimination based on race. This declaration excited not only us but the world at large. I am afraid that very little of this movement has been in evidence so far. It is not to move substantially from discrimination when some signs are removed from park benches. These are only superficial changes which do not fundamentally affect the lives of Blacks. Husbands and fathers are still separated from their loved ones as a result of the pernicious system of migratory labour which a D.R.C. Synod once castigated as a cancer in South African society, one which had deleterious consequences on Black family life, thus undermining the stability of society which I referred to earlier. We don't see this much longed-for movement when we look at the overcrowded schools in Black townships, at the inadequate housing and woefully inadequate system of transport etc.

I write to you, Sir, to give you all the credit due to you for your efforts at promoting detente and dialogue. In these efforts many of us here wanted to support you eagerly, but we feel we cannot in honesty do this, when external detente is not paralleled by equally vigorous efforts at internal detente. Blacks are grateful for all that has been done for them, but now they claim *an inalienable right to do things for themselves,* in co-operation with their fellow South Africans of all races.

I write to you, Sir, because like you, I am deeply commited to real reconciliation with justice for all, and to peaceful change to a more just and open South African society in which the wonderful riches and wealth of our country will be shared more equitably. I write to you, Sir, to say with all the eloquence I can command that the security of our country ultimately depends not on military strength and a Security Police being given more and more draconian power to do virtually as they please without being accountable to the courts of our land, courts which have a splendid reputation throughout the world for fairness and justice. That is why we have called and continue to call for the release of all detainees or that they be brought before the courts where they should be punished if they have been found guilty of indictable offences. There is much disquiet in our land that people can be held for such long periods in detention and then often either released without being charged or, when charged, usually acquitted; but this does not free them from police harassment. Though often declared innocent by the courts, they are often punished by being banned or placed under house arrest or immediately re-detained. How long can a people, do you think, bear such blatant injustice and suffering? Much of the White community by and large, with all its prosperity, its privilege, its beautiful homes, its servants, its leisure, is hagridden by a fear and a sense of insecurity. And this will continue to be the case until South Africans of all races are free. Freedom, Sir, is indivisible. The Whites in this land will not be free until all sections of our community are genuinely free. Then we will have a security that does not require such astronomical sums to maintain it, huge funds which could have been used in far more creative and profitable ways for the good of our whole community, which would take its rightful place as a leader in Africa and elsewhere, demonstrating as it will that people of different races can live amicably together. We need one another and Blacks have tried to assure Whites that they don't want to drive them into the sea. How long can they go on giving these assurances and have them thrown back in their faces with contempt? They say even the worm will turn.

I am writing to you, Sir, because I have a growing nightmarish fear that unless something drastic is done very soon then bloodshed and violence are going to happen in South Africa almost inevitably. A people can take only so much and no more. The history of your own people which I referred to earlier demonstrated this. Vietnam has shown this, the struggle against Portugal has shown this. I wish to God that I am wrong and that I have misread history and the situation in my beloved homeland, my mother country South Africa. A people made desperate by despair, injustice and oppression will use desperate means. I am frightened, dreadfully frightened, that we may soon reach a a point of no return, when events will generate a momentum of their own, when nothing will stop their reaching a bloody denouement which is "too ghastly to contemplate", to quote your words, Sir.

I am frightened because I have some experience of the awfulness of violence. My wife and I with our two youngest children stayed for two months in Jerusalem in 1966 and we saw the escalating violence and the mounting tensions between Jew and Arab which preceded the Six Day War. I was in Addis Ababa when there was rioting in the streets, a prelude to the overthrow of the dynasty of Haile Selassie. I was in Uganda just before the expulsion of the Asians from that country and have returned there since and experienced the fear and the evil of things there. I have visited the Sudan, admittedly after the end of the seventeen years of civil strife, but I could see what this internecine war had done to people and their property. I have visited Nigeria and the former Biafra and have seen there the awful ravages of that ghastly civil war on property and on the souls of the defeated Biafrans. Last year I was privileged to address the General Assembly of the Presbyterian Church in Ireland in Belfast—and what I saw shook me to the core of my being. We saw daily on television in Britain horrific pictures of the pillage and destruction being perpetrated in Vietnam: children screaming from the excruciating agony of burns caused by napalm bombing, a people rushing helter skelter, looking so forlorn and bewildered that one wanted to cry out 'But is there no God who cares in heaven'. No, I know violence and bloodshed and I and many of our people don't want that at all.

But we Blacks are exceedingly patient and peace-loving. We are aware that politics is the art of the possible. We cannot expect you to move so far in advance of your voters that you alienate their support. We are ready to accept some meaningful signs which would demonstrate that you and your Government and all Whites really mean business when you say you want peaceful change. First, accept the urban Black as a permanent inhabitant of what is wrongly called White South Africa, with consequent freehold property rights. He will have a stake in the land and would not easily join those who wish to destroy his country. Indeed, he would be willing to die to defend his mother country and his birthright. Secondly, and also as a matter of urgency, repeal the pass laws which demonstrate to Blacks more clearly than anything else that they are third rate citizens in their beloved country. Thirdly, it is imperative, Sir, that you call a National Convention made up of the genuine leaders (i.e. leaders recognised as such by their section of the community,) to try to work out an orderly evolution of South Africa into a nonracial, open and just society. I believe firmly that your leadership is quite unassailable and that you have been given virtually a blank cheque by the White electorate and that you have little to fear from a so-called right wing backlash. For if the things which I suggest are not done soon, and a rapidly deteriorating situation arrested, then there will be no right wing to fear—there will be nothing.

I am writing this letter to you, Sir, during a three day clergy retreat in Johannesburg, when in the atmosphere of deep silence, worship and adoration and daily services of the Lord's Supper we seek to draw closer to our Lord and try to discover what is the will of God for us and what are the promptings and inspirations of God's Holy Spirit. It is during this time that God seemed to move me to write this letter.

I hope to hear from you, Sir, as soon as you can conveniently respond, because I want to make this correspondence available to the Press, preferably with your concurrence, so that all our people, both Black and White, will know that from our side we have done all that is humanly possible to do, to appeal, not only to the rank and file of Whites, but to the highest political figure in the land, and to have issued the grave warning contained in my letter. This flows from a deep love and anguish for my country. I shall soon become Bishop of Lesotho, when I must reside in my new diocese. But I am quite clear in my own mind, and my wife supports me in this resolve, that we should retain our South African citizenship no matter how long we have to remain in Lesotho.

Please may God inspire you to hear us before it is too late, and may He bless you and your Government now and always.

Should you think it might serve any useful purpose, I am more than willing to meet with you to discuss the issues I raise here as you say in Afrikaans, *onder vier oë*.

Since coming to this Cathedral last year, we have had a regular service, praying for Justice and Reconciliation in this country every Friday. And at all services in the Cathedral we pray:

God bless Africa
Guard her children
Guide her rulers and
Give her peace,
For Jesus Christ's sake.

And:

O Lord, make us instruments of Thy peace: where there is hatred, let us sow love; where there is injury, pardon; where there is despair, hope; where there is darkness, light; where there is sadness, joy.
O divine Master, grant that we may not so much seek to be consoled as to console, to be understood as to understand, to be loved as to love: for it is in giving that we receive, it is in pardoning that we are pardoned, it is in dying that we are born to eternal life.
Amen.

And we mean it.
Yours respectfully,
Desmond Tutu

SOUTH AFRICAN CATHOLIC BISHOPS CONFERENCE

SOCIAL JUSTICE AND RACE RELATIONS WITHIN THE CHURCH, 1977

Assembled in plenary session, we, the South African Catholic Bishops' Conference, accept that the Catholic Church in South Africa is lagging behind in witness to the Gospel in matters of social justice. We are encouraged by the support given to our policy of opening Catholic schools to all pupils regardless of race; and now, after prayerful reflection and in humble reliance on the wisdom and strength that come from God's Spirit, we commit ourselves to the following programme:

A. CONCERNING SOCIAL ATTITUDES AND CUSTOMS

1. To strive for the elimination of terms which of themselves or in their South African context, are derogatory and even insulting, even when no slight is intended, such as "native", "Bantu" (except where this word is unavoidable on official documents), "boy" or "girl" for adults, "non-whites", "non-Europeans", "location" and "mission" (when used in the sense of parish); and to combat the unnecessary use of racial and national designations that emphasize differences and foster the apartheid mentality.

2. To eradicate all differentiation on purely racial grounds in the treatment of persons at presbyteries, convents, other church institutions and private homes.

3. To suppress the custom still lingering in some places of having different sections of churches appropriated to different race groups and to ensure that church halls and similar premises in any area are available to all.

4. To insist that all Catholic associations and parish councils review their policy and actual achievement or failure in bringing various races together.

5. To commend the witness of persons who in their desire to identify with the deprived and to make the Church recognisable as the Church of the poor, refrain from using privileges arising from race or wealth.

6. To aim at a simple life-style for ourselves and where necessary to encourage other church and religious personnel to do the same.

B. CONCERNING THE SHARING OF RESPONSIBILITY

7. To do all in our power to speed up the promotion of Black persons to responsible functions and high positions in the Church, to encourage them to accept such functions and responsibilities, so that the multi-cultural nature of the Church in South Africa may be clearly recognised, and to provide the training necessary for this purpose.

[Source: Southern African Catholic Bishops Conference, plenary session, Feb. 1977.]

8. To encourage priests, especially those working in Black parishes from which White priests may be excluded in times of crisis likely to recur, to give the fullest responsibility to parish councils and lay ministers, including allowing for learning by trial and error.

C. CONCERNING SOCIAL JUSTICE, LIBERATION AND DEVELOPMENT

9. To re-assess the distribution and function of church personnel, clergy and religious, in relation to the needs and numbers of racial and ethnic groups and, where necessary, to bring about a more equitable distribution.

10. To be mindful of the Church's duty to minister to Christ where he most suffers in society and therefore to make more strenuous efforts to direct special attention to the growing numbers of unemployed, to industrial workers in general and migrant workers in particular, to worker organisations, to the thousands of squatters living on the periphery of large cities, to political prisoners, detainees, banned people and their dependants, and to other distressed and displaced groups discovered; and to provide as far as possible for the care of these groups and the creation of communities among them by special appointed priests, religious and lay workers.

11. To signify, by the appointment of Black priests to the charge of White parishes, the breaking away by the Church from the prevailing social and political system.

12. To push forward with the policy of integrating our institutions, and in such a way as to enable the poor as well as the better-off to benefit.

13. To accept the establishment of equal pay for equal work as the aim of deliberate progressive budgetting and meanwhile to accept as basic the standards proposed by the Justice and Reconciliation Department and to insist on periodical reviews of all wages and conditions of work in our dioceses.

14. To promote the awakening of social conscience and the awareness of injustice and social problems as central to evangelisation and an essential element of preaching, liturgy and catechetics and of priestly religious and lay formation, of church work and witness.

15. To give practical expression to the conviction that the Church's mission includes work for complete human liberation and to the teaching of "Evangelii Nuntiandi" that evangelisation includes transforming the concrete structures that oppress people; and in the light of this, to strive that the Church be seen in solidarity with the legitimate aspirations of oppressed people; on the side, therefore, of Black Consciousness, in regard both to those who promote it and those who suffer for it.

16. To urge that, in addition to the campaign for public social justice Christians be urged to give their time and energy to assisting in development work, such as literacy campaigns and tutoring, co-operative ventures and self-help associations and advisory bodies to aid in such matters as welfare services, legal problems, budgetting and the use of hire purchase; that those who have any technique to offer should be willing to help; that projects should be limited and

carefully selected; that work should aim at the development of the whole person and the formation of basic groups and communities; and that those engaged in this work should, however, not see themselves as dispensed from the broader social apostolate for human rights.

17. To aim at the employment in every diocese or region of a full-time worker in justice and reconciliation and development work, who will give his time to each activity according to needs, and whose financial support will be a priority in diocesan or regional budgetting.

18. To encourage clergy, religious and lay associations to undertake development work less exclusively within the Catholic Church and to move towards the whole of society, showing there the power of the Spirit in union with other Christian churches and in co-operation with local communities, so as not to further divide people on lines of church affiliation in ordinary citizen and political action but to promote harmony.

19. To encourage, under the aegis of Church bodies, including religious congregations, the launching of local community groups to promote training and development projects and the timely handing over to the groups of the institutions, property and funds connected with the projects.

D. CONCERNING CHURCH FINANCE

20. To recognise, in accordance with resolution 12 of the 1975 meeting of the Southern African Council of Priests, the importance for community witness of making the principle of sharing more visible in church finance and to devote serious study to:

(1) the re-evaluation of the meaning and use of money, as to how much should be seen as belonging to the local parish and how much to the Church collectively;

(2) to communalising of parochial funds within each diocese to form a central fund which will be evenly distributed enabling standards of churches, presbyteries and works of mercy to be more consistent;

(3) to the application of the principle of communalising church funds not only within dioceses but also on a national level between poor and richer dioceses.

E. CONCERNING A PASTORAL CONSULTATION

21. To take into account the singular situation and resultant tensions of the Church in South Africa, where 80% of the laity are Black and 80% of the clergy White, and to investigate as a matter of extreme urgency the feasibility of a Pastoral Consultation in which lay people, religious and priests, in large majority Black, may participate with the bishops, in arriving at policy on Church life and Apostolate but not on doctrinal and canonical matters.

ALLAN BOESAK

LETTER TO THE SOUTH AFRICAN MINISTER OF JUSTICE

The Honourable A. Schlebusch
Minister of Justice
Union Building
Pretoria 0002

24th August 1979

Your Honour,

A short while ago you thought it right to address the South African Council of Churches as well as church leaders sharply and seriously over the radio and television and in the press in connection with the SACC resolution on civil disobedience. Although the decision was not taken as a result of my address, I expressed my point of view openly at this occasion and was one of the people who supported the SACC in this respect.

You are Minister of Justice and in this capacity you have issued your serious warning. I take your words seriously. Hence my reaction which I express to you in full respect and which you must read particularly as a personal declaration of faith.

Your warning has become almost customary in South Africa. It consists in the Government's continually pointing out to pastors and churches that they must keep themselves "out of politics" and confine themselves to their "proper" task: the preaching of the Gospel.

Here already an extremely important question emerges: what is the Gospel of Jesus Christ which the churches have been called to preach? Surely it is the message of the salvation of God which has come to all people through Jesus Christ. It is the proclamation of the kingdom, and the lordship of Christ. But this salvation is the making whole of the *whole person.* It is not meant for his "inner life", his soul, only. It is meant for his whole human existence. This Jesus who proclaimed the church was surely not only a spiritual being with spiritual qualities estranged from the reality of our human existence. No, He is the Word become flesh, who took on complete human form, and his message of liberation is meant for the total person in his *full humanity.*

But besides, the fact that the term Kingdom is so politically loaded must already say a great deal to us. For example, the fact that reformed Christians have rightly professed with conviction throughout the centuries that the lordship of Christ applies to *all* spheres of our lives. The political, social and economic spheres also. The Lord rules over all these spheres and the church and the Christian looks for his sovereignty and respect in all these spheres. Surely it is a

---

[Source: *International Review of Mission,* 69 (Jan. 1983).]

holy duty and calling for every Christian to participate in political life so that there also God's law and justice may prevail, and there also obedience to Him and his Word can be shown.

The Dutch Reformed Church professes this in its report "Ras, Volk en Nasie in die lig van die heilige Skrif". The report states plainly that the church in its proclaiming must appeal to its members to apply the principles of the Kingdom of God in the social and political sphere. When the Word of God demands it, the church must fulfill its prophetic function with regard to the State in spite of popular opinion. The witness of the church with regard to the government is a part of its essential being, says the report. The Dutch Reformed Church professes this because it is Reformed. Why then is this profession and participation not granted to other Christians (and other Reformed Christians!)?

There is still another problem. Your government through its spokesmen has often warned that clergymen "must keep out of politics". Yet at the same time it is your own colleagues in the cabinet who want to involve churchmen in political dialogue!

The only conclusion which I can come to is that you do not object in principle to the participation of churchmen in politics—as long as it happens on your terms. This seems to me to be a standpoint which is neither tenable nor honest. In addition, are you not denying your own history by taking up this standpoint? Did not the church of the Afrikaner, even in the Anglo-Boer War, stand right in the middle of the struggle? Why do you today reject with a sort of political pietism that which yesterday and the day before you embraced to your bosom with thankfulness to God.

But, your Honour, there is something more in your warning. It is associated with the exceptionally difficult and sensitive issue of a Christian's obedience to the government.

It is important that you understand clearly that I made my call for civil disobedience as a Christian to other Christians.

It surprises me that some people see in this a call for violence. It is precisely an alternative to violence! I look to this alternative because I still do not find the way of violence to be the proper way.

Or is it the case of people fearing that should Christians perform their duty of being more obedient to God than to men, then the idolized nature of the state will be exposed? Surely the State in which Christ reigns shouldn't have to be afraid of this? In addition, I am of the opinion that I have done nothing more than place myself fairly and squarely within the Reformed tradition.

But essential to all of this is the following: It is my conviction that, for a Christian, obedience to the state or any authority is always linked to the obedience to God. That is to say, that obedience to human institutions is always relative. The human institution can never have the same authority as God, and human laws must always be subordinate to the Word of God. This is how the Christian understands it. Since God does not expect blind obedience from his children, Christians cannot give unconditional obedience to a worldly sovereignty.

Over the years gone by it has become clear to me that your government expects precisely this sort of unconditional, blind obedience. I want to be honest with you, this I cannot give you. The believer in Christ has not only the right, but also the responsibility, to be more obedient to God and *his* law than to the government, should this government deviate from God's law.

Over the years gone by, nearly all the large Christian churches in South Africa have condemned the policy of your government as sinful and wrong. My own church, the D.R. Mission church, last year condemned the policy of this government as being "in conflict with the Gospel of Jesus Christ, a policy which cannot stand up to the demands of the Gospel". I heartily endorse this statement of my church. Your policy is unjust, it denies people their basic human rights and it undermines their humanity. So many of the laws which you make are in conflict with the Word of God.

Your policy, and its execution, are a tremendous obstacle for reconciliation between the people of South Africa. Some of the laws are more hurtful than others and have been condemned especially by the churches. Now the churches have reached a point where we say: if we condemn laws on the grounds of God's Word, how can we then obey those very same laws?

In my view, Christians do not stand alone in this decision. The Scriptures know the familiar disobedience to powers when these powers disregard the Word of the Living God.

Daniel was refusing to obey the king's law when he refused to bow down before the graven image of Nebuchadnezzar (Dan. 3:17-18). He regarded the king's law as being in conflict with the instructions of his God.

Peter's refusal to obey the Sanhedrin command and not to witness about Jesus any more, is the classical example of disobedience to a worldly authority. Today still his answer resounds like a bell in the Church of Christ: "We must obey God rather than men" (Acts 5:29).

There are still other examples. Paul displayed nothing of a servile obedience when the magistrate of Philippi wanted to release him from prison after confining him unlawfully (without a trial!). "They gave us a public flogging, though we are Roman citizens and have not been found guilty; they threw us into prison, and are they now to smuggle us out privately? No indeed!" (Acts 16:37).

This despite the fact that in the case of Peter and John the Sanhedrin was the highest authority, not only in religious matters, but in everything which did not lie directly in the sphere of the Roman procurator.

In the case of Paul, the judges were the highest officials in the Roman colony of Philippi. For both Peter and Paul it was clear that occasions could arise when the only way out would be disobedience to the unjust authority. Still more of these examples, Luke 23:6-12, Mark 15:1-5 and John 18:8-11, teach us that Jesus did not always demonstrate obedience to state authority. Before Herod, he refused to say a word: "He answered him without a word." Also before Pilate, according to Mark, Jesus gave no answer, neither to the questions of Pilate, nor to the charges of the high priests.

John tells us that Jesus reminded Pilate of something of which every worldly bearer of authority since must be reminded: " 'You would have no authority at all over me', Jesus replied, 'if it had not been granted you from above; and therefore the deeper guilt lies with the man who handed me over to you' " (John 19:11).

I am not saying that there is "proof" from these actions of Jesus, Peter and Paul, that a revolutionary overthrow of the state can be approved. That question is a completely different issue. I am saying instead that blind obedience to civil authorities is alien to the Bible and that loyalty and obedience is first and foremost to God for a Christian.

May I point out, in parenthesis, that the issue on which everything hinges is definitely not servile submissiveness of citizens, but co-responsibility for the affairs of State. And it is precisely this which the policy of your government denies millions of citizens.

Here is not the place to present a full explanation on Romans 13. However, I would simply point out that the first verse of Romans 13, which is often taken as a blank legitimization of state interference, is in fact a very serious point of criticism. A government yields authority because (and as long as) it reflects the authority of God: liberating, creative, serving. Thus Paul can refer to a government as a servant of God, "for your good". Thus throughout the years, it has been taken for granted in the Reformed thinking that a government wields authority for as long as there is evidence that it is accepting responsibility for the law and for justice. Where justice is lacking, however, the government's authority is no longer derived from God but is in conflict with God. In such a case, resistance against such a government is justified and demanded.

Even Augustine, who is one of the old Fathers of the Church who was particularly concerned with protecting the state and who defended state authority with extraordinary energy, had this to say: "Justice is the only thing that can give a worldly power worth. What is worldly wealth if justice is lacking? It is none other than a bunch of plunderers."

Calvin also saw this and said: "Worldly princes" will lose all their power when they rise up against God. He stated clearly that Christians should resist such a power rather than obey it.

The point is of course to decide *when* a government collides with the demands of God's Word. In this the church should be led by the Word itself through the justice of the Kingdom of God, and also by the actual experience of people. Because it is in the concrete situation of people that the Word shows itself alive and more powerful and sharper than any two-edged sword.

In this the church should find its criteria, not from those who make the laws, or from those who are favoured by the laws, but rather from those who are touched by these laws, who are hurt at their deepest level of being: those who have no votes, the oppressed, the "least of these my brethren".

And in the mouths of the least of the brethren in our country, your government and your policy are condemned. I don't have to repeat the accusations again. I just want to draw your attention to the fact.

The suffering of men, women and children, the bitterness of too many already, the wounds made by your policy through the years can never be compensated for by "concessions". The superficial adjustment already made by your government doesn't touch the root of the matter. This is as one of your colleagues has said: "The fact that a black man carries a springbok emblem doesn't give him political rights." Indeed. We can add: it doesn't give him either his God-given humanity.

It is because of your policy that so many churches and so many Christians find themselves against you. Because the church of Christ in South Africa must obey God more than people. I plead with you: stop your disastrous policy.

May I end with a personal word? I don't write this letter in order to be brave or arrogant. I must honestly confess that I'm afraid of you. You are the Minister of Justice. You have at your disposal a mighty power such as only a fool would underestimate. The victims of this power are sown across the path of South Africa's recent history.

I, like any other South African, want to live a normal life with my wife and children and to serve the church without fear. I want a country where freedom is seen as the right of every citizen and not as a gift from the government. I want, along with millions of other people, to have co-responsibility in our native country, with everything you grant yourself and your children. I also want peace, but then real peace. Not the fearful silence which we have now, but *that* peace, which is the fruit of active justice for everybody.

But my wish for a "normal life" must not undermine the service I am called to. That would be intolerable. And my service is also towards you. That is why I write this letter. I stand guilty before God if I do not witness against the government.

I think the time has come that your government has to make a choice between the servant of God in Romans 13 and the demon in Revelation 13. And unless the right choice becomes evident (through a whole-hearted and fundamental change of your policy), Christians in South Africa will have to continue resisting. Because for the Christian the obedience to God and His Word must be first priority.

Resistance against a government is not an easy decision. That is why the synod of the Dutch Reformed Mission Church made this so clear last year: "If a Christian finds himself bound by his conscience to follow the way of criticism, which brings himself into conflict with the state, then he should obey God more than the people. In this case, however, he must be prepared to accept to suffer in the spirit of Christ and his apostles."

Once again, this is not a matter of being brave. Rather I would like to use the occasion seriously to urge you to realize that peace and salvation and a happy future for South Africa do not lie in more "safety laws" or in more threats or in an ever-growing defense budget. They lie rather in providing justice for everybody.

You as whites are not in a position to achieve this on your own. That is why from the churches we plead for a national convention of chosen and authentic leaders of all the people of South Africa. Give us the right to vote, so that our citizenship of South Africa becomes meaningful. Give us the right to vote, so that we ourselves can express our political will. Give us the right to vote—you grant this to yourself, don't you?

My plea is that you make a real use of the opportunity to talk. An honest conversation in view of a genuine new sharing *together* in South Africa is always better than to stand against each other as enemies, isn't it?

I am using this letter as an open witness and thus will make it available to the press.

I thank you for giving your time,

May God give you wisdom in everything,

Yours sincerely,
Dr A. A. Boesak

NEDERDUITSE GEREFORMEERDE SENDINGKERK
(NG MISSION CHURCH)

CONFESSION OF FAITH, 1982

A STATUS CONFESSIONIS

Because the secular Gospel of apartheid threatens in the deepest possible way the witness of reconciliation in Jesus Christ and the unity of the Church of Jesus Christ in its very essence, the NG Mission Church in South Africa declares that this constitutes a *status confessionis* for the Church of Jesus Christ. (A *status confessionis* means that we regard this matter as a concern about which it is impossible to differ without it affecting the integrity of our communal confession as Reformed Churches.)

We declare that apartheid (separate development) is a sin, that the moral and theological justification of it makes a mockery of the Gospel, and that its consistent disobedience to the Word of God is a theological heresy.

The decision of Ottawa and the decisions with regard to racism and therefore apartheid (separate development) cannot be regarded as an alternative to the decision of the Synod of 1978, but rather as a consequence.

According to the conviction of the Synod the NGK believes in the ideology of apartheid, which is in direct conflict with the evangelical message of reconciliation and the visible unity of the Church. Therefore the 1978 decision of the Mission Church makes it clear that we can do no other than with the deepest regret accuse the NGK of theological heresy and idolatry. This is done in the light of her theologically formulated standpoint and its implementation in practice.

The NG Mission Church makes this statement in deep humility and self-examination so that we may keep ourselves 'from being disqualified after having called others to the contest' (I Cor. 9:27).

THE CONFESSION OF FAITH

1. We believe in the triune God, Father, Son, and Holy Spirit, who gathers, protects, and cares for his Church by his Word and his Spirit, as he has done since the beginning of the world and will do to the end.

2. We believe in one holy, universal Christian Church, the communion of saints called from the entire human family.

[Source: Synod of the NG Sendingkerk, Belhar, Sept. 22–Oct. 6, 1982.]

We believe

Eph. 2:11–22	that Christ's work of reconciliation is made manifest in the Church as the community of believers who have been reconciled with God and with one another;
Eph. 4:1–16	that unity is, therefore, both a gift and an obligation for the Church of Jesus Christ; that through the working of God's Spirit it is a binding force, yet simultaneously a reality which must be earnestly pursued and sought: one which the people of God must continually be built up to attain;
John 17:20, 23	that this unity must become visible so that the world may believe; that separation, enmity, and hatred between people and groups is sin which Christ has already conquered, and accordingly that anything which threatens this unity may have no place in the Church and must be resisted;
Phil. 2:1–5 1 Cor. 12:4–31 John 13:1–17 1 Cor. 1:10–13 Eph. 4:1–6 Eph. 3:14–20 1 Cor. 10:16–17 1 Cor. 11:17–34 Gal. 6:2 2 Cor. 1:3–4	that this unity of the people of God must be manifested and be active in a variety of ways: in that we experience, practice, and pursue community with one another, that we are obligated to give ourselves willingly and joyfully to be of benefit and blessing to one another; that we share one faith, have one calling, are of one soul and one mind; have one God and Father, are filled with one Spirit, are baptized with one baptism, eat of one bread and drink of one cup, confess one name, are obedient to one Lord, work for one cause, and share one hope; together come to know the height and the breadth and the depth of the love of Christ; together are built up to the stature of Christ, to the new humanity; together know and bear one another's burdens, thereby fulfilling the law of Christ; that we need one another and upbuild one another, admonishing and comforting one another; that we suffer with one another for the sake of righteousness; pray together; together serve God in this world; and together fight against all which may threaten or hinder this unity;
Rom. 12:3–8 1 Cor. 12:1–11 Eph. 4:7–13 Gal. 3:27–28 James 2:1–13	that this unity can be established only in freedom and not under constraint; that the variety of spiritual gifts, opportunities, backgrounds, convictions, as well as the various languages and cultures, are by virtue of the reconciliation in Christ opportunities for mutual service and enrichment within the one visible people of God;
	that true faith in Jesus Christ is the only condition for membership of this Church.

Therefore, we reject any doctrine

which absolutizes either natural diversity or the sinful separation of people in such a way that this absolutization hinders or breaks the visible and active unity of the Church, or even leads to the establishment of a separate church formation;

which professes that this spiritual unity is truly being maintained in the bond of peace while believers of the same confession are in effect alienated from one another for the sake of diversity and in despair of reconciliation;

which denies that a refusal earnestly to pursue this visible unity as a priceless gift is sin;

which explicitly or implicitly maintains that descent or any other human or social factor should be a consideration in determining membership of the Church.

2 Cor. 5:17–21
Matt. 5:13–16
Matt. 5:9
2 Pet. 3:13
Rev. 21–22

3. We believe that God has entrusted to his Church the message of reconciliation in and through Jesus Christ; and the Church is called to be the salt of the earth and the light of the world; that the Church is called blessed because it is a peacemaker; that the Church is witness both by word and by deed to the new heaven and the new earth in which righteousness dwells;

Eph. 4:17–6:23
Rom. 6
Col. 1:9–14
Col. 2:13–19
Col. 3:1–4:6

that God by his lifegiving Word and Spirit has conquered the powers of sin and death, and therefore also of irreconciliation and hatred, bitterness and enmity; that God by his lifegiving Word and Spirit will enable his people to live in a new obedience which can open new possibilities of life for society and the world;

that the credibility of this message is seriously affected and its beneficial work obstructed when it is proclaimed in a land which professes to be Christian, but in which the enforced separation of people on a racial basis promotes and perpetuates alienation, hatred, and enmity;

that any teaching which attempts to legitimate such forced separation by appeal to the gospel and is not prepared to venture on the road of obedience and reconciliation, but rather, out of prejudice, fear, selfishness, and unbelief, denies in advance the reconciling power of the gospel, must be considered ideology and false doctrine.

Therefore, we reject any doctrine which, in such a situation, sanctions in the name of the gospel or of the will of God the forced separation of people on the grounds of race and color and thereby in advance obstructs and weakens the ministry and experience of reconciliation in Christ.

Deut. 32:4
Luke 2:14
John 14:27
Eph. 2:14
Isa. 1:16–17
James 1:27
James 5:1–6
Luke 1:46–55
Luke 6:20–26
Luke 7:22
Luke 16:19–31
Ps. 146
Luke 4:16–19
Rom. 6:13–18
Amos 5

4. We believe that God has revealed himself as the one who wishes to bring about justice and true peace among men; that in a world full of injustice and enmity he is in a special way the God of the destitute, the poor, and the wronged and that he calls his Church to follow him in this; that he brings justice to the oppressed and gives bread to the hungry; that he frees the prisoner and restores sight to the blind; that he supports the downtrodden, protects the stranger, helps orphans and widows, and blocks the path of the ungodly; that for him pure and undefiled religion is to visit the orphans and the widows in their suffering; that he wishes to teach his people to do what is good and to seek the right;

that the Church must therefore stand by people in any form of suffering and need, which implies, among other things, that the Church must witness against any form of injustice, so that justice may roll down like waters, and righteousness like an ever-flowing stream;

that the Church as the possession of God must stand where he stands, namely against injustice and with the wronged; that in following Christ the Church must witness against all the powerful and privileged and selfishly seek their own interests and thus control and harm others.

Therefore, we reject any ideology which would legitimate forms of injustice and any doctrine which is unwilling to resist such an ideology in the name of the gospel.

Eph. 4:15–16
Acts 5:29–33
1 Pet. 2:18–25
1 Pet. 3:15–18

5. We believe that, in obedience to Jesus Christ, its only head, the Church is called to confess and to do all these things, even though the authorities and human laws might forbid them and punishment and suffering be the consequence.

Jesus is Lord.
To the one and only God, Father, Son and Holy Spirit, be the honor and the glory for ever and ever.

SOUTHERN AFRICAN CATHOLIC BISHOPS CONFERENCE

CALL FOR AN END TO CONSCRIPTION, 1985

Our concern as Bishops in Southern Africa is for a speedy and just solution to the problems experienced by the people of RSA and Namibia, a solution in which all sectors of the population are called to play their part.

THE SITUATION

In our report on Namibia, issued in 1982, we drew your attention to the fact that the majority of Namibians regard the SADF as an army of occupation which is hindering the granting of independence to that country in terms of Resolution 435 of the UN Security Council.

During the unrest in the Vaal and East Rand townships in late 1984 the army was deployed in a support capacity to the SAP operating in those areas. This action was greeted with shock and horror by the inhabitants of those townships and by other South Africans concerned about how and where the army is deployed.

This use of the army to enforce "law and order" within the country has been further extended in 1985 to include the townships in the Eastern Cape, despite all the protests that the legitimate use of an army is in the defence of the country against its enemies.

Many young men who are conscripted each year into the SADF are experiencing crises of conscience as they become aware of the role that they are being expected to play in the black townships, and elsewhere in RSA. As far back as 1977 in our statement "On Conscientious Objection" which we issued in our concern for the nature of the armed struggle and the escalating violence in Southern Africa, we defended the right of every individual to follow his own conscience; the right therefore to conscientious objection both on the grounds of universal pacificism and on the grounds that a person may seriously believe the war to be unjust.

We believe that a serious decision of this nature is a moral judgment and must be made after deep and prayerful examination of the facts available. In 1977 we urged the RSA government to make provision for alternative forms of non-military national service, as is found in other parts of the world. Sixty six countries do not have conscription. In 1983, in a letter to the Minister of Defence about the proposed Defence Amendment Act, Cardinal McCann, on our behalf, pointed out to the minister that the proposed amendments, making it possible for Christian pacifists to refuse military training, did not go far enough. Provision should also be made for so-called moral or ethical objectors. At that time we stated that if such an amendment was not included in the Defence Amendment Act we would find it necessary to reject the Act as unjust.

[Source: Southern African Catholic Bishops Conference, 1985.]

OUR SUGGESTION

Our suggested amendment was not included in the Defence Amendment Act. The situation in Southern Africa has continued to deteriorate and in 1985 we find ourselves in a situation of grave crisis.

We are concerned at the growing numbers of young men faced with a crisis of conscience caused by their conscription. The choices for them are:

- Serving in an army with whose mode of operation they cannot agree.
- Doing 6 years alternate service if they are recognised as religious pacifists.
- Serving a 6 year jail sentence if they object to the war on the grounds that they believe it to be unjust.
- Leaving the country and living in exile.

They are faced with these choices because of the system of compulsory conscription in RSA which does not prevail in most other countries around the world.

We recognise that an end to conscription would leave membership of the SADF open to those who are in sympathy with it and would grant individuals freedom of conscience in determining their response to the situation. Therefore we join our voices with those who have already asked for an end to conscription. We call on the Government to amend the Defence Act to make this possible. We also encourage Catholics to help promote peace by working for an end to conscription in whatever ways lie open to them.

SOUTH AFRICAN COUNCIL OF CHURCHES

A THEOLOGICAL RATIONALE AND A CALL TO PRAYER FOR THE END TO UNJUST RULE, 1985

Soweto, 16 June 1976, is South Africa's most potent symbol of black resistance. Approximately 700 people were killed and hundreds more wounded in unrest which soon extended beyond that day and place to encompass the entire country. These events have come to constitute a fundamental crisis in South African society which the authorities are apparently incapable of resolving. They represent a phase of resistance which began on 21 March 1960 when the police killed 69 people and wounded a further 180 people in the notorious Sharpeville shootings. In the short term black unrest was quelled and white dominance firmly re-affirmed. It is, however, clear that Sharpeville was a turning point in the history of African self-determination. Protest hardened into resistance, and blacks were forced to think more sharply and clearly of the need for fundamental change. The reality of the Sharpeville atrocity was recognized throughout the world, in the wake of which South African and world church leaders met at Cottesloe in December 1960 to reject the apartheid system as unChristian. The Soweto unrest again compelled the Christian Church to address itself to the crisis within the country—a crisis that continues to this day, as is evidenced in the killing of people at Uitenhage. In response to this reality, those churches who enjoy fraternity through the SACC and other ecumenical forms of contact, have consistently condemned the structures of racial and economic oppression in this land as being contrary to the declared will of God, made known in the Scriptures and the traditions of the Church.

Now, on 16 June, and twenty-five years after the dawning of this phase of resistance it is right to remember those whose blood has been shed in resistance and protest against an unjust system. It is also right that we as Christians reassess our response to a system that all right-thinking people identify as unjust. We have prayed for our rulers, as is demanded of us in the Scriptures. We have entered into consultation with them as is required by our faith. We have taken the reluctant and drastic step of declaring apartheid to be contrary to the declared will of God, and some churches have declared its theological justification to be a heresy. We now pray that God will replace the present structures of oppression with ones that are just, and remove from power those who persist in defying his laws, installing in their place leaders who will govern with justice and mercy.

A FIRM THEOLOGICAL TRADITION

We do this conscious of a broad and compelling tradition of faith that unites us in a common loyalty to the sole lordship of Jesus Christ. The Scriptural record

[Source: South African Council of Churches, Apr. 16, 1985.]

is clear. Civil authority is instituted of God, in order to rule with justice, goodness and love (Romans 13). This same record is equally clear that civil authority can be a source of blasphemy against God (Revelation 13). In this awareness Christians have through the ages prayed that they may be godly and quietly governed.

With Tertullian, in the spirit of the early church, we recognize that if civil law is not the source of social justice it is tyranny, and that such authority has no right to exist.[1] In the same spirit Augustine defined the objective of "government" to be human peace, and "the republic" as the welfare of the people.[2] St. Thomas taught that "human law has the true nature of law only in so far as it corresponds to right reason, and therefore is derived from the eternal law. In so far as it falls short of right reason, a law is said to be a wicked law; and so lacking the true nature of law, it is rather a kind of violence.[3]

In this tradition the Reformers addressed themselves to the nature of legitimate government. Luther counselled people themselves to be willing to accept injustices, but warned of the obligation to oppose injustice shown towards one's neighbour. He also warned the tyrant that people would not accept their presumption indefinitely, and allowed that it was not their duty to obey such authority which contradicted the rule of God. In calling the people to turn in prayer to God in their need, he believed that God would not tolerate such rule for long.[4] Calvin recognized the obligation of citizens to be subject even to the wicked ruler, while at the same time rejecting unjust laws as no laws at all. He stressed that obedience to civil authority should never be allowed to contradict obedience to God, who is the Lord of all and the King of Kings.[5] He understood the hunger for justice to be implanted in the human soul by God himself. "And this feeling, is it not implanted in us by the Lord?" he asked. "It is then the same as though God hears himself, when he hears the cries and groanings of those who cannot bear injustice."[6]

In more recent times Karl Barth spoke of the obligation of the Church to pray for the state, never as an object of worship, but on its behalf, that it might be legitimate, governing according to the rule of God. In so doing he recognized that such prayer cannot be offered without a corresponding commitment to work for good and legitimate government.[7] He left us with no doubt in this regard that the Church is obliged to be unconditionally and passionately for the lowly and against the exalted.[8] The Dutch Calvinist, Abraham Kuyper, has also spoken of the obligation of government: "In order that it may be able to rule people, the government must respect this deepest ethical power of our human existence. A nation consisting of citizens whose consciences are bruised, is itself broken in its national strength." For this reason, he continued, "we must ever watch against the danger which lurks, for our personal liberty, in the power of the state." Indeed, "the struggle for liberty is not only declared permissible, but is made a duty for each individual in his own sphere."[9]

It is this affirmation that stands central to the contemporary emphasis of the Roman Catholic Church, which proclaims a preferential option for the poor. It is this option which requires the theologian to analyze the process of authority from the perspective of the poor, the marginalized and the oppressed—an option reaffirmed by Pope John Paul II in his recent commentary on Latin American theology.[10] Pope John XXIII has stated that "if civil authorities legislate for or allow anything that is contrary to that order and therefore contrary to the will of God, neither the laws nor the authorizations granted can be binding on the consciences of the citizens, since God has more right to be obeyed than men."[11] Paul VI, in turn, recognising that governments can become tyrannical, declared: "There are certainly situations whose injustice cries to heaven . . . whole populations destitute of necessities live in a state of dependence barring them from initiative and responsibility, and all opportunity to advance culturally and share in social and political life." "We want to be clearly understood," he concluded, "the situation must be faced with courage and the injustices linked with it must be fought against and overcome."[12] It is this affirmation which forms the basis of Vatican II theology which states: "Where citizens are oppressed by a public authority which exceeds its competence, they should not on that account refuse what is objectively required of them for the common good, but it must be allowable for them, within the limits of the law of nature and the Gospel, to defend their rights and those of their fellow citizens against this abuse of authority."[13]

THE CHURCH IN SOUTH AFRICA

The considered judgement of every synod, assembly and conference of the Roman Catholic and mainline Protestant Churches (with the exception of the Afrikaans Reformed Churches), has been that the present regime, together with its structures of domination, stands in contradiction to the Christian Gospel to which the churches of the land seek to remain faithful.[14] We have continually prayed for the authorities, that they may govern wisely and justly. Now, in solidarity with those who suffer most, in this hour of crisis we pray that God in His grace may remove from His people the tyrannical structures of oppression and the present rulers in our country who persistently refuse to heed the cry for justice, as reflected in the Word of God as proclaimed through His Church both within this land and beyond. In constant and solemn awareness of the responsibility we take on ourselves in this regard, we pray that God's rule may be established in this land. We pledge ourselves to work for that day, knowing that this rule is good news to the poor, because the captives will be released, the blind healed, the oppressed set at liberty, and the acceptable year of the Lord proclaimed (Luke 4:18-19).

A CALL TO PRAYER

We invite Christians, and all people of goodwill, to join consistently in prayer for a new and just order in this land. In so doing we share in a community of those who believe throughout this world, who will pray on June 16, in commemoration of those who died at Soweto and other places such as Sharpeville, Crossroads and Uitenhage, in commitment to a new South Africa for all its people.

NOTES

1. Tertullian, *Apology*, in Alexander Roberts and James Donaldson, eds., *The Ante-Nicene Fathers*, vol. 3: *Latin Christianity: Its Founder, Tertullian* (Grand Rapids: Eerdmans, n.d.), p. 21.

2. St. Augustine, *The City of God*, XIX, 21 (New York: Doubleday, 1958), p. 470.
3. St. Thomas Aquinas, *Summa Theologica*, 2/1. 93, 3 (London: Paternoster, 1915), p. 32.
4. Martin Luther, "On Secular Authority," *Works of Martin Luther* (Philadelphia: Holman and Castle, 1930), vol. 3, pp. 374, 397.
5. John Calvin, *Institutes of the Christian Religion*, trans. Ford Lewis Battles (Philadelphia: Westminster, 1960), IV xx, 15 and IV, xx, 32.
6. John Calvin, *Commentary on Habakkuk (Calvin's Commentaries: Minor Prophets*, vol. 4 [Grand Rapids: Eerdmans, 1950]), pp. 93–94.
7. Karl Barth, "Church and State," in *Community, State and Church*, ed. Will Herberg (Garden City: Anchor Books, 1960), pp. 135, 145.
8. Karl Barth, *Church Dogmatics*, II/I (Edinburgh: T. and T. Clark, 1964), p. 386.
9. Abraham Kuyper, *Lectures on Calvinism* (Grand Rapids: Eerdmans, 1931), pp. 107, 108, 81, 98–99.
10. Pope John Paul II. "Instruction on Certain Aspects of the Theology of Liberation," *Pastoral Action*, number 38 (Pretoria: South African Catholic Bishops' Conference), nn. 5 and 10.
11. Pope John XXIII, *Pacem in Terris*, 1963.
12. Pope Paul VI, *Populorum Progressio*, 1967.
13. Vatican II Ecumenical Council, *Gaudium et Spes*, 1965.
14. See documentation in *Apartheid Is a Heresy*, ed. John W. de Gruchy and Charles Villa-Vicencio (Cape Town: David Philip and Grand Rapids: Eerdmans, 1983), pp. 144–84.

THE KAIROS THEOLOGIANS

THE KAIROS DOCUMENT, 1985

CHAPTER ONE: THE MOMENT OF TRUTH

The time has come. The moment of truth has arrived. South Africa has been plunged into a crisis that is shaking the foundations and there is every indication that the crisis has only just begun and that it will deepen and become even more threatening in the months to come. It is the KAIROS or moment of truth not only for apartheid but also for the Church.

We as a group of theologians have been trying to understand the theological significance of this moment in our history. It is serious, very serious. For very many Christians in South Africa this is the KAIROS, the moment of grace and opportunity, the favourable time in which God issues a challenge to decisive action. It is a dangerous time because, if this opportunity is missed and allowed to pass by, the loss for the Church, for the Gospel and for all the people of South Africa will be immeasurable. Jesus wept over Jerusalem. He wept over the tragedy of the destruction of the city and the massacre of the people that was imminent, "and all because you did not recognise your opportunity (KAIROS) when God offered it" (Lk 19:44).

A crisis is a judgment that brings out the best in some people and the worst in others. A crisis is a moment of truth that shows us up for what we really are. There will be no place to hide and no way of pretending to be what we are not in fact. At this moment in South Africa the Church is about to be shown up for what it really is and no cover-up will be possible.

What the present crisis shows up, although many of us have known it all along, is that *the Church is divided*. More and more people are now saying that there are in fact two Churches in South Africa—a White Church and a Black Church. Even within the same denomination there are in fact two Churches. In the life and death conflict between different social forces that has come to a head in South Africa today, there are Christians (or at least people who profess to be Christians) on both sides of the conflict—and some who are trying to sit on the fence!

Does this prove that Christian faith has no real meaning or relevance for our times? Does it show that the Bible can be used for any purpose at all? Such problems would be critical enough for the Church in any circumstances, but when we also come to see that the conflict in South Africa is between the oppressor and the oppressed, the crisis for the Church as an institution becomes much more acute. Both oppressor and oppressed claim loyalty to the same Church. They are both baptised in the same baptism and participate together in the breaking of the

---

[Source: The Kairos Theologians, *The Kairos Document: Challenge to the Church* (Braamfontein, 1985).]

same bread, the same body and blood of Christ. There we sit in the same Church while outside Christian policemen and soldiers are beating up and killing Christian children or torturing Christian prisoners to death while yet other Christians stand by and weakly plead for peace.

The Church is divided and its day of judgment has come.

The moment of truth has compelled us to analyse more carefully the different theologies in our Churches and to speak out more clearly and boldly about the real significance of these theologies. We have been able to isolate three theologies and we have chosen to call them 'State Theology', 'Church Theology' and 'Prophetic Theology'. In our thoroughgoing criticism of the first and second theologies we do not wish to mince our words. The situation is too critical for that.

CHAPTER TWO: CRITIQUE OF STATE THEOLOGY

The South African apartheid State has a theology of its own and we have chosen to call it 'State Theology'. 'State Theology' is simply the theological justification of the status quo with its racism, capitalism and totalitarianism. It blesses injustice, canonises the will of the powerful and reduces the poor to passivity, obedience and apathy.

How does 'State Theology' do this? It does it by misusing theological concepts and biblical texts for its own political purposes. In this document we would like to draw your attention to four key examples of how this is done in South Africa. The first would be the use of Romans 13:1-7 to give an absolute and 'divine' authority to the State. The second would be the use of the idea of 'Law and Order' to determine and control what the people may be permitted to regard as just and unjust. The third would be the use of the word 'communist' to brand anyone who rejects 'State Theology'. And finally there is the use that is made of the name of God.

2.1 Romans 13:1-7 The misuse of this famous text is not confined to the present government in South Africa. Throughout the history of Christianity totalitarian regimes have tried to legitimise an attitude of blind obedience and absolute servility towards the state by quoting this text. The well-known theologian Oscar Cullmann pointed this out thirty years ago:

> As soon as Christians, out of loyalty to the gospel of Jesus, offer resistance to a State's totalitarian claim, the representatives of the State or their collaborationist theological advisers are accustomed to appeal to this saying of Paul, as if Christians are here commended to endorse and thus to abet all the crimes of a totalitarian State.
> (*The State in the New Testament* [1957], p 56.)

But what then is the meaning of Romans 13:1-7 and why is the use made of it by 'State Theology' unjustifiable from a biblical point of view?

'State Theology' assumes that in this text Paul is presenting us with the absolute and definitive Christian doctrine about the State, in other words an absolute and universal principle that is equally valid for all times and in all circumstances. The falseness of this assumption has been pointed out by numerous biblical scholars (see, for example, E Kasemann, *Commentary on Romans* [1980]; O Cullmann, *The State in the New Testament* [1957]).

What has been overlooked here is one of the most fundamental of all principles of biblical interpretation: every text must be interpreted *in its context.* To abstract a text from its context and to interpret it in the abstract is to distort the meaning of God's Word. Moreover, the context here is not only the chapters and verses that precede and succeed this particular text nor is it even limited to the total context of the Bible. The context includes also the *circumstances* in which Paul's statement was made. Paul was writing to a particular Christian community in Rome, a community that had its own particular problems in relation to the State at that time and in those circumstances. That is part of the context of our text.

Many authors have drawn attention to the fact that in the rest of the Bible God does not demand obedience to oppressive rulers. Examples can be given ranging from Pharaoh to Pilate and through into Apostolic times. The Jews and later the Christians did not believe that their imperial overlords, the Egyptians, the Babylonians, the Greeks or the Romans, had some kind of divine right to rule them and oppress them. These empires were the beasts described in the Book of Daniel and the Book of Revelation. God *allowed* them to rule for a while but he did not *approve* of what they did. It was not God's will. His will was the freedom and liberation of Israel. Romans 13:1-7 cannot be contradicting all of this.

But most revealing of all is the circumstances of the Roman Christians to whom Paul was writing. They were not revolutionaries. They were not trying to overthrow the State. They were not calling for a change of government. They were what has been called 'antinomians' or 'enthusiasts,' and their belief was that Christians, and only Christians, were exonerated from obeying any State at all, any government or political authority at all, *because* Jesus alone was their Lord and King. This is of course heretical, and Paul is compelled to point out to these Christians that before the second coming of Christ there will always be some kind of State, some kind of secular government and that Christians are not exonerated from subjection to some kind of political authority.

Paul is simply not addressing the issue of a just or unjust State or the need to change one government for another. He is simply establishing the fact that there will be some kind of secular authority and that Christians as such are not exonerated from subjection to secular laws and authorities. He does not say anything at all about what they should do when the State becomes unjust and oppressive. That is another question.

Consequently those who try to find answers to the very different questions and problems of our time in the text of Romans 13:1-7 are doing a great disservice to Paul. The use that 'State Theology' makes of this text tells us more about the political options of those who construct this theology than it does about the meaning of God's Word in this text. As one biblical scholar puts it: "The primary concern is to justify the interests of the State, and the text is pressed into its service without respect for the context and the intention of Paul".

If we wish to search the Bible for guidance in a situation where the State that is supposed to be "the servant of God" (Romans 13:16) betrays that calling and begins to serve Satan instead, then we can study chapter 13 of the Book of Revelation. Here the Roman State becomes the servant of the dragon (the devil) and takes on the appearance of a horrible beast. Its days are numbered because God will not permit his unfaithful servant to reign forever.

2.2 Law and Order The State makes use of the concept of law and order to maintain the status quo which it depicts as 'normal'. But this *law* is the unjust and discriminatory laws of apartheid and this *order* is the organised and institutionalised disorder of oppression. Anyone who wishes to change this law and this order is made to feel that they are lawless and disorderly. In other words they are made to feel guilty of sin.

It is indeed the duty of the State to maintain law and order, but it has not divine mandate to maintain any kind of law and order. Something does not become moral and just simply because the State has declared it to be a law, and the organisation of a society is not a just and right order simply because it has been instituted by the State. We cannot accept any kind of law and any kind of order. The concern of Christians is that we should have in our country a just law and a right order.

In the present crisis and especially during the State of Emergency, 'State Theology' has tried to re-establish the status quo of orderly discrimination, exploitation and oppression by appealing to the consciences of its citizens in the name of law and order. It tries to make those who reject this law and this order feel that they are ungodly. The State here is not only usurping the right of the Church to make judgments about what would be right and just in our circumstances; it is going even further than that and demanding of us, in the name of law and order, an obedience that must be reserved for God alone. The South African State recognises no authority beyond itself and therefore it will not allow anyone to question what it has chosen to define as 'law and order'. However, there are millions of Christians in South Africa today who are saying with Peter: "We must obey God rather than man (human beings)" (Acts 5:29).

2.3 The Threat of Communism We all know how the South African State makes use of the label 'communist'. Anything that threatens the status quo is labelled 'communist'. Anyone who opposes the State and especially anyone who rejects its theology is simply dismissed as a 'communist'. No account is taken of what communism really means. No thought is given to why some people have indeed opted for communism or for some form of socialism. Even people who have not rejected capitalism are called 'communists' when they reject 'State Theology'. The State uses the label 'communist' in an uncritical and unexamined way as its symbol of evil.

'State Theology' like every other theology needs to have its own concrete symbol of evil. It must be able to symbolise what it regards as godless behaviour and what ideas must be regarded as atheistic. It must have its own version of hell. And so it has invented, or rather taken over, the myth of communism. All evil is communistic and all communist or socialist ideas are atheistic and godless. Threats about hell-fire and eternal damnation are replaced by threats and warnings about the horrors of a tyrannical, totalitarian, atheistic and terrorist communist regime—a kind of hell-on-earth. This is a very convenient way of frightening some people into accepting any kind of domination and exploitation by a capitalist minority.

The South African State has its own heretical theology, and according to that theology millions of Christians in South Africa (not to mention the rest of the world) are to be regarded as 'atheists'. It is significant that in earlier times when Christians rejected the gods of the Roman Empire they were branded as 'atheists'—by the State.

2.4 The God of the State The State in its oppression of the people makes use again and again of the name of God. Military chaplains use it to encourage the South African Defence Force, police chaplains use it to strengthen policemen and cabinet ministers use it in their propaganda speeches. But perhaps the most revealing of all is the blasphemous use of God's holy name in the preamble to the new apartheid constitution.

> In humble submission to Almighty God, who controls the destinies of nations and the history of peoples; who gathered our forebears together from many lands and gave them this their own; who has guided them from generation to generation; who has wondrously delivered them from the dangers that beset them.

This god is an idol. It is as mischievous, sinister and evil as any of the idols that the prophets of Israel had to contend with. Here we have a god who is historically on the side of the white settlers, who dispossesses black people of their land and who gives the major part of the land to his "chosen people".

It is the god of superior weapons who conquered those who were armed with nothing but spears. It is the god of the casspirs and hippos, the god of teargas, rubber bullets, sjamboks, prison cells and death sentences. Here is a god who exalts the proud and humbles the poor—the very opposite of the God of the Bible who "scatters the proud of heart, pulls down the mighty from their thrones and exalts the humble" (Lk 1:51-52). From a theological point of view the opposite of the God of the Bible is the devil, Satan. The god of the South African State is not merely an idol or false god, it is the devil disguised as Almighty God—the antichrist.

The oppressive South African regime will always be particularly abhorrent to Christians precisely because it makes use of Christianity to justify its evil ways. As Christians we simply cannot tolerate this blasphemous use of God's name and God's Word. 'State Theology' is not only heretical, it is blasphemous. Christians who are trying to remain faithful to the God of the Bible are even more horrified when they see that there are Churches, like the White Dutch Reformed Churches and other groups of Christians, who actually subscribe to this heretical theology. 'State Theology' needs its own prophets and it manages to find them from the ranks of those who profess to be ministers of God's Word in some of our Churches. What is particularly tragic for a Christian is to see the number of people who are fooled and confused by these false prophets and their heretical theology.

CHAPTER THREE: CRITIQUE OF 'CHURCH THEOLOGY'

We have analysed the statements that are made from time to time by the so-called 'English-speaking' Churches. We have looked at what Church leaders tend to say in their speeches and press statements about the apartheid regime and the present crisis. What we found running through all these pronouncements is a series of inter-related theological assumptions. These we have chosen to call 'Church Theology'. We are well aware of the fact that this theology does *not* express the faith of the majority of Christians in South Africa today who form the greater part of most of our Churches. Nevertheless the opinions expressed by Church leaders are regarded in the media and generally in our society as the official opinions of the Churches. We have therefore chosen to call these opinions 'Church Theology'. The crisis in which we find ourselves today compels us to question this theology, to question its assumptions, its implications and its practicality.

In a limited, guarded and cautious way this theology is critical of apartheid. Its criticism, however, is superficial and counter-productive because instead of engaging in an in-depth analysis of the signs of our times, it relies upon a few stock ideas derived from Christian tradition and then uncritically and repeatedly applies them to our situation. The stock ideas used by almost all these Church leaders that we would like to examine here are: reconciliation (or peace), justice and non-violence.

3.1 Reconciliation 'Church Theology' takes 'reconciliation' as the key to problem resolution. It talks about the need for reconciliation between white and black, or between all South Africans. 'Church Theology' often describes the Christian stance in the following way: "We must be fair. We must listen to both sides of the story. If the two sides can only meet to talk and negotiate they will sort out their differences and misunderstandings, and the conflict will be resolved". On the face of it this may sound very Christian. But is it?

The fallacy here is that 'reconciliation' has been made into an absolute principle that must be applied in all cases of conflict or dissension. But not all cases of conflict are the same. We can imagine a private quarrel between two people or two groups whose differences are based upon misunderstandings. In such cases it would be appropriate to talk and negotiate to sort out the misunderstandings and to reconcile the two sides. But there are other conflicts in which one side is right and the other wrong. There are conflicts where one side is a fully armed and violent oppressor while the other side is defenceless and oppressed. There are conflicts that can only be described as the struggle between justice and injustice, good and evil, God and the devil. To speak of reconciling these two is not only a mistaken application of the Christian idea of reconciliation, it is a total betrayal of all that Christian faith has ever meant. Nowhere in the Bible or in Christian tradition has it ever been suggested that we ought to try to reconcile good and evil, God and the devil. We are supposed to do away with evil, injustice, oppression and sin—not come to terms with it. We are supposed to oppose, confront and reject the devil and not try to sup with the devil.

In our situation in South Africa today it would be totally unChristian to plead for reconciliation and peace before the present injustices have been removed. Any such plea plays into the hands of the oppressor by trying to persuade those of us who are oppressed to accept our oppression and to become reconciled to the intolerable crimes that are committed against us. That is not Christian reconciliation, it is sin. It is asking us to become accomplices in our own oppression, to become servants of the devil. No reconciliation is possible in South Africa *without justice*.

What this means in practice is that no reconciliation, no forgiveness and no negotiations are possible *without repentance*. The Biblical teaching on reconciliation and forgiveness makes it quite clear that nobody can be forgiven and reconciled with God unless he or she repents of their sins. Nor are *we* expected to forgive the unrepentant sinner. When he or she repents we must be willing to forgive seventy times seven times, but before that, we are expected to preach repentance to those who sin against us or against anyone. Reconciliation, forgiveness and negotiations will become our Christian duty in South Africa only when the apartheid regime shows signs of genuine repentance. The recent speech of P W Botha in Durban, the continued military repression of the people in the townships and the jailing of all its opponents is clear proof of the total lack of repentance on the part of the present regime.

There is nothing that we want more than true reconciliation and genuine peace—the peace that God wants and not the peace the world wants (Jn 14:27). The peace that God wants is based upon truth, repentance, justice and love. The peace that the world offers us is a unity that compromises the truth, covers over injustice and oppression and is totally motivated by selfishness. At this stage, like Jesus, we must expose this false peace, confront our oppressors and sow dissension. As Christians we must say with Jesus: "Do you suppose that I am here to bring peace on earth. No, I tell you, but rather dissension" (Lk 12:51). There can be no real peace without justice and it would be quite wrong to try to preserve 'peace' and 'unity' at all costs, even at the cost of truth and justice and, worse still, at the cost of thousands of young lives. As disciples of Jesus we should rather promote truth and justice and life at all costs, even at the cost of creating conflict, disunity and dissension along the way. To be truly biblical our Church leaders must adopt a theology that millions of Christians have already adopted—a biblical theology of direct confrontation with the forces of evil rather than a theology of reconciliation with sin and the devil.

3.2 Justice It would be quite wrong to give the impression that 'Church Theology' in South Africa is not particularly concerned about the need for justice. There have been some very strong and very sincere demands for justice. But the question we need to ask here, the very serious theological question is: What kind of justice? An examination of Church statements and pronouncements gives the distinct impression that the justice that is envisaged is *the justice of reform*, that is to say, a justice that is determined by the oppressor, by the white minority and that is offered to the people as a kind of concession. It does not appear to be the more radical justice that comes from below and is determined by the people of South Africa.

One of our main reasons for drawing this conclusion is the simple fact that almost all Church statements and appeals are made to the State or to the white community. The assumption seems to be that changes must come from whites or at least from people who are at the top of the pile. The general idea appears to be that one must simply appeal to the conscience and the goodwill of those who are responsible for injustice in our land and that once they have repented of their sins and after some consultation with others they will introduce the necessary reforms to the system. Why else would Church leaders be having talks with P W Botha if this is not the vision of a just and peaceful solution to our problems?

At the heart of this approach is the reliance upon 'individual conversions' in response to 'moralising demands' to change the structures of a society. It has not worked and it never will work. The present crisis with all its cruelty, brutality and callousness is ample proof of the ineffectiveness of years and years of Christian 'moralising' about the need for love. The problem that we are dealing with here in South Africa is not merely a problem of personal guilt, it is a problem of structural injustice. People are suffering, people are being maimed and killed and tortured every day. We cannot just sit back and wait for the oppressor to see the light so that the oppressed can put out their hands and beg for the crumbs of some small reforms. That in itself would be degrading and oppressive.

There have been reforms and, no doubt, there will be further reforms in the near future. And it may well be that the Church's appeal to the consciences of whites has contributed marginally to the introduction of some of these reforms. But can such reforms ever be regarded as real change, as the introduction of a true and lasting justice. Reforms that come from the top are never satisfactory. They seldom do more than make the oppression more effective and more acceptable. If the oppressor does ever introduce reforms that might lead to real change this will come about because of strong pressure from those who are oppressed. True justice, God's justice, demands a radical change of structures. This can only come from below, from the oppressed themselves. God will bring about change through the oppressed as he did through the oppressed Hebrew slaves in Egypt. God does not bring his justice through reforms introduced by the Pharaohs of this world.

Why then does 'Church Theology' appeal to the top rather than to the people who are suffering? Why does this theology not demand that the oppressed stand up for their rights and wage a struggle against their oppressors? Why does it not tell them that it is *their* duty to work for justice and to change the unjust structures? Perhaps the answer to these questions is that appeals from the 'top' in the Church tend very easily to be appeals to the 'top' in society. An appeal to the conscience of those who perpetuate the system of injustice must be made. But real change and true justice can only come from below, from the people—most of whom are Christians.

3.3 Non-Violence The stance of 'Church Theology' on non-violence, expressed as a blanket condemnation of all that is *called* violence, has not only been unable to curb the violence of our situation, it has actually, although unwittingly, been a major contributing factor in the recent escalation of State violence. Here again non-violence has been made into an absolute principle that applies to anything anyone *calls* violence without regard for who is using it, which side they are on or what purpose they may have in mind. In our situation, this is simply counter-productive.

The problem for the Church here is the way the word violence is being used in the propaganda of the State. The State and the media have chosen to call violence what some people do in the townships as they struggle for their liberation, i.e. throwing stones, burning cars and buildings and sometimes killing collaborators. But this *excludes* the structural, institutional and unrepentant violence of the State and especially the oppressive and naked violence of the police and the army. These things are not counted as violence. And even when they are acknowledged to be 'excessive', they are called 'misconduct' or even 'atrocities' but never violence. Thus the phrase 'violence in the townships' comes to mean what the young people are doing and not what the police are doing or what apartheid in general is doing to people. If one calls for non-violence in such circumstances one appears to be criticising the resistance of the people while justifying or at least overlooking the violence of the police and the State. That is how it is understood not only by the State and its supporters but also by the people who are struggling for their freedom. Violence, especially in our circumstances, is a loaded word.

It is true that Church statements and pronouncements do also condemn the violence of the police. They do say that they condemn *all violence*. But is it legitimate, especially in our circumstances, to use the same word violence in a blanket condemnation to cover the ruthless and repressive activities of the State and the desperate attempts of the people to defend themselves? Do such abstractions and generalisations not confuse the issue? How can acts of oppression, injustice and domination be equated with acts of resistance and self-defence? Would it be legitimate to describe both the physical force used by a rapist and the physical force used by a woman trying to resist the rapist as violence?

Moreover, there is nothing in the Bible or in our Christian tradition that would permit us to make such generalisations. Throughout the Bible the word violence is used to describe everything that is done by a wicked oppressor (e.g. Ps 72:12-14; Is 59:1-8; Jer 22:13-17; Amos 3:9-10; 6:3; Mic 2:2; 3:1-3; 6:12). It is never used to describe the activities of Israel's armies in attempting to liberate themselves or to resist aggression. When Jesus says that we should turn the other cheek he is telling us that we must not take revenge; he is not saying that we should never defend ourselves or others. There is a long and consistent Christian tradition about the use of physical force to defend oneself against aggressors and tyrants. In other words there are circumstances when physical force may be used. They are very restrictive circumstances, only as the very last resort and only as the lesser of two evils, or, as Bonhoeffer put it, "the lesser of two guilts". But it is simply not true to say that every possible use of physical force is violence and that no matter what the circumstances may be it is never permissible.

This is not to say that any use of force at any time by people who are oppressed is permissible simply because they are struggling for their liberation. There have been cases of killing and maiming that no Christian would want to approve of. But then our disapproval is based upon a concern for genuine liberation and a conviction that such acts are unnecessary, counter-productive and unjustifiable and not because they fall under a blanket condemnation of any use of physical force in any circumstances.

And finally what makes the professed non-violence of 'Church Theology' extremely suspect in the eyes of very many people, including ourselves, is the tacit support that many Church leaders give to the growing *militarisation* of the South African State. How can one condemn all violence and then appoint chaplains to a very violent and oppressive army? How can one condemn all violence and then allow young white males to accept their conscription into the armed forces? Is it because the activities of the armed forces and the police are counted as defensive? That raises very serious questions about whose side such Church leaders might be on. Why are the activities of young blacks in the townships not regarded as defensive?

In practice what one calls 'violence' and what one calls 'self-defence' seems to depend upon which side one is on. To call all physical force 'violence' is to try to be neutral and to refuse to make a judgment about who is right and who is wrong. The attempt to remain neutral in this kind of conflict is futile. Neutrality enables the status quo of oppression (and therefore violence) to continue. It is a way of giving tacit support to the oppressor.

3.4 The Fundamental Problem It is not enough to criticise 'Church Theology'; we must also try to account for it. What is behind the mistakes and misunderstandings and inadequacies of this theology?

In the first place we can point to a lack of *social analysis.* We have seen how 'Church Theology' tends to make use of absolute principles like reconciliation, negotiation, non-violence and peaceful solutions and applies them indiscriminately and uncritically to all situations. Very little attempt is made to analyse what is actually happening in our society and why it is happening. It is not possible to make valid moral judgments about a society without first understanding that society. The analysis of apartheid that underpins 'Church Theology' is simply inadequate. The present crisis has now made it very clear that the efforts of Church leaders to promote effective and practical ways of changing our society have failed. This failure is due in no small measure to the fact that 'Church Theology' has not developed a social analysis that would enable it to understand the mechanics of injustice and oppression.

Closely linked to this is the lack in 'Church Theology' of an adequate understanding of *politics and political strategy.* Changing the structures of a society is fundamentally a matter of politics. It requires a political strategy based upon a clear social or political analysis. The Church has to address itself to these strategies and to the analysis upon which they are based. It is into this political situation that the Church has to bring the gospel. Not as an alternative solution to our problems as if the gospel provided us with a non-political solution to political problems. There is no specifically Christian solution. There will be a Christian way of approaching the political solutions, a Christian spirit and motivation and attitude. But there is no way of bypassing politics and political strategies.

But we have still not pinpointed the fundamental problem. Why has 'Church

Theology' not developed a social analysis? Why does it have an inadequate understanding of the need for political strategies? And why does it make a virtue of neutrality and sitting on the sidelines?

The answer must be sought in the *type of faith and spirituality* that has dominated Church life for centuries. As we all know, spirituality has tended to be an other-worldly affair that has very little, if anything at all, to do with the affairs of this world. Social and political matters were seen as worldly affairs that have nothing to do with the spiritual concerns of the Church. Moreover, spirituality has also been understood to be purely private and individualistic. Public affairs and social problems were thought to be beyond the sphere of spirituality. And finally the spirituality we inherit tends to rely upon God to intervene in his own good time to put right what is wrong in the world. That leaves very little for human beings to do except to pray for God's intervention.

It is precisely this kind of spirituality that, when faced with the present crisis in South Africa, leaves so many Christians and Church leaders in a state of near paralysis.

It hardly needs saying that this kind of faith and this type of spirituality has no biblical foundation. The Bible does not separate the human person from the world in which he or she lives; it does not separate the individual from the social or one's private life from one's public life. God redeems the whole person as part of his whole creation (Rom 8:18-24). A truly biblical spirituality would penetrate into every aspect of human existence and would exclude nothing from God's redemptive will. Biblical faith is prophetically relevant to everything that happens in the world.

CHAPTER FOUR: TOWARDS A PROPHETIC THEOLOGY

Our present KAIROS calls for a response from Christians that is biblical, spiritual, pastoral and, above all, prophetic. It is not enough in these circumstances to repeat generalised Christian principles. We need a bold and incisive response that is prophetic because it speaks to the particular circumstances of this crisis, a response that does not give the impression of sitting on the fence but is clearly and unambiguously taking a stand.

4.1 Social Analysis The first task of a prophetic theology for our times would be an attempt at social analysis or what Jesus would call "reading the signs of the times" (Mt 16:3) or "interpreting this KAIROS" (Lk 12:56). It is not possible to do this in any detail in this document but we must start with at least the broad outlines of an analysis of the conflict in which we find ourselves.

It would be quite wrong to see the present conflict as simply a racial war. The racial component is there, but we are not dealing with two equal races or nations each with its own selfish group interests. The situation we are dealing with here is one of oppression. The conflict is between an oppressor and the oppressed. The conflict is between two irreconcilable *causes* or *interests* in which the one is just and the other is unjust.

On the one hand we have the interests of those who benefit from the status quo and who are determined to maintain it at any cost, even at the cost of millions of lives. It is in their interests to introduce a number of reforms in order to ensure that the system is not radically changed and that they can continue to benefit from it as they have done in the past. They benefit from the system because it favours them and enables them to accumulate a great deal of wealth and to maintain an exceptionally high standard of living. And they want to make sure that it stays that way even if some adjustments are needed.

On the other hand we have those who do not benefit in any way from the system the way it is now. They are treated as mere labour units, paid starvation wages, separated from their families by migratory labour, moved about like cattle and dumped in homelands to starve—and all for the benefit of a privileged minority. They have no say in the system and are supposed to be grateful for the concessions that are offered to them like crumbs. It is not in their interests to allow this system to continue even in some 'reformed' or 'revised' form. They are no longer prepared to be crushed, oppressed and exploited. They are determined to change the system radically so that it no longer benefits only the privileged few. And they are willing to do this even at the cost of their own lives. What they want is justice for all.

This is our situation of civil war or revolution. The one side is committed to maintaining the system at all costs and the other side is committed to changing it at all costs. There are two conflicting projects here and no compromise is possible. Either we have full and equal justice for all or we don't.

The Bible has a great deal to say about this kind of conflict, about a world that is divided into oppressors and oppressed.

4.2 Oppression in the Bible When we search the Bible for a message about oppression we discover, as others throughout the world are discovering, that oppression is a central theme that runs right through the Old and New Testaments. The biblical scholars who have taken the trouble to study the theme of oppression in the Bible have discovered that there are no less than twenty different root words in Hebrew to describe oppression. As one author says, oppression is "a basic structural category of biblical theology" (T D Hanks, *God So Loved the Third World* [1983], p 4).

Moreover the description of oppression in the Bible is concrete and vivid. The Bible describes oppression as the experience of being crushed, degraded, humiliated, exploited, impoverished, defrauded, deceived and enslaved. And the oppressors are described as cruel, ruthless, arrogant, greedy, violent and tyrannical and as the enemy. Such descriptions could only have been written originally by people who had had a long and painful experience of what it means to be oppressed. And indeed nearly 90 percent of the history of the Jewish and later the Christian people whose story is told in the Bible is a history of domestic or international oppression. Israel as a nation was built upon the painful experience of oppression and repression as slaves in Egypt. But what made all the difference for this particular group of oppressed people was the revelation of Yahweh. God revealed himself as Yahweh, the one who has compassion on those who suffer and who liberates them from their oppressors.

> I have seen the miserable state of my people in Egypt. I have heard their appeal to be free of their slave-drivers. I mean to deliver them out of the hands of the Egyptians. . . . The cry of the sons of Israel has come to me, and I have witnessed the way in which the Egyptians oppress them (Ex 3:7-9).

Throughout the Bible God appears as the liberator of the oppressed. He is not neutral. He does not attempt to reconcile Moses and Pharaoh, to reconcile the Hebrew slaves with their Egyptian oppressors or to reconcile the Jewish people with any of their later oppressors. Oppression is sin and it cannot be compromised with, it must be done away with. God takes sides with the oppressed. As we read in Psalm 103:6 (JB), "God, who does what is right, is always on the side of the oppressed."

Nor is this identification with the oppressed confined to the Old Testament. When Jesus stood up in the synagogue at Nazareth to announce his mission he made use of the words of Isaiah.

> The Spirit of the Lord has been given to me, for he has anointed me. He has sent me to bring the good news to the poor, to proclaim liberty to captives and to the blind new sight, to set the downtrodden free, to proclaim the Lord's year of favour (Lk 4:18-19).

There can be no doubt that Jesus is here taking up the cause of the poor and the oppressed. He has identified himself with their interests. Not that he is unconcerned about the rich and the oppressor. These he calls to repentance. The oppressed Christians of South Africa have known for a long time that they are united to Christ in their sufferings. By his own suffering and his death on the cross he became a victim of oppression and violence. He is with us in our oppression.

4.3 Tyranny in the Christian Tradition There is a long Christian tradition relating to oppression, but the word that has been used most frequently to describe this particular form of sinfulness is the word 'tyranny'. According to this tradition once it is established beyond doubt that a particular ruler is a tyrant or that a particular regime is tyrannical, it forfeits the moral right to govern and the people acquire the right to resist and to find the means to protect their own interests against injustice and oppression. In other words a tyrannical regime has no *moral legitimacy*. It may be the *de facto* government and it may even be recognised by other governments and therefore be the *de iure* or legal government. But if it is a tyrannical regime, it is, from a moral and a theological point of view, *illegitimate.*

There are indeed some differences of opinion in the Christian tradition about the means that might be used to replace a tyrant *but* there has not been any doubt about our Christian duty to refuse to co-operate with tyranny and to do whatever we can to remove it.

Of course everything hinges on the definition of a tyrant. At what point does a government become a tyrannical regime?

The traditional Latin definition of a tyrant is *hostis boni communis*—an enemy of the common good. The purpose of all government is the promotion of what is called the common good of the people governed. To promote the common good is to govern in the interest of, and for the benefit of, all the people. Many governments fail to do this at times. There might be this or that injustice done to some of the people. And such lapses would indeed have to be criticised. But occasional acts of injustice would not make a government into an enemy of the people, a tyrant.

To be an enemy of the people a government would have to be hostile to the common good *in principle*. Such a government would be acting against the interests of the people as a whole and permanently. This would be clearest in cases where the very policy of a government is hostile towards the common good and where the government has a mandate to rule in the interests of some of the people rather than in the interests of all the people. Such a government would be in principle *irreformable*. Any reform that it might try to introduce would not be calculated to serve the common good but to serve the interests of the minority from whom it received its mandate.

A tyrannical regime cannot continue to rule for very long without becoming more and more *violent*. As the majority of the people begin to demand their rights and to put pressure on the tyrant, so will the tyrant resort more and more to desperate, cruel, gross and ruthless forms of tyranny and repression. The reign of a tyrant always ends up as a reign of terror. It is inevitable because from the start the tyrant is an enemy of the common good.

This account of what we mean by a tyrant or a tyrannical regime can best be summed up in the words of a well-known moral theologian: "a regime which is openly the enemy of the people and which violates the common good permanently and in the grossest manner" (B Häring, *The Law of Christ*, Vol 3, p 150).

That leaves us with the question of whether the present government of South Africa is tyrannical or not. There can be no doubt what the majority of the people of South Africa think. For them the apartheid regime is indeed the enemy of the people and that is precisely what they call it: the enemy. In the present crisis, more than ever before, the regime has lost any legitimacy that it might have had in the eyes of the people. Are the people right or wrong?

Apartheid is a system whereby a minority regime elected by one small section of the population is given an explicit mandate to govern in the interests of, and for the benefit of, the white community. Such a mandate or policy is by definition hostile to the common good of all the people. In fact because it tries to rule in the exclusive interests of whites and not in the interests of all, it ends up ruling in a way that is not even in the interests of those same whites. It becomes an enemy of all the people. A tyrant. A totalitarian regime. A reign of terror.

This also means that the apartheid minority regime is irreformable. We cannot expect the apartheid regime to experience a conversion or change of heart and totally abandon the policy of apartheid. It has no mandate from its electorate to do so. Any reforms or adjustments it might make would have to be done in the interests of those who elected it. Individual members of the government could experience a real conversion and repent but, if they did, they would simply have to follow this through by leaving a regime that was elected and put into power precisely because of its policy of apartheid.

And that is why we have reached the present impasse. As the oppressed majority becomes more insistent and puts more and more pressure on the tyrant by means of boycotts, strikes, uprisings, burnings and even armed struggle, the more tyrannical will this regime become. On the one hand it will use repressive measures: detentions, trials, killings, torture, bannings, propaganda, states of emergency and other desperate and tyrannical methods. And on the other hand it will introduce reforms that will always be unacceptable to the majority because all its reforms must ensure that the white minority remains on top.

A regime that is in principle the enemy of the people cannot suddenly begin to rule in the interests of all the people. It can only be replaced by another government—one that has been elected by the majority of the people with an explicit mandate to govern in the interests of all the people.

A regime that has made itself the enemy of the people has thereby also made itself the enemy of God. People are made in the image and likeness of God and whatever we do to the least of them we do to God (Mt 25:40, 45).

To say that the State or the regime is the enemy of God is not to say that all those who support the system are aware of this. On the whole they simply do not know what they are doing. Many people have been blinded by the regime's propaganda. They are frequently quite ignorant of the consequences of their stance. However, such blindness does not make the State any less tyrannical or any less of an enemy of the people and an enemy of God.

On the other hand the fact that the State is tyrannical and an enemy of God is no excuse for hatred. As Christians we are called upon to love our enemies (Mt 5:44). It is not said that we should not or will not have enemies or that we should not identify tyrannical regimes as indeed our enemies. But once we have identified our enemies, we must endeavour to love them. That is not always easy. But then we must also remember that the most loving thing we can do for *both* the oppressed *and* for our enemies who are oppressors is to eliminate the oppression, remove the tyrants from power and establish a just government for the common good of *all the people*.

4.4 A Message of Hope At the very heart of the gospel of Jesus Christ and at the very centre of all true prophecy is a message of hope. Nothing could be more relevant and more necessary at this moment of crisis in South Africa than the Christian message of hope.

Jesus has taught us to speak of this hope as the coming of God's kingdom. We believe that God is at work in our world turning hopeless and evil situations to good so that his "Kingdom may come" and his "Will may be done on earth as it is in heaven". We believe that goodness and justice and love will triumph in the end and that tyranny and oppression cannot last forever. One day "all tears will be wiped away" (Rev 7:17; 21:4) and "the lamb will lie down with the lion" (Is 11:6). True peace and true reconciliation are not only desirable, they are assured and guaranteed. This is our faith and our hope.

Why is it that this powerful message of hope has not been highlighted in 'Church Theology', in the statements and pronouncements of Church leaders? Is it because they have been addressing themselves to the oppressor rather than to the oppressed? Is it because they do not want to encourage the oppressed to be too hopeful for too much?

As the crisis deepens day by day, what both the oppressor and the oppressed can legitimately demand of the Churches is a message of hope. Most of the oppressed people in South Africa today and especially the youth do have hope. They are acting courageously and fearlessly because they have a sure hope that liberation will come. Often enough their bodies are broken but nothing can now break their spirit. But hope needs to be confirmed. Hope needs to be maintained and strengthened. Hope needs to be spread. The people need to hear it said again and again that God is with them.

On the other hand the oppressor and those who believe the propaganda of the oppressor are desperately fearful. They must be made aware of the diabolical evils of the present system and they must be called to repentance but they must also be given something to hope for. At present they have false hopes. They hope to maintain the status quo and their special privileges with perhaps some adjustments and they fear any real alternative. But there is much more than that to hope for and nothing to fear. Can the Christian message of hope not help them in this matter?

There is hope. There is hope for all of us. But the road to that hope is going to be very hard and very painful. The conflict and the struggle will have to intensify in the months and years ahead because there is no other way to remove the injustice and oppression. But God is with us. We can only learn to become the instruments of *his* peace even unto death. We must participate in the cross of Christ if we are to have the hope of participating in his resurrection.

CHAPTER FIVE: CHALLENGE TO ACTION

5.1 God Sides with the Oppressed To say that the Church must now take sides unequivocally and consistently with the poor and the oppressed is to overlook the fact that the majority of Christians in South Africa have already done so. By far the greater part of the Church in South Africa *is* poor and oppressed. Of course it cannot be taken for granted that everyone who is oppressed has taken up their own cause and is struggling for their own liberation. Nor can it be assumed that all oppressed Christians are fully aware of the fact that their cause is God's cause. Nevertheless it remains true that the Church is already on the side of the oppressed because that is where the majority of its members are to be found. This fact needs to be appropriated and confirmed by the Church as a whole.

At the beginning of this document it was pointed out that the present crisis has highlighted the divisions in the Church. We are a divided Church precisely because not all the members of our Churches have taken sides against oppression. In other words not all Christians have united themselves with God "who is always on the side of the oppressed" (Ps 103:6). As far as the present crisis is concerned, there is only one way forward to Church unity, and that is for those Christians who find themselves on the side of the oppressor or sitting on the fence to cross over to the other side to be united in faith and action with those who are oppressed.

Unity and reconciliation within the Church itself is only possible around God and Jesus Christ who are to be found on the side of the poor and the oppressed.

If this is what the Church must become, if this is what the Church as a whole must have as its project, how then are we to translate it into concrete and effective action?

5.2 Participation in the Struggle Christians, if they are not doing so already, must quite simply participate in the struggle for liberation and for a just society. The campaigns of the people, from consumer boycotts to stayaways, need to be supported and encouraged by the Church. Criticism will sometimes be necessary but encouragement and support will also be necessary. In other words the present crisis challenges the whole Church to move beyond a mere 'ambulance ministry' to a ministry of involvement and participation.

5.3 Transforming Church Activities The Church has its own specific activities: Sunday services, communion services, baptisms, Sunday school, funerals and so forth. It also has its specific way of expressing its faith and its commitment, i.e. in the form of confessions of faith. All of these activities must be re-shaped to be more fully consistent with a prophetic faith related to the KAIROS that God is offering us today. The evil forces we speak of in baptism must be named. We know what these evil forces are in South Africa today. The unity and sharing we profess in our communion services or Masses must be named. It is the solidarity of the people inviting all to join in the struggle for God's peace in South Africa. The repentance we preach must be named. It is repentance for our share of the guilt for the suffering and oppression in our country.

Much of what we do in our Church services has lost its relevance to the poor and the oppressed. Our services and sacraments have been appropriated to serve the need of the individual for comfort and security. Now these same Church activities must be reappropriated to serve the real religious needs of all the people and to further the liberating mission of God and the Church in the world.

5.4 Special Campaigns Over and above its regular activities the Church would need to have special programmes, projects and campaigns because of the special needs of the struggle for liberation in South Africa today. But there is a very important caution here. The Church must avoid becoming a 'Third Force', a force between the oppressor and the oppressed. The Church's programmes and campaigns must not duplicate what the people's organisations are already doing and, even more seriously, the Church must not confuse the issue by having programmes that run counter to the struggles of those political organisations that truly represent the grievances and demands of the people. Consultation, co-ordination and co-operation will be needed. We all have the same goals even when we differ about the final significance of what we are struggling for.

5.5 Civil Disobedience Once it is established that the present regime has no moral legitimacy and is in fact a tyrannical regime certain things follow for the Church and its activities. In the first place *the Church cannot collaborate with tyranny*. It cannot or should not do anything that appears to give legitimacy to a morally illegitimate regime. Secondly, the Church should not only pray for a change of government, it should also mobilise its members in every parish to begin to think and work and plan for a change of government in South Africa. We must begin to look ahead and begin working now with firm hope and faith for a better future. And finally the moral illegitimacy of the apartheid regime means that the Church will have to be involved at times in *civil disobedience*. A Church that takes its responsibilities seriously in these circumstances will sometimes have to confront and to disobey the State in order to obey God.

5.6 Moral Guidance The people look to the Church, especially in the midst of our present crisis, for moral guidance. In order to provide this the Church must first make its stand absolutely clear and never tire of explaining and dialoguing about it. It must then help people to understand their rights and their duties. There must be no misunderstanding about the *moral duty* of all who are oppressed to resist oppression and to struggle for liberation and justice. The Church will also find that at times it does need to curb excesses and to appeal to the consciences of those who act thoughtlessly and wildly.

But the Church of Jesus Christ is not called to be a bastion of caution and moderation. The Church should challenge, inspire and motivate people. It has a message of the cross that inspires us to make sacrifices for justice and liberation. It has a message of hope that challenges us to wake up and to act with hope and confidence. The Church must preach this message not only in words and sermons and statements but also through its actions, programmes, campaigns and divine services.

CONCLUSION

As we said in the beginning, there is nothing final about this document. Our hope is that it will stimulate discussion, debate, reflection and prayer, but, above all, that it will lead to action. We invite all committed Christians to take this matter further, to do more research, to develop the themes we have presented here or to criticise them and to return to the Bible, as we have tried to do, with the question raised by the crisis of our times.

Although the document suggests various modes of involvement it does not prescribe the particular actions anyone should take. We call upon all those who are committed to this prophetic form of theology to use the document for discussion in groups, small and big, to determine an appropriate form of action, depending on their particular situation, and to take up the action with other related groups and organisations.

The challenge to renewal and action that we have set out here is addressed to the Church. But that does not mean that it is intended only for Church leaders. The challenge of the faith and of our present KAIROS is addressed to all who bear the name Christian. None of us can simply sit back and wait to be told what to do by our Church leaders or by anyone else. We must all accept responsibility for acting and living out our Christian faith in these circumstances. We pray that God will help all of us to translate the challenge of our times into action.

We, as theologians (both lay and professional), have been greatly challenged by our own reflections, our exchange of ideas and our discoveries as we met together in smaller and larger groups to prepare this document or to suggest amendments to it. We are convinced that this challenge comes from God and that it is addressed to all of us. We see the present crisis or KAIROS as indeed a divine visitation.

And finally we also like to call upon our Christian brothers and sisters throughout the world to give us the necessary support in this regard so that the daily loss of so many young lives may be brought to a speedy end.